Abstract Dynamic Programming

Dimitri P. Bertsekas

Massachusetts Institute of Technology

WWW site for book information and orders

http://www.athenasc.com

Athena Scientific, Belmont, Massachusetts

Athena Scientific
Post Office Box 805
Nashua, NH 03061-0805
U.S.A.

Email: info@athenasc.com
WWW: http://www.athenasc.com

Publisher's Cataloging-in-Publication Data

Bertsekas, Dimitri P.
Abstract Dynamic Programming
Includes bibliographical references and index
1. Mathematical Optimization. 2. Dynamic Programming. I. Title.

QA402.5 .B465 2013 519.703 01-75941

ISBN-10: 1-886529-42-6, ISBN-13: 978-1-886529-42-7

Contents

Preface

This book aims at a unified and economical development of the core theory and algorithms of total cost sequential decision problems, based on the strong connections of the subject with fixed point theory. The analysis focuses on the abstract mapping that underlies dynamic programming (DP for short) and defines the mathematical character of the associated problem. Our discussion centers on two fundamental properties that this mapping may have: *monotonicity* and (weighted sup-norm) *contraction*. It turns out that the nature of the analytical and algorithmic DP theory is determined primarily by the presence or absence of these two properties, and the rest of the problem's structure is largely inconsequential.

In this book, with some minor exceptions, we will assume that monotonicity holds. Consequently, we organize our treatment around the contraction property, and we focus on four main classes of models:

(a) **Contractive models**, discussed in Chapter 2, which have the richest and strongest theory, and are the benchmark against which the theory of other models is compared. Prominent among these models are discounted stochastic optimal control problems. The development of these models is quite thorough and includes the analysis of recent approximation algorithms for large-scale problems (neuro-dynamic programming, reinforcement learning).

(b) **Semicontractive models**, discussed in Chapter 3 and parts of Chapter 4. The term "semicontractive" is used qualitatively here, to refer to a variety of models where some policies have a regularity/contraction-like property but others do not. A prominent example is stochastic shortest path problems, where one aims to drive the state of a Markov chain to a termination state at minimum expected cost. These models also have a strong theory under certain conditions, often nearly as strong as those of the contractive models.

(c) **Noncontractive models**, discussed in Chapter 4, which rely on just monotonicity. These models are more complex than the preceding ones and much of the theory of the contractive models generalizes in weaker form, if at all. For example, in general the associated Bellman equation need not have a unique solution, the value iteration method may work starting with some functions but not with others, and the policy iteration method may not work at all. Infinite horizon examples of these models are the classical positive and negative DP problems, first analyzed by Dubins and Savage, Blackwell, and

Strauch, which are discussed in various sources. Some new semicontractive models are also discussed in this chapter, further bridging the gap between contractive and noncontractive models.

(d) **Restricted policies and Borel space models**, which are discussed in Chapter 5. These models are motivated in part by the complex measurability questions that arise in mathematically rigorous theories of stochastic optimal control involving continuous probability spaces. Within this context, the admissible policies and DP mapping are restricted to have certain measurability properties, and the analysis of the preceding chapters requires modifications. Restricted policy models are also useful when there is a special class of policies with favorable structure, which is "closed" with respect to the standard DP operations, in the sense that analysis and algorithms can be confined within this class.

We do not consider average cost DP problems, whose character bears a much closer connection to stochastic processes than to total cost problems. We also do not address specific stochastic characteristics underlying the problem, such as for example a Markovian structure. Thus our results apply equally well to Markovian decision problems and to sequential minimax problems. While this makes our development general and a convenient starting point for the further analysis of a variety of different types of problems, it also ignores some of the interesting characteristics of special types of DP problems that require an intricate probabilistic analysis.

Let us describe the research content of the book in summary, deferring a more detailed discussion to the end-of-chapter notes. A large portion of our analysis has been known for a long time, but in a somewhat fragmentary form. In particular, the contractive theory, first developed by Denardo [Den67], has been known for the case of the unweighted sup-norm, but does not cover the important special case of stochastic shortest path problems where all policies are proper. Chapter 2 transcribes this theory to the weighted sup-norm contraction case. Moreover, Chapter 2 develops extensions of the theory to approximate DP, and includes material on asynchronous value iteration (based on the author's work [Ber82], [Ber83]), and asynchronous policy iteration algorithms (based on the author's joint work with Huizhen (Janey) Yu [BeY10a], [BeY10b], [YuB11a]). Most of this material is relatively new, having been presented in the author's recent book [Ber12a] and survey paper [Ber12b], with detailed references given there. The analysis of infinite horizon noncontractive models in Chapter 4 was first given in the author's paper [Ber77], and was also presented in the book by Bertsekas and Shreve [BeS78], which in addition contains much of the material on finite horizon problems, restricted policies models, and Borel space models. These were the starting point and main sources for our development.

The new research presented in this book is primarily on the semicontractive models of Chapter 3 and parts of Chapter 4. Traditionally, the theory of total cost infinite horizon DP has been bordered by two extremes: discounted models, which have a contractive nature, and positive and negative models, which do not have a contractive nature, but rely on an enhanced monotonicity structure (monotone increase and monotone decrease models, or in classical DP terms, positive and negative models). Between these two extremes lies a gray area of problems that are not contractive, and either do not fit into the categories of positive and negative models, or possess additional structure that is not exploited by the theory of these models. Included are stochastic shortest path problems, search problems, linear-quadratic problems, a host of queueing problems, multiplicative and exponential cost models, and others. Together these problems represent an important part of the infinite horizon total cost DP landscape. They possess important theoretical characteristics, not generally available for positive and negative models, such as the uniqueness of solution of Bellman's equation within a subset of interest, and the validity of useful forms of value and policy iteration algorithms.

Our semicontractive models aim to provide a unifying abstract DP structure for problems in this gray area between contractive and noncontractive models. The analysis is motivated in part by stochastic shortest path problems, where there are two types of policies: *proper*, which are the ones that lead to the termination state with probability one from all starting states, and *improper*, which are the ones that are not proper. Proper and improper policies can also be characterized through their Bellman equation mapping: for the former this mapping is a contraction, while for the latter it is not. In our more general semicontractive models, policies are also characterized in terms of their Bellman equation mapping, through a notion of *regularity*, which generalizes the notion of a proper policy and is related to classical notions of asymptotic stability from control theory.

In our development a policy is regular within a certain set if its cost function is the unique asymptotically stable equilibrium (fixed point) of the associated DP mapping within that set. *We assume that some policies are regular while others are not*, and impose various assumptions to ensure that attention can be focused on the regular policies. From an analytical point of view, this brings to bear the theory of fixed points of monotone mappings. From the practical point of view, this allows application to a diverse collection of interesting problems, ranging from stochastic shortest path problems of various kinds, where the regular policies include the proper policies, to linear-quadratic problems, where the regular policies include the stabilizing linear feedback controllers.

The definition of regularity is introduced in Chapter 3, and its theoretical ramifications are explored through extensions of the classical stochastic shortest path and search problems. In Chapter 4, semicontractive models are discussed in the presence of additional monotonicity structure, which brings to bear the properties of positive and negative DP models. With the aid of this structure, the theory of semicontractive models can be strengthened and can be applied to several additional problems, including risk-sensitive/exponential cost problems.

The book has a theoretical research monograph character, but requires a modest mathematical background for all chapters except the last one, essentially a first course in analysis. Of course, prior exposure to DP will definitely be very helpful to provide orientation and context. A few exercises have been included, either to illustrate the theory with examples and counterexamples, or to provide applications and extensions of the theory. Solutions of all the exercises can be found in Appendix D, at the book's internet site

http://www.athenasc.com/abstractdp.html

and at the author's web site

http://www.mit.edu:8001/people/dimitrib/books.htm

Additional exercises and other related material may be added to these sites over time.

I would like to express my appreciation to a few colleagues for interactions, recent and old, which have helped shape the form of the book. My collaboration with Steven Shreve on our 1978 book provided the motivation and the background for the material on models with restricted policies and associated measurability questions. My collaboration with John Tsitsiklis on stochastic shortest path problems provided inspiration for the work on semicontractive models. My collaboration with Janey Yu played an important role in the book's development, and is reflected in our joint work on asynchronous policy iteration, on perturbation models, and on risk-sensitive models. Moreover Janey contributed significantly to the material on semicontractive models with many insightful suggestions. Finally, I am thankful to Mengdi Wang, who went through portions of the book with care, and gave several helpful comments.

Dimitri P. Bertsekas

dimitrib@mit.edu

Spring 2013

1
Introduction

Contents

1.1 STRUCTURE OF DYNAMIC PROGRAMMING PROBLEMS

Dynamic programming (DP for short) is the principal method for analysis of a large and diverse class of sequential decision problems. Examples are deterministic and stochastic optimal control problems with a continuous state space, Markov and semi-Markov decision problems with a discrete state space, minimax problems, and sequential zero sum games. While the nature of these problems may vary widely, their underlying structures turn out to be very similar. In all cases there is an underlying mapping that depends on an associated controlled dynamic system and corresponding cost per stage. This mapping, the DP operator, provides a "compact signature" of the problem. It defines the cost function of policies and the optimal cost function, and it provides a convenient shorthand notation for algorithmic description and analysis.

More importantly, the structure of the DP operator defines the mathematical character of the associated problem. The purpose of this book is to provide an analysis of this structure, centering on two fundamental properties: *monotonicity* and (weighted sup-norm) *contraction*. It turns out that the nature of the analytical and algorithmic DP theory is determined primarily by the presence or absence of these two properties, and the rest of the problem's structure is largely inconsequential.

A Deterministic Optimal Control Example

To illustrate our viewpoint, let us consider a discrete-time deterministic optimal control problem described by a system equation

$$x_{k+1} = f(x_k, u_k), \qquad k = 0, 1, \ldots. \tag{1.1}$$

Here x_k is the state of the system taking values in a set X (the state space), and u_k is the control taking values in a set U (the control space). At stage k, there is a cost

$$\alpha^k g(x_k, u_k)$$

incurred when u_k is applied at state x_k, where α is a scalar in $(0, 1]$ that has the interpretation of a discount factor when $\alpha < 1$. The controls are chosen as a function of the current state, subject to a constraint that depends on that state. In particular, at state x the control is constrained to take values in a given set $U(x) \subset U$. Thus we are interested in optimization over the set of (nonstationary) policies

$$\Pi = \big\{\{\mu_0, \mu_1, \ldots\} \mid \mu_k \in \mathcal{M},\ k = 0, 1, \ldots\big\},$$

where $\mathcal{M}$ is the set of functions $\mu : X \mapsto U$ defined by

$$\mathcal{M} = \big\{\mu \mid \mu(x) \in U(x),\ \forall\ x \in X\big\}.$$

The total cost of a policy $\pi = \{\mu_0, \mu_1, \ldots\}$ over an infinite number of stages and starting at an initial state x_0 is

$$J_\pi(x_0) = \sum_{k=0}^{\infty} \alpha^k g\big(x_k, \mu_k(x_k)\big), \tag{1.2}$$

where the state sequence $\{x_k\}$ is generated by the deterministic system (1.1) under the policy π:

$$x_{k+1} = f\big(x_k, \mu_k(x_k)\big), \quad k = 0, 1, \ldots$$

The optimal cost function is †

$$J^*(x) = \inf_{\pi \in \Pi} J_\pi(x), \qquad x \in X.$$

For any policy $\pi = \{\mu_0, \mu_1, \ldots\}$, consider the policy $\pi_1 = \{\mu_1, \mu_2, \ldots\}$ and write by using Eq. (1.2),

$$J_\pi(x) = g\big(x, \mu_0(x)\big) + \alpha J_{\pi_1}\big(f(x, \mu_0(x)\big).$$

We have for all $x \in X$

$$\begin{aligned} J^*(x) &= \inf_{\pi = \{\mu_0, \pi_1\} \in \Pi} \Big\{ g\big(x, \mu_0(x)\big) + \alpha J_{\pi_1}\big(f(x, \mu_0(x)\big) \Big\} \\ &= \inf_{\mu_0 \in \mathcal{M}} \Big\{ g\big(x, \mu_0(x)\big) + \alpha \inf_{\pi_1 \in \Pi} J_{\pi_1}\big(f(x, \mu_0(x)\big) \Big\} \\ &= \inf_{\mu_0 \in \mathcal{M}} \Big\{ g\big(x, \mu_0(x)\big) + \alpha J^*\big(f(x, \mu_0(x)\big) \Big\}. \end{aligned}$$

The minimization over $\mu_0 \in \mathcal{M}$ can be written as minimization over all $u \in U(x)$, so we can write the preceding equation as

$$J^*(x) = \inf_{u \in U(x)} \Big\{ g(x, u) + \alpha J^*\big(f(x, u)\big) \Big\}, \qquad \forall\, x \in X. \tag{1.3}$$

This equation is an example of *Bellman's equation*, which plays a central role in DP analysis and algorithms. If it can be solved for J^*, an optimal stationary policy $\{\mu^*, \mu^*, \ldots\}$ may typically be obtained by minimization of the right-hand side for each x, i.e.,

$$\mu^*(x) \in \arg\min_{u \in U(x)} \Big\{ g(x, u) + \alpha J^*\big(f(x, u)\big) \Big\}, \qquad \forall\, x \in X. \tag{1.4}$$

† For the informal discussion of this section, we will disregard a few mathematical issues. In particular, we assume that the series defining J_π in Eq. (1.2) is convergent for all allowable π, and that the optimal cost function J^* is real-valued. We will address such issues later.

We now note that both Eqs. (1.3) and (1.4) can be stated in terms of the expression

$$H(x, u, J) = g(x, u) + \alpha J\big(f(x, u)\big), \qquad x \in X,\ u \in U(x).$$

Defining

$$(T_\mu J)(x) = H\big(x, \mu(x), J\big), \qquad x \in X,$$

and

$$(TJ)(x) = \inf_{u \in U(x)} H(x, u, J) = \inf_{\mu \in \mathcal{M}} (T_\mu J)(x), \qquad x \in X,$$

we see that Bellman's equation (1.3) can be written compactly as

$$J^* = TJ^*,$$

i.e., J^* is the fixed point of T, viewed as a mapping from the set of real-valued functions on X into itself. Moreover, it can be similarly seen that J_μ, the cost function of the stationary policy $\{\mu, \mu, \ldots\}$, is a fixed point of T_μ. In addition, the optimality condition (1.4) can be stated compactly as

$$T_{\mu^*} J^* = TJ^*.$$

We will see later that additional properties, as well as a variety of algorithms for finding J^* can be analyzed using the mappings T and T_μ.

One more property that holds in some generality is worth noting. For a given policy $\pi = \{\mu_0, \mu_1, \ldots\}$ and a terminal cost $\alpha^N \bar{J}(x_N)$ for the state x_N at the end of N stages, consider the N-stage cost function

$$J_{\pi,N}(x_0) = \alpha^N \bar{J}(x_N) + \sum_{k=0}^{N-1} \alpha^k g\big(x_k, \mu_k(x_k)\big). \tag{1.5}$$

Then it can be verified by induction that for all initial states x_0, we have

$$J_{\pi,N}(x_0) = (T_{\mu_0} T_{\mu_1} \cdots T_{\mu_{N-1}} \bar{J})(x_0). \tag{1.6}$$

Here $T_{\mu_0} T_{\mu_1} \cdots T_{\mu_{N-1}}$ is the composition of the mappings $T_{\mu_0}, T_{\mu_1}, \ldots T_{\mu_{N-1}}$, i.e., for all J,

$$(T_{\mu_0} T_{\mu_1} J)(x) = \big(T_{\mu_0}(T_{\mu_1} J)\big)(x), \qquad x \in X,$$

and more generally

$$(T_{\mu_0} T_{\mu_1} \cdots T_{\mu_{N-1}} J)(x) = \big(T_{\mu_0}(T_{\mu_1}(\cdots (T_{\mu_{N-1}} J)))\big)(x), \qquad x \in X,$$

(our notational conventions are summarized in Appendix A). Thus the finite horizon cost functions $J_{\pi,N}$ of π can be defined in terms of the mappings T_μ [cf. Eq. (1.6)], and so can their infinite horizon limit J_π:

$$J_\pi(x) = \lim_{N \to \infty} (T_{\mu_0} T_{\mu_1} \cdots T_{\mu_{N-1}} \bar{J})(x), \qquad x \in X, \tag{1.7}$$

where $\bar{J}$ is the zero function, $\bar{J}(x) = 0$ for all $x \in X$ (assuming the limit exists).

Connection with Fixed Point Methodology

The Bellman equation (1.3) and the optimality condition (1.4), stated in terms of the mappings T_μ and T, highlight the central theme of this book, which is that DP theory is intimately connected with the theory of abstract mappings and their fixed points. Analogs of the Bellman equation, $J^* = TJ^*$, optimality conditions, and other results and computational methods hold for a great variety of DP models, and can be stated compactly as described above in terms of the corresponding mappings T_μ and T. The gain from this abstraction is greater generality and mathematical insight, as well as a more unified, economical, and streamlined analysis.

1.2 ABSTRACT DYNAMIC PROGRAMMING MODELS

In this section we formally introduce and illustrate with examples an abstract DP model, which embodies the ideas discussed in the preceding section.

1.2.1 Problem Formulation

Let X and U be two sets, which we loosely refer to as a set of "states" and a set of "controls," respectively. For each $x \in X$, let $U(x) \subset U$ be a nonempty subset of controls that are feasible at state x. We denote by $\mathcal{M}$ the set of all functions $\mu : X \mapsto U$ with $\mu(x) \in U(x)$, for all $x \in X$.

In analogy with DP, we refer to sequences $\pi = \{\mu_0, \mu_1, \ldots\}$, with $\mu_k \in \mathcal{M}$ for all k, as "nonstationary policies," and we refer to a sequence $\{\mu, \mu, \ldots\}$, with $\mu \in \mathcal{M}$, as a "stationary policy." In our development, stationary policies will play a dominant role, and with slight abuse of terminology, we will also refer to any $\mu \in \mathcal{M}$ as a "policy" when confusion cannot arise.

Let $R(X)$ be the set of real-valued functions $J : X \mapsto \Re$, and let $H : X \times U \times R(X) \mapsto \Re$ be a given mapping.† For each policy $\mu \in \mathcal{M}$, we consider the mapping $T_\mu : R(X) \mapsto R(X)$ defined by

$$(T_\mu J)(x) = H\big(x, \mu(x), J\big), \qquad \forall\, x \in X,\ J \in R(X),$$

and we also consider the mapping T defined by‡

$$(TJ)(x) = \inf_{u \in U(x)} H(x, u, J), \qquad \forall\, x \in X,\ J \in R(X).$$

---

† Our notation and mathematical conventions are outlined in Appendix A. In particular, we denote by $\Re$ the set of real numbers, and by $\Re^n$ the space of n-dimensional vectors with real components.

‡ We assume that H, $T_\mu J$, and TJ are real-valued for $J \in R(X)$ in the present chapter and in Chapter 2. In Chapters 3-5 we will allow $H(x, u, J)$, and hence also $(T_\mu J)(x)$ and $(TJ)(x)$, to take the values ∞ and $-\infty$.

Similar to the deterministic optimal control problem of the preceding section, the mappings T_μ and T serve to define a multistage optimization problem and a DP-like methodology for its solution. In particular, for some function $\bar J \in R(X)$, and nonstationary policy $\pi = \{\mu_0, \mu_1, \ldots\}$, we define for each integer $N \geq 1$ the functions

$$J_{\pi,N}(x) = (T_{\mu_0} T_{\mu_1} \cdots T_{\mu_{N-1}} \bar J)(x), \qquad x \in X,$$

where $T_{\mu_0} T_{\mu_1} \cdots T_{\mu_{N-1}}$ denotes the composition of the mappings $T_{\mu_0}, T_{\mu_1}, \ldots, T_{\mu_{N-1}}$, i.e.,

$$T_{\mu_0} T_{\mu_1} \cdots T_{\mu_{N-1}} J = \big(T_{\mu_0}(T_{\mu_1}(\cdots (T_{\mu_{N-2}}(T_{\mu_{N-1}} J))) \cdots)\big), \quad J \in R(X).$$

We view $J_{\pi,N}$ as the "N-stage cost function" of π [cf. Eq. (1.5)]. Consider also the function

$$J_\pi(x) = \limsup_{N\to\infty} J_{\pi,N}(x) = \limsup_{N\to\infty} (T_{\mu_0} T_{\mu_1} \cdots T_{\mu_{N-1}} \bar J)(x), \qquad x \in X,$$

which we view as the "infinite horizon cost function" of π [cf. Eq. (1.7); we use lim sup for generality, since we are not assured that the limit exists]. We want to minimize J_π over π, i.e., to find

$$J^*(x) = \inf_\pi J_\pi(x), \qquad x \in X,$$

and a policy π^* that attains the infimum, if one exists.

The key connection with fixed point methodology is that J^* "typically" (under mild assumptions) can be shown to satisfy

$$J^*(x) = \inf_{u \in U(x)} H(x, u, J^*), \qquad \forall\, x \in X,$$

i.e., it is a fixed point of T. We refer to this as *Bellman's equation* [cf. Eq. (1.3)]. Another fact is that if an optimal policy π^* exists, it "typically" can be selected to be stationary, $\pi^* = \{\mu^*, \mu^*, \ldots\}$, with $\mu^* \in \mathcal{M}$ satisfying an optimality condition, such as for example

$$T_{\mu^*} J^* = T J^*$$

[cf. Eq. (1.4)]. Several other results of an analytical or algorithmic nature also hold under appropriate conditions, which will be discussed in detail later.

However, Bellman's equation and other related results may not hold without T_μ and T having some special structural properties. Prominent among these are a monotonicity assumption that typically holds in DP problems, and a contraction assumption that holds for some important classes of problems.

1.2.2 Monotonicity and Contraction Assumptions

Let us now formalize the monotonicity and contraction assumptions. We will require that both of these assumptions hold throughout the next chapter, and we will gradually relax the contraction assumption in Chapters 3-5. Recall also our assumption that T_μ and T map $R(X)$ (the space of real-valued functions over X) into $R(X)$. In Chapters 3-5 we will relax this assumption as well.

Assumption 1.2.1: (Monotonicity) If $J, J' \in R(X)$ and $J \leq J'$, then

$$H(x, u, J) \leq H(x, u, J'), \qquad \forall\, x \in X,\ u \in U(x).$$

Note that by taking infimum over $u \in U(x)$, we have

$$J \leq J' \qquad \Rightarrow \qquad \inf_{u \in U(x)} H(x, u, J) \leq \inf_{u \in U(x)} H(x, u, J'), \quad \forall\, x \in X,$$

or equivalently,

$$J \leq J' \qquad \Rightarrow \qquad TJ \leq TJ'.$$

Another way to arrive at this relation, is to note that the monotonicity assumption is equivalent to

$$J \leq J' \quad \Rightarrow \quad T_\mu J \leq T_\mu J', \qquad \forall\, \mu \in \mathcal{M},$$

and to use the simple but important fact

$$\inf_{u \in U(x)} H(x, u, J) = \inf_{\mu \in \mathcal{M}} (T_\mu J)(x), \qquad \forall\, x \in X,\ J \in R(x),$$

i.e., *infimum over u is equivalent to infimum over μ*, which holds in view of the definition $\mathcal{M} = \big\{\mu \mid \mu(x) \in U(x),\ \forall\, x \in X\big\}$. We will be writing this relation as $TJ = \inf_{\mu \in \mathcal{M}} T_\mu J$.

For the contraction assumption, we introduce a function $v : X \mapsto \Re$ with

$$v(x) > 0, \qquad \forall\, x \in X.$$

Let us denote by $B(X)$ the space of real-valued functions J on X such that $J(x)/v(x)$ is bounded as x ranges over X, and consider the weighted sup-norm

$$\|J\| = \sup_{x \in X} \frac{\big|J(x)\big|}{v(x)}$$

on $B(X)$. The properties of $B(X)$ and some of the associated fixed point theory are discussed in Appendix B. In particular, as shown there, $B(X)$

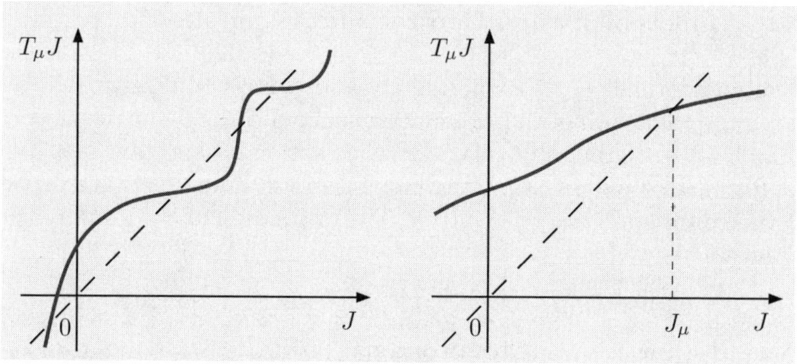

Figure 1.2.1. Illustration of the monotonicity and the contraction assumptions in one dimension. The mapping T_μ on the left is monotone but is not a contraction. The mapping T_μ on the right is both monotone and a contraction. It has a unique fixed point at J_μ.

is a complete normed space, so any mapping from $B(X)$ to $B(X)$ that is a contraction or an m-stage contraction for some integer $m > 1$, with respect to $\|\cdot\|$, has a unique fixed point (cf. Props. B.1 and B.2).

Assumption 1.2.2: (Contraction) For all $J \in B(X)$ and $\mu \in \mathcal{M}$, the functions $T_\mu J$ and TJ belong to $B(X)$. Furthermore, for some $\alpha \in (0, 1)$, we have

$$\|T_\mu J - T_\mu J'\| \leq \alpha \|J - J'\|, \qquad \forall\, J, J' \in B(X),\ \mu \in \mathcal{M}. \tag{1.8}$$

Figure 1.2.1 illustrates the monotonicity and the contraction assumptions. It is important to note that the contraction condition (1.8) implies that

$$\|TJ - TJ'\| \leq \alpha \|J - J'\|, \qquad \forall\, J, J' \in B(X), \tag{1.9}$$

so that T is also a contraction with modulus α. To see this we use Eq. (1.8) to write

$$(T_\mu J)(x) \leq (T_\mu J')(x) + \alpha \|J - J'\|\, v(x), \qquad \forall\, x \in X,$$

from which, by taking infimum of both sides over $\mu \in \mathcal{M}$, we have

$$\frac{(TJ)(x) - (TJ')(x)}{v(x)} \leq \alpha \|J - J'\|, \qquad \forall\, x \in X.$$

Reversing the roles of J and J', we also have

$$\frac{(TJ')(x) - (TJ)(x)}{v(x)} \leq \alpha \|J - J'\|, \qquad \forall\, x \in X,$$

and combining the preceding two relations, and taking the supremum of the left side over $x \in X$, we obtain Eq. (1.9).

Nearly all mappings related to DP satisfy the monotonicity assumption, and many important ones satisfy the weighted sup-norm contraction assumption as well. When both assumptions hold, the most powerful analytical and computational results can be obtained, as we will show in Chapter 2. These are:

(a) Bellman's equation has a unique solution, i.e., T and T_μ have unique fixed points, which are the optimal cost function J^* and the cost functions J_μ of the stationary policies $\{\mu, \mu, \ldots\}$, respectively [cf. Eq. (1.3)].

(b) A stationary policy $\{\mu^*, \mu^*, \ldots\}$ is optimal if and only if

$$T_{\mu^*} J^* = T J^*,$$

[cf. Eq. (1.4)].

(c) J^* and J_μ can be computed by the *value iteration* method,

$$J^* = \lim_{k\to\infty} T^k J, \qquad J_\mu = \lim_{k\to\infty} T_\mu^k J,$$

starting with any $J \in B(X)$.

(d) J^* can be computed by the *policy iteration* method, whereby we generate a sequence of stationary policies via

$$T_{\mu^{k+1}} J_{\mu^k} = T J_{\mu^k},$$

starting from some initial policy μ^0 [here J_{μ^k} is obtained as the fixed point of T_{μ^k} by several possible methods, including value iteration as in (c) above].

These are the most favorable types of results one can hope for in the DP context, and they are supplemented by a host of other results, involving approximate and/or asynchronous implementations of the value and policy iteration methods, and other related methods that combine features of both. As the contraction property is relaxed and is replaced by various weaker assumptions, some of the preceding results may hold in weaker form. For example J^* turns out to be a solution of Bellman's equation in all the models to be discussed, but it may not be the unique solution. The interplay between the monotonicity and contraction-like properties, and the associated results of the form (a)-(d) described above is the recurring analytical theme in this book.

1.2.3 Some Examples

In what follows in this section, we describe a few special cases, which indicate the connections of appropriate forms of the mapping H with the most popular total cost DP models. In all these models the monotonicity Assumption 1.2.1 (or some closely related version) holds, but the contraction Assumption 1.2.2 may not hold, as we will indicate later. Our descriptions are by necessity brief, and the reader is referred to the relevant textbook literature for more detailed discussion.

Example 1.2.1 (Stochastic Optimal Control - Markovian Decision Problems)

Consider the stationary discrete-time dynamic system

$$x_{k+1} = f(x_k, u_k, w_k), \qquad k = 0, 1, \ldots, \tag{1.10}$$

where for all k, the state x_k is an element of a space X, the control u_k is an element of a space U, and w_k is a random "disturbance," an element of a space W. We consider problems with infinite state and control spaces, as well as problems with discrete (finite or countable) state space (in which case the underlying system is a Markov chain). However, for technical reasons that relate to measure theoretic issues to be explained later in Chapter 5, we assume that W is a countable set.

The control u_k is constrained to take values in a given nonempty subset $U(x_k)$ of U, which depends on the current state x_k [$u_k \in U(x_k)$, for all $x_k \in X$]. The random disturbances w_k, $k = 0, 1, \ldots$, are characterized by probability distributions $P(\cdot \mid x_k, u_k)$ that are identical for all k, where $P(w_k \mid x_k, u_k)$ is the probability of occurrence of w_k, when the current state and control are x_k and u_k, respectively. Thus the probability of w_k may depend explicitly on x_k and u_k, but not on values of prior disturbances $w_{k-1}, \ldots, w_0$.

Given an initial state x_0, we want to find a policy $\pi = \{\mu_0, \mu_1, \ldots\}$, where $\mu_k : X \mapsto U$, $\mu_k(x_k) \in U(x_k)$, for all $x_k \in X$, $k = 0, 1, \ldots$, that minimizes the cost function

$$J_\pi(x_0) = \limsup_{N \to \infty} \mathop{E}_{\substack{w_k \\ k=0,1,\ldots}} \left\{ \sum_{k=0}^{N-1} \alpha^k g\big(x_k, \mu_k(x_k), w_k\big) \right\}, \tag{1.11}$$

subject to the system equation constraint

$$x_{k+1} = f\big(x_k, \mu_k(x_k), w_k\big), \qquad k = 0, 1, \ldots.$$

This is a classical problem, which is discussed extensively in various sources, including the author's text [Ber12a]. It is usually referred to as the *stochastic optimal control problem* or the *Markovian Decision Problem* (MDP for short).

Note that the expected value of the N-stage cost of π,

$$\mathop{E}_{\substack{w_k \\ k=0,1,\ldots}} \left\{ \sum_{k=0}^{N-1} \alpha^k g\big(x_k, \mu_k(x_k), w_k\big) \right\},$$

is defined as a (possibly countably infinite) sum, since the disturbances w_k, $k = 0, 1, \ldots$, take values in a countable set. Indeed, the reader may verify that all the subsequent mathematical expressions that involve an expected value can be written as summations over a finite or a countable set, so they make sense without resort to measure-theoretic integration concepts.†

In what follows we will often impose appropriate assumptions on the cost per stage g and the scalar α, which guarantee that the infinite horizon cost $J_\pi(x_0)$ is defined as a limit (rather than as a lim sup):

$$J_\pi(x_0) = \lim_{N\to\infty} \mathop{E}_{\substack{w_k\\ k=0,1,\ldots}} \left\{ \sum_{k=0}^{N-1} \alpha^k g\big(x_k, \mu_k(x_k), w_k\big) \right\}.$$

In particular, it can be shown that the limit exists if $\alpha < 1$ and g is uniformly bounded, i.e., for some $B > 0$,

$$\big|g(x,u,w)\big| \le B, \qquad \forall\ x \in X,\ u \in U(x),\ w \in W. \tag{1.12}$$

In this case, we obtain the classical discounted infinite horizon DP problem, which generally has the most favorable structure of all infinite horizon stochastic DP models (see [Ber12a], Chapters 1 and 2).

To make the connection with abstract DP, let us define

$$H(x,u,J) = E\big\{g(x,u,w) + \alpha J\big(f(x,u,w)\big)\big\},$$

so that

$$(T_\mu J)(x) = E\big\{g\big(x,\mu(x),w\big) + \alpha J\big(f(x,\mu(x),w)\big)\big\},$$

and

$$(TJ)(x) = \inf_{u\in U(x)} E\big\{g(x,u,w) + \alpha J\big(f(x,u,w)\big)\big\}.$$

Similar to the deterministic optimal control problem of Section 1.1, the N-stages cost of π, can be expressed in terms of T_μ:

$$(T_{\mu_0}\cdots T_{\mu_{N-1}}\bar J)(x_0) = \mathop{E}_{\substack{w_k\\ k=0,1,\ldots}} \left\{ \sum_{k=0}^{N-1} \alpha^k g\big(x_k, \mu_k(x_k), w_k\big) \right\},$$

---

† As noted in Appendix A, the formula for the expected value of a random variable w defined over a space Ω is

$$E\{w\} = E\{w^+\} + E\{w^-\},$$

where w^+ and w^- are the positive and negative parts of w,

$$w^+(\omega) = \max\big\{0, w(\omega)\big\}, \qquad w^-(\omega) = \min\big\{0, w(\omega)\big\}, \qquad \forall\ \omega \in \Omega.$$

In this way, taking also into account the rule $\infty - \infty = \infty$ (see Appendix A), $E\{w\}$ is well-defined as an extended real number if Ω is finite or countably infinite.

where $\bar{J}$ is the zero function, $\bar{J}(x) = 0$ for all $x \in X$. The same is true for the infinite stages cost [cf. Eq. (1.11)]:

$$J_\pi(x_0) = \limsup_{N \to \infty} (T_{\mu_0} \cdots T_{\mu_{N-1}} \bar{J})(x_0).$$

It can be seen that the mappings T_μ and T are monotone, and it is well-known that if $\alpha < 1$ and the boundedness condition (1.12) holds, they are contractive as well (under the unweighted sup-norm); see e.g., [Ber12a], Chapter 1. In this case, the model has the powerful analytical and algorithmic properties (a)-(d) mentioned at the end of the preceding subsection. In particular, the optimal cost function J^* [i.e., $J^*(x) = \inf_\pi J_\pi(x)$ for all $x \in X$] can be shown to be the unique solution of the fixed point equation $J^* = TJ^*$, also known as Bellman's equation, which has the form

$$J^*(x) = \inf_{u \in U(x)} E\bigl\{g(x,u,w) + \alpha J^*\bigl(f(x,u,w)\bigr)\bigr\}, \qquad x \in X,$$

and parallels the one given for deterministic optimal control problems [cf. Eq. (1.3)].

These properties can be expressed and analyzed in an abstract setting by using just the mappings T_μ and T, both when T_μ and T are contractive (see Chapter 2), and when they are only monotone and not contractive (see Chapter 4). Moreover, under some conditions, it is possible to analyze these properties in cases where T_μ is contractive for some but not all μ (see Chapter 3, and Sections 4.4-4.5).

Example 1.2.2 (Finite-State Discounted Markovian Decision Problems)

In the special case of the preceding example where the number of states is finite, the system equation (1.10) may be defined in terms of the transition probabilities

$$p_{xy}(u) = \text{Prob}\bigl(y = f(x,u,w) \mid x\bigr), \qquad x, y \in X,\ u \in U(x),$$

so H takes the form

$$H(x,u,J) = \sum_{y \in X} p_{xy}(u)\bigl(g(x,u,y) + \alpha J(y)\bigr).$$

When $\alpha < 1$ and the boundedness condition

$$\bigl|g(x,u,y)\bigr| \le B, \qquad \forall\ x, y \in X,\ u \in U(x),$$

[cf. Eq. (1.12)] holds (or more simply when U is a finite set), the mappings T_μ and T are contraction mappings with respect to the standard (unweighted) sup-norm. This is a classical problem, referred to as *discounted finite-state MDP*, which has a favorable theory and has found extensive applications (cf. [Ber12a], Chapters 1 and 2). The model is additionally important, because it is often used for computational solution of continuous state space problems via discretization.

Example 1.2.3 (Discounted Semi-Markov Problems)

With x, y, and u as in Example 1.2.2, consider a mapping of the form

$$H(x, u, J) = G(x, u) + \sum_{y \in X} m_{xy}(u) J(y),$$

where G is some function representing expected cost per stage, and $m_{xy}(u)$ are nonnegative scalars with

$$\sum_{y \in X} m_{xy}(u) < 1, \qquad \forall\, x \in X,\, u \in U(x).$$

The equation $J^* = TJ^*$ is Bellman's equation for a finite-state continuous-time semi-Markov decision problem, after it is converted into an equivalent discrete-time problem (cf. [Ber12a], Section 1.4). Again, the mappings T_μ and T are monotone and can be shown to be contraction mappings with respect to the unweighted sup-norm.

Example 1.2.4 (Discounted Zero-Sum Dynamic Games)

Let us consider a zero sum game analog of the finite-state MDP Example 1.2.2. Here there are two players that choose actions at each stage: the first (called the *minimizer*) may choose a move i out of n moves and the second (called the *maximizer*) may choose a move j out of m moves. Then the minimizer gives a specified amount a_{ij} to the maximizer, called a *payoff*. The minimizer wishes to minimize a_{ij}, and the maximizer wishes to maximize a_{ij}.

The players use mixed strategies, whereby the minimizer selects a probability distribution $u = (u_1, \ldots, u_n)$ over his n possible moves and the maximizer selects a probability distribution $v = (v_1, \ldots, v_m)$ over his m possible moves. Since the probability of selecting i and j is $u_i v_j$, the expected payoff for this stage is $\sum_{i,j} a_{ij} u_i v_j$ or $u'Av$, where A is the $n \times m$ matrix with components a_{ij}.

In a single-stage version of the game, the minimizer must minimize $\max_{v \in V} u'Av$ and the maximizer must maximize $\min_{u \in U} u'Av$, where U and V are the sets of probability distributions over $\{1, \ldots, n\}$ and $\{1, \ldots, m\}$, respectively. A fundamental result (which will not be proved here) is that these two values are equal:

$$\min_{u \in U} \max_{v \in V} u'Av = \max_{v \in V} \min_{u \in U} u'Av. \tag{1.13}$$

Let us consider the situation where a separate game of the type just described is played at each stage. The game played at a given stage is represented by a "state" x that takes values in a finite set X. The state evolves according to transition probabilities $q_{xy}(i, j)$ where i and j are the moves selected by the minimizer and the maximizer, respectively (here y represents the next game to be played after moves i and j are chosen at the game represented by x). When the state is x, under $u \in U$ and $v \in V$, the one-stage expected payoff is $u'A(x)v$, where $A(x)$ is the $n \times m$ payoff matrix, and the state transition probabilities are

$$p_{xy}(u,v) = \sum_{i=1}^{n} \sum_{j=1}^{m} u_i v_j q_{xy}(i,j) = u' Q_{xy} v,$$

where Q_{xy} is the $n \times m$ matrix that has components $q_{xy}(i,j)$. Payoffs are discounted by $\alpha \in (0,1)$, and the objectives of the minimizer and maximizer, roughly speaking, are to minimize and to maximize the total discounted expected payoff. This requires selections of u and v to strike a balance between obtaining favorable current stage payoffs and playing favorable games in future stages.

We now introduce an abstract DP framework related to the sequential move selection process just described. We consider the mapping G given by

$$\begin{aligned} G(x,u,v,J) &= u'A(x)v + \alpha \sum_{y \in X} p_{xy}(u,v) J(y) \\ &= u' \left(A(x) + \alpha \sum_{y \in X} Q_{xy} J(y) \right) v, \end{aligned} \tag{1.14}$$

where $\alpha \in (0,1)$ is discount factor, and the mapping H given by

$$H(x,u,J) = \max_{v \in V} G(x,u,v,J).$$

The corresponding mappings T_μ and T are

$$(T_\mu J)(x) = \max_{v \in V} G\big(x, \mu(x), v, J\big), \qquad x \in X,$$

and

$$(TJ)(x) = \min_{u \in U} \max_{v \in V} G(x,u,v,J).$$

It can be shown that T_μ and T are monotone and (unweighted) sup-norm contractions. Moreover, the unique fixed point J^* of T satisfies

$$J^*(x) = \min_{u \in U} \max_{v \in V} G(x,u,v,J^*), \qquad \forall\, x \in X,$$

(see [Ber12a], Section 1.6.2).

We now note that since

$$A(x) + \alpha \sum_{y \in X} Q_{xy} J(y)$$

[cf. Eq. (1.14)] is a matrix that is independent of u and v, we may view $J^*(x)$ as the value of a static game (which depends on the state x). In particular, from the fundamental minimax equality (1.13), we have

$$\min_{u \in U} \max_{v \in V} G(x,u,v,J^*) = \max_{v \in V} \min_{u \in U} G(x,u,v,J^*), \qquad \forall\, x \in X.$$

This implies that J^* is also the unique fixed point of the mapping

$$(\overline{T}J)(x) = \max_{v \in V} \overline{H}(x, v, J),$$

where

$$\overline{H}(x, v, J) = \min_{u \in U} G(x, u, v, J),$$

i.e., J^* is the fixed point regardless of the order in which minimizer and maximizer select mixed strategies at each stage.

In the preceding development, we have introduced J^* as the unique fixed point of the mappings T and $\overline{T}$. However, J^* also has an interpretation in game theoretic terms. In particular, it can be shown that $J^*(x)$ is the value of a dynamic game, whereby at state x the two opponents choose multistage (possibly nonstationary) policies that consist of functions of the current state, and continue to select moves using these policies over an infinite horizon. For further discussion of this interpretation, we refer to [Ber12a] and to books on dynamic games such as [FiV96]; see also [PaB99] and [Yu11] for an analysis of the undiscounted case ($\alpha = 1$) where there is a termination state, as in the stochastic shortest path problems of the subsequent Example 1.2.6.

Example 1.2.5 (Minimax Problems)

Consider a minimax version of Example 1.2.1, where w is not random but is rather chosen by an antagonistic player from a set $W(x, u)$. Let

$$H(x, u, J) = \sup_{w \in W(x,u)} \Big[g(x, u, w) + \alpha J\big(f(x, u, w)\big) \Big].$$

Then the equation $J^* = TJ^*$ is Bellman's equation for an infinite horizon minimax DP problem. A special case of this mapping arises in zero-sum dynamic games (cf. Example 1.2.4).

Example 1.2.6 (Stochastic Shortest Path Problems)

The stochastic shortest path (SSP for short) problem is the special case of the stochastic optimal control Example 1.2.1 where:

(a) There is no discounting ($\alpha = 1$).

(b) The state space is $X = \{0, 1, \ldots, n\}$ and we are given transition probabilities, denoted by

$$p_{xy}(u) = P(x_{k+1} = y \mid x_k = x, u_k = u), \qquad x, y \in X, \ u \in U(x).$$

(c) The control constraint set $U(x)$ is finite for all $x \in X$.

(d) A cost $g(x, u)$ is incurred when control $u \in U(x)$ is selected at state x.

(e) State 0 is a special termination state, which is absorbing and cost-free, i.e.,

$$p_{00}(u) = 1,$$

and for all $u \in U(0)$, $g(0, u) = 0$.

To simplify the notation, we have assumed that the cost per stage does not depend on the successor state, which amounts to using expected cost per stage in all calculations.

Since the termination state 0 is cost-free and absorbing, the cost starting from 0 is zero for every policy. Accordingly, for all cost functions, we ignore the component that corresponds to 0, and define

$$H(x, u, J) = g(x, u) + \sum_{y=1}^{n} p_{xy}(u)J(y), \quad x = 1, \ldots, n, \ u \in U(x), \ J \in \Re^n.$$

The mappings T_μ and T are defined by

$$(T_\mu J)(x) = g\big(x, \mu(x)\big) + \sum_{y=1}^{n} p_{xy}\big(\mu(x)\big) J(y), \qquad x = 1, \ldots, n,$$

$$(TJ)(x) = \min_{u \in U(x)} \left[g(x, u) + \sum_{y=1}^{n} p_{xy}(u)J(y) \right], \qquad x = 1, \ldots, n.$$

Note that the matrix that has components $p_{xy}(u)$, $x, y = 1, \ldots, n$, is substochastic (some of its row sums may be less than 1) because there may be positive transition probability from a state x to the termination state 0. Consequently T_μ may be a contraction for some μ, but not necessarily for all $\mu \in \mathcal{M}$.

The SSP problem has been discussed in many sources, including the books [Pal67], [Der70], [Whi82], [Ber87], [BeT89], [HeL99], and [Ber12a], where it is sometimes referred to by earlier names such as "first passage problem" and "transient programming problem." In the framework that is most relevant to our purposes, there is a classification of stationary policies for SSP into *proper* and *improper*. We say that $\mu \in \mathcal{M}$ is proper if, when using μ, there is positive probability that termination will be reached after at most n stages, regardless of the initial state; i.e., if

$$\rho_\mu = \max_{x=1,\ldots,n} P\{x_n \neq 0 \mid x_0 = x, \mu\} < 1.$$

Otherwise, we say that μ is improper. It can be seen that μ is proper if and only if in the Markov chain corresponding to μ, each state x is connected to the termination state with a path of positive probability transitions.

For a proper policy μ, it can be shown that T_μ is a weighted sup-norm contraction, as well as an n-stage contraction with respect to the unweighted sup-norm. For an improper policy μ, T_μ is not a contraction with respect to any norm. Moreover, T also need not be a contraction with respect to any norm (think of the case where there is only one policy, which is improper).

However, T is a weighted sup-norm contraction in the important special case where all policies are proper (see [BeT96], Prop. 2.2, or [Ber12a], Prop. 3.3.1).

Nonetheless, even in the case where there are improper policies and T is not a contraction, results comparable to the case of discounted finite-state MDP are available for SSP problems assuming that:

(a) There exists at least one proper policy.

(b) For every improper policy there is an initial state that has infinite cost under this policy.

Under the preceding two assumptions, it was shown in [BeT91] that T has a unique fixed point J^*, the optimal cost function of the SSP problem. Moreover, a policy $\{\mu^*, \mu^*, \ldots\}$ is optimal if and only if

$$T_{\mu^*} J^* = T J^*.$$

In addition, J^* and J_μ can be computed by value iteration,

$$J^* = \lim_{k \to \infty} T^k J, \qquad J_\mu = \lim_{k \to \infty} T_\mu^k J,$$

starting with any $J \in \Re^n$ (see [Ber12a], Chapter 3, for a textbook account). These properties are in analogy with the desirable properties (a)-(c), given at the end of the preceding subsection in connection with contractive models.

Regarding policy iteration, it works in its strongest form when there are no improper policies, in which case the mappings T_μ and T are weighted sup-norm contractions. When there are improper policies, modifications to the policy iteration method are needed; see [YuB11a], [Ber12a], and also Sections 3.3.2, 3.3.3, where these modifications will be discussed in an abstract setting.

Let us also note that there is an alternative line of analysis of SSP problems, whereby favorable results are obtained assuming that there exists an optimal proper policy, and the one-stage cost is nonnegative, $g(x, u) \geq 0$ for all (x, u) (see [Pal67], [Der70], [Whi82], and [Ber87]). This analysis will also be generalized in Chapter 3 and in Section 4.4, and the nonnegativity assumption on g will be relaxed.

Example 1.2.7 (Deterministic Shortest Path Problems)

The special case of the SSP problem where the state transitions are deterministic is the classical shortest path problem. Here, we have a graph of n nodes $x = 1, \ldots, n$, plus a destination 0, and an arc length a_{xy} for each directed arc (x, y). At state/node x, a policy μ chooses an outgoing arc from x. Thus the controls available at x can be identified with the outgoing neighbors of x [the nodes u such that (x, u) is an arc]. The corresponding mapping H is

$$H(x, u, J) = \begin{cases} a_{xu} + J(u) & \text{if } u \neq 0, \\ a_{x0} & \text{if } u = 0, \end{cases} \qquad x = 1, \ldots, n.$$

A stationary policy μ defines a graph whose arcs are $\big(x, \mu(x)\big)$, $x = 1, \ldots, n$. The policy μ is proper if and only if this graph is acyclic (it consists of a tree of directed paths leading from each node to the destination). Thus there exists a proper policy if and only if each node is connected to the destination with a directed path. Furthermore, an improper policy has finite cost starting from every initial state if and only if all the cycles of the corresponding graph have nonnegative cycle cost. It follows that the favorable analytical and algorithmic results described for SSP in the preceding example hold if the given graph is connected and the costs of all its cycles are positive. We will see later that significant complications result if the cycle costs are allowed to be nonpositive, even though the shortest path problem is still well posed in the sense that shortest paths exist if the given graph is connected (see Section 3.1.2).

Example 1.2.8 (Multiplicative and Risk-Sensitive Models)

With x, y, u, and transition probabilities $p_{xy}(u)$, as in the finite-state MDP of Example 1.2.2, consider the mapping

$$H(x,u,J) = \sum_{y\in X} p_{xy}(u) g(x,u,y) J(y) = E\big\{g(x,u,y)J(y) \mid x,u\big\}, \tag{1.15}$$

where g is a scalar function with $g(x,u,y) \geq 0$ for all x, y, u (this is necessary for H to be monotone). This mapping corresponds to the multiplicative model of minimizing over all $\pi = \{\mu_0, \mu_1, \ldots\}$ the cost

$$\begin{aligned} J_\pi(x_0) = \limsup_{N\to\infty} E\Big\{ & g\big(x_0,\mu_0(x_0),x_1\big) g\big(x_1,\mu_1(x_1),x_2\big)\cdots \\ & g\big(x_{N-1},\mu_{N-1}(x_{N-1}),x_N\big) \;\Big|\, x_0\Big\}, \end{aligned} \tag{1.16}$$

where the state sequence $\{x_0, x_1, \ldots\}$ is generated using the transition probabilities $p_{x_k x_{k+1}}\big(\mu_k(x_k)\big)$.

To see that the mapping H of Eq. (1.15) corresponds to the cost function (1.16), let us consider the unit function

$$\bar J(x) \equiv 1, \qquad x \in X,$$

and verify that for all $x_0 \in X$, we have

$$\begin{aligned} (T_{\mu_0}T_{\mu_1}\cdots T_{\mu_{N-1}}\bar J)(x_0) = E\Big\{ & g\big(x_0,\mu_0(x_0),x_1\big) g\big(x_1,\mu_1(x_1),x_2\big)\cdots \\ & g\big(x_{N-1},\mu_{N-1}(x_{N-1}),x_N\big) \;\Big|\; x_0\Big\}, \end{aligned} \tag{1.17}$$

so that

$$J_\pi(x) = \limsup_{N\to\infty} (T_{\mu_0}T_{\mu_1}\cdots T_{\mu_{N-1}}\bar J)(x), \qquad x \in X.$$

Indeed, taking into account that $\bar J(x) \equiv 1$, we have

$$\begin{aligned} (T_{\mu_{N-1}}\bar J)(x_{N-1}) &= E\big\{g\big(x_{N-1},\mu_{N-1}(x_{N-1}),x_N\big)\bar J(x_N) \mid x_{N-1}\big\} \\ &= E\big\{g\big(x_{N-1},\mu_{N-1}(x_{N-1}),x_N\big) \mid x_{N-1}\big\}, \end{aligned}$$

$$\begin{aligned}(T_{\mu_{N-2}}T_{\mu_{N-1}}\bar{J})(x_{N-2}) &= \big((T_{\mu_{N-2}}(T_{\mu_{N-1}}\bar{J})\big)(x_{N-2})\\ &= E\big\{g\big(x_{N-2},\mu_{N-2}(x_{N-2}),x_{N-1}\big)\\ &\qquad \cdot E\big\{g\big(x_{N-1},\mu_{N-1}(x_{N-1}),x_N\big)\mid x_{N-1}\big\}\mid x_{N-2}\big\},\end{aligned}$$

and continuing similarly,

$$\begin{aligned}(T_{\mu_0}T_{\mu_1}\cdots T_{\mu_{N-1}}\bar{J})(x_0) = E\Big\{&g\big(x_0,\mu_0(x_0),x_1\big)E\big\{g\big(x_1,\mu_1(x_1),x_2\big)\cdots\\ &E\big\{g\big(x_{N-1},\mu_{N-1}(x_{N-1}),x_N\big)\mid x_{N-1}\big\}\mid x_{N-2}\big\}\cdots\big\}\mid x_0\Big\},\end{aligned}$$

which by using the iterated expectations formula (see e.g., [BeT08]) proves the expression (1.17).

An important special case of a multiplicative model is when g has the form

$$g(x,u,y)=e^{h(x,u,y)}$$

for some one-stage cost function h. We then obtain a finite-state MDP with an exponential cost function,

$$J_\pi(x_0)=\limsup_{N\to\infty} E\Big\{e^{\big(h(x_0,\mu_0(x_0),x_1)+\cdots+h(x_{N-1},\mu_{N-1}(x_{N-1}),x_N)\big)}\Big\},$$

which is often used to introduce risk aversion in the choice of policy through the convexity of the exponential.

There is also a multiplicative version of the infinite state space stochastic optimal control problem of Example 1.2.1. The mapping H takes the form

$$H(x,u,J)=E\big\{g(x,u,w)J\big(f(x,u,w)\big)\big\},$$

where $x_{k+1}=f(x_k,u_k,w_k)$ is the underlying discrete-time dynamic system; cf. Eq. (1.10).

Multiplicative models and related risk-sensitive models are discussed extensively in the literature, mostly for the exponential cost case and under different assumptions than ours; see e.g., [HoM72], [Jac73], [Rot84], [ChS87], [Whi90], [JBE94], [FlM95], [HeM96], [FeM97], [BoM99], [CoM99], [BoM99], [BoM02], [BBB08]. The works of references [DeR79], [Pat01], and [Pat07] relate to the stochastic shortest path problems of Example 1.2.6, and are the closest to the semicontractive models discussed in Chapters 3 and 4.

Issues of risk-sensitivity have also been dealt within frameworks that do not quite conform to the multiplicative model of the preceding example, and are based on the theory of multi-stage risk measures; see e.g., [Rus10], [CaR12], and the references quoted there. Still these formulations involve abstract monotone DP mappings and are covered by our theory.

Example 1.2.9 (Distributed Aggregation)

The abstract DP framework is useful not only in modeling DP problems, but also in modeling algorithms arising in DP and even other contexts. We illustrate this with an example from [BeY10b] that relates to the distributed solution of large-scale discounted finite-state MDP using cost function approximation based on aggregation.† It involves a partition of the n states into m subsets for the purposes of distributed computation, and yields a corresponding approximation $(V_1, \ldots, V_m)$ to the cost vector J^*.

In particular, we have a discounted n-state MDP (cf. Example 1.2.2), and we introduce aggregate states $S_1, \ldots, S_m$, which are disjoint subsets of the original state space $\{1, \ldots, n\}$. We assume that these sets form a partition, i.e., each $x \in \{1, \ldots, n\}$ belongs to one and only one of the aggregate state/subsets. We envision a network of processors $\ell = 1, \ldots, m$, each assigned to the computation of a local cost function V_ℓ, defined on the corresponding aggregate state/subset S_ℓ:

$$V_\ell = \{V_{\ell y} \mid y \in S_\ell\}.$$

Processor ℓ also maintains a scalar aggregate cost R_ℓ for its aggregate state, which is a weighted average of the detailed cost values $V_{\ell x}$ within S_ℓ:

$$R_\ell = \sum_{x \in S_\ell} d_{\ell x} V_{\ell x},$$

where $d_{\ell x}$ are given probabilities with $d_{\ell x} \geq 0$ and $\sum_{x \in S_\ell} d_{\ell x} = 1$. The aggregate costs R_ℓ are communicated between processors and are used to perform the computation of the local cost functions V_ℓ (we will discuss computation models of this type in Section 2.6).

We denote $J = (V_1, \ldots, V_m, R_1, \ldots, R_m)$, so that J is a vector of dimension $n + m$. We introduce the mapping $H(x, u, J)$ defined for each of the n states x by

$$H(x, u, J) = W_\ell(x, u, V_\ell, R_1, \ldots, R_m), \qquad \text{if } x \in S_\ell.$$

where for $x \in S_\ell$

$$\begin{aligned} W_\ell(x, u, V_\ell, R_1, \ldots, R_m) = \sum_{y=1}^{n} p_{xy}(u) g(x, u, y) + \alpha \sum_{y \in S_\ell} p_{xy}(u) V_{\ell y} \\ + \alpha \sum_{y \notin S_\ell} p_{xy}(u) R_{s(y)}; \end{aligned}$$

and for each original system state y, we denote by $s(y)$ the index of the subset to which y belongs [i.e., $y \in S_{s(y)}$].

We may view H as an abstract mapping on the space of J, and aim to find its fixed point $J^* = (V_1^*, \ldots, V_m^*, R_1^*, \ldots, R_m^*)$. Then, for $\ell = 1, \ldots, m$, we

† See [Ber12a], Section 6.5.2, for a more detailed discussion. Other examples of algorithmic mappings that come under our framework arise in asynchronous policy iteration (see Sections 2.6.3, 3.3.2, and [BeY10a], [BeY10b], [YuB11a]), and in constrained forms of policy iteration (see [Ber11c], or [Ber12a], Exercise 2.7).

may view V_ℓ^* as an approximation to the optimal cost vector of the original MDP starting at states $x \in S_\ell$, and we may view R_ℓ^* as a form of aggregate cost for S_ℓ. The advantage of this formulation is that it involves significant decomposition and parallelization of the computations among the processors, when performing various DP algorithms. In particular, the computation of $W_\ell(x, u, V_\ell, R_1, \ldots, R_m)$ depends on just the local vector V_ℓ, whose dimension may be potentially much smaller than n.

1.2.4 Approximation-Related Mappings

Given an abstract DP model described by a mapping H, we may be interested in fixed points of related mappings other than T and T_μ. Such mappings may arise in various contexts; we have seen one that is related to distributed asynchronous aggregation in Example 1.2.9. An important context is subspace approximation, whereby T_μ and T are restricted onto a subspace of functions for the purpose of approximating their fixed points. Much of the theory of approximate DP and reinforcement learning relies on such approximations (see e.g., the books by Bertsekas and Tsitsiklis [BeT96], Sutton and Barto [SuB98], Gosavi [Gos03], Cao [Cao07], Chang, Fu, Hu, and Marcus [CFH07], Meyn [Mey07], Powell [Pow07], Borkar [Bor08], Haykin [Hay08], Busoniu, Babuska, De Schutter, and Ernst [BBD10], Szepesvari [Sze10], Bertsekas [Ber12a], and Vrabie, Vamvoudakis, and Lewis [VVL13]).

For an illustration, consider the approximate evaluation of the cost vector of a discrete-time Markov chain with states $i = 1, \ldots, n$. We assume that state transitions (i, j) occur at time k according to given transition probabilities p_{ij}, and generate a cost $\alpha^k g(i, j)$, where $\alpha \in (0, 1)$ is a discount factor. The cost function over an infinite number of stages can be shown to be the unique fixed point of the Bellman equation mapping $T : \Re^n \mapsto \Re^n$ whose components are given by

$$(TJ)(i) = \sum_{j=1}^{n} p_{ij}(u)\big(g(i, j) + \alpha J(j)\big), \qquad i = 1, \ldots, n, \ J \in \Re^n.$$

This is the same as the mapping T in the discounted finite-state MDP Example 1.2.2, except that we restrict attention to a single policy. Finding the cost function of a fixed policy is the important policy evaluation subproblem which arises prominently within the context of policy iteration.

The approximation of the fixed point of T is often based on the solution of lower-dimensional equations defined on the subspace $\{\Phi R \mid R \in \Re^s\}$ that is spanned by the columns of a given $n \times s$ matrix Φ. Two such approximating equations have been studied extensively (see [Ber12a], Chapter 6, for a detailed account and references; also [BeY07], [BeY09], [YuB10], [Ber11a] for extensions to abstract contexts beyond approximate DP). These are:

(a) The projected equation

$$\Phi R = \Pi_\xi T(\Phi R), \tag{1.18}$$

where Π_ξ denotes projection onto S with respect to a weighted Euclidean norm

$$\|J\|_\xi = \sum_{i=1}^{n} \xi_i J(i) \tag{1.19}$$

with $\xi = (\xi_1, \ldots, \xi_n)$ being a probability distribution with positive components.

(b) The aggregation equation

$$\Phi R = \Phi D T(\Phi R), \tag{1.20}$$

with D being an $s \times n$ matrix whose rows are restricted to be probability distributions; these are known as the disaggregation probabilities. Also, in this approach, the rows of Φ are restricted to be probability distributions; they are known as the aggregation probabilities.

We now see that solution of the projected equation (1.18) and the aggregation equation (1.20) amounts to finding a fixed point of the mappings $\Pi_\xi T$ and $\Phi D T$, respectively. These mappings derive their structure from the DP operator T, so they have some DP-like properties, which can be exploited for analysis and computation.

An important fact is that the aggregation mapping $\Phi D T$ preserves the monotonicity and the sup-norm contraction property of T, while the projected equation mapping $\Pi_\xi T$ does not. The reason for preservation of monotonicity is the nonnegativity of the components of the matrices Φ and D. The reason for preservation of sup-norm contraction is that the matrices Φ and D are sup-norm nonexpansive, because their rows are probability distributions. In fact, it can be shown that the solution R of Eq. (1.20) can be viewed as the *exact* DP solution of an "aggregate" DP problem that represents a lower-dimensional approximation of the original (see [Ber12a], Section 6.5).

By contrast, the projected equation mapping $\Pi_\xi T$ need not be monotone, because the components of Π_ξ need not be nonnegative. Moreover while the projection Π_ξ is nonexpansive with respect to the projection norm $\|\cdot\|_\xi$, it need not be nonexpansive with respect to the sup-norm. As a result the projected equation mapping $\Pi_\xi T$ need not be a sup-norm contraction. These facts play a significant role in approximate DP methodology.

Let us also mention that multistep versions of the mapping T have been used widely for approximations, particularly in connection with the projected equation approach. For example, the popular temporal difference methods, such as TD(λ), LSTD(λ), and LSPE(λ) (see the book references on reinforcement learning and approximate DP cited earlier), are based on the mapping $T^{(\lambda)} : \Re^n \mapsto \Re^n$ whose components are given by

$$\big(T^{(\lambda)} J\big)(i) = (1 - \lambda) \sum_{k=1}^{\infty} \lambda^{\ell-1} (T^\ell J)(i), \qquad i = 1, \ldots, n,\ J \in \Re^n,$$

for $\lambda \in (0, 1]$, where T^ℓ is the ℓ-fold composition of T with itself ℓ times. Here the mapping $T^{(\lambda)}$ is used in place of T in the projected equation (1.18). In the context of the aggregation equation approach, a multistep method based on the mapping $T^{(\lambda)}$ is the λ-aggregation method, given for the case of hard aggregation in [Ber12a], Section 6.5, as well as other forms of aggregation (see [Ber12a], [YuB12]).

A more general form of multistep approach, introduced and studied in [YuB12], uses instead the mapping $T^{(w)} : \Re^n \mapsto \Re^n$, with components

$$\big(T^{(w)}J\big)(i) = \sum_{\ell=1}^{\infty} w_{i\ell}(T^\ell J)(i), \qquad i = 1, \ldots, n,\ J \in \Re^n,$$

where for each i, $(w_{i1}, w_{i2}, \ldots)$ is a probability distribution over the positive integers. Then the multistep analog of the projected Eq. (1.18) is

$$\Phi R = \Pi_\xi T^{(w)}(\Phi R), \tag{1.21}$$

while the multistep analog of the aggregation Eq. (1.20) is

$$\Phi R = \Phi D T^{(w)}(\Phi R). \tag{1.22}$$

The mapping $T^{(\lambda)}$ is obtained for $w_{i\ell} = (1 - \lambda)\lambda^{\ell-1}$, independently of the state i. The solution of Eqs. (1.21) and (1.22) by simulation-based methods is discussed in [YuB12] and [Yu12].

In fact, a connection between projected equations of the form (1.21) and aggregation equations of the form (1.22) was established in [YuB12] through the use of a seminorm [this is given by the same expression as the norm $\|\cdot\|_\xi$ of Eq. (1.19), with some of the components of ξ allowed to be 0]. In particular, the most prominent classes of aggregation equations can be viewed as seminorm projected equations because it turns out that ΦD is a seminorm projection (see [Ber12a], p. 639, [YuB12], Section 4). Moreover they can be viewed as projected equations where the projection is oblique (see [Ber12a], Section 7.3.6).

The preceding observations are important for our purposes, as they indicate that much of the theory developed in this book applies to approximation-related mappings based on aggregation. However, this is not true to nearly the same extent for approximation-related mappings based on projection.

1.3 ORGANIZATION OF THE BOOK

The examples of the preceding section have illustrated how the monotonicity assumption is satisfied for many DP models, while the contraction assumption may or may not be satisfied. In particular, the contraction assumption is satisfied for the mapping H in Examples 1.2.1-1.2.5, assuming that there is discounting and that the cost per stage is bounded, but it need not hold in the SSP Example 1.2.6 and the multiplicative Example 1.2.8.

The main theme of this book is that the presence or absence of monotonicity and contraction is the primary determinant of the analytical and algorithmic theory of a typical total cost DP model. In our development, with some minor exceptions, we will assume that monotonicity holds. Consequently, the rest of the book is organized around the presence or absence of the contraction property. In the next four chapters we will discuss the following four types of models.

(a) **Contractive models:** These models, discussed in Chapter 2, have the richest and strongest algorithmic theory, and are the benchmark against which the theory of other models is compared. Prominent among them are discounted stochastic optimal control problems (cf. Example 1.2.1), finite-state discounted MDP (cf. Example 1.2.2), and some special types of SSP problems (cf. Example 1.2.6).

(b) **Semicontractive models:** In these models T_μ is monotone but it need not be a contraction for all $\mu \in \mathcal{M}$. Instead policies are separated into those that "behave well" with respect to our optimization framework and those that do not. It turns out that the notion of contraction is not sufficiently general for our purposes. We will thus introduce a related notion of "regularity," which is based on the idea that a policy μ should be considered "well-behaved" if the dynamic system defined by T_μ has J_μ as an asymptotically stable equilibrium within some domain. Our models and analysis are patterned to a large extent after the SSP problems of Example 1.2.6 (the regular μ correspond to the proper policies). One of the complications here is that policies that are not regular, may have cost functions that take the value $+\infty$ or $-\infty$. Still under certain conditions, which directly or indirectly guarantee that there exists an optimal regular policy, the complications can be dealt with, and we can prove strong properties for these models, sometimes almost as strong as those of the contractive models.

(c) **Noncontractive models:** These models rely on just the monotonicity property of T_μ, and are more complex than the preceding ones. As in semicontractive models, the various cost functions of the problem may take the values $+\infty$ or $-\infty$, and the mappings T_μ and T must accordingly be allowed to deal with such functions. However, the optimal cost function may take the values ∞ and $-\infty$ as a matter of course (rather than on an exceptional basis, as in semicontractive models). The complications are considerable, and much of the theory of the contractive models generalizes in weaker form, if at all. For example, in general the fixed point equation $J = TJ$ need not have a unique solution, the value iteration method may work starting with some functions but not with others, and the policy iteration method may not work at all. Of course some of these weaknesses may not appear in the presence of additional structure, and we will discuss noncontractive models that also have some semicontractive structure, and corresponding favorable properties.

(d) **Restricted Policies Models:** These models are variants of some of the preceding ones, where there are restrictions of the set of policies, so that $\mathcal{M}$ may be a strict subset of the set of functions $\mu : X \mapsto U$ with $\mu(x) \in U(x)$ for all $x \in X$. Such restrictions may include measurability (needed to establish a mathematically rigorous probabilistic framework) or special structure that enhances the characterization of optimal policies and facilitates their computation.

Examples of DP problems from each of the above model categories, mostly special cases of the specific DP models discussed in Section 1.2, are scattered throughout the book, both to illustrate the theory and its exceptions, and to illustrate the beneficial role of additional special structure. The discussion of algorithms centers on abstract forms of value and policy iteration, and is organized along three characteristics: *exact, approximate, and asynchronous.*

The exact algorithms represent idealized versions, the approximate represent implementations that use approximations of various kinds, and the asynchronous involve irregular computation orders, where the costs and controls at different states are updated at different iterations (for example the cost of a single state being iterated at a time, as in Gauss-Seidel and other methods; see [Ber12a]). Approximate and asynchronous implementations have been the subject of intensive investigations in the last twenty five years, in the context of the solution of large-scale problems. Some of this methodology relies on the use of simulation, which is asynchronous by nature and is prominent in approximate DP and reinforcement learning.

1.4 NOTES, SOURCES, AND EXERCISES

The connection between DP and fixed point theory may be traced to Shapley [Sha53], who exploited contraction mappings in analysis of the two-player dynamic game model of Example 1.2.4. Since that time the underlying contraction properties of discounted DP problems with bounded cost per stage have been explicitly or implicitly used by most authors that have dealt with the subject. Moreover, the value of the abstract viewpoint as the basis for economical and insightful analysis has been widely recognized.

An abstract DP model, based on unweighted sup-norm contraction assumptions, was introduced in the paper by Denardo [Den67]. This model pointed to the fundamental connections between DP and fixed point theory, and provided generality and insight into the principal analytical and algorithmic ideas underlying the discounted DP research up to that time. Abstract DP ideas were also researched earlier, notably in the paper by Mitten (Denardo's Ph.D. thesis advisor) [Mit64]; see also Denardo and Mitten [DeM67]. The properties of monotone contractions were also used in the analysis of sequential games by Zachrisson [Zac64].

Denardo's model motivated a related abstract DP model by the author [Ber77], which relies only on monotonicity properties, and was patterned after the positive DP problem of Blackwell [Bla65] and the negative DP problem of Strauch [Str66]. These two abstract DP models were used extensively in the book by Bertsekas and Shreve [BeS78] for the analysis of both discounted and undiscounted DP problems, ranging over MDP, minimax, multiplicative, Borel space models, and models based on outer integration. Extensions of the analysis of [Ber77] were given by Verdu and Poor [VeP87], which considered additional structure that allows the development of backward and forward value iterations, and in the thesis by Szepesvari [Sze98a], [Sze98b], which introduced non-Markovian policies into the abstract DP framework. The model of [Ber77] was also used by Bertsekas [Ber82], and Bertsekas and Yu [BeY10b], to develop asynchronous value and policy iteration methods for abstract contractive and noncontractive DP models. Another line of related research involving abstract DP mappings that are not necessarily scalar-valued was initiated by Mitten [Mit74], and was followed up by a number of authors, including Sobel [Sob75], Morin [Mor82], and Carraway and Morin [CaM88].

Restricted policies models that aim to address measurability issues in the context of abstract DP were first considered in [BeS98]. Followup research on this highly technical subject has been limited, and some issues have not been fully worked out beyond the classical discounted, positive, and negative stochastic optimal control problems; see Chapter 5.

Generally, noncontractive total cost DP models with some special structure beyond monotonicity, fall in three major categories: monotone increasing models principally represented by negative DP, monotone decreasing models principally represented by positive DP, and transient models, exemplified by the SSP model of Example 1.2.6, where the decision process terminates after a period that is random and subject to control. Abstract DP models patterned after the first two categories have been known since [Ber77] and are further discussed in Section 4.3. The semicontractive models of Chapters 3 and 4, are patterned after the third category, and their analysis is based on the idea of separating policies into those that are well-behaved (have contraction-like properties) and those that are not (but their detrimental effects can be effectively limited thanks to the problem's structure). As far as the author knows, this idea is new in the context of abstract DP. One of the aims of the present monograph is to develop this idea and to show that it leads to an important and insightful paradigm for conceptualization and solution of major classes of practical DP problems.

EXERCISES

1.1 (Multistep Contraction Mappings)

This exercise shows how starting with an abstract mapping, we can obtain multistep mappings with the same fixed points and a stronger contraction modulus. Consider a set of mappings $T_\mu : B(X) \mapsto B(X)$, $\mu \in \mathcal{M}$, satisfying the contraction Assumption 1.2.2, let m be a positive integer, and let $\mathcal{M}_m$ be the set of m-tuples $\nu = (\mu_0, \ldots, \mu_{m-1})$, where $\mu_k \in \mathcal{M}$, $k = 1, \ldots, m-1$. For each $\nu = (\mu_0, \ldots, \mu_{m-1}) \in \mathcal{M}_m$, define the mapping $\overline{T}_\nu$, by

$$\overline{T}_\nu J = T_{\mu_0} \cdots T_{\mu_{m-1}} J, \qquad \forall\, J \in B(X).$$

Show that we have the contraction properties

$$\|\overline{T}_\nu J - \overline{T}_\nu J'\| \le \alpha^m \|J - J'\|, \qquad \forall\, J, J' \in B(X), \tag{1.23}$$

and

$$\|\overline{T} J - \overline{T} J'\| \le \alpha^m \|J - J'\|, \qquad \forall\, J, J' \in B(X), \tag{1.24}$$

where $\overline{T}$ is defined by

$$(\overline{T} J)(x) = \inf_{(\mu_0, \ldots, \mu_{m-1}) \in \mathcal{M}_m} (T_{\mu_0} \cdots T_{\mu_{m-1}} J)(x), \qquad \forall\, J \in B(X),\ x \in X.$$

1.2 (State-Dependent Weighted Multistep Mappings [YuB12])

Consider a set of mappings $T_\mu : B(X) \mapsto B(X)$, $\mu \in \mathcal{M}$, satisfying the contraction Assumption 1.2.2. Consider also the mappings $T_\mu^{(w)} : B(X) \mapsto B(X)$ defined by

$$(T_\mu^{(w)} J)(x) = \sum_{\ell=1}^{\infty} w_\ell(x) \big(T_\mu^\ell J\big)(x), \qquad x \in X,\ J \in B(X),$$

where $w_\ell(x)$ are nonnegative scalars such that for all $x \in X$,

$$\sum_{\ell=1}^{\infty} w_\ell(x) = 1.$$

Show that

$$\frac{\big|(T_\mu^{(w)} J)(x) - (T_\mu^{(w)} J')(x)\big|}{v(x)} \le \sum_{\ell=1}^{\infty} w_\ell(x) \alpha^\ell \|J - J'\|, \qquad \forall\, x \in X,$$

where α is the contraction modulus of T_μ, so that $T_\mu^{(w)}$ is a contraction with modulus

$$\bar{\alpha} = \sup_{x \in X} \sum_{\ell=1}^{\infty} w_\ell(x)\, \alpha^\ell \le \alpha.$$

Show also that T_μ and $T_\mu^{(w)}$ have a common fixed point for all $\mu \in \mathcal{M}$.

2

Contractive Models

Contents

In this chapter we consider the abstract DP model of Section 1.2 under the most favorable assumptions: monotonicity and weighted sup-norm contraction. Important special cases of this model are the discounted problems with bounded cost per stage (Example 1.2.1-1.2.5), the stochastic shortest path problem of Example 1.2.6 in the case where all policies are proper, as well as other problems involving special structures. We first provide some basic analytical results and then focus on two types of algorithms: *value iteration and policy iteration.* In addition to exact forms of these algorithms, we discuss combinations and approximate versions, as well as asynchronous distributed versions.

2.1 FIXED POINT EQUATION AND OPTIMALITY CONDITIONS

In this section we recall the abstract DP model of Section 1.2, and derive some of its basic properties under the monotonicity and contraction assumptions of Section 1.3. We consider a set X of states and a set U of controls, and for each $x \in X$, a nonempty control constraint set $U(x) \subset U$. We denote by $\mathcal{M}$ the set of all functions $\mu : X \mapsto U$ with $\mu(x) \in U(x)$ for all $x \in X$, which we refer to as policies.

We denote by $R(X)$ the set of real-valued functions $J : X \mapsto \Re$. We have a mapping $H : X \times U \times R(X) \mapsto \Re$ and for each policy $\mu \in \mathcal{M}$, we consider the mapping $T_\mu : R(X) \mapsto R(X)$ defined by

$$(T_\mu J)(x) = H\big(x, \mu(x), J\big), \qquad \forall\, x \in X.$$

We also consider the mapping T defined by

$$(TJ)(x) = \inf_{u \in U(x)} H(x, u, J) = \inf_{\mu \in \mathcal{M}} (T_\mu J)(x), \qquad \forall\, x \in X.$$

We want to find a function $J^* \in R(X)$ such that

$$J^*(x) = \inf_{u \in U(x)} H(x, u, J^*), \qquad \forall\, x \in X,$$

i.e., to find a fixed point of T within $R(X)$. We also want to obtain a policy $\mu^* \in \mathcal{M}$ such that $T_{\mu^*} J^* = TJ^*$.

Let us restate for convenience the contraction and monotonicity assumptions of Section 1.2.2.

Assumption 2.1.1: (Monotonicity) If $J, J' \in R(X)$ and $J \leq J'$, then

$$H(x, u, J) \leq H(x, u, J'), \qquad \forall\, x \in X,\ u \in U(x).$$

Note that the monotonicity assumption implies the following properties, for all $J, J' \in R(X)$ and $k = 0, 1, \ldots$, which we will use extensively:

$$J \leq J' \quad \Rightarrow \quad T^k J \leq T^k J', \qquad T_\mu^k J \leq T_\mu^k J', \quad \forall\, \mu \in \mathcal{M},$$

$$J \leq TJ \quad \Rightarrow \quad T^k J \leq T^{k+1} J, \qquad T_\mu^k J \leq T_\mu^{k+1} J, \quad \forall\, \mu \in \mathcal{M}.$$

Here T^k and T_μ^k denotes the k-fold composition of T and T_μ, respectively.

For the contraction assumption, we introduce a function $v : X \mapsto \Re$ with

$$v(x) > 0, \qquad \forall\, x \in X.$$

We consider the weighted sup-norm

$$\|J\| = \sup_{x \in X} \frac{\big|J(x)\big|}{v(x)}$$

on $B(X)$, the space of real-valued functions J on X such that $J(x)/v(x)$ is bounded over $x \in X$ (see Appendix B for a discussion of the properties of this space).

Assumption 2.1.2: (Contraction) For all $J \in B(X)$ and $\mu \in \mathcal{M}$, the functions $T_\mu J$ and TJ belong to $B(X)$. Furthermore, for some $\alpha \in (0, 1)$, we have

$$\|T_\mu J - T_\mu J'\| \leq \alpha \|J - J'\|, \qquad \forall\, J, J' \in B(X),\ \mu \in \mathcal{M}.$$

The classical DP models where both the monotonicity and contraction assumptions are satisfied are the discounted finite-state Markovian decision problem of Example 1.2.2, and the stochastic shortest path problem of Example 1.2.6 in the special case where all policies are proper. We refer the reader to the textbook [Ber12a] for an extensive discussion of these problems.

The following proposition summarizes some of the basic consequences of the contraction assumption.

Proposition 2.1.1: Let the contraction Assumption 2.1.2 hold. Then:

(a) The mappings T_μ and T are contraction mappings with modulus α over $B(X)$, and have unique fixed points in $B(X)$, denoted J_μ and J^*, respectively.

(b) For any $J \in B(X)$ and $\mu \in \mathcal{M}$,

$$\lim_{k\to\infty} \|J^* - T^k J\| = 0, \qquad \lim_{k\to\infty} \|J_\mu - T_\mu^k J\| = 0.$$

(c) We have $T_\mu J^* = TJ^*$ if and only if $J_\mu = J^*$.

(d) For any $J \in B(X)$,

$$\|J^* - J\| \le \frac{1}{1-\alpha}\|TJ - J\|, \qquad \|J^* - TJ\| \le \frac{\alpha}{1-\alpha}\|TJ - J\|.$$

(e) For any $J \in B(X)$ and $\mu \in \mathcal{M}$,

$$\|J_\mu - J\| \le \frac{1}{1-\alpha}\|T_\mu J - J\|, \qquad \|J_\mu - T_\mu J\| \le \frac{\alpha}{1-\alpha}\|T_\mu J - J\|.$$

Proof: We showed in Section 1.2.2 that T is a contraction with modulus α over $B(X)$. Parts (a) and (b) follow from Prop. B.1 of Appendix B.

To show part (c), note that if $T_\mu J^* = TJ^*$, then in view of $TJ^* = J^*$, we have $T_\mu J^* = J^*$, which implies that $J^* = J_\mu$, since J_μ is the unique fixed point of T_μ. Conversely, if $J_\mu = J^*$, we have $T_\mu J^* = T_\mu J_\mu = J_\mu = J^* = TJ^*$.

To show part (d), we use the triangle inequality to write for every k,

$$\|T^k J - J\| \le \sum_{\ell=1}^{k} \|T^\ell J - T^{\ell-1} J\| \le \sum_{\ell=1}^{k} \alpha^{\ell-1}\|TJ - J\|.$$

Taking the limit as $k \to \infty$ and using part (b), the left-hand side inequality follows. The right-hand side inequality follows from the left-hand side and the contraction property of T. The proof of part (e) is similar to part (d) [indeed it is the special case of part (d) where T is equal to T_μ, i.e., when $U(x) = \{\mu(x)\}$ for all $x \in X$]. **Q.E.D.**

Part (c) of the preceding proposition shows that there exists a $\mu \in \mathcal{M}$ such that $J_\mu = J^*$ if and only if the minimum of $H(x, u, J^*)$ over $U(x)$ is attained for all $x \in X$. Of course the minimum is attained if $U(x)$ is finite for every x, but otherwise this is not guaranteed in the absence of additional assumptions. Part (d) provides a useful error bound: we can evaluate the proximity of any function $J \in B(X)$ to the fixed point J^* by applying T to J and computing $\|TJ - J\|$. The left-hand side inequality of part (e) (with $J = J^*$) shows that for every $\epsilon > 0$, there exists a $\mu_\epsilon \in \mathcal{M}$ such that $\|J_{\mu_\epsilon} - J^*\| \le \epsilon$, which may be obtained by letting $\mu_\epsilon(x)$ minimize $H(x, u, J^*)$ over $U(x)$ within an error of $(1-\alpha)\epsilon\, v(x)$, for all $x \in X$.

The preceding proposition and some of the subsequent results may also be proved if $B(X)$ is replaced by a closed subset $\overline{B}(X) \subset B(X)$. This is because the contraction mapping fixed point theorem (Prop. B.1) applies to closed subsets of complete spaces. For simplicity, however, we will disregard this possibility in the present chapter.

An important consequence of monotonicity of H, when it holds in addition to contraction, is that it implies an optimality property of J^*.

Proposition 2.1.2: Let the monotonicity and contraction Assumptions 2.1.1 and 2.1.2 hold. Then

$$J^*(x) = \inf_{\mu \in \mathcal{M}} J_\mu(x), \qquad \forall\, x \in X.$$

Furthermore, for every $\epsilon > 0$, there exists $\mu_\epsilon \in \mathcal{M}$ such that

$$J^*(x) \leq J_{\mu_\epsilon}(x) \leq J^*(x) + \epsilon, \qquad \forall\, x \in X. \tag{2.1}$$

Proof: We note that the right-hand side of Eq. (2.1) holds by Prop. 2.1.1(e) (see the remark following its proof). Thus $\inf_{\mu \in \mathcal{M}} J_\mu(x) \leq J^*(x)$ for all $x \in X$. To show the reverse inequality as well as the left-hand side of Eq. (2.1), we note that for all $\mu \in \mathcal{M}$, we have $TJ^* \leq T_\mu J^*$, and since $J^* = TJ^*$, it follows that $J^* \leq T_\mu J^*$. By applying repeatedly T_μ to both sides of this inequality and by using the monotonicity Assumption 2.1.1, we obtain $J^* \leq T_\mu^k J^*$ for all $k > 0$. Taking the limit as $k \to \infty$, we see that $J^* \leq J_\mu$ for all $\mu \in \mathcal{M}$. **Q.E.D.**

Note that without monotonicity, we may have $\inf_{\mu \in \mathcal{M}} J_\mu(x) < J^*(x)$ for some x. This is illustrated by the following example.

Example 2.1.1 (Counterexample Without Monotonicity)

Let $X = \{x_1, x_2\}$, $U = \{u_1, u_2\}$, and let

$$H(x_1, u, J) = \begin{cases} -\alpha J(x_2) & \text{if } u = u_1, \\ -1 + \alpha J(x_1) & \text{if } u = u_2, \end{cases} \qquad H(x_2, u, J) = \begin{cases} 0 & \text{if } u = u_1, \\ B & \text{if } u = u_2, \end{cases}$$

where B is a positive scalar. Then it can be seen that

$$J^*(x_1) = -\frac{1}{1-\alpha}, \qquad J^*(x_2) = 0,$$

and $J_{\mu^*} = J^*$ where $\mu^*(x_1) = u_2$ and $\mu^*(x_2) = u_1$. On the other hand, for $\mu(x_1) = u_1$ and $\mu(x_2) = u_2$, we have $J_\mu(x_1) = -\alpha B$ and $J_\mu(x_2) = B$, so $J_\mu(x_1) < J^*(x_1)$ for B sufficiently large.

Optimality over Nonstationary Policies

The connection with DP motivates us to consider the set Π of all sequences $\pi = \{\mu_0, \mu_1, \ldots\}$ with $\mu_k \in \mathcal{M}$ for all k (nonstationary policies in the DP context), and define

$$J_\pi(x) = \limsup_{k\to\infty} (T_{\mu_0} \cdots T_{\mu_k} \bar{J})(x), \qquad \forall\, x \in X,$$

with $\bar{J}$ being some function in $B(X)$, where $T_{\mu_0} \cdots T_{\mu_k} J$ denotes the composition of the mappings $T_{\mu_0}, \ldots, T_{\mu_k}$ applied to J, i.e,

$$T_{\mu_0} \cdots T_{\mu_k} J = T_{\mu_0}\big(T_{\mu_1} \cdots (T_{\mu_{k-1}}(T_{\mu_k} J)) \cdots\big).$$

Note that under the contraction Assumption 2.1.2, the choice of $\bar{J}$ in the definition of J_π does not matter, since for any two $J, J' \in B(X)$, we have

$$\|T_{\mu_0} T_{\mu_1} \cdots T_{\mu_k} J - T_{\mu_0} T_{\mu_1} \cdots T_{\mu_k} J'\| \le \alpha^{k+1} \|J - J'\|,$$

so the value of $J_\pi(x)$ is independent of $\bar{J}$. Since by Prop. 2.1.1(b), $J_\mu(x) = \lim_{k\to\infty} (T_\mu^k J)(x)$ for all $\mu \in \mathcal{M}$, $J \in B(X)$, and $x \in X$, in the DP context we recognize J_μ as the cost function of the stationary policy $\{\mu, \mu, \ldots\}$.

We now claim that under the monotonicity and contraction Assumptions 2.1.1 and 2.1.2, J^*, *which was defined as the unique fixed point of* T, *is equal to the optimal value of* J_π, i.e.,

$$J^*(x) = \inf_{\pi\in\Pi} J_\pi(x), \qquad \forall\, x \in X.$$

Indeed, since $\mathcal{M}$ defines a subset of Π, we have from Prop. 2.1.2,

$$J^*(x) = \inf_{\mu\in\mathcal{M}} J_\mu(x) \ge \inf_{\pi\in\Pi} J_\pi(x), \qquad \forall\, x \in X,$$

while for every $\pi \in \Pi$ and $x \in X$, we have

$$J_\pi(x) = \limsup_{k\to\infty} (T_{\mu_0} T_{\mu_1} \cdots T_{\mu_k} \bar{J})(x) \ge \lim_{k\to\infty} (T^{k+1} \bar{J})(x) = J^*(x)$$

[the monotonicity Assumption 2.1.1 can be used to show that

$$T_{\mu_0} T_{\mu_1} \cdots T_{\mu_k} \bar{J} \ge T^{k+1} \bar{J},$$

and the last equality holds by Prop. 2.1.1(b)]. Combining the preceding relations, we obtain $J^*(x) = \inf_{\pi\in\Pi} J_\pi(x)$.

Thus, in DP terms, *we may view* J^* *as an optimal cost function over all policies.* At the same time, Prop. 2.1.2 states that stationary policies are sufficient in the sense that *the optimal cost can be attained to within arbitrary accuracy with a stationary policy* [uniformly for all $x \in X$, as Eq. (2.1) shows].

Error Bounds and Other Inequalities

The analysis of abstract DP algorithms and related approximations requires the use of some basic inequalities that follow from the assumptions of contraction and monotonicity. We have obtained two such results in Prop. 2.1.1(d),(e), which assume only the contraction assumption. These results can be strengthened if in addition to contraction, we have monotonicity. To this end we first show the following useful characterization.

Proposition 2.1.3: The monotonicity and contraction Assumptions 2.1.1 and 2.1.2 hold if and only if for all $J, J' \in B(X)$, $\mu \in \mathcal{M}$, and scalar $c \geq 0$, we have

$$J \leq J' + c\,v \quad \Rightarrow \quad T_\mu J \leq T_\mu J' + \alpha c\,v, \tag{2.2}$$

where v is the weight function of the weighted sup-norm $\|\cdot\|$.

Proof: Let the contraction and monotonicity assumptions hold. If $J' \leq J + c\,v$, we have

$$H(x,u,J') \leq H(x,u,J+c\,v) \leq H(x,u,J) + \alpha c\,v(x), \qquad \forall\, x \in X,\, u \in U(x), \tag{2.3}$$

where the left-side inequality follows from the monotonicity assumption and the right-side inequality follows from the contraction assumption, which together with $\|v\| = 1$, implies that

$$\frac{H(x,u,J+c\,v) - H(x,u,J)}{v(x)} \leq \alpha \|J + c\,v - J\| = \alpha c.$$

The condition (2.3) implies the desired condition (2.2). Conversely, condition (2.2) for $c = 0$ yields the monotonicity assumption, while for $c = \|J' - J\|$ it yields the contraction assumption. **Q.E.D.**

We can now derive the following useful variant of Prop. 2.1.1(d),(e), which involves one-sided inequalities. This variant will be used in the derivation of error bounds for various computational methods.

Proposition 2.1.4: (Error Bounds Under Contraction and Monotonicity) Let the monotonicity and contraction Assumptions 2.1.1 and 2.1.2 hold.

(a) For any $J \in B(X)$ and $c \geq 0$, we have

$$TJ \leq J + c\,v \quad \Rightarrow \quad J^* \leq J + \frac{c}{1-\alpha} v,$$

$$J \leq TJ + c\,v \quad \Rightarrow \quad J \leq J^* + \frac{c}{1-\alpha} v.$$

(b) For any $J \in B(X)$, $\mu \in \mathcal{M}$, and $c \geq 0$, we have

$$T_\mu J \leq J + c\,v \quad \Rightarrow \quad J_\mu \leq J + \frac{c}{1-\alpha} v,$$

$$J \leq T_\mu J + c\,v \quad \Rightarrow \quad J \leq J_\mu + \frac{c}{1-\alpha} v.$$

(c) For all $J \in B(X)$, $c \geq 0$, and $k = 0, 1, \ldots$, we have

$$TJ \leq J + c\,v \qquad \Rightarrow \qquad J^* \leq T^k J + \frac{\alpha^k c}{1-\alpha} v,$$

$$J \leq TJ + c\,v \qquad \Rightarrow \qquad T^k J \leq J^* + \frac{\alpha^k c}{1-\alpha} v.$$

Proof: (a) We show the first relation. Applying Eq. (2.2) with J' and J replaced by J and TJ, respectively, and taking infimum over $\mu \in \mathcal{M}$, we see that if $TJ \leq J + c\,v$, then $T^2 J \leq TJ + \alpha c\,v$. Proceeding similarly, it follows that

$$T^\ell J \leq T^{\ell-1} J + \alpha^{\ell-1} c\,v.$$

We now write for every k,

$$T^k J - J = \sum_{\ell=1}^{k} (T^\ell J - T^{\ell-1} J) \leq \sum_{\ell=1}^{k} \alpha^{\ell-1} c\,v,$$

from which, by taking the limit as $k \to \infty$, we obtain $J^* \leq J + \big(c/(1-\alpha)\big)v$. The second relation follows similarly.

(b) This part is the special case of part (a) where T is equal to T_μ.

(c) We show the first relation. From part (a), the inequality $TJ \leq J + c\,v$ implies that

$$J^* \leq J + \frac{c}{1-\alpha} v.$$

Applying T^k to both sides of this inequality, and using the monotonicity and fixed point property of T^k, we have

$$J^* \leq T^k \left(J + \frac{c}{1-\alpha} v \right).$$

Using Eq. (2.2) with T_μ and α replaced by T^k and α^k, respectively, we obtain

$$T^k \left(J + \frac{c}{1-\alpha} v \right) \leq T^k J + \frac{\alpha^k c}{1-\alpha} v,$$

and the first relation to be shown follows from the preceding two relations. The second relation follows similarly. **Q.E.D.**

2.2 LIMITED LOOKAHEAD POLICIES

In this section, we discuss a basic building block in the algorithmic methodology of abstract DP. Given some function $\tilde{J}$ that approximates J^*, we obtain a policy by solving a finite-horizon problem where $\tilde{J}$ is the terminal cost function. The simplest possibility is a *one-step lookahead policy* $\overline{\mu}$ defined by

$$\overline{\mu}(x) \in \arg\min_{u \in U(x)} H(x, u, \tilde{J}), \qquad x \in X. \tag{2.4}$$

The following proposition gives some bounds for its performance.

Proposition 2.2.1: (One-Step Lookahead Error Bounds) Let the contraction Assumption 2.1.2 hold, and let $\overline{\mu}$ be a one-step lookahead policy obtained by minimization in Eq. (2.4), i.e., satisfying $T_{\overline{\mu}}\tilde{J} = T\tilde{J}$. Then

$$\|J_{\overline{\mu}} - T\tilde{J}\| \leq \frac{\alpha}{1-\alpha} \|T\tilde{J} - \tilde{J}\|, \tag{2.5}$$

where $\|\cdot\|$ denotes the weighted sup-norm. Moreover

$$\|J_{\overline{\mu}} - J^*\| \leq \frac{2\alpha}{1-\alpha} \|\tilde{J} - J^*\|, \tag{2.6}$$

and

$$\|J_{\overline{\mu}} - J^*\| \leq \frac{2}{1-\alpha} \|T\tilde{J} - \tilde{J}\|. \tag{2.7}$$

Proof: Equation (2.5) follows from the second relation of Prop. 2.1.1(e) with $J = \tilde{J}$. Also from the first relation of Prop. 2.1.1(e) with $J = J^*$, we have

$$\|J_{\overline{\mu}} - J^*\| \le \frac{1}{1-\alpha}\|T_{\overline{\mu}}J^* - J^*\|.$$

By using the triangle inequality, and the relations $T_{\overline{\mu}}\tilde{J} = T\tilde{J}$ and $J^* = TJ^*$, we obtain

$$\begin{aligned}
\|T_{\overline{\mu}}J^* - J^*\| &\le \|T_{\overline{\mu}}J^* - T_{\overline{\mu}}\tilde{J}\|| + \|T_{\overline{\mu}}\tilde{J} - T\tilde{J}\|| + \|T\tilde{J} - J^*\| \\
&= \|T_{\overline{\mu}}J^* - T_{\overline{\mu}}\tilde{J}\|| + \|T\tilde{J} - TJ^*\| \\
&\le \alpha\|J^* - \tilde{J}\| + \alpha\|\tilde{J} - J^*\| \\
&= 2\alpha\,\|\tilde{J} - J^*\|,
\end{aligned}$$

and Eq. (2.6) follows by combining the preceding two relations.

Also, from the first relation of Prop. 2.1.1(d) with $J = \tilde{J}$,

$$\|J^* - \tilde{J}\| \le \frac{1}{1-\alpha}\|T\tilde{J} - \tilde{J}\|. \tag{2.8}$$

Thus

$$\begin{aligned}
\|J_{\overline{\mu}} - J^*\| &\le \|J_{\overline{\mu}} - T\tilde{J}\| + \|T\tilde{J} - \tilde{J}\| + \|\tilde{J} - J^*\| \\
&\le \frac{\alpha}{1-\alpha}\|T\tilde{J} - \tilde{J}\| + \|T\tilde{J} - \tilde{J}\| + \frac{1}{1-\alpha}\|T\tilde{J} - \tilde{J}\| \\
&= \frac{2}{1-\alpha}\|T\tilde{J} - \tilde{J}\|,
\end{aligned}$$

where the second inequality follows from Eqs. (2.5) and (2.8). This proves Eq. (2.7). **Q.E.D.**

Equation (2.5) provides a computable bound on the cost function $J_{\overline{\mu}}$ of the one-step lookahead policy. The bound (2.6) says that if the one-step lookahead approximation $\tilde{J}$ is within ϵ of the optimal, the performance of the one-step lookahead policy is within $2\alpha\epsilon/(1-\alpha)$ of the optimal. Unfortunately, this is not very reassuring when α is close to 1, in which case the error bound is very large relative to ϵ. Nonetheless, the following example from [BeT96], Section 6.1.1, shows that this bound is tight in the sense that for any $\alpha < 1$, there is a problem with just two states where the error bound is satisfied with equality. What is happening is that an $O(\epsilon)$ difference in single stage cost between two controls can generate an $O\big(\epsilon/(1-\alpha)\big)$ difference in policy costs, yet it can be "nullified" in the fixed point equation $J^* = TJ^*$ by an $O(\epsilon)$ difference between J^* and $\tilde{J}$.

Example 2.2.1

Consider a discounted optimal control problem with two states, 1 and 2, and deterministic transitions. State 2 is absorbing, but at state 1 there are two possible decisions: move to state 2 (policy μ^*) or stay at state 1 (policy μ).

The cost of each transition is 0 except for the transition from 1 to itself under policy μ, which has cost $2\alpha\epsilon$, where ϵ is a positive scalar and $\alpha \in [0, 1)$ is the discount factor. The optimal policy μ^* is to move from state 1 to state 2, and the optimal cost-to-go function is $J^*(1) = J^*(2) = 0$. Consider the vector $\tilde{J}$ with $\tilde{J}(1) = -\epsilon$ and $\tilde{J}(2) = \epsilon$, so that

$$\|\tilde{J} - J^*\| = \epsilon,$$

as assumed in Eq. (2.6) (cf. Prop. 2.2.1). The policy μ that decides to stay at state 1 is a one-step lookahead policy based on $\tilde{J}$, because

$$2\alpha\epsilon + \alpha\tilde{J}(1) = \alpha\epsilon = 0 + \alpha\tilde{J}(2).$$

We have

$$J_\mu(1) = \frac{2\alpha\epsilon}{1-\alpha} = \frac{2\alpha}{1-\alpha}\|\tilde{J} - J^*\|,$$

so the bound of Eq. (2.6) holds with equality.

Multistep Lookahead Policies with Approximations

Let us now consider a more general form of lookahead involving multiple stages as well as other approximations of the type that we will consider later in the implementation of various approximate value and policy iteration algorithms. In particular, we will assume that given any $J \in B(X)$, we cannot compute exactly TJ, but instead we can compute $\tilde{J} \in B(X)$ and $\mu \in \mathcal{M}$ such that

$$\|\tilde{J} - TJ\| \leq \delta, \qquad \|T_\mu J - TJ\| \leq \epsilon, \tag{2.9}$$

where δ and ϵ are nonnegative scalars. These scalars may be unknown, so the resulting analysis will have a mostly qualitative character.

The case $\delta > 0$ arises when the state space is either infinite or it is finite but very large. Then instead of calculating $(TJ)(x)$ for all states x, one may do so only for some states and estimate $(TJ)(x)$ for the remaining states x by some form of interpolation. Alternatively, one may use simulation data [e.g., noisy values of $(TJ)(x)$ for some or all x] and some kind of least-squares error fit of $(TJ)(x)$ with a function from a suitable parametric class. The function $\tilde{J}$ thus obtained will satisfy $\|\tilde{J} - TJ\| \leq \delta$ with $\delta > 0$. Note that δ may not be small in this context, and the resulting performance degradation may be a primary concern.

Cases where $\epsilon > 0$ may arise when the control space is infinite or finite but large, and the minimization involved in the calculation of $(TJ)(x)$ cannot be done exactly. Note, however, that it is possible that

$$\delta > 0, \qquad \epsilon = 0,$$

and in fact this occurs often in practice. In an alternative scenario, we may first obtain the policy μ subject to a restriction that it belongs to a certain subset of structured policies, so it satisfies

$$\|T_\mu J - TJ\| \leq \epsilon$$

for some $\epsilon > 0$, and then we may set $\tilde{J} = T_\mu J$. In this case we have $\epsilon = \delta$ in Eq. (2.9).

In a multistep method with approximations, we are given a positive integer m and a lookahead function J_m, and we successively compute (backwards in time) $J_{m-1}, \ldots, J_0$ and policies $\mu_{m-1}, \ldots, \mu_0$ satisfying

$$\|J_k - TJ_{k+1}\| \leq \delta, \quad \|T_{\mu_k} J_{k+1} - TJ_{k+1}\| \leq \epsilon, \qquad k = 0, \ldots, m-1. \tag{2.10}$$

Note that in the context of MDP, J_k can be viewed as an approximation to the optimal cost function of an $(m-k)$-stage problem with terminal cost function J_m. We have the following proposition.

Proposition 2.2.2: (Multistep Lookahead Error Bound) Let the contraction Assumption 2.1.2 hold. The periodic policy

$$\pi = \{\mu_0, \ldots, \mu_{m-1}, \mu_0, \ldots, \mu_{m-1}, \ldots\}$$

generated by the method of Eq. (2.10) satisfies

$$\|J_\pi - J^*\| \leq \frac{2\alpha^m}{1-\alpha^m}\|J_m - J^*\| + \frac{\epsilon}{1-\alpha^m} + \frac{\alpha(\epsilon + 2\delta)(1-\alpha^{m-1})}{(1-\alpha)(1-\alpha^m)}. \tag{2.11}$$

Proof: Using the triangle inequality, Eq. (2.10), and the contraction property of T, we have for all k

$$\begin{aligned} \|J_{m-k} - T^k J_m\| &\leq \|J_{m-k} - TJ_{m-k+1}\| + \|TJ_{m-k+1} - T^2 J_{m-k+2}\| \\ &\quad + \cdots + \|T^{k-1} J_{m-1} - T^k J_m\| \\ &\leq \delta + \alpha\delta + \cdots + \alpha^{k-1}\delta, \end{aligned} \tag{2.12}$$

showing that

$$\|J_{m-k} - T^k J_m\| \leq \frac{\delta(1-\alpha^k)}{1-\alpha}, \qquad k = 1, \ldots, m. \tag{2.13}$$

From Eq. (2.10), we have $\|J_k - T_{\mu_k} J_{k+1}\| \le \delta + \epsilon$, so for all k

$$\begin{aligned}\|J_{m-k} - T_{\mu_{m-k}} \cdots T_{\mu_{m-1}} J_m\| &\le \|J_{m-k} - T_{\mu_{m-k}} J_{m-k+1}\| \\ &\quad + \|T_{\mu_{m-k}} J_{m-k+1} - T_{\mu_{m-k}} T_{\mu_{m-k+1}} J_{m-k+2}\| \\ &\quad + \cdots \\ &\quad + \|T_{\mu_{m-k}} \cdots T_{\mu_{m-2}} J_{m-1} - T_{\mu_{m-k}} \cdots T_{\mu_{m-1}} J_m\| \\ &\le (\delta+\epsilon) + \alpha(\delta+\epsilon) + \cdots + \alpha^{k-1}(\delta+\epsilon),\end{aligned}$$

showing that

$$\|J_{m-k} - T_{\mu_{m-k}} \cdots T_{\mu_{m-1}} J_m\| \le \frac{(\delta+\epsilon)(1-\alpha^k)}{1-\alpha}, \qquad k = 1, \ldots, m. \tag{2.14}$$

Using the fact $\|T_{\mu_0} J_1 - T J_1\| \le \epsilon$ [cf. Eq. (2.10)], we obtain

$$\begin{aligned}\|T_{\mu_0} \cdots T_{\mu_{m-1}} J_m - T^m J_m\| &\le \|T_{\mu_0} \cdots T_{\mu_{m-1}} J_m - T_{\mu_0} J_1\| \\ &\quad + \|T_{\mu_0} J_1 - T J_1\| + \|T J_1 - T^m J_m\| \\ &\le \alpha \|T_{\mu_1} \cdots T_{\mu_{m-1}} J_m - J_1\| + \epsilon + \alpha \|J_1 - T^{m-1} J_m\| \\ &\le \epsilon + \frac{\alpha(\epsilon + 2\delta)(1-\alpha^{m-1})}{1-\alpha},\end{aligned}$$

where the last inequality follows from Eqs. (2.13) and (2.14) for $k = m-1$.

From this relation and the fact that $T_{\mu_0} \cdots T_{\mu_{m-1}}$ and T^m are contractions with modulus α^m, we obtain

$$\begin{aligned}\|T_{\mu_0} \cdots T_{\mu_{m-1}} J^* - J^*\| &\le \|T_{\mu_0} \cdots T_{\mu_{m-1}} J^* - T_{\mu_0} \cdots T_{\mu_{m-1}} J_m\| \\ &\quad + \|T_{\mu_0} \cdots T_{\mu_{m-1}} J_m - T^m J_m\| + \|T^m J_m - J^*\| \\ &\le 2\alpha^m \|J^* - J_m\| + \epsilon + \frac{\alpha(\epsilon+2\delta)(1-\alpha^{m-1})}{1-\alpha}.\end{aligned}$$

We also have using Prop. 2.1.1(e), applied in the context of the multistep mapping of Example 1.3.1,

$$\|J_\pi - J^*\| \le \frac{1}{1-\alpha^m} \|T_{\mu_0} \cdots T_{\mu_{m-1}} J^* - J^*\|.$$

Combining the last two relations, we obtain the desired result. **Q.E.D.**

Note that for $m = 1$ and $\delta = \epsilon = 0$, i.e., the case of one-step lookahead policy $\overline{\mu}$ with lookahead function J_1 and no approximation error in the minimization involved in TJ_1, Eq. (2.11) yields the bound

$$\|J_{\overline{\mu}} - J^*\| \le \frac{2\alpha}{1-\alpha} \|J_1 - J^*\|,$$

which coincides with the bound (2.6) derived earlier.

Also, in the special case where $\epsilon = \delta$ and $J_k = T_{\mu_k} J_{k+1}$ (cf. the discussion preceding Prop. 2.2.2), the bound (2.11) can be strengthened somewhat. In particular, we have for all k, $J_{m-k} = T_{\mu_{m-k}} \cdots T_{\mu_{m-1}} J_m$, so the right-hand side of Eq. (2.14) becomes 0 and the preceding proof yields, with some calculation,

$$\begin{aligned} \|J_\pi - J^*\| &\leq \frac{2\alpha^m}{1-\alpha^m}\|J_m - J^*\| + \frac{\delta}{1-\alpha^m} + \frac{\alpha\delta(1-\alpha^{m-1})}{(1-\alpha)(1-\alpha^m)} \\ &= \frac{2\alpha^m}{1-\alpha^m}\|J_m - J^*\| + \frac{\delta}{1-\alpha}. \end{aligned}$$

We finally note that Prop. 2.2.2 shows that as the lookahead size m increases, the corresponding bound for $\|J_\pi - J^*\|$ tends to $\epsilon + \alpha(\epsilon + 2\delta)/(1-\alpha)$, or

$$\limsup_{m\to\infty} \|J_\pi - J^*\| \leq \frac{\epsilon + 2\alpha\delta}{1-\alpha}.$$

We will see that this error bound is superior to corresponding error bounds for approximate versions of value and policy iteration by essentially a factor $1/(1-\alpha)$.

There is an alternative and often used form of multistep lookahead, whereby at each stage we compute a multistep policy $\{\mu_0, \ldots, \mu_{m-1}\}$, we apply the first component μ_0 of that policy, then at the next stage we recompute a new multistep policy $\{\bar\mu_0, \ldots, \bar\mu_{m-1}\}$, apply $\bar\mu_0$, etc. However, no error bound for this type of lookahead is currently known.

2.3 VALUE ITERATION

In this section, we discuss value iteration (VI for short), the algorithm that starts with some $J \in B(X)$, and generates $TJ, T^2J, \ldots$. Since T is a weighted sup-norm contraction under Assumption 2.1.2, the algorithm converges to J^*, and the rate of convergence is governed by

$$\|T^kJ - J^*\| \leq \alpha^k \|J - J^*\|, \qquad k = 0, 1, \ldots.$$

Similarly, for a given policy $\mu \in \mathcal{M}$, we have

$$\|T_\mu^kJ - J_\mu\| \leq \alpha^k \|J - J_\mu\|, \qquad k = 0, 1, \ldots.$$

From Prop. 2.1.1(d), we also have the error bound

$$\|T^{k+1}J - J^*\| \leq \frac{\alpha}{1-\alpha}\|T^{k+1}J - T^kJ\|, \qquad k = 0, 1, \ldots.$$

This bound does not rely on the monotonicity Assumption 2.1.1.

The VI algorithm is often used to compute an approximation $\tilde{J}$ to J^*, and then to obtain a policy $\overline{\mu}$ by minimization of $H(x, u, \tilde{J})$ over $u \in U(x)$ for each $x \in X$. In other words $\tilde{J}$ and $\overline{\mu}$ satisfy

$$\|\tilde{J} - J^*\| \leq \gamma, \qquad T_{\overline{\mu}}\tilde{J} = T\tilde{J},$$

where γ is some positive scalar. Then by using Eq. (2.6), we have

$$\|J_{\overline{\mu}} - J^*\| \leq \frac{2\alpha\,\gamma}{1-\alpha}. \tag{2.15}$$

If the set of policies is finite, this procedure can be used to compute an optimal policy with a finite but sufficiently large number of exact VI, as shown in the following proposition.

Proposition 2.3.1: Let the contraction Assumption 2.1.2 hold and let $J \in B(X)$. If the set of policies $\mathcal{M}$ is finite, there exists an integer $\overline{k} \geq 0$ such that $J_{\mu^*} = J^*$ for all μ^* and $k \geq \overline{k}$ with $T_{\mu^*}T^kJ = T^{k+1}J$.

Proof: Let $\tilde{\mathcal{M}}$ be the set of policies such that $J_\mu \neq J^*$. Since $\tilde{\mathcal{M}}$ is finite, we have

$$\inf_{\mu \in \tilde{\mathcal{M}}} \|J_\mu - J^*\| > 0,$$

so by Eq. (2.15), there exists sufficiently small $\beta > 0$ such that

$$\|\tilde{J} - J^*\| \leq \beta \ \text{ and } \ T_\mu\tilde{J} = T\tilde{J} \quad \Rightarrow \quad \|J_\mu - J^*\| = 0 \quad \Rightarrow \quad \mu \notin \tilde{\mathcal{M}}. \tag{2.16}$$

It follows that if k is sufficiently large so that $\|T^kJ - J^*\| \leq \beta$, then $T_{\mu^*}T^kJ = T^{k+1}J$ implies that $\mu^* \notin \tilde{\mathcal{M}}$ so $J_{\mu^*} = J^*$. **Q.E.D.**

2.3.1 Approximate Value Iteration

We will now consider situations where the VI method may be implementable only through approximations. In particular, given a function J, assume that we may only be able to calculate an approximation $\tilde{J}$ to TJ such that

$$\|\tilde{J} - TJ\| \leq \delta,$$

where δ is a given positive scalar. In the corresponding approximate VI method, we start from an arbitrary bounded function J_0, and we generate a sequence $\{J_k\}$ satisfying

$$\|J_{k+1} - TJ_k\| \leq \delta, \qquad k = 0, 1, \ldots. \tag{2.17}$$

This approximation may be the result of representing J_{k+1} compactly, as a linear combination of basis functions, through a projection or aggregation process, as is common in approximate DP.

We may also simultaneously generate a sequence of policies $\{\mu^k\}$ such that

$$\|T_{\mu^k} J_k - T J_k\| \leq \epsilon, \qquad k = 0, 1, \ldots, \tag{2.18}$$

where ϵ is some scalar [which could be equal to 0, as in case of Eq. (2.10), considered earlier]. The following proposition shows that the corresponding cost functions J_{μ^k} "converge" to J^* to within an error of order $O\big(\delta/(1-\alpha)^2\big)$ [plus a less significant error of order $O\big(\epsilon/(1-\alpha)\big)$].

Proposition 2.3.2: (Error Bounds for Approximate VI) Let the contraction Assumption 2.1.2 hold. A sequence $\{J_k\}$ generated by the approximate VI method (2.17)-(2.18) satisfies

$$\limsup_{k\to\infty} \|J_k - J^*\| \leq \frac{\delta}{1-\alpha}, \tag{2.19}$$

while the corresponding sequence of policies $\{\mu^k\}$ satisfies

$$\limsup_{k\to\infty} \|J_{\mu^k} - J^*\| \leq \frac{\epsilon}{1-\alpha} + \frac{2\alpha\delta}{(1-\alpha)^2}. \tag{2.20}$$

Proof: Using the triangle inequality, Eq. (2.17), and the contraction property of T, we have

$$\begin{aligned}\|J_k - T^k J_0\| &\leq \|J_k - T J_{k-1}\| \\ &\quad + \|T J_{k-1} - T^2 J_{k-2}\| + \cdots + \|T^{k-1} J_1 - T^k J_0\| \\ &\leq \delta + \alpha\delta + \cdots + \alpha^{k-1}\delta,\end{aligned}$$

and finally

$$\|J_k - T^k J_0\| \leq \frac{(1-\alpha^k)\delta}{1-\alpha}, \qquad k = 0, 1, \ldots. \tag{2.21}$$

By taking limit as $k \to \infty$ and by using the fact $\lim_{k\to\infty} T^k J_0 = J^*$, we obtain Eq. (2.19).

We also have using the triangle inequality and the contraction property of T_{μ^k} and T,

$$\begin{aligned}\|T_{\mu^k} J^* - J^*\| &\leq \|T_{\mu^k} J^* - T_{\mu^k} J_k\| + \|T_{\mu^k} J_k - T J_k\| + \|T J_k - J^*\| \\ &\leq \alpha\|J^* - J_k\| + \epsilon + \alpha\|J_k - J^*\|,\end{aligned}$$

while by using also Prop. 2.1.1(e), we obtain

$$\|J_{\mu^k} - J^*\| \leq \frac{1}{1-\alpha}\|T_{\mu^k}J^* - J^*\| \leq \frac{\epsilon}{1-\alpha} + \frac{2\alpha}{1-\alpha}\|J_k - J^*\|.$$

By combining this relation with Eq. (2.19), we obtain Eq. (2.20). **Q.E.D.**

The error bound (2.20) relates to stationary policies obtained from the functions J_k by one-step lookahead. We may also obtain an m-step periodic policy π from J_k by using m-step lookahead. Then Prop. 2.2.2 shows that the corresponding bound for $\|J_\pi - J^*\|$ tends to $\epsilon + 2\alpha\delta/(1-\alpha)$ as $m \to \infty$, which improves on the error bound (2.20) by a factor $1/(1-\alpha)$.

Finally, let us note that the error bound of Prop. 2.3.2 is predicated upon generating a sequence $\{J_k\}$ satisfying $\|J_{k+1} - TJ_k\| \leq \delta$ for all k [cf. Eq. (2.17)]. Unfortunately, some practical approximation schemes guarantee the existence of such a δ only if $\{J_k\}$ is a bounded sequence. The following example shows that boundedness of the iterates is not automatically guaranteed, and is a serious issue that should be addressed in approximate VI schemes.

Example 2.3.1 (Error Amplification in Approximate Value Iteration)

Consider a two-state discounted MDP with states 1 and 2, and a single policy. The transitions are deterministic: from state 1 to state 2, and from state 2 to state 2. These transitions are also cost-free. Thus we have $J^*(1) = J^*(2) = 0$.

We consider a VI scheme that approximates cost functions within the one-dimensional subspace of linear functions $S = \big\{(r, 2r) \mid r \in \Re\big\}$ by using a weighted least squares minimization; i.e., we approximate a vector J by its weighted Euclidean projection onto S. In particular, given $J_k = (r_k, 2r_k)$, we find $J_{k+1} = (r_{k+1}, 2r_{k+1})$, where for weights $w_1, w_2 > 0$, r_{k+1} is obtained as

$$r_{k+1} = \arg\min_r \Big[w_1\big(r - (TJ_k)(1)\big)^2 + w_2\big(2r - (TJ_k)(2)\big)^2\Big].$$

Since for a zero cost per stage and the given deterministic transitions, we have $TJ_k = (2\alpha r_k, 2\alpha r_k)$, the preceding minimization is written as

$$r_{k+1} = \arg\min_r \big[w_1(r - 2\alpha r_k)^2 + w_2(2r - 2\alpha r_k)^2\big],$$

which by writing the corresponding optimality condition yields $r_{k+1} = \alpha\beta r_k$, where $\beta = 2(w_1 + 2w_2)(w_1 + 4w_2) > 1$. Thus if $\alpha > 1/\beta$, the sequence $\{r_k\}$ diverges and so does $\{J_k\}$. Note that in this example the optimal cost function $J^* = (0, 0)$ belongs to the subspace S. The difficulty here is that the approximate VI mapping that generates J_{k+1} as the weighted Euclidean projection of TJ_k is not a contraction (this is a manifestation of an important issue in approximate DP and projected equation approximation; see [Ber12a]). At the same time there is no δ such that $\|J_{k+1} - TJ_k\| \leq \delta$ for all k, because of error amplification in each approximate VI.

2.4 POLICY ITERATION

In this section, we discuss policy iteration (PI for short), an algorithm whereby we maintain and update a policy μ^k, starting from some initial policy μ^0. The typical iteration has the following form.

Policy iteration given the current policy μ^k:

Policy evaluation: We compute J_{μ^k} as the unique solution of the equation

$$J_{\mu^k} = T_{\mu^k} J_{\mu^k}.$$

Policy improvement: We obtain a policy μ^{k+1} that satisfies

$$T_{\mu^{k+1}} J_{\mu^k} = T J_{\mu^k}.$$

We assume that the minimum of $H(x, u, J_{\mu^k})$ over $u \in U(x)$ is attained for all $x \in X$, so that the improved policy μ^{k+1} is defined (we use this assumption for all the PI algorithms of the book). The following proposition establishes a basic cost improvement property, as well as finite convergence for the case where the set of policies is finite.

Proposition 2.4.1: (Convergence of PI) Let the monotonicity and contraction Assumptions 2.1.1 and 2.1.2 hold, and let $\{\mu^k\}$ be a sequence generated by the PI algorithm. Then for all k, we have $J_{\mu^{k+1}} \leq J_{\mu^k}$, with equality if and only if $J_{\mu^k} = J^*$. Moreover,

$$\lim_{k \to \infty} \|J_{\mu^k} - J^*\| = 0,$$

and if the set of policies is finite, we have $J_{\mu^k} = J^*$ for some k.

Proof: We have

$$T_{\mu^{k+1}} J_{\mu^k} = T J_{\mu^k} \leq T_{\mu^k} J_{\mu^k} = J_{\mu^k}.$$

Applying $T_{\mu^{k+1}}$ to this inequality while using the monotonicity Assumption 2.1.1, we obtain

$$T^2_{\mu^{k+1}} J_{\mu^k} \leq T_{\mu^{k+1}} J_{\mu^k} = T J_{\mu^k} \leq T_{\mu^k} J_{\mu^k} = J_{\mu^k}.$$

Similarly, we have for all $m > 0$,

$$T^m_{\mu^{k+1}} J_{\mu^k} \leq T J_{\mu^k} \leq J_{\mu^k},$$

and by taking the limit as $m \to \infty$, we obtain

$$J_{\mu^{k+1}} \le TJ_{\mu^k} \le J_{\mu^k}, \qquad k = 0, 1, \ldots. \tag{2.22}$$

If $J_{\mu^{k+1}} = J_{\mu^k}$, it follows that $TJ_{\mu^k} = J_{\mu^k}$, so J_{μ^k} is a fixed point of T and must be equal to J^*. Moreover by using induction, Eq. (2.22) implies that

$$J_{\mu^k} \le T^k J_{\mu^0}, \qquad k = 0, 1, \ldots,$$

Since

$$J^* \le J_{\mu^k}, \qquad \lim_{k\to\infty} \|T^k J_{\mu^0} - J^*\| = 0,$$

it follows that $\lim_{k\to\infty} \|J_{\mu^k} - J^*\| = 0$. Finally, if the number of policies is finite, Eq. (2.22) implies that there can be only a finite number of iterations for which $J_{\mu^{k+1}}(x) < J_{\mu^k}(x)$ for some x, so we must have $J_{\mu^{k+1}} = J_{\mu^k}$ for some k, at which time $J_{\mu^k} = J^*$ as shown earlier. **Q.E.D.**

In the case where the set of policies is infinite, we may assert the convergence of the sequence of generated policies under some compactness and continuity conditions. In particular, we will assume that the state space is finite, $X = \{1, \ldots, n\}$, and that each control constraint set $U(x)$ is a compact subset of $\Re^m$. We will view a cost function J as an element of $\Re^n$, and a policy μ as an element of the compact set $U(1) \times \cdots \times U(n) \subset \Re^{mn}$. Then $\{\mu^k\}$ has at least one limit point $\overline{\mu}$, which must be an admissible policy. The following proposition guarantees, under an additional continuity assumption for $H(x, \cdot, \cdot)$, that every limit point $\overline{\mu}$ is optimal.

Assumption 2.4.1: (Compactness and Continuity)

(a) The state space is finite, $X = \{1, \ldots, n\}$.

(b) Each control constraint set $U(x)$, $x = 1, \ldots, n$, is a compact subset of $\Re^m$.

(c) Each function $H(x, \cdot, \cdot)$, $x = 1, \ldots, n$, is continuous over $U(x) \times \Re^n$.

Proposition 2.4.2: Let the monotonicity and contraction Assumptions 2.1.1 and 2.1.2 hold, together with Assumption 2.4.1, and let $\{\mu^k\}$ be a sequence generated by the PI algorithm. Then for every limit point $\overline{\mu}$ of $\{\mu^k\}$, we have $J_{\overline{\mu}} = J^*$.

Proof: We have $J_{\mu^k} \to J^*$ by Prop. 2.4.1. Let $\overline{\mu}$ be the limit of a subsequence $\{\mu^k\}_{k\in\mathcal{K}}$. We will show that $T_{\overline{\mu}}J^* = TJ^*$, from which it follows that $J_{\overline{\mu}} = J^*$ [cf. Prop. 2.1.1(c)]. Indeed, we have $T_{\overline{\mu}}J^* \geq TJ^*$, so we focus on showing the reverse inequality. From the equation $T_{\mu^k}J_{\mu^{k-1}} = TJ_{\mu^{k-1}}$ we have

$$H\big(x, \mu^k(x), J_{\mu^{k-1}}\big) \leq H(x, u, J_{\mu^{k-1}}), \qquad x = 1, \ldots, n,\ u \in U(x).$$

By taking limit in this relation as $k \to \infty$, $k \in \mathcal{K}$, and by using the continuity of $H(x, \cdot, \cdot)$ [cf. Assumption 2.4.1(c)], we obtain

$$H\big(x, \overline{\mu}(x), J^*\big) \leq H(x, u, J^*), \qquad x = 1, \ldots, n,\ u \in U(x).$$

By taking the minimum of the right-hand side over $u \in U(x)$, we obtain $T_{\overline{\mu}}J^* \leq TJ^*$. **Q.E.D.**

2.4.1 Approximate Policy Iteration

We now consider the PI method where the policy evaluation step and/or the policy improvement step of the method are implemented through approximations. This method generates a sequence of policies $\{\mu^k\}$ and a corresponding sequence of approximate cost functions $\{J_k\}$ satisfying

$$\|J_k - J_{\mu^k}\| \leq \delta, \qquad \|T_{\mu^{k+1}}J_k - TJ_k\| \leq \epsilon, \qquad k = 0, 1, \ldots, \tag{2.23}$$

where δ and ϵ are some scalars, $\|\cdot\|$ denotes the sup-norm and v is the weight function of the weighted sup-norm (it is important to use v rather than the unit function in the above equation, in order for the bounds obtained to have a clean form). The following proposition provides an error bound for this algorithm.

Proposition 2.4.3: (Error Bound for Approximate PI) Let the monotonicity and contraction Assumptions 2.1.1 and 2.1.2 hold. The sequence $\{\mu^k\}$ generated by the approximate PI algorithm (2.23) satisfies

$$\limsup_{k\to\infty} \|J_{\mu^k} - J^*\| \leq \frac{\epsilon + 2\alpha\delta}{(1-\alpha)^2}. \tag{2.24}$$

The essence of the proof is contained in the following proposition, which quantifies the amount of approximate policy improvement at each iteration.

Proposition 2.4.4: Let the monotonicity and contraction Assumptions 2.1.1 and 2.1.2 hold. Let J, $\overline{\mu}$, and μ satisfy

$$\|J - J_\mu\| \le \delta, \qquad \|T_{\overline{\mu}}J - TJ\| \le \epsilon,$$

where δ and ϵ are some scalars. Then

$$\|J_{\overline{\mu}} - J^*\| \le \alpha\|J_\mu - J^*\| + \frac{\epsilon + 2\alpha\delta}{1-\alpha}. \tag{2.25}$$

Proof: Using Eq. (2.25) and the contraction property of T and $T_{\overline{\mu}}$, which implies that $\|T_{\overline{\mu}}J_\mu - T_{\overline{\mu}}J\| \le \alpha\delta$ and $\|TJ - TJ_\mu\| \le \alpha\delta$, and hence $T_{\overline{\mu}}J_\mu \le T_{\overline{\mu}}J + \alpha\delta\, v$ and $TJ \le TJ_\mu + \alpha\delta\, v$, we have

$$T_{\overline{\mu}}J_\mu \le T_{\overline{\mu}}J + \alpha\delta\, v \le TJ + (\epsilon + \alpha\delta)\, v \le TJ_\mu + (\epsilon + 2\alpha\delta)\, v. \tag{2.26}$$

Since $TJ_\mu \le T_\mu J_\mu = J_\mu$, this relation yields

$$T_{\overline{\mu}}J_\mu \le J_\mu + (\epsilon + 2\alpha\delta)\, v,$$

and applying Prop. 2.1.4(b) with $\mu = \overline{\mu}$, $J = J_\mu$, and $\epsilon = \epsilon + 2\alpha\delta$, we obtain

$$J_{\overline{\mu}} \le J_\mu + \frac{\epsilon + 2\alpha\delta}{1-\alpha}\, v. \tag{2.27}$$

Using this relation, we have

$$J_{\overline{\mu}} = T_{\overline{\mu}}J_{\overline{\mu}} = T_{\overline{\mu}}J_\mu + (T_{\overline{\mu}}J_{\overline{\mu}} - T_{\overline{\mu}}J_\mu) \le T_{\overline{\mu}}J_\mu + \frac{\alpha(\epsilon + 2\alpha\delta)}{1-\alpha}\, v,$$

where the inequality follows by using Prop. 2.1.3 and Eq. (2.27). Subtracting J^* from both sides, we have

$$J_{\overline{\mu}} - J^* \le T_{\overline{\mu}}J_\mu - J^* + \frac{\alpha(\epsilon + 2\alpha\delta)}{1-\alpha}\, v, \tag{2.28}$$

Also by subtracting J^* from both sides of Eq. (2.26), and using the contraction property

$$TJ_\mu - J^* = TJ_\mu - TJ^* \le \alpha\|J_\mu - J^*\|\, v,$$

we obtain

$$T_{\overline{\mu}}J_\mu - J^* \le TJ_\mu - J^* + (\epsilon + 2\alpha\delta)\, v \le \alpha\|J_\mu - J^*\|\, v + (\epsilon + 2\alpha\delta)\, v.$$

Combining this relation with Eq. (2.28), yields

$$J_{\overline{\mu}}-J^* \leq \alpha \| J_\mu-J^* \| \, v+\frac{\alpha(\epsilon+2\alpha\delta)}{1-\alpha} \, v+(\epsilon+\alpha\delta)e = \alpha \| J_\mu-J^* \| \, v+\frac{\epsilon+2\alpha\delta}{1-\alpha} \, v,$$

which is equivalent to the desired relation (2.25). **Q.E.D.**

Proof of Prop. 2.4.3: Applying Prop. 2.4.4, we have

$$\| J_{\mu^{k+1}} - J^* \| \leq \alpha \| J_{\mu^k} - J^* \| + \frac{\epsilon+2\alpha\delta}{1-\alpha},$$

which by taking the lim sup of both sides as $k \to \infty$ yields the desired result. **Q.E.D.**

We note that the error bound of Prop. 2.4.3 is tight, as can be shown with an example from [BeT96], Section 6.2.3. The error bound is comparable to the one for approximate VI, derived earlier in Prop. 2.3.2. In particular, the error $\| J_{\mu^k} - J^* \|$ is asymptotically proportional to $1/(1-\alpha)^2$ and to the approximation error in policy evaluation or value iteration, respectively. This is noteworthy, as it indicates that contrary to the case of exact implementation, approximate PI need not hold a convergence rate advantage over approximate VI, despite its greater overhead per iteration.

On the other hand, approximate PI does not exhibit the same kind of error amplification difficulty that was illustrated by Example 2.3.1 for approximate VI. In particular, if the set of policies is finite, so that the sequence $\{J_{\mu^k}\}$ is guaranteed to be bounded, the assumption of Eq. (2.23) is not hard to satisfy in practice with commonly used function approximation methods.

Note that when $\delta = \epsilon = 0$, Eq. (2.25) yields

$$\| J_{\mu^{k+1}} - J^* \| \leq \alpha \| J_{\mu^k} - J^* \|.$$

Thus in the case of an infinite state space and/or control space, exact PI converges at a geometric rate under the contraction and monotonicity assumptions of this section. This rate is the same as the rate of convergence of exact VI.

The Case Where Policies Converge

Generally, the policy sequence $\{\mu^k\}$ generated by approximate PI may oscillate between several policies. However, under some circumstances this sequence may be guaranteed to converge to some $\overline{\mu}$, in the sense that

$$\mu^{\overline{k}+1} = \mu^{\overline{k}} = \overline{\mu} \qquad \text{for some } \overline{k}. \tag{2.29}$$

An example arises when the policy sequence $\{\mu^k\}$ is generated by *exact PI* applied with a *different* mapping $\tilde{H}$ in place of H, but the bounds of Eq. (2.23) are satisfied. The mapping $\tilde{H}$ may for example correspond to an approximation of the original problem (as in aggregation methods; see [Ber12a] for further discussion). In this case we can show the following bound, which is much more favorable than the one of Prop. 2.4.3.

Proposition 2.4.5: (Error Bound for Approximate PI when Policies Converge) Let the monotonicity and contraction Assumptions 2.1.1 and 2.1.2 hold, and let $\overline{\mu}$ be a policy generated by the approximate PI algorithm (2.23) and satisfying condition (2.29). Then we have

$$\|J_{\overline{\mu}} - J^*\| \leq \frac{\epsilon + 2\alpha\delta}{1-\alpha}. \tag{2.30}$$

Proof: Let $\tilde{J}$ be the cost function obtained by approximate policy evaluation of $\overline{\mu}$ [i.e., $\tilde{J} = J_{\overline{k}}$, where $\overline{k}$ satisfies the condition (2.29)]. Then we have

$$\|\tilde{J} - J_{\overline{\mu}}\| \leq \delta, \qquad \|T_{\overline{\mu}}\tilde{J} - T\tilde{J}\| \leq \epsilon, \tag{2.31}$$

where the latter inequality holds since we have

$$\|T_{\overline{\mu}}\tilde{J} - T\tilde{J}\| = \|T_{\mu^{\overline{k}+1}}J_{\overline{k}} - TJ_{\overline{k}}\| \leq \epsilon,$$

cf. Eq. (2.23). Using Eq. (2.31) and the fact $J_{\overline{\mu}} = T_{\overline{\mu}}J_{\overline{\mu}}$, we have

$$\begin{aligned}\|TJ_{\overline{\mu}} - J_{\overline{\mu}}\| &\leq \|TJ_{\overline{\mu}} - T\tilde{J}\| + \|T\tilde{J} - T_{\overline{\mu}}\tilde{J}\| + \|T_{\overline{\mu}}\tilde{J} - J_{\overline{\mu}}\| \\ &= \|TJ_{\overline{\mu}} - T\tilde{J}\| + \|T\tilde{J} - T_{\overline{\mu}}\tilde{J}\| + \|T_{\overline{\mu}}\tilde{J} - T_{\overline{\mu}}J_{\overline{\mu}}\| \\ &\leq \alpha\|J_{\overline{\mu}} - \tilde{J}\| + \epsilon + \alpha\|\tilde{J} - J_{\overline{\mu}}\| \\ &\leq \epsilon + 2\alpha\delta.\end{aligned} \tag{2.32}$$

Using Prop. 2.1.1(d) with $J = J_{\overline{\mu}}$, we obtain the error bound (2.30). **Q.E.D.**

The preceding error bound can be extended to the case where two successive policies generated by the approximate PI algorithm are "not too different" rather than being identical. In particular, suppose that μ and $\overline{\mu}$ are successive policies, which in addition to

$$\|\tilde{J} - J_{\mu}\| \leq \delta, \qquad \|T_{\overline{\mu}}\tilde{J} - T\tilde{J}\| \leq \epsilon,$$

[cf. Eq. (2.23)], also satisfy

$$\|T_{\mu}\tilde{J} - T_{\overline{\mu}}\tilde{J}\| \leq \zeta,$$

where ζ is some scalar (instead of $\mu = \overline{\mu}$, which is the case where policies converge exactly). Then we also have

$$\|T\tilde{J} - T_\mu \tilde{J}\| \leq \|T\tilde{J} - T_{\overline{\mu}}\tilde{J}\| + \|T_{\overline{\mu}}\tilde{J} - T_\mu \tilde{J}\| \leq \epsilon + \zeta,$$

and by replacing ϵ with $\epsilon + \zeta$ and $\overline{\mu}$ with μ in Eq. (2.32), we obtain

$$\|J_\mu - J^*\| \leq \frac{\epsilon + \zeta + 2\alpha\delta}{1-\alpha}.$$

When ζ is small enough to be of the order of $\max\{\delta, \epsilon\}$, this error bound is comparable to the one for the case where policies converge.

2.5 OPTIMISTIC POLICY ITERATION

In this section, we discuss optimistic PI (also called "modified" PI, see e.g., [Put94]), a variant of the PI algorithm of the preceding section, which tends to be more computationally efficient, based on empirical evidence. Here each policy μ^k is evaluated by solving the equation $J_{\mu^k} = T_{\mu^k} J_{\mu^k}$ approximately, using a finite number of VI. Thus, starting with a function $J_0 \in B(X)$, we generate sequences $\{J_k\}$ and $\{\mu^k\}$ with the algorithm

$$T_{\mu^k} J_k = T J_k, \qquad J_{k+1} = T_{\mu^k}^{m_k} J_k, \qquad k = 0, 1, \ldots, \tag{2.33}$$

where $\{m_k\}$ is a sequence of positive integers. There is no systematic guideline for selecting the integers m_k. Usually their best values are chosen empirically, and tend to be considerably larger than 1 (in which case the optimistic PI method would be identical to the VI method).

2.5.1 Convergence of Optimistic Policy Iteration

The following two propositions provide the convergence properties of the optimistic PI algorithm (2.33).

Proposition 2.5.1: (Convergence of Optimistic PI) Let the monotonicity and contraction Assumptions 2.1.1 and 2.1.2 hold, and let $\{(J_k, \mu^k)\}$ be a sequence generated by the optimistic PI algorithm (2.33). Then

$$\lim_{k\to\infty} \|J_k - J^*\| = 0,$$

and if the number of policies is finite, we have $J_{\mu^k} = J^*$ for all k greater than some index $\bar{k}$.

Proposition 2.5.2: Let the monotonicity and contraction Assumptions 2.1.1 and 2.1.2 hold, together with Assumption 2.4.1, and let $\{(J_k, \mu^k)\}$ be a sequence generated by the optimistic PI algorithm (2.33). Then every limit point $\overline{\mu}$ of $\{\mu^k\}$, satisfies $J_{\overline{\mu}} = J^*$.

We develop the proofs of the propositions through four lemmas. The first lemma collects some properties of monotone weighted sup-norm contractions, variants of which we noted earlier, and we restate for convenience.

Lemma 2.5.1: Let $W : B(X) \mapsto B(X)$ be a mapping that satisfies the monotonicity assumption

$$J \leq J' \quad \Rightarrow \quad WJ \leq WJ', \qquad \forall\, J, J' \in B(X),$$

and the contraction assumption

$$\|WJ - WJ'\| \leq \alpha \|J - J'\|, \qquad \forall\, J, J' \in B(X),$$

for some $\alpha \in (0, 1)$.

(a) For all $J, J' \in B(X)$ and scalar $c \geq 0$, we have

$$J \geq J' - c\,v \quad \Rightarrow \quad WJ \geq WJ' - \alpha c\, v. \tag{2.34}$$

(b) For all $J \in B(X)$, $c \geq 0$, and $k = 0, 1, \ldots$, we have

$$J \geq WJ - c\,v \quad \Rightarrow \quad W^k J \geq J^* - \frac{\alpha^k}{1-\alpha} c\,v, \tag{2.35}$$

$$WJ \geq J - c\,v \quad \Rightarrow \quad J^* \geq W^k J - \frac{\alpha^k}{1-\alpha} c\,v, \tag{2.36}$$

where J^* is the fixed point of W.

Proof: The proof of part (a) follows the one of Prop. 2.1.4(b), while the proof of part (b) follows the one of Prop. 2.1.4(c). **Q.E.D.**

Lemma 2.5.2: Let the monotonicity and contraction Assumptions 2.1.1 and 2.1.2 hold, and let $J \in B(X)$ and $c \geq 0$ satisfy

$$J \geq TJ - c\,v,$$

and let $\mu \in \mathcal{M}$ be such that $T_\mu J = TJ$. Then for all $k > 0$, we have

$$TJ \geq T_\mu^k J - \frac{\alpha}{1-\alpha} c\,v, \tag{2.37}$$

and

$$T_\mu^k J \geq T(T_\mu^k J) - \alpha^k c\,v. \tag{2.38}$$

Proof: Since $J \geq TJ - c\,v = T_\mu J - c\,v$, by using Lemma 2.5.1(a) with $W = T_\mu^j$ and $J' = T_\mu J$, we have for all $j \geq 1$,

$$T_\mu^j J \geq T_\mu^{j+1} J - \alpha^j c\,v. \tag{2.39}$$

By adding this relation over $j = 1, \ldots, k-1$, we have

$$TJ = T_\mu J \geq T_\mu^k J - \sum_{j=1}^{k-1} \alpha^j c\,v = T_\mu^k J - \frac{\alpha - \alpha^k}{1-\alpha} c\,v \geq T_\mu^k J - \frac{\alpha}{1-\alpha} c\,v,$$

showing Eq. (2.37). From Eq. (2.39) for $j = k$, we obtain

$$T_\mu^k J \geq T_\mu^{k+1} J - \alpha^k c\,v = T_\mu(T_\mu^k J) - \alpha^k c\,v \geq T(T_\mu^k J) - \alpha^k c\,v,$$

showing Eq. (2.38). **Q.E.D.**

The next lemma applies to the optimistic PI algorithm (2.33) and proves a preliminary bound.

Lemma 2.5.3: Let the monotonicity and contraction Assumptions 2.1.1 and 2.1.2 hold, let $\{(J_k, \mu^k)\}$ be a sequence generated by the PI algorithm (2.33), and assume that for some $c \geq 0$ we have

$$J_0 \geq TJ_0 - c\,v.$$

Then for all $k \geq 0$,

$$TJ_k + \frac{\alpha}{1-\alpha} \beta_k c\,v \geq J_{k+1} \geq TJ_{k+1} - \beta_{k+1} c\,v, \tag{2.40}$$

where β_k is the scalar given by

$$\beta_k = \begin{cases} 1 & \text{if } k = 0, \\ \alpha^{m_0 + \cdots + m_{k-1}} & \text{if } k > 0, \end{cases} \tag{2.41}$$

with m_j, $j = 0, 1, \ldots$, being the integers used in the algorithm (2.33).

Proof: We prove Eq. (2.40) by induction on k, using Lemma 2.5.2. For $k = 0$, using Eq. (2.37) with $J = J_0$, $\mu = \mu^0$, and $k = m_0$, we have

$$TJ_0 \geq J_1 - \frac{\alpha}{1-\alpha} c\, v = J_1 - \frac{\alpha}{1-\alpha} \beta_0 c\, v,$$

showing the left-hand side of Eq. (2.40) for $k = 0$. Also by Eq. (2.38) with $\mu = \mu^0$ and $k = m_0$, we have

$$J_1 \geq TJ_1 - \alpha^{m_0} c\, v = TJ_1 - \beta_1 c\, v.$$

showing the right-hand side of Eq. (2.40) for $k = 0$.

Assuming that Eq. (2.40) holds for $k - 1 \geq 0$, we will show that it holds for k. Indeed, the right-hand side of the induction hypothesis yields

$$J_k \geq TJ_k - \beta_k c\, v.$$

Using Eqs. (2.37) and (2.38) with $J = J_k$, $\mu = \mu^k$, and $k = m_k$, we obtain

$$TJ_k \geq J_{k+1} - \frac{\alpha}{1-\alpha} \beta_k c\, v,$$

and

$$J_{k+1} \geq TJ_{k+1} - \alpha^{m_k} \beta_k c\, v = TJ_{k+1} - \beta_{k+1} c\, v,$$

respectively. This completes the induction. **Q.E.D.**

The next lemma essentially proves the convergence of the optimistic PI (Prop. 2.5.1) and provides associated error bounds.

Lemma 2.5.4: Let the monotonicity and contraction Assumptions 2.1.1 and 2.1.2 hold, let $\{(J_k, \mu^k)\}$ be a sequence generated by the PI algorithm (2.33), and let $c \geq 0$ be a scalar such that

$$\|J_0 - TJ_0\| \leq c. \tag{2.42}$$

Then for all $k \geq 0$,

$$J_k + \frac{\alpha^k}{1-\alpha} c\, v \geq J_k + \frac{\beta_k}{1-\alpha} c\, v \geq J^* \geq J_k - \frac{(k+1)\alpha^k}{1-\alpha} c\, v, \tag{2.43}$$

where β_k is defined by Eq. (2.41).

Proof: Using the relation $J_0 \geq TJ_0 - c\, v$ [cf. Eq. (2.42)] and Lemma 2.5.3, we have

$$J_k \geq TJ_k - \beta_k c\, v, \quad k = 0, 1, \ldots.$$

Using this relation in Lemma 2.5.1(b) with $W = T$ and $k = 0$, we obtain

$$J_k \geq J^* - \frac{\beta_k}{1-\alpha} c\, v,$$

which together with the fact $\alpha^k \geq \beta_k$, shows the left-hand side of Eq. (2.43).

Using the relation $TJ_0 \geq J_0 - c\, v$ [cf. Eq. (2.42)] and Lemma 2.5.1(b) with $W = T$, we have

$$J^* \geq T^k J_0 - \frac{\alpha^k}{1-\alpha} c\, v, \qquad k = 0, 1, \ldots. \tag{2.44}$$

Using again the relation $J_0 \geq TJ_0 - c\, v$ in conjunction with Lemma 2.5.3, we also have

$$TJ_j \geq J_{j+1} - \frac{\alpha}{1-\alpha} \beta_j c\, v, \qquad j = 0, \ldots, k-1.$$

Applying T^{k-j-1} to both sides of this inequality and using the monotonicity and contraction properties of T^{k-j-1}, we obtain

$$T^{k-j} J_j \geq T^{k-j-1} J_{j+1} - \frac{\alpha^{k-j}}{1-\alpha} \beta_j c\, v, \qquad j = 0, \ldots, k-1,$$

cf. Lemma 2.5.1(a). By adding this relation over $j = 0, \ldots, k-1$, and using the fact

$$\beta_j \leq \alpha^j,$$

it follows that

$$T^k J_0 \geq J_k - \sum_{j=0}^{k-1} \frac{\alpha^{k-j}}{1-\alpha} \alpha^j c\, v = J_k - \frac{k\alpha^k}{1-\alpha} c\, v. \tag{2.45}$$

Finally, by combining Eqs. (2.44) and (2.45), we obtain the right-hand side of Eq. (2.43). **Q.E.D.**

Proof of Props. 2.5.1 and 2.5.2: Let c be a scalar satisfying Eq. (2.42). Then the error bounds (2.43) show that $\lim_{k\to\infty} \|J_k - J^*\| = 0$, i.e., the first part of Prop. 2.5.1. The second part (finite termination when the number of policies is finite) follows similar to Prop. 2.4.1. The proof of Prop. 2.5.2 follows using the compactness and continuity Assumption 2.4.1, and the convergence argument of Prop. 2.4.2. **Q.E.D.**

Convergence Rate Issues

Let us consider the convergence rate bounds of Lemma 2.5.4 for optimistic PI, and write them in the form

$$\|J_0 - TJ_0\| \leq c \quad \Rightarrow \quad J_k - \frac{(k+1)\alpha^k}{1-\alpha} c\, v \leq J^* \leq J_k + \frac{\alpha^{m_0+\cdots+m_k}}{1-\alpha} c\, v. \tag{2.46}$$

We may contrast these bounds with the ones for VI, where

$$\|J_0 - TJ_0\| \leq c \quad \Rightarrow \quad T^k J_0 - \frac{\alpha^k}{1-\alpha} c\, v \leq J^* \leq T^k J_0 + \frac{\alpha^k}{1-\alpha} c\, v \tag{2.47}$$

[cf. Prop. 2.1.4(c)].

In comparing the bounds (2.46) and (2.47), we should also take into account the associated overhead for a single iteration of each method: optimistic PI requires at iteration k a single application of T and $m_k - 1$ applications of T_{μ^k} (each being less time-consuming than an application of T), while VI requires a single application of T. It can then be seen that the upper bound for optimistic PI is better than the one for VI (same bound for less overhead), while the lower bound for optimistic PI is worse than the one for VI (worse bound for more overhead). This suggests that the choice of the initial condition J_0 is important in optimistic PI, and in particular it is preferable to have $J_0 \geq TJ_0$ (implying convergence to J^* from above) rather than $J_0 \leq TJ_0$ (implying convergence to J^* from below). This is consistent with the results of other works, which indicate that the convergence properties of the method are fragile when the condition $J_0 \geq TJ_0$ does not hold (see [WiB93], [BeT96], [BeY10a], [BeY10b], [YuB11a]).

2.5.2 Approximate Optimistic Policy Iteration

We will now derive error bounds for the case where the policy evaluation and policy improvement operations are approximate, similar to the nonoptimistic PI case of Section 2.4.1. In particular, we consider a method that generates a sequence of policies $\{\mu^k\}$ and a corresponding sequence of approximate cost functions $\{J_k\}$ satisfying

$$\|J_k - T_{\mu^k}^{m_k} J_{k-1}\| \leq \delta, \qquad \|T_{\mu^{k+1}} J_k - TJ_k\| \leq \epsilon, \qquad k = 0, 1, \ldots, \tag{2.48}$$

[cf. Eq. (2.23)]. For example, we may compute (perhaps approximately, by simulation) the values $T_{\mu^k}^{m_k}(x)$ for a subset of states x, and use a least squares fit of these values to select J_k from some parametric class of functions.

We will prove the same error bound as for the nonoptimistic case, cf. Eq. (2.24). However, for this we will need the following condition, which is stronger than the contraction and monotonicity conditions that we have been using so far.

Assumption 2.5.1: (Semilinear Monotonic Contraction) For all $J \in B(X)$ and $\mu \in \mathcal{M}$, the functions $T_\mu J$ and TJ belong to $B(X)$. Furthermore, for some $\alpha \in (0,1)$, we have for all $J, J' \in B(X)$, $\mu \in \mathcal{M}$, and $x \in X$,

$$\frac{(T_\mu J')(x) - (T_\mu J)(x)}{v(x)} \leq \alpha \sup_{y \in X} \frac{J'(y) - J(y)}{v(y)}. \tag{2.49}$$

This assumption implies both the monotonicity and contraction Assumptions 2.1.1 and 2.1.2, as can be easily verified. Moreover the assumption is satisfied in the discounted DP examples of Section 1.2, as well as the stochastic shortest path problem of Example 1.2.6. It holds if T_μ is a linear mapping involving a matrix with nonnegative components that has spectral radius less than 1 (or more generally if T_μ is the minimum or the maximum of a finite number of such linear mappings).

For any function $y \in B(X)$, let us use the notation

$$M(y) = \sup_{x \in X} \frac{y(x)}{v(x)}.$$

Then the condition (2.49) can be written for all $J, J' \in B(X)$, and $\mu \in \mathcal{M}$ as

$$M(T_\mu J - T_\mu J') \leq \alpha M(J - J'), \tag{2.50}$$

and also implies the following multistep versions, for $\ell \geq 1$,

$$T_\mu^\ell J - T_\mu^\ell J' \leq \alpha^\ell M(J - J')v, \quad M(T_\mu^\ell J - T_\mu^\ell J') \leq \alpha^\ell M(J - J'), \tag{2.51}$$

which can be proved by induction using Eq. (2.50). We have the following proposition.

Proposition 2.5.3: (Error Bound for Optimistic Approximate PI) Let Assumption 2.5.1 hold. Then the sequence $\{\mu^k\}$ generated by the optimistic approximate PI algorithm (2.48) satisfies

$$\limsup_{k \to \infty} \|J_{\mu^k} - J^*\| \leq \frac{\epsilon + 2\alpha\delta}{(1-\alpha)^2}.$$

Proof: Let us fix $k \geq 1$ and for simplicity let us denote

$$\underline{J} = J_{k-1}, \qquad J = J_k,$$

$$\mu = \mu^k, \qquad \bar{\mu} = \mu^{k+1}, \qquad m = m_k, \qquad \bar{m} = m_{k+1},$$

$$s = J_\mu - T_\mu^m \underline{J}, \qquad \bar{s} = J_{\bar{\mu}} - T_{\bar{\mu}}^{\bar{m}} J, \qquad t = T_\mu^m \underline{J} - J^*, \qquad \bar{t} = T_{\bar{\mu}}^{\bar{m}} J - J^*.$$

We have

$$J_\mu - J^* = J_\mu - T_\mu^m \underline{J} + T_\mu^m \underline{J} - J^* = s + t. \tag{2.52}$$

We will derive recursive relations for s and t, which will also involve the residual functions

$$r = T_\mu \underline{J} - \underline{J}, \qquad \bar{r} = T_{\bar{\mu}} J - J.$$

We first obtain a relation between r and $\bar{r}$. We have

$$\begin{aligned}
\bar{r} &= T_{\bar{\mu}} J - J \\
&= (T_{\bar{\mu}} J - T_\mu J) + (T_\mu J - J) \\
&\leq (T_{\bar{\mu}} J - TJ) + \big(T_\mu J - T_\mu (T_\mu^m \underline{J})\big) + (T_\mu^m \underline{J} - J) + \big(T_\mu^m (T_\mu \underline{J}) - T_\mu^m \underline{J}\big) \\
&\leq \epsilon v + \alpha M(J - T_\mu^m \underline{J}) v + \delta v + \alpha^m M(T_\mu \underline{J} - \underline{J}) v \\
&\leq (\epsilon + \delta) v + \alpha \delta v + \alpha^m M(r) v,
\end{aligned}$$

where the first inequality follows from $T_{\bar{\mu}} J \geq TJ$, and the second and third inequalities follow from Eqs. (2.48) and (2.51). From this relation we have

$$M(\bar{r}) \leq \big(\epsilon + (1 + \alpha)\delta\big) + \beta M(r),$$

where $\beta = \alpha^m$. Taking lim sup as $k \to \infty$ in this relation, we obtain

$$\limsup_{k \to \infty} M(r) \leq \frac{\epsilon + (1 + \alpha)\delta}{1 - \hat{\beta}}, \tag{2.53}$$

where $\hat{\beta} = \alpha^{\liminf_{k \to \infty} m_k}$.

Next we derive a relation between s and r. We have

$$\begin{aligned}
s &= J_\mu - T_\mu^m \underline{J} \\
&= T_\mu^m J_\mu - T_\mu^m \underline{J} \\
&\leq \alpha^m M(J_\mu - \underline{J}) v \\
&\leq \frac{\alpha^m}{1 - \alpha} M(T_\mu \underline{J} - \underline{J}) v \\
&= \frac{\alpha^m}{1 - \alpha} M(r) v,
\end{aligned}$$

where the first inequality follows from Eq. (2.51) and the second inequality follows by using Prop. 2.1.4(b). Thus we have $M(s) \leq \frac{\alpha^m}{1-\alpha} M(r)$, from which by taking lim sup of both sides and using Eq. (2.53), we obtain

$$\limsup_{k\to\infty} M(s) \leq \frac{\hat{\beta}\big(\epsilon + (1+\alpha)\delta\big)}{(1-\alpha)(1-\hat{\beta})}. \tag{2.54}$$

Finally we derive a relation between t, $\bar{t}$, and r. We first note that

$$\begin{aligned} TJ - TJ^* &\leq \alpha M(J - J^*)v \\ &= \alpha M(J - T_\mu^m \underline{J} + T_\mu^m \underline{J} - J^*)v \\ &\leq \alpha M(J - T_\mu^m \underline{J})v + \alpha M(T_\mu^m \underline{J} - J^*)v \\ &\leq \alpha\delta v + \alpha M(t)v. \end{aligned}$$

Using this relation, and Eqs. (2.48) and (2.51), we have

$$\begin{aligned} \bar{t} &= T_{\bar{\mu}}^{\bar{m}} J - J^* \\ &= (T_{\bar{\mu}}^{\bar{m}} J - T_{\bar{\mu}}^{\bar{m}-1} J) + \cdots + (T_{\bar{\mu}}^2 J - T_{\bar{\mu}} J) + (T_{\bar{\mu}} J - TJ) + (TJ - TJ^*) \\ &\leq (\alpha^{\bar{m}-1} + \cdots + \alpha) M(T_{\bar{\mu}} J - J)v + \epsilon v + \alpha\delta v + \alpha M(t)v, \end{aligned}$$

so finally

$$M(\bar{t}) \leq \frac{\alpha - \alpha^{\bar{m}}}{1-\alpha} M(\bar{r}) + (\epsilon + \alpha\delta) + \alpha M(t).$$

By taking lim sup of both sides and using Eq. (2.53), it follows that

$$\limsup_{k\to\infty} M(t) \leq \frac{(\alpha - \hat{\beta})\big(\epsilon + (1+\alpha)\delta\big)}{(1-\alpha)^2(1-\hat{\beta})} + \frac{\epsilon + \alpha\delta}{1-\alpha}. \tag{2.55}$$

We now combine Eqs. (2.52), (2.54), and (2.55). We obtain

$$\begin{aligned} \limsup_{k\to\infty} M(J_{\mu^k} - J^*) &\leq \limsup_{k\to\infty} M(s) + \limsup_{k\to\infty} M(t) \\ &\leq \frac{\hat{\beta}\big(\epsilon + (1+\alpha)\delta\big)}{(1-\alpha)(1-\hat{\beta})} + \frac{(\alpha - \hat{\beta})\big(\epsilon + (1+\alpha)\delta\big)}{(1-\alpha)^2(1-\hat{\beta})} + \frac{\epsilon + \alpha\delta}{1-\alpha} \\ &= \frac{\big(\hat{\beta}(1-\alpha) + (\alpha - \hat{\beta})\big)\big(\epsilon + (1+\alpha)\delta\big)}{(1-\alpha)^2(1-\hat{\beta})} + \frac{\epsilon + \alpha\delta}{1-\alpha} \\ &= \frac{\alpha\big(\epsilon + (1+\alpha)\delta\big)}{(1-\alpha)^2} + \frac{\epsilon + \alpha\delta}{1-\alpha} \\ &= \frac{\epsilon + 2\alpha\delta}{(1-\alpha)^2}. \end{aligned}$$

This proves the result, since in view of $J_{\mu^k} \geq J^*$, we have $M(J_{\mu^k} - J^*) = \|J_{\mu^k} - J^*\|$. **Q.E.D.**

Note that optimistic PI with approximations is susceptible to the error amplification difficulty illustrated by Example 2.3.1. In particular, when $m_k = 1$ for all k in Eq. (2.48), the method becomes essentially identical to approximate VI. However, it appears that choices of m_k that are significantly larger than 1 should be helpful in connection with this difficulty. In particular, it can be verified that in Example 2.3.1, the method converges to the optimal cost function if m_k is sufficiently large.

A remarkable fact is that approximate VI, approximate PI, and approximate optimistic PI have very similar error bounds (cf. Props. 2.3.2, 2.4.3, and 2.5.3). Approximate VI has a slightly better bound, but insignificantly so in practical terms. When approximate PI produces a convergent sequence of policies, the associated error bound is much better (cf. Prop. 2.4.5).

2.6 ASYNCHRONOUS ALGORITHMS

In this section, we extend further the computational methods of VI and PI for abstract DP models, by embedding them within an asynchronous computation framework.

2.6.1 Asynchronous Value Iteration

Each VI of the form described in Section 2.3 applies the mapping T defined by

$$(TJ)(x) = \inf_{u \in U(x)} H(x, u, J), \qquad \forall\, x \in X,$$

for all states simultaneously, thereby producing the sequence $TJ, T^2J, \ldots$ starting with some $J \in B(X)$. In a more general form of VI, at any one iteration, $J(x)$ may be updated and replaced by $(TJ)(x)$ only for a subset of states. An example is the Gauss-Seidel method for the finite-state case, where at each iteration, $J(x)$ is updated only for a single selected state $\overline{x}$ and $J(x)$ is left unchanged for all other states $x \neq \overline{x}$ (see [Ber12a]). In that method the states are taken up for iteration in a cyclic order, but more complex iteration orders are possible, deterministic as well as randomized.

Methods of the type just described are called *asynchronous VI methods* and may be motivated by several considerations such as:

(a) *Faster convergence.* Generally, computational experience with DP as well as analysis, have shown that convergence is accelerated by incorporating the results of VI updates for some states as early as possible into subsequent VI updates for other states. This is known as the *Gauss-Seidel effect*, which is discussed in some detail in the book [BeT89].

(b) *Parallel and distributed asynchronous computation.* In this context, we have several processors, each applying VI for a subset of states, and communicating the results to other processors (perhaps with some delay). One objective here may be faster computation by taking advantage of parallelism. Another objective may be computational convenience in problems where useful information is generated and processed locally at geographically dispersed points. An example is data or sensor network computations, where nodes, gateways, sensors, and data collection centers collaborate to route and control the flow of data, using DP or shortest path-type computations.

(c) *Simulation-based implementations.* In simulation-based versions of VI, iterations at various states are often performed in the order that the states are generated by some form of simulation.

With these contexts in mind, we introduce a model of asynchronous distributed solution of abstract fixed point problems of the form $J = TJ$. Let $R(X)$ be the set of real-valued functions defined on some given set X and let T map $R(X)$ into $R(X)$. We consider a partition of X into disjoint nonempty subsets $X_1, \ldots, X_m$, and a corresponding partition of J as $J = (J_1, \ldots, J_m)$, where J_ℓ is the restriction of J on the set X_ℓ. Our computation framework involves a network of m processors, each updating corresponding components of J. In a (synchronous) distributed VI algorithm, processor ℓ updates J_ℓ at iteration t according to

$$J_\ell^{t+1}(x) = T(J_1^t, \ldots, J_m^t)(x), \qquad \forall\, x \in X_\ell,\ \ell = 1, \ldots, m. \tag{2.56}$$

Here to accommodate the distributed algorithmic framework and its overloaded notation, we will use superscript t to denote iterations/times where some (but not all) processors update their corresponding components, reserving the index k for computation stages involving all processors, and also reserving subscript ℓ to denote component/processor index.

In an asynchronous VI algorithm, processor ℓ updates J_ℓ only for t in a selected subset $\mathcal{R}_\ell$ of iterations, and with components J_j, $j \neq \ell$, supplied by other processors with communication "delays" $t - \tau_{\ell j}(t)$,

$$J_\ell^{t+1}(x) = \begin{cases} T\left(J_1^{\tau_{\ell 1}(t)}, \ldots, J_m^{\tau_{\ell m}(t)}\right)(x) & \text{if } t \in \mathcal{R}_\ell,\ x \in X_\ell, \\ J_\ell^t(x) & \text{if } t \notin \mathcal{R}_\ell,\ x \in X_\ell. \end{cases} \tag{2.57}$$

Communication delays arise naturally in the context of asynchronous distributed computing systems of the type described in many sources (an extensive reference is the book [BeT89]). Such systems are interesting for solution of large DP problems, particularly for methods that are based on simulation, which is naturally well-suited for distributed computation. On the other hand, if the entire algorithm is centralized at a single physical processor, the algorithm (2.57) ordinarily will not involve communication delays, i.e., $\tau_{\ell j}(t) = t$ for all ℓ, j, and t.

The simpler case where X is a finite set and each subset X_ℓ consists of a single element ℓ arises often, particularly in the context of simulation.

In this case we may simplify the notation of iteration (2.57) by writing J_ℓ^t in place of the scalar component $J_\ell^t(\ell)$, as we do in the following example.

Example 2.6.1 (One-State-at-a-Time Iterations)

Assuming $X = \{1, \ldots, n\}$, let us view each state as a processor by itself, so that $X_\ell = \{\ell\}$, $\ell = 1, \ldots, n$, and execute VI one-state-at-a-time, according to some state sequence $\{x^0, x^1, \ldots\}$, which is generated in some way, possibly by simulation. Thus, starting from some initial vector J^0, we generate a sequence $\{J^t\}$, with $J^t = (J_1^t, \ldots, J_n^t)$, as follows:

$$J_\ell^{t+1} = \begin{cases} T(J_1^t, \ldots, J_n^t)(\ell) & \text{if } \ell = x^t, \\ J_\ell^t & \text{if } \ell \neq x^t, \end{cases}$$

where $T(J_1^t, \ldots, J_n^t)(\ell)$ denotes the ℓ-th component of the vector

$$T(J_1^t, \ldots, J_n^t) = TJ^t,$$

and for simplicity we write J_ℓ^t instead of $J_\ell^t(\ell)$. This algorithm is a special case of iteration (2.57) where the set of times at which J_ℓ is updated is $\mathcal{R}_\ell = \{t \mid x^t = \ell\}$, and there are no communication delays (as in the case where the entire algorithm is centralized at a single physical processor).

Note also that if X is finite, we can assume without loss of generality that each state is assigned to a separate processor. The reason is that a physical processor that updates a group of states may be replaced by a group of fictitious processors, each assigned to a single state, and updating their corresponding components of J simultaneously.

We will now discuss the convergence of the asynchronous algorithm (2.57). To this end we introduce the following assumption.

Assumption 2.6.1: (Continuous Updating and Information Renewal)

(1) The set of times $\mathcal{R}_\ell$ at which processor ℓ updates J_ℓ is infinite, for each $\ell = 1, \ldots, m$.

(2) $\lim_{t\to\infty} \tau_{\ell j}(t) = \infty$ for all $\ell, j = 1, \ldots, m$.

Assumption 2.6.1 is natural, and is essential for any kind of convergence result about the algorithm.† In particular, the condition $\tau_{\ell j}(t) \to \infty$

† Generally, convergent distributed iterative asynchronous algorithms are classified in totally and partially asynchronous (cf. Chapters 6 and 7 of the book [BeT89]). In the former, there is no bound on the communication delays, while in the latter there must be a bound (which may be unknown). The algorithms of the present section are totally asynchronous, as reflected by Assumption 2.6.1.

guarantees that outdated information about the processor updates will eventually be purged from the computation. It is also natural to assume that $\tau_{\ell j}(t)$ is monotonically increasing with t, but this assumption is not necessary for the subsequent analysis.

We wish to show that $J_\ell^t \to J_\ell^*$ for all ℓ, and to this end we employ the following convergence theorem for totally asynchronous iterations from the author's paper [Ber83], which has served as the basis for the treatment of totally asynchronous iterations in the book [BeT89] (Chapter 6), and their application to DP (i.e., VI and PI), and asynchronous gradient-based optimization. For the statement of the theorem, we say that a sequence $\{J^k\} \subset R(X)$ *converges pointwise* to $J \in R(X)$ if $\lim_{k\to\infty} J^k(x) = J(x)$ for all $x \in X$.

Proposition 2.6.1 (Asynchronous Convergence Theorem): Let T have a unique fixed point J^*, let Assumption 2.6.1 hold, and assume that there is a sequence of nonempty subsets $\big\{S(k)\big\} \subset R(X)$ with

$$S(k+1) \subset S(k), \quad k = 0, 1, \ldots,$$

and is such that if $\{V^k\}$ is any sequence with $V^k \in S(k)$, for all $k \geq 0$, then $\{V^k\}$ converges pointwise to J^*. Assume further the following:

(1) *Synchronous Convergence Condition:* We have

$$TJ \in S(k+1), \qquad \forall\ J \in S(k),\ k = 0, 1, \ldots.$$

(2) *Box Condition:* For all k, $S(k)$ is a Cartesian product of the form

$$S(k) = S_1(k) \times \cdots \times S_m(k),$$

where $S_\ell(k)$ is a set of real-valued functions on X_ℓ, $\ell = 1, \ldots, m$.

Then for every $J^0 \in S(0)$, the sequence $\{J^t\}$ generated by the asynchronous algorithm (2.57) converges pointwise to J^*.

Proof: To explain the idea of the proof, let us note that the given conditions imply that updating any component J_ℓ, by applying T to a function $J \in S(k)$, while leaving all other components unchanged, yields a function in $S(k)$. Thus, once enough time passes so that the delays become "irrelevant," then after J enters $S(k)$, it stays within $S(k)$. Moreover, once a component J_ℓ enters the subset $S_\ell(k)$ and the delays become "irrelevant," J_ℓ gets permanently within the smaller subset $S_\ell(k+1)$ at the first time that J_ℓ is iterated on with $J \in S(k)$. Once each component J_ℓ, $\ell = 1, \ldots, m$, gets within $S_\ell(k+1)$, the entire function J is within $S(k+1)$ by the Box

Condition. Thus the iterates from $S(k)$ eventually get into $S(k+1)$ and so on, and converge pointwise to J^* in view of the assumed properties of $\{S(k)\}$.

With this idea in mind, we show by induction that for each $k \geq 0$, there is a time t_k such that:

(1) $J^t \in S(k)$ for all $t \geq t_k$.

(2) For all ℓ and $t \in \mathcal{R}_\ell$ with $t \geq t_k$, we have

$$\left(J_1^{\tau_{\ell 1}(t)}, \ldots, J_m^{\tau_{\ell m}(t)}\right) \in S(k).$$

[In words, after some time, all fixed point estimates will be in $S(k)$ and all estimates used in iteration (2.57) will come from $S(k)$.]

The induction hypothesis is true for $k = 0$ since $J^0 \in S(0)$. Assuming it is true for a given k, we will show that there exists a time t_{k+1} with the required properties. For each $\ell = 1, \ldots, m$, let $t(\ell)$ be the first element of $\mathcal{R}_\ell$ such that $t(\ell) \geq t_k$. Then by the Synchronous Convergence Condition, we have $TJ^{t(\ell)} \in S(k+1)$, implying (in view of the Box Condition) that

$$J_\ell^{t(\ell)+1} \in S_\ell(k+1).$$

Similarly, for every $t \in \mathcal{R}_\ell$, $t \geq t(\ell)$, we have $J_\ell^{t+1} \in S_\ell(k+1)$. Between elements of $\mathcal{R}_\ell$, J_ℓ^t does not change. Thus,

$$J_\ell^t \in S_\ell(k+1), \qquad \forall\, t \geq t(\ell) + 1.$$

Let $t_k' = \max_\ell\{t(\ell)\} + 1$. Then, using the Box Condition we have

$$J^t \in S(k+1), \qquad \forall\, t \geq t_k'.$$

Finally, since by Assumption 2.6.1, we have $\tau_{\ell j}(t) \to \infty$ as $t \to \infty$, $t \in \mathcal{R}_\ell$, we can choose a time $t_{k+1} \geq t_k'$ that is sufficiently large so that $\tau_{\ell j}(t) \geq t_k'$ for all ℓ, j, and $t \in \mathcal{R}_\ell$ with $t \geq t_{k+1}$. We then have, for all $t \in \mathcal{R}_\ell$ with $t \geq t_{k+1}$ and $j = 1, \ldots, m$, $J_j^{\tau_{j\ell}(t)} \in S_j(k+1)$, which (by the Box Condition) implies that

$$\left(J_1^{\tau_{\ell 1}(t)}, \ldots, J_m^{\tau_{\ell m}(t)}\right) \in S(k+1).$$

The induction is complete. **Q.E.D.**

Figure 2.6.1 illustrates the assumptions of the preceding convergence theorem. The challenge in applying the theorem is to identify the set sequence $\{S(k)\}$ and to verify the assumptions of Prop. 2.6.1. In abstract DP, these assumptions are satisfied in two primary contexts of interest. The first is when $S(k)$ are weighted sup-norm spheres centered at J^*, and

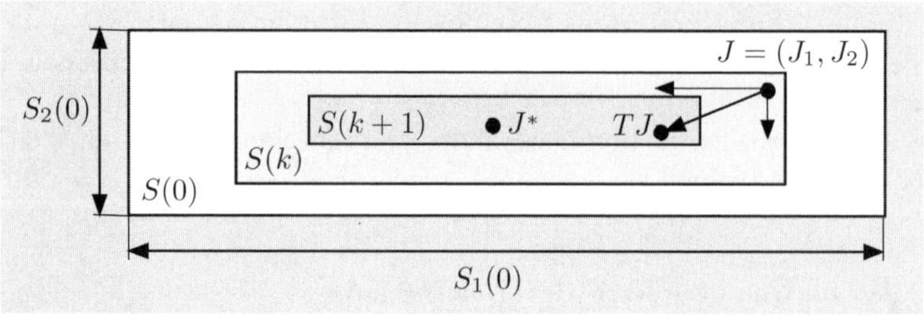

Figure 2.6.1 Geometric interpretation of the conditions of asynchronous convergence theorem. We have a nested sequence of boxes $\{S(k)\}$ such that $TJ \in S(k+1)$ for all $J \in S(k)$.

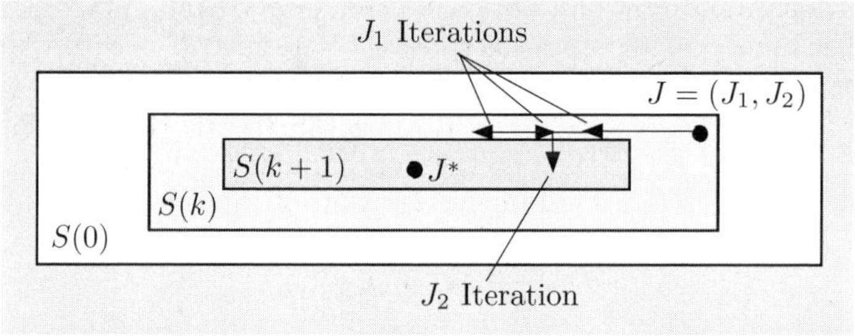

Figure 2.6.2 Geometric interpretation of the mechanism for asynchronous convergence. Iteration on a single component of a function $J \in S(k)$, say J_ℓ, keeps J in $S(k)$, while it moves J_ℓ into the corresponding component $S_\ell(k+1)$ of $S(k+1)$, where it remains throughout the subsequent iterations. Once all components J_ℓ have been iterated on at least once, the iterate is guaranteed to be in $S(k+1)$.

can be used in conjunction with the contraction framework of the preceding section (see the following proposition). The second context is based on monotonicity conditions. It will be used in Section 3.3 in conjunction with semicontractive models for which there is no underlying sup-norm contraction. It is also relevant to the noncontractive models of Section 4.3 where again there is no underlying contraction. Figure 2.6.2 illustrates the mechanism by which asynchronous convergence is achieved.

We note a few extensions of the theorem. It is possible to allow T to be time-varying, so in place of T we operate with a sequence of mappings T_k, $k = 0, 1, \ldots$. Then if all T_k have a common fixed point J^*, the conclusion of the theorem holds (see Exercise 2.2 for a more precise statement). This extension is useful in some of the algorithms to be discussed later. Another extension is to allow T to have multiple fixed points and introduce an assumption that roughly says that $\cap_{k=0}^{\infty} S(k)$ is the set of fixed points. Then the conclusion is that any limit point (in an appropriate sense) of $\{J^t\}$ is a fixed point.

We now apply the preceding convergence theorem to the totally asynchronous VI algorithm under the contraction assumption. Note that the monotonicity Assumption 2.1.1 is not necessary (just like it is not needed for the synchronous convergence of $\{T^k J\}$ to J^*).

Proposition 2.6.2: Let the contraction Assumption 2.1.2 hold, together with Assumption 2.6.1. Then if $J^0 \in B(X)$, a sequence $\{J^t\}$ generated by the asynchronous VI algorithm (2.57) converges pointwise to J^*.

Proof: We apply Prop. 2.6.1 with

$$S(k) = \big\{J \in B(X) \mid \|J^k - J^*\| \leq \alpha^k \|J^0 - J^*\|\big\}, \qquad k = 0, 1, \ldots.$$

Since T is a contraction with modulus α, the synchronous convergence condition is satisfied. Since T is a weighted sup-norm contraction, the box condition is also satisfied, and the result follows. **Q.E.D.**

2.6.2 Asynchronous Policy Iteration

We will now develop asynchronous PI algorithms that have comparable properties to the asynchronous VI algorithm of the preceding subsection. The processors collectively maintain and update an estimate J^t of the optimal cost function, and an estimate μ^t of an optimal policy. The local portions of J^t and μ^t of processor ℓ are denoted J_ℓ^t and μ_ℓ^t, respectively, i.e., $J_\ell^t(x) = J^t(x)$ and $\mu_\ell^t(x) = \mu^t(x)$ for all $x \in X_\ell$.

For each processor ℓ, there are two disjoint subsets of times $\mathcal{R}_\ell, \overline{\mathcal{R}}_\ell \subset \{0, 1, \ldots\}$, corresponding to policy improvement and policy evaluation iterations, respectively. At the times $t \in \mathcal{R}_\ell \cup \overline{\mathcal{R}}_\ell$, the local cost function J_ℓ^t of processor ℓ is updated using "delayed" local costs $J_j^{\tau_{\ell j}(t)}$ of other processors $j \neq \ell$, where $0 \leq \tau_{\ell j}(t) \leq t$. At the times $t \in \mathcal{R}_\ell$ (the local policy improvement times), the local policy μ_ℓ^t is also updated. For various choices of $\mathcal{R}_\ell$ and $\overline{\mathcal{R}}_\ell$, the algorithm takes the character of VI (when $\mathcal{R}_\ell = \{0, 1, \ldots\}$), and PI (when $\overline{\mathcal{R}}_\ell$ contains a large number of time indices between successive elements of $\mathcal{R}_\ell$). As before, we view $t - \tau_{\ell j}(t)$ as a "communication delay," and we require Assumption 2.6.1.†

In a natural asynchronous version of optimistic PI, at each time t, each processor ℓ does one of the following:

---

† As earlier in all PI algorithms we assume that the infimum over $u \in U(x)$ in the policy improvement operation is attained, and we write min in place of inf.

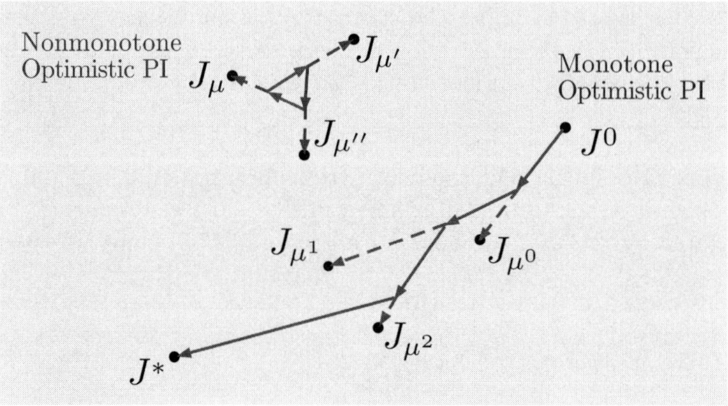

Figure 2.6.3 Illustration of optimistic asynchronous PI. When started with J^0 and μ^0 satisfying

$$J^0 \geq TJ^0 = T_{\mu^0} J^0,$$

the algorithm converges monotonically to J^* (see the trajectory on the right). However, for other initial conditions, there is a possibility for oscillations, since with changing values of μ, the mappings T_μ have different fixed points and "aim at different targets." It turns out that such oscillations are not possible when the algorithm is implemented synchronously (cf. Prop. 2.5.1), but may occur in asynchronous implementations (see the trajectory on the left, which illustrates a cycle between three policies μ, μ', μ'').

(a) *Local policy improvement*: If $t \in \mathcal{R}_\ell$, processor ℓ sets for all $x \in X_\ell$,

$$J_\ell^{t+1}(x) = \min_{u \in U(x)} H\big(x, u, J_1^{\tau_{\ell 1}(t)}, \ldots, J_m^{\tau_{\ell m}(t)}\big), \tag{2.58}$$

$$\mu_\ell^{t+1}(x) = \arg\min_{u \in U(x)} H\big(x, u, J_1^{\tau_{\ell 1}(t)}, \ldots, J_m^{\tau_{\ell m}(t)}\big). \tag{2.59}$$

(b) *Local policy evaluation*: If $t \in \overline{\mathcal{R}}_\ell$, processor ℓ sets for all $x \in X_\ell$,

$$J_\ell^{t+1}(x) = H\big(x, \mu^t(x), J_1^{\tau_{\ell 1}(t)}, \ldots, J_m^{\tau_{\ell m}(t)}\big), \tag{2.60}$$

and leaves μ_ℓ unchanged, i.e., $\mu_\ell^{t+1}(x) = \mu_\ell^t(x)$ for all $x \in X_\ell$.

(c) *No local change*: If $t \notin \mathcal{R}_\ell \cup \overline{\mathcal{R}}_\ell$, processor ℓ leaves J_ℓ and μ_ℓ unchanged, i.e., $J_\ell^{t+1}(x) = J_\ell^t(x)$ and $\mu_\ell^{t+1}(x) = \mu_\ell^t(x)$ for all $x \in X_\ell$.

Unfortunately, even when implemented without the delays $\tau_{\ell j}(t)$, the preceding PI algorithm is unreliable. The difficulty is that the algorithm involves a mix of applications of T and various mappings T_μ that have different fixed points, so in the absence of some systematic tendency towards J^* there is the possibility of oscillation (see Fig. 2.6.3). While this does not happen in synchronous versions (cf. Prop. 2.5.1), asynchronous versions of the algorithm (2.33) may oscillate unless J^0 satisfies some special condition such as

$$TJ^0 \leq J^0$$

(examples of this type of oscillation have been constructed in the paper [WiB93]; see also [Ber10], which translates an example from [WiB93] to the notation of the present book).

In this subsection and the next we will develop two distributed asynchronous PI algorithms, each embodying a mechanism that precludes the oscillatory behavior just described. In the first algorithm, there is a simple randomization scheme, according to which a policy evaluation of the form (2.60) is replaced by a policy improvement (2.58)-(2.59) with some positive probability. In the second algorithm, we introduce a mapping F_μ, which has a common fixed point property: its fixed point is related to J^* and is the same for all μ, so the anomaly illustrated in Fig. 2.6.3 cannot occur. The first algorithm is simple but requires some restrictions, including that the set of policies is finite. The second algorithm is more sophisticated and does not require this restriction.

An Optimistic Asynchronous Algorithm with Randomization

We introduce a scheme that provides a randomization mechanism for avoiding oscillatory behavior. It is defined by a small probability $p > 0$, according to which a policy evaluation iteration is replaced by a policy improvement iteration with probability p, independently of the results of past iterations. We model this randomization by assuming that before the algorithm is started, we restructure the sets $\mathcal{R}_\ell$ and $\overline{\mathcal{R}}_\ell$ as follows: we take each element of each set $\overline{\mathcal{R}}_\ell$, and with probability p, remove it from $\overline{\mathcal{R}}_\ell$, and add it to $\mathcal{R}_\ell$ (independently of other elements).

We will assume the following:

Assumption 2.6.2:

(a) The set of policies $\mathcal{M}$ is finite.

(b) There exists an integer $B \geq 0$ such that

$$(\mathcal{R}_\ell \cup \overline{\mathcal{R}}_\ell) \cap \{\tau \mid t < \tau \leq t + B\} \neq \emptyset, \qquad \forall\, t,\, \ell.$$

(c) There exists an integer $B' \geq 0$ such that

$$0 \leq t - \tau_{\ell j}(t) \leq B', \qquad \forall\, t,\, \ell,\, j.$$

Assumption 2.6.2 guarantees that each processor ℓ will execute at least one policy evaluation or policy improvement iteration within every block of B consecutive iterations, and places a bound B' on the communication delays. The convergence of the algorithm is shown in the following proposition.

Proposition 2.6.3: Under the contraction Assumption 2.1.2, and Assumptions 2.6.1, and 2.6.2, for the preceding algorithm with randomization, we have

$$\lim_{t\to\infty} J^t(x) = J^*(x), \qquad \forall\, x \in X,$$

with probability one.

Proof: Let J^* and J_μ be the fixed points of T and T_μ, respectively, and denote by $\mathcal{M}^*$ the set of optimal policies:

$$\mathcal{M}^* = \{\mu \in \mathcal{M} \mid J_\mu = J^*\} = \{\mu \in \mathcal{M} \mid T_\mu J^* = TJ^*\}.$$

We will show that the algorithm eventually (with probability one) enters a small neighborhood of J^* within which it remains, generates policies in $\mathcal{M}^*$, becomes equivalent to asynchronous VI, and therefore converges to J^* by Prop. 2.6.2. The idea of the proof is twofold.

(1) There exists a small enough weighted sup-norm sphere centered at J^*, call it $\mathcal{S}^*$, within which policy improvement generates only policies in $\mathcal{M}^*$, so policy evaluation with such policies as well as policy improvement keep the algorithm within $\mathcal{S}^*$ if started there, and reduce the weighted sup-norm distance to J^*, in view of the contraction and common fixed point property of T and T_μ, $\mu \in \mathcal{M}^*$. This is a consequence of Prop. 2.3.1 [cf. Eq. (2.16)].

(2) With probability one, thanks to the randomization device, the algorithm will eventually enter permanently $\mathcal{S}^*$ with a policy in $\mathcal{M}^*$.

We now establish (1) and (2) in suitably refined form to account for the presence of delays and asynchronism. We first define a bounded set within which the algorithm remains at all times. Consider the set

$$A_b = \big\{J \mid \|J - J_\mu\| \le b,\ \forall\, \mu \in \mathcal{M}\big\},$$

where $\|\cdot\|$ denotes weighted sup-norm and b is sufficiently large so that A_b is nonempty. Then A_b is bounded since $\mathcal{M}$ is a finite set by Assumption 2.6.2. Note that we have $T_\mu J \in A_b$ for all $\mu \in \mathcal{M}$ and $J \in A_b$, since

$$\|T_\mu J - J_\mu\| = \|T_\mu J - T_\mu J_\mu\| \le \alpha\|J - J_\mu\| \le \alpha b < b.$$

Let b be sufficiently large so that $J^0 \in A_b$, and define

$$S(k) = \{J \mid \|J - J^*\| \leq \alpha^k c\},$$

where c is sufficiently large so that $A_b \subset S(0)$. Then $J^t \in A_b$ and hence $J^t \in S(0)$ for all t.

Let k^* be such that

$$J \in S(k^*) \text{ and } T_\mu J = TJ \qquad \Rightarrow \qquad \mu \in \mathcal{M}^*. \tag{2.61}$$

Such a k^* exists in view of the finiteness of $\mathcal{M}$ and Prop. 2.3.1 [cf. Eq. (2.16)].

We now claim that with probability one, for any given $k \geq 1$, J^t will eventually enter $S(k)$ and stay within $S(k)$ for at least B' additional consecutive iterations. This is because our randomization scheme is such that for any t and k, with probability at least $p^{k(B+B')}$ the next $k(B+B')$ iterations are policy improvements, so that $J^{t+k(B+B')-\xi} \in S(k)$ for all ξ with $0 \leq \xi < B'$ [if $t \geq B'-1$, we have $J^{t-\xi} \in S(0)$ for all ξ with $0 \leq \xi < B'$, so $J^{t+B+B'-\xi} \in S(1)$ for $0 \leq \xi < B'$, which implies that $J^{t+2(B+B')-\xi} \in S(2)$ for $0 \leq \xi < B'$, etc].

It follows that with probability one, for some $\bar{t}$ we will have $J^\tau \in S(k^*)$ for all τ with $\bar{t} - B' \leq \tau \leq \bar{t}$, as well as $\mu^{\bar{t}} \in \mathcal{M}^*$ [cf. Eq. (2.61)]. Based on property (2.61) and the definition (2.59)-(2.60) of the algorithm, we see that at the next iteration, we have $\mu^{\bar{t}+1} \in \mathcal{M}^*$ and

$$\|J^{\bar{t}+1} - J^*\| \leq \|J^{\bar{t}} - J^*\| \leq \alpha^{k^*} c,$$

so $J^{\bar{t}+1} \in S(k^*)$; this is because in view of $J_{\mu^{\bar{t}}} = J^*$, and the contraction property of T and $T_{\mu^{\bar{t}}}$, we have

$$\frac{\big|J_\ell^{\bar{t}+1}(x) - J_\ell^*(x)\big|}{v(x)} \leq \alpha\|J^{\bar{t}} - J^*\| \leq \alpha^{k^*+1} c, \tag{2.62}$$

for all $x \in X_\ell$ and ℓ such that $\bar{t} \in \overline{\mathcal{R}}_\ell \cup \mathcal{R}_\ell$, while $J^{\bar{t}+1}(x) = J^{\bar{t}}(x)$ for all other x. Proceeding similarly, it follows that for all $t > \bar{t}$ we will have $J^\tau \in S(k^*)$ for all τ with $t - B' \leq \tau \leq t$, as well as $\mu^t \in \mathcal{M}^*$. Thus, after at most B iterations following $\bar{t}$ [after all components J_ℓ are updated through policy evaluation or policy improvement at least once so that

$$\frac{\big|J_\ell^{t+1}(x) - J_\ell^*(x)\big|}{v(x)} \leq \alpha\|J^{\bar{t}} - J^*\| \leq \alpha^{k^*+1} c,$$

for every i, $x \in X_\ell$, and some t with $\bar{t} \leq t < \bar{t} + B$, cf. Eq. (2.62)], J^t will enter $S(k^*+1)$ permanently, with $\mu^t \in \mathcal{M}^*$ (since $\mu^t \in \mathcal{M}^*$ for all $t \geq \bar{t}$ as shown earlier). Then, with the same reasoning, after at most another

$B' + B$ iterations, J^t will enter $S(k^* + 2)$ permanently, with $\mu^t \in \mathcal{M}^*$, etc. Thus J^t will converge to J^* with probability one. **Q.E.D.**

The proof of Prop. 2.6.3 shows that eventually (with probability one after some iteration) the algorithm will become equivalent to asynchronous VI (each policy evaluation will produce the same results as a policy improvement), while generating optimal policies exclusively. However, the expected number of iterations for this to happen can be very large. Moreover the proof depends on the set of policies being finite. These observations raise questions regarding the practical effectiveness of the algorithm. However, it appears that for many problems the algorithm works well, particularly when oscillatory behavior is a rare occurrence.

A potentially important issue is the choice of the randomization probability p. If p is too small, convergence may be slow because oscillatory behavior may go unchecked for a long time. On the other hand if p is large, a correspondingly large number of policy improvement iterations may be performed, and the hoped for benefits of optimistic PI may be lost. Adaptive schemes which adjust p based on algorithmic progress may be an interesting possibility for addressing this issue.

2.6.3 Policy Iteration with a Uniform Fixed Point

We will now discuss another approach to address the convergence difficulties of the "natural" asynchronous PI algorithm (2.58)-(2.60). As illustrated in Fig. 2.6.3 in connection with optimistic PI, the mappings T and T_μ have different fixed points. As a result, optimistic and distributed PI, which involve an irregular mixture of applications of T_μ and T, do not have a "consistent target" at which to aim.

With this in mind, we introduce a new mapping that is parametrized by μ and has a common fixed point for all μ, which in turn yields J^*. This mapping is a weighted sup-norm contraction with modulus α, so it may be used in conjunction with asynchronous VI and PI. An additional benefit is that the monotonicity Assumption 2.1.1 is not needed for convergence (see Exercise 2.3 where the algorithm of the present section is applied to a nonmonotonic contractive model).

The mapping operates on a pair (V, Q) where:

- V is a function with a component $V(x)$ for each x (in the DP context it may be viewed as a cost function).

- Q is a function with a component $Q(x, u)$ for each pair (x, u) [in the DP context $Q(x, u)$ is known as a Q-factor].

The mapping produces a pair

$$\big(MF_\mu(V, Q), F_\mu(V, Q)\big),$$

where

- $F_\mu(V,Q)$ is a function with a component $F_\mu(V,Q)(x,u)$ for each (x,u), defined by

$$F_\mu(V,Q)(x,u) = H\big(x,u,\min\{V,Q_\mu\}\big), \tag{2.63}$$

where for any Q and μ, we denote by Q_μ the function of x defined by

$$Q_\mu(x) = Q\big(x,\mu(x)\big), \qquad x \in X,$$

and for any two functions V_1 and V_2 of x, we denote by $\min\{V_1,V_2\}$ the function of x given by

$$\min\{V_1,V_2\}(x) = \min\big\{V_1(x),V_2(x)\big\}, \qquad x \in X.$$

- $MF_\mu(V,Q)$ is a function with a component $\big(MF_\mu(V,Q)\big)(x)$ for each x, where M denotes minimization over u, so that

$$\big(MF_\mu(V,Q)\big)(x) = \min_{u\in U(x)} F_\mu(V,Q)(x,u). \tag{2.64}$$

Example 2.6.2 (Asynchronous Optimistic Policy Iteration for Discounted Finite-State MDP)

Consider the special case of the finite-state discounted MDP of Example 1.2.2. We have

$$H(x,u,J) = \sum_{y=1}^n p_{xy}(u)\big(g(x,u,y)+\alpha J(y)\big),$$

and

$$\begin{aligned} F_\mu(V,Q)(x,u) &= H\big(x,u,W_\mu(V,Q)\big) \\ &= \sum_{y=1}^n p_{xy}(u)\Big(g(x,u,y)+\alpha\min\big\{V(y),Q\big(y,\mu(y)\big)\big\}\Big), \end{aligned}$$

$$\big(MF_\mu(V,Q)\big)(x) = \min_{u\in U(x)} \sum_{y=1}^n p_{xy}(u)\Big(g(x,u,y)+\alpha\min\big\{V(y),Q\big(y,\mu(y)\big)\big\}\Big),$$

[cf. Eqs. (2.63)-(2.64)]. Note that $F_\mu(V,Q)$ is the mapping that defines Bellman's equation for the Q-factors of a policy μ in an optimal stopping problem where the stopping cost at state y is equal to $V(y)$.

We now consider the mapping G_μ given by

$$G_\mu(V,Q) = \big(MF_\mu(V,Q),F_\mu(V,Q)\big), \tag{2.65}$$

and show that it has a uniform contraction property and a corresponding uniform fixed point. To this end, we introduce the norm

$$\big\|(V,Q)\big\| = \max\big\{\|V\|, \|Q\|\big\}$$

in the space of (V,Q), where $\|V\|$ is the weighted sup-norm of V, and $\|Q\|$ is defined by

$$\|Q\| = \sup_{x\in X,\, u\in U(x)} \frac{\big|Q(x,u)\big|}{v(x)}.$$

We have the following proposition.

Proposition 2.6.4: Let the contraction Assumption 2.1.2 hold. Consider the mapping G_μ defined by Eqs. (2.63)-(2.65). Then for all μ:

(a) (J^*,Q^*) is the unique fixed point of G_μ, where Q^* is defined by

$$Q^*(x,u) = H(x,u,J^*), \qquad x\in X,\ u\in U(x). \tag{2.66}$$

(b) The following uniform contraction property holds for all (V,Q), $(\tilde V,\tilde Q)$:

$$\big\|G_\mu(V,Q) - G_\mu(\tilde V,\tilde Q)\big\| \le \alpha\big\|(V,Q)-(\tilde V,\tilde Q)\big\|.$$

Proof: (a) Using the definition (2.66) of Q^*, we have

$$J^*(x) = (TJ^*)(x) = \inf_{u\in U(x)} H(x,u,J^*) = \inf_{u\in U(x)} Q^*(x,u), \qquad \forall\, x\in X,$$

so that

$$\min\big\{J^*(x),\, Q^*\big(x,\mu(x)\big)\big\} = J^*(x), \qquad \forall\, x\in X,\ \mu\in\mathcal{M}.$$

Using the definition (2.63) of F_μ, it follows that $F_\mu(J^*,Q^*) = Q^*$ and also that $MF_\mu(J^*,Q^*) = J^*$, so (J^*,Q^*) is a fixed point of G_μ for all μ. The uniqueness of this fixed point will follow from the contraction property of part (b).

(b) Using the definition (2.63) of F_μ, it can be shown that for all (V,Q), $(\tilde V,\tilde Q)$,

$$\begin{aligned}\big\|F_\mu(V,Q) - F_\mu(\tilde V,\tilde Q)\big\| &\le \alpha\big\|\min\{V,Q_\mu\} - \min\{\tilde V,\tilde Q_\mu\}\big\|\\ &\le \alpha\max\big\{\|V-\tilde V\|,\ \|Q-\tilde Q\|\big\}.\end{aligned} \tag{2.67}$$

Indeed, the first inequality follows from the contraction Assumption 2.1.2 and the second inequality follows from a nonexpansiveness property of the minimization map: for any J_1, J_2, $\tilde{J}_1$, $\tilde{J}_2$, we have

$$\big\| \min\{J_1, J_2\} - \min\{\tilde{J}_1, \tilde{J}_2\}\big\| \le \max\big\{\|J_1 - \tilde{J}_1\|, \|J_2 - \tilde{J}_2\|\big\}; \tag{2.68}$$

[to see this, write for every x,

$$\frac{J_m(x)}{v(x)} \le \max\big\{\|J_1 - \tilde{J}_1\|, \|J_2 - \tilde{J}_2\|\big\} + \frac{\tilde{J}_m(x)}{v(x)}, \qquad m = 1, 2,$$

take the minimum of both sides over m, exchange the roles of J_m and $\tilde{J}_m$, and take supremum over x]. Here we use the relation (2.68) for $J_1 = V$, $\tilde{J}_1 = \tilde{V}$, and $J_2(x) = Q\big(x, \mu(x)\big)$, $\tilde{J}_2(x) = \tilde{Q}\big(x, \mu(x)\big)$, for all $x \in X$.

We next note that for all $Q, \tilde{Q}$, †

$$\|MQ - M\tilde{Q}\| \le \|Q - \tilde{Q}\|,$$

which together with Eq. (2.67) yields

$$\max\big\{\big\|MF_\mu(V,Q) - MF_\mu(\tilde{V},\tilde{Q})\big\|, \big\|F_\mu(V,Q) - F_\mu(\tilde{V},\tilde{Q})\big\|\big\} \\ \le \alpha \max\big\{\|V - \tilde{V}\|, \|Q - \tilde{Q}\|\big\},$$

or equivalently $\big\|G_\mu(V,Q) - G_\mu(\tilde{V},\tilde{Q})\big\| \le \alpha\big\|(V,Q) - (\tilde{V},\tilde{Q})\big\|$. **Q.E.D.**

Because of the uniform contraction property of Prop. 2.6.4(b), a distributed fixed point iteration, like the VI algorithm of Eq. (2.57), can be used in conjunction with the mapping (2.65) to generate asynchronously a sequence $\{(V^t, Q^t)\}$ that is guaranteed to converge to (J^*, Q^*) for any sequence $\{\mu^t\}$. This can be verified using the proof of Prop. 2.6.2 (more precisely, a proof that closely parallels the one of that proposition); the mapping (2.65) plays the role of T in Eq. (2.57). ‡

---

† For a proof, we write

$$\frac{Q(x,u)}{v(x)} \le \|Q - \tilde{Q}\| + \frac{\tilde{Q}(x,u)}{v(x)}, \qquad \forall\, u \in U(x),\ x \in X,$$

take infimum of both sides over $u \in U(x)$, exchange the roles of Q and $\tilde{Q}$, and take supremum over $x \in X$ and $u \in U(x)$.

‡ Because F_μ and G_μ depend on μ, which changes as the algorithm progresses, it is necessary to use a minor extension of the asynchronous convergence theorem, given in Exercise 2.2, for the convergence proof.

Asynchronous PI Algorithm

We now describe a PI algorithm, which applies asynchronously the components $MF_\mu(V,Q)$ and $F_\mu(V,Q)$ of the mapping $G_\mu(V,Q)$ of Eq. (2.65). The first component is used for local policy improvement and makes a local update to V and μ, while the second component is used for local policy evaluation and makes a local update to Q. The algorithm draws its validity from the weighted sup-norm contraction property of Prop. 2.6.4(b) and the asynchronous convergence theory (Prop. 2.6.2 and Exercise 2.2).

For the asynchronous computation framework, we consider again m processors, a partition of X into sets $X_1,\ldots,X_m$, and assignment of each subset X_ℓ to a processor $\ell \in \{1,\ldots,m\}$. The following modification of the "natural" asynchronous PI algorithm (2.59)-(2.60) [without the "communication delays" $t-\tau_{\ell j}(t)$] can be shown to converge, in the sense that $V^t \to J^*$, $Q^t \to Q^*$. For each ℓ, there are two infinite disjoint subsets of times $\mathcal{R}_\ell, \overline{\mathcal{R}}_\ell \subset \{0,1,\ldots\}$, corresponding to policy improvement and policy evaluation iterations, respectively. Each processor ℓ operates on $V^t(x)$, $Q^t(x,u)$, and $\mu^t(x)$, only for x in its "local" state space X_ℓ. In particular, at each time t, each processor ℓ does one of the following:

(a) *Local policy improvement*: If $t \in \mathcal{R}_\ell$, processor ℓ sets for all $x \in X_\ell$, †

$$V^{t+1}(x) = \min_{u\in U(x)} H\big(x,u,\min\{V^t,Q^t_{\mu^t}\}\big) = \big(MF_{\mu^t}(V^t,Q^t)\big)(x),$$

sets $\mu^{t+1}(x)$ to a u that attains the minimum, and leaves Q unchanged, i.e., $Q^{t+1}(x,u) = Q^t(x,u)$ for all $x \in X_\ell$ and $u \in U(x)$.

(b) *Local policy evaluation*: If $t \in \overline{\mathcal{R}}_\ell$, processor ℓ sets for all $x \in X_\ell$ and $u \in U(x)$,

$$Q^{t+1}(x,u) = H\big(x,u,\min\{V^t,Q^t_{\mu^t}\}\big) = F_{\mu^t}(V^t,Q^t)(x,u),$$

and leaves V and μ unchanged, i.e., $V^{t+1}(x) = V^t(x)$ and $\mu^{t+1}(x) = \mu^t(x)$ for all $x \in X_\ell$.

(c) *No local change*: If $t \notin \mathcal{R}_\ell \cup \overline{\mathcal{R}}_\ell$, processor ℓ leaves Q, V, and μ unchanged, i.e., $Q^{t+1}(x,u) = Q^t(x,u)$ for all $x \in X_\ell$ and $u \in U(x)$, $V^{t+1}(x) = V^t(x)$, and $\mu^{t+1}(x) = \mu^t(x)$ for all $x \in X_\ell$.

Note that while this algorithm does not involve the "communication delays" $t-\tau_{\ell j}(t)$, it can clearly be extended to include them. The reason is that our asynchronous convergence analysis framework in combination with the uniform weighted sup-norm contraction property of Prop. 2.6.4 can tolerate the presence of such delays.

---

† As earlier we assume that the infimum over $u \in U(x)$ in the policy improvement operation is attained, and we write min in place of inf.

Reduced Space Implementation

The preceding PI algorithm is well-suited for the calculation of both J^* and Q^*. However, if the objective is just to calculate J^*, a simpler and more efficient algorithm is possible. To this end, we observe that the preceding algorithm can be operated so that it does not require the maintenance of the entire function Q. The reason is that the values $Q^t(x,u)$ with $u \neq \mu^t(x)$ do not appear in the calculations, and hence we need only the values $Q\big(x,\mu^t(x)\big)$, which we store in a function J^t:

$$J^t(x) = Q\big(x,\mu^t(x)\big).$$

This observation is the basis for the following algorithm.

At each time t and for each processor ℓ:

(a) *Local policy improvement*: If $t \in \mathcal{R}_\ell$, processor ℓ sets for all $x \in X_\ell$,

$$J^{t+1}(x) = V^{t+1}(x) = \min_{u \in U(x)} H\big(x,u,\min\{V^t,J^t\}\big), \tag{2.69}$$

and sets $\mu^{t+1}(x)$ to a u that attains the minimum.

(b) *Local policy evaluation*: If $t \in \overline{\mathcal{R}}_\ell$, processor ℓ sets for all $x \in X_\ell$,

$$J^{t+1}(x) = H\big(x,\mu^t(x),\min\{V^t,J^t\}\big), \tag{2.70}$$

and leaves V and μ unchanged, i.e., for all $x \in X_\ell$,

$$V^{t+1}(x) = V^t(x), \qquad \mu^{t+1}(x) = \mu^t(x).$$

(c) *No local change*: If $t \notin \mathcal{R}_\ell \cup \overline{\mathcal{R}}_\ell$, processor ℓ leaves J, V, and μ unchanged, i.e., for all $x \in X_\ell$,

$$J^{t+1}(x) = J^t(x), \quad V^{t+1}(x) = V^t(x), \quad \mu^{t+1}(x) = \mu^t(x).$$

Example 2.6.3 (Asynchronous Optimistic Policy Iteration for Discounted Finite-State MDP - Continued)

As an illustration of the preceding reduced space implementation, consider the special case of the finite-state discounted MDP of Example 1.2.2. Here

$$H(x,u,J) = \sum_{y=1}^n p_{xy}(u)\big(g(x,u,y) + \alpha J(y)\big),$$

and the mapping $F_\mu(V,Q)$ given by

$$F_\mu(V,Q)(x,u) = \sum_{y=1}^n p_{xy}(u)\Big(g(x,u,y) + \alpha \min\big\{V(y), Q(y,\mu(y))\big\}\Big),$$

defines the Q-factors of μ in a corresponding stopping problem. In the PI algorithm (2.69)-(2.70), policy evaluation of μ aims to solve this stopping problem, rather than solve a linear system of equations, as in classical PI. In particular, the policy evaluation iteration (2.70) is

$$J^{t+1}(x) = \sum_{y=1}^{n} p_{xy}\big(\mu^t(x)\big)\Big(g\big(x,\mu^t(x),y\big) + \alpha \min\big\{V^t(y), J^t(y)\big\}\Big),$$

for all $x \in X_\ell$. The policy improvement iteration (2.69) is a VI for the stopping problem:

$$J^{t+1}(x) = V^{t+1}(x) = \min_{u\in U(x)} \sum_{y=1}^{n} p_{xy}(u)\Big(g(x,u,y) + \alpha \min\big\{V^t(y), J^t(y)\big\}\Big),$$

for all $x \in X_\ell$, while the current policy is locally updated by

$$\mu^{t+1}(x) = \arg\min_{u\in U(x)} \sum_{y=1}^{n} p_{xy}(u)\Big(g(x,u,y) + \alpha \min\big\{V^t(y), J^t(y)\big\}\Big),$$

for all $x \in X_\ell$. The "stopping cost" $V^t(y)$ is the most recent cost value, obtained by local policy improvement at y.

Example 2.6.4 (Asynchronous Optimistic Policy Iteration for Dynamic Games)

Consider the optimistic PI algorithm (2.69)-(2.70) for the case of the discounted dynamic game problem of Example 1.2.4 of Chapter 1. In the context of this problem, a local policy evaluation step [cf. Eq. (2.70)] consists of a local VI for the maximizer's DP problem assuming a fixed policy for the minimizer, and a stopping cost V^t as per Eq. (2.70). A local policy improvement step [cf. Eq. (2.69)] at state x consists of the solution of a static game with a payoff matrix that also involves $\min\{V^t, J^t\}$ in place of J^t, as per Eq. (2.69).

A Variant with Interpolation

While the use of $\min\{V^t, J^t\}$ (rather than J^t) in Eq. (2.70) provides a convergence enforcement mechanism for the algorithm, it may also become a source of inefficiency, particularly when $V^t(x)$ approaches its limit $J^*(x)$ from lower values for many x. Then $J^{t+1}(x)$ is set to a lower value than the iterate

$$\hat{J}^{t+1}(x) = H\big(x, \mu^t(x), J^t\big), \tag{2.71}$$

given by the "standard" policy evaluation iteration, and in some cases this may slow down the algorithm.

A possible way to address this is to use an algorithmic variation that modifies appropriately Eq. (2.70), using interpolation with a parameter $\gamma_t \in (0, 1]$, with $\gamma_t \to 0$. In particular, for $t \in \overline{\mathcal{R}}_\ell$ and $x \in X_\ell$, we calculate the values $J^{t+1}(x)$ and $\hat{J}^{t+1}(x)$ given by Eqs. (2.70) and (2.71), and if

$$J^{t+1}(x) < \hat{J}^{t+1}(x), \tag{2.72}$$

we reset $J^{t+1}(x)$ to

$$(1 - \gamma_t) J^{t+1}(x) + \gamma_t \hat{J}^{t+1}(x). \tag{2.73}$$

The idea of the algorithm is to aim for a larger value of $J^{t+1}(x)$ when the condition (2.72) holds. Asymptotically, as $\gamma_t \to 0$, the iteration (2.72)-(2.73) becomes identical to the convergent update (2.70). For a more detailed analysis of an algorithm of this type, we refer to the paper [BeY10b].

2.7 NOTES, SOURCES, AND EXERCISES

The abstract contractive DP model of this chapter was introduced by Denardo [Den67], who focused on unweighted sup-norm contractions. We have transcribed his model and results in Section 2.1 so that they apply under weighted sup-norm contraction assumptions.

The abstraction of the computational methodology for finite-state discounted MDP within the broad framework of weighted sup-norm contractions follows the author's survey [Ber12b], and relies on several earlier analyses that use more specialized assumptions. In particular, the multistage error bound of Prop. 2.2.2 follows the work of Scherrer [Sch12], which explores the use of periodic policies in approximate VI and PI in finite-state discounted MDP (see also Scherrer and Lesner [ShL12], who give an example showing that the bound for approximate VI of Prop. 2.3.2 is essentially sharp for discounted finite-state MDP). For a related discussion of approximate VI, including the error amplification phenomenon of Example 2.3.1, and associated error bounds, see Munos and Szepesvari [MuS08]. The error bound and approximate PI analysis of Section 2.4.1 (Prop. 2.4.3) extends the one of Bertsekas and Tsitsiklis [BeT96] (Section 6.2.2), which was given for finite-state discounted MDP, and was shown to be tight by an example.

Optimistic PI has received a lot of attention in the literature, particularly for finite-state discounted MDP, and it is generally thought to be computationally more efficient than ordinary PI (see e.g., Puterman [Put94], who refers to the method as "modified PI"). The convergence analysis of the synchronous optimistic PI (Section 2.5.1) follows Rothblum [Rot79], who considered the case of an unweighted sup-norm ($v = e$); see also Canbolat and Rothblum [CaR11], which considers optimistic PI methods where the minimization in the policy improvement operation is approximate, within some $\epsilon > 0$. The error bound for optimistic PI (Section 2.5.2) is due to Thierry and Scherrer [ThS10b], given for the case of a finite-state discounted MDP. We follow closely their proof. Related error bounds and analysis are given by Scherrer [Sch11].

An alternative form of optimistic PI is the λ-PI method, introduced by Bertsekas and Ioffe [BeI96] (see also [BeT96]), and further studied in approximate DP contexts by Thierry and Scherrer [ThS10a], Bertsekas [Ber11b], and Scherrer [Sch11], and in a modified form by Yu and Bertsekas [YuB12]. The λ-PI method is defined by

$$T_{\mu^k} J_k = T J_k, \qquad J_{k+1} = T_{\mu^k}^{(\lambda)} J_k,$$

where J_0 is an initial function in $B(X)$, and for any policy μ and $\lambda \in (0,1)$, the mapping $T_\mu^{(\lambda)}$ is defined by

$$T_\mu^{(\lambda)} J = (1-\lambda) \sum_{\ell=0}^{\infty} \lambda^\ell T_\mu^{\ell+1} J.$$

To compare λ-PI and optimistic PI, where

$$J_{k+1} = T_{\mu^k}^{m_k} J_k,$$

note that they both involve multiple applications of the VI mapping T_{μ^k}: a fixed number m_k in the latter case, and a geometrically weighted number in the former case. We will revisit λ-PI in Section 4.3.3, where we will show that it offers some implementation advantages in the contexts discussed there.

Asynchronous VI (Section 2.6.1) for finite-state discounted MDP and games, shortest path problems, and abstract DP models, was proposed in Bertsekas [Ber82]. The asynchronous convergence theorem (Prop. 2.6.1) was first given in the author's paper [Ber83], where it was applied to a variety of algorithms, including VI for discounted and undiscounted DP, and gradient methods for unconstrained optimization (see also Bertsekas and Tsitsiklis [BeT89], where a textbook account is presented). There are earlier references on distributed asynchronous iterative algorithms, including the early work of Chazan and Miranker [ChM69] on linear relaxation methods (who attributed the original idea to Rosenfeld [Ros67]), and also Baudet [Bau78] on sup-norm contractive iterations. We refer to [BeT89] for detailed references.

Asynchronous algorithms have also been studied and applied to simulation-based DP, particularly in the context of Q-learning, which may be viewed as a stochastic version of VI. Two principal approaches for the convergence analysis of such algorithms have been suggested. The first approach, initiated in the paper by Tsitsiklis [Tsi94], considers the totally asynchronous computation of fixed points of abstract sup-norm contractive mappings and monotone mappings, which are defined in terms of an expected value. The algorithm of [Tsi94] contains as special cases Q-learning algorithms for finite-spaces discounted MDP and SSP problems. The analysis of [Tsi94] shares some ideas with the theory of Section 2.6.1, and also relies on the theory of stochastic approximation methods. For a subsequent analysis of the convergence of Q-learning for SSP, which addresses the issue of boundedness of the iterates, we refer to Yu and Bertsekas [YuB11b]. The second approach, treats asynchronous algorithms of the stochastic approximation type under some restrictions on the size of the communication delays or on the time between consecutive updates of a typical component. This approach was initiated in the paper by Tsitsiklis, Bertsekas, and Athans [TBA86], and was also developed in the book by Bertsekas and Tsitsiklis [BeT89] for stochastic gradient optimization methods. A related analysis that uses the ODE approach for more general fixed point problems was given in the paper by Borkar [Bor98], and was refined in the papers by Abounadi, Bertsekas, and Borkar [ABB02], and Borkar and Meyn [BeM00], which also considered applications to Q-learning. We refer to the monograph by Borkar [Bor08] for a more comprehensive discussion.

The convergence of asynchronous PI for finite-state discounted MDP under the condition $J^0 \geq T_{\mu^0} J^0$ was shown by Williams and Baird [WiB93], who also gave examples showing that without this condition, cycling of the algorithm may occur. The asynchronous PI algorithms of Sections 2.6.2 and 2.6.3 belong to the algorithmic framework of the papers by Bertsekas and Yu [BeY10a], [BeY10b], which address this difficulty. Our analysis follows closely the analysis of these papers, which also propose related Q-learning algorithms with and without cost function approximation.

In addition to discounted finite-state MDP, the results of this chapter find application in the context of the stochastic shortest path problem of Example 1.2.6, in the special case where all policies are proper. Then it can be shown that T and T_μ are weighted sup-norm contractions with respect to a special norm. It follows that the analysis and algorithms of this chapter fully apply in this special case. For a detailed discussion, we refer to [BeT96], and the survey [Ber12b]. Some of the theory and algorithms also extend to the case of countable state space; see the textbook [Ber12a], Section 3.3, and Hinderer and Waldmann [HiW05].

E X E R C I S E S

2.1 (Periodic Policies)

Consider the multistep mappings $\overline{T}_\nu = T_{\mu_0} \cdots T_{\mu_{m-1}}$, $\nu \in \mathcal{M}_m$, defined in Exercise 1.1 of Chapter 1, where $\mathcal{M}_m$ is the set of m-tuples $\nu = (\mu_0, \ldots, \mu_{m-1})$, with $\mu_k \in \mathcal{M}$, $k = 1, \ldots, m-1$, and m is a positive integer. Assume that the mappings T_μ satisfy the monotonicity and contraction Assumptions 2.1.1 and 2.1.2, so that the same is true for the mappings $\overline{T}_\nu$ (with the contraction modulus of $\overline{T}_\nu$ being α^m, cf. Exercise 1.1).

(a) Show that the unique fixed point of $\overline{T}_\nu$ is J_π, where π is the nonstationary but periodic policy

$$\pi = \{\mu_0, \ldots, \mu_{m-1}, \mu_0, \ldots, \mu_{m-1}, \ldots\}.$$

(b) Show that the multistep mappings $T_{\mu_0} \cdots T_{\mu_{m-1}}$, $T_{\mu_1} \cdots T_{\mu_{m-1}} T_{\mu_0}$, $\ldots$, $T_{\mu_{m-1}} T_{\mu_0} \cdots T_{\mu_{m-2}}$, have unique corresponding fixed points $J_0, J_1, \ldots$, J_{m-1}, which satisfy

$$J_0 = T_{\mu_0} J_1, \quad J_1 = T_{\mu_1} J_2, \quad \ldots \quad J_{\mu_{m-2}} = T_{\mu_{m-2}} J_{\mu_{m-1}}, \quad J_{\mu_{m-1}} = T_{\mu_{m-1}} J_0.$$

Hint: Apply T_{μ_0} to the fixed point relation

$$J_1 = T_{\mu_1} \cdots T_{\mu_{m-1}} T_{\mu_0} J_1$$

to show that $T_{\mu_0} J_1$ is the fixed point of $T_{\mu_0} \cdots T_{\mu_{m-1}}$, i.e., is equal to J_0. Similarly, apply T_{μ_1} to the fixed point relation

$$J_2 = T_{\mu_2} \cdots T_{\mu_{m-1}} T_{\mu_0} T_{\mu_1} J_2,$$

to show that $T_{\mu_1} J_2$ is the fixed point of $T_{\mu_1} \cdots T_{\mu_{m-1}} T_{\mu_0}$, i.e., is equal to J_1, etc.

2.2 (Asynchronous Convergence Theorem for Time-Varying Maps)

In reference to the asynchronous computation framework of Section 2.6.1, let $\{T_t\}$ be a sequence of mappings from $R(X)$ to $R(X)$ that have a common unique fixed point J^*, let Assumption 2.6.1 hold, and assume that there is a sequence of nonempty subsets $\big\{S(k)\big\} \subset R(X)$ with $S(k+1) \subset S(k)$ for all k, and with the following properties:

(1) *Synchronous Convergence Condition:* Every sequence $\{J^k\}$ with $J^k \in S(k)$ for each k, converges pointwise to J^*. Moreover, we have

$$T_t J \in S(k+1), \qquad \forall\ J \in S(k),\ k, t = 0, 1, \ldots.$$

(2) *Box Condition:* For all k, $S(k)$ is a Cartesian product of the form

$$S(k) = S_1(k) \times \cdots \times S_m(k),$$

where $S_\ell(k)$ is a set of real-valued functions on X_ℓ, $\ell = 1, \ldots, m$.

Then for every $J^0 \in S(0)$, the sequence $\{J^t\}$ generated by the asynchronous algorithm

$$J_\ell^{t+1}(x) = \begin{cases} T_t(J_1^{\tau_{\ell 1}(t)}, \ldots, J_m^{\tau_{\ell m}(t)})(x) & \text{if } t \in \mathcal{R}_\ell,\ x \in X_\ell, \\ J_\ell^t(x) & \text{if } t \notin \mathcal{R}_\ell,\ x \in X_\ell, \end{cases}$$

[cf. Eq. (2.57)] converges pointwise to J^*. *Hint*: Use the proof of Prop. 2.6.1.

2.3 (Nonmonotonic Contractive Models – Fixed Points of Concave Sup-Norm Contractions)

The purpose of this exercise is to make a connection between our abstract DP model and the problem of finding the fixed point of a mapping that is a sup-norm contraction and has concave components. Let $T : \Re^n \mapsto \Re^n$ be a real-valued function whose n scalar components are concave. Then the components of T can be represented as

$$(TJ)(x) = \inf_{u \in U(x)} \big\{F(x,u) - J'u\big\}, \qquad x = 1,\ldots,n, \tag{2.74}$$

where $u \in \Re^n$, $J'u$ denotes the inner product of J and u, $F(x,\cdot)$ is the conjugate convex function of the convex function $-(TJ)(x)$, and $U(x) = \big\{u \in \Re^n \mid F(x,u) < \infty\big\}$ is the effective domain of $F(x,\cdot)$ (for the definition of these terms, we refer to books on convex analysis, such as [Roc70] and [Ber09]). Assuming that the infimum in Eq. (2.74) is attained for all x, show how the VI algorithm of Section 2.6.1 and the PI algorithm of Section 2.6.3 can be used to find the fixed point of T in the case where T is a sup-norm contraction, but not necessarily monotone.

2.4 (Discounted Problems with Unbounded Cost per Stage)

Consider a countable-state MDP, where $X = \{1,2,\ldots\}$, the discount factor is $\alpha \in (0,1)$, the transition probabilities are denoted $p_{xy}(u)$ for $x,y \in X$ and $u \in U(x)$, and the expected cost per stage is denoted by $g(x,u)$, $x \in X$, $u \in U(x)$. The constraint set $U(x)$ may be infinite. For a positive weight sequence $v = \big\{v(1),v(2),\ldots\big\}$, we consider the space $B(X)$ of sequences $J = \big\{J(1),J(2),\ldots\big\}$ such that $\|J\| < \infty$, where $\|\cdot\|$ is the corresponding weighted sup-norm. We assume the following.

(1) The sequence $G = \big\{G_1, G_2, \ldots\big\}$, where

$$G_x = \sup_{u \in U(x)} \big|g(x,u)\big|, \qquad x \in X,$$

belongs to $B(X)$.

(2) The sequence $V = \big\{V_1, V_2, \ldots\big\}$, where

$$V_x = \sup_{u \in U(x)} \sum_{y \in X} p_{xy}(u)\, v(y), \qquad x \in X,$$

belongs to $B(X)$.

(3) We have

$$\frac{\sum_{y \in X} p_{xy}(u) v(y)}{v(x)} \le 1, \qquad \forall\, x \in X.$$

Consider the monotone mappings T_μ and T, given by

$$(T_\mu J)(x) = g\big(x, \mu(x)\big) + \alpha \sum_{y \in X} p_{xy}\big(\mu(x)\big) J(y), \qquad x \in X,$$

$$(TJ)(x) = \inf_{u \in U(x)} \left[g(x,u) + \alpha \sum_{y \in X} p_{xy}(u) J(y) \right], \qquad x \in X.$$

Show that T_μ and T map $B(X)$ into $B(X)$, and are contraction mappings with modulus α.

2.5 (Solution by Mathematical Programming)

Let the monotonicity and contraction Assumptions 2.1.1 and 2.1.2 hold. Show that if $J \leq TJ$ and $J \in B(X)$, then $J \leq J^*$, and use this fact to show that if $X = \{1, \ldots, n\}$ and $U(i)$ is finite for each $i = 1, \ldots, n$, then $J^*(1), \ldots, J^*(n)$ solves the following problem (in $z_1, \ldots, z_n$):

$$\begin{aligned} &\text{maximize} \quad \sum_{i=1}^{n} z_i \\ &\text{subject to} \quad z_i \leq H(i, u, z), \qquad i = 1, \ldots, n, \quad u \in U(i), \end{aligned}$$

where $z = (z_1, \ldots, z_n)$. *Note*: This is a linear or nonlinear program (depending on whether H is linear in J or not) with n variables and as many as $n \times m$ constraints, where m is the maximum number of elements in the sets $U(i)$.

2.6 (Convergence of Nonexpansive Monotone Fixed Point Iterations)

Consider the mapping H of Section 2.1 under the monotonicity Assumption 2.1.1. Assume that X is a finite set and that instead of the contraction Assumption 2.1.2, H satisfies the following:

(1) For every $J \in B(X)$, the function TJ belongs to $B(X)$.

(2) For all $J, J' \in B(X)$, H satisfies

$$\frac{\big|H(x,u,J) - H(x,u,J')\big|}{v(x)} \leq \|J - J'\|, \qquad \forall\, x \in X,\ u \in U(x).$$

(3) T has a unique fixed point within $B(X)$, denoted J^*.

Show that for every $J \in B(X)$, we have $\|T^k J - J^*\| \to 0$.

3

Semicontractive Models

Contents

We will now consider abstract DP models that are intermediate between the contractive models of Chapter 2, where all stationary policies involve a contraction mapping, and noncontractive models to be discussed in Chapter 4, where there are no contraction-like assumptions. A representative example of such an intermediate model is the stochastic shortest path problem of Example 1.2.6 (SSP for short). In one of the main versions of an SSP theory, there are two types of policies: those that are *proper* where the mapping T_μ is a contraction with respect to a weighted sup-norm, and those that are *improper*, where T_μ is not a contraction with respect to any norm. As noted in Example 1.2.6, results that are comparable to the ones for discounted finite-state MDP have been obtained with appropriate assumptions that guarantee among others that improper policies are "bad" in the sense that they have infinite cost from some initial state.

In this chapter we introduce models where, as in SSP problems, policies are divided into two groups, one of which has favorable characteristics. We loosely refer to such models as *semicontractive* to indicate that these favorable characteristics include contraction-like properties of the mapping T_μ. To develop a more broadly applicable theory, we replace the notion of contraction of T_μ with a notion of *regularity of μ within an appropriate set S* (roughly, this is a form of "local stability" of T_μ, which ensures that the cost function J_μ is the unique fixed point of T_μ within S, and that $T_\mu^k J$ converges to J_μ regardless of the choice of J from within S). We allow that some policies are regular in this sense while others are not, and impose further conditions ensuring that there exist optimal policies that are regular. Under a variety of assumptions, we show results that resemble those available for SSP problems: that J^* is a fixed point of T, that the Bellman equation $J = TJ$ has a unique solution, at least within a suitable class of functions, and that variants of the VI and PI algorithms are valid.

We note that the term "semicontractive" is not used in a precise mathematical sense here. Rather it refers qualitatively to a collection of models where some policies have a regularity/contraction-like property but others do not. In particular, in this chapter and the next one, we consider several alternative assumptions for different semicontractive models.

The chapter is organized as follows. In Section 3.1, we introduce the notion of a regular policy, and we develop some of the basic results. In Section 3.2, we discuss related lines of analysis to address some major special cases that bear similarity to SSP problems. In Section 3.3, we focus on VI and PI-type algorithms.

3.1 SEMICONTRACTIVE MODELS AND REGULAR POLICIES

Our basic model for this chapter and the next one is similar to the one of Chapter 2, but the assumptions are different. We will maintain the monotonicity assumption, but we will weaken the contraction assumption, and we will introduce some other conditions in its place.

In our analysis of this chapter, the optimal cost function J^* will typically be real-valued. However, the cost function J_μ of some policies μ may take infinite values for some states. To accommodate this, we will use the set of extended real numbers $\Re^* = \Re \cup \{\infty, -\infty\}$, and the set of all extended real-valued functions $J : X \mapsto \Re^*$, which we denote by $E(X)$. We denote by $R(X)$ the set of real-valued functions $J : X \mapsto \Re$, and by $B(X)$ the set of real-valued functions $J : X \mapsto \Re$ that are bounded with respect to a given weighted sup-norm. Throughout this chapter and the next two, when we write lim, lim sup, or lim inf of a sequence of functions we mean it to be pointwise. We also write $J_k \to J$ to mean that $J_k(x) \to J(x)$ for each $x \in X$; see our notational conventions in Appendix A.

As in Chapters 1 and 2, we introduce the set X of states and the set U of controls, and for each $x \in X$, the nonempty control constraint set $U(x) \subset U$. We denote by $\mathcal{M}$ the set of all functions $\mu : X \mapsto U$ with $\mu(x) \in U(x)$, for all $x \in X$, and by Π the set of nonstationary policies $\pi = \{\mu_0, \mu_1, \ldots\}$, with $\mu_k \in \mathcal{M}$ for all k. We refer to a stationary policy $\{\mu, \mu, \ldots\}$ simply as μ. We introduce a mapping $H : X \times U \times E(X) \mapsto \Re^*$, satisfying the following condition.

Assumption 3.1.1: (Monotonicity) If $J, J' \in E(X)$ and $J \leq J'$, then

$$H(x, u, J) \leq H(x, u, J'), \qquad \forall\, x \in X,\ u \in U(x).$$

The preceding monotonicity assumption will be in effect throughout this chapter. Consequently, *we will not mention it explicitly in various propositions*. We define the mapping $T : E(X) \mapsto E(X)$ by

$$(TJ)(x) = \inf_{u \in U(x)} H(x, u, J), \qquad \forall\, x \in X,\ J \in E(X),$$

and for each $\mu \in \mathcal{M}$ the mapping $T_\mu : E(X) \mapsto E(X)$ by

$$(T_\mu J)(x) = H\big(x, \mu(x), J\big), \qquad \forall\, x \in X,\ J \in E(X).$$

The monotonicity assumption implies the following properties for all $J, J' \in E(X)$ and $k = 0, 1, \ldots,$

$$J \leq J' \qquad \Rightarrow \qquad T^k J \leq T^k J', \qquad T_\mu^k J \leq T_\mu^k J', \quad \forall\, \mu \in \mathcal{M},$$

$$J \leq TJ \qquad \Rightarrow \qquad T^k J \leq T^{k+1} J, \qquad T_\mu^k J \leq T_\mu^{k+1} J, \quad \forall\, \mu \in \mathcal{M}.$$

We now define cost functions associated with T_μ and T. In Chapter 2 our starting point was to define J_μ and J^* as the unique fixed points of T_μ and T, respectively, based on the contraction assumption used there.

However, under our assumptions in this chapter this is not possible, so we use a different definition, which nonetheless is consistent with the one of Chapter 2 (see Section 2.1, following Prop. 2.1.2). We introduce a function $\bar{J} \in E(X)$, and we define the infinite horizon cost of a policy in terms of the limit of its finite horizon costs with $\bar{J}$ being the cost function at the end of the horizon.

Definition 3.1.1: Given a function $\bar{J} \in E(X)$, for a policy $\pi \in \Pi$ with $\pi = \{\mu_0, \mu_1, \ldots\}$, we define the cost function of π by

$$J_\pi(x) = \limsup_{k\to\infty} (T_{\mu_0} \cdots T_{\mu_k} \bar{J})(x), \qquad \forall\, x \in X.$$

In the case of a stationary policy $\mu \in \mathcal{M}$, the cost function of μ is denoted by J_μ and is given by

$$J_\mu(x) = \limsup_{k\to\infty} (T_\mu^k \bar{J})(x), \qquad \forall\, x \in X.$$

The optimal cost function J^* is given by

$$J^*(x) = \inf_{\pi\in\Pi} J_\pi(x), \qquad \forall\, x \in X.$$

An optimal policy $\pi^* \in \Pi$ is one for which $J_{\pi^*} = J^*$. Note two important differences from Chapter 2:

(1) J_μ is defined in terms of a pointwise lim sup rather than lim, since we don't know whether the limit exists.

(2) J_π and J_μ in general depend on $\bar{J}$, so $\bar{J}$ becomes an important part of the problem definition.

Similar to Chapter 2, under the assumptions to be introduced in this chapter, stationary policies will turn out to be "sufficient" in the sense that the optimal cost obtained with nonstationary policies is matched by the one obtained by stationary ones.

Regular Policies

Our objective in this chapter is to construct an analytical framework with a strong connection to fixed point theory, based on the idea of separating policies into those that have "favorable" characteristics and those that do not. It would then appear that a favorable property for a policy μ is that J_μ is a fixed point of T_μ. However, J_μ may depend on $\bar{J}$, even though T_μ does not depend on $\bar{J}$. It would thus appear that another favorable property for μ is that J_μ stays the same if $\bar{J}$ is changed arbitrarily within some set S. We express these two properties with the following definition.

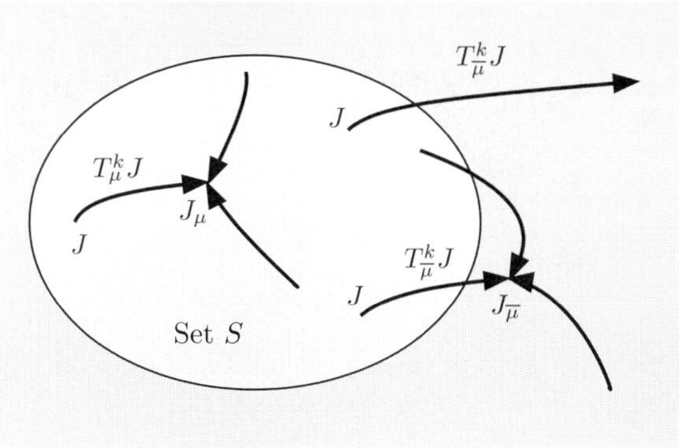

Figure 3.1.1. Illustration of S-regular and S-irregular policies. Policy μ is S-regular because $J_\mu \in S$ and $T_\mu^k J \to J_\mu$ for all $J \in S$. Policy $\overline{\mu}$ is S-irregular.

Definition 3.1.2: Given a set of functions $S \subset E(X)$, we say that a stationary policy μ is S-*regular* if:

(a) $J_\mu \in S$, $J_\mu = T_\mu J_\mu$, and J_μ is the only fixed point of T_μ in S.

(b) $T_\mu^k J \to J_\mu$ for all $J \in S$.

A policy that is not S-regular is called S-*irregular*.

Thus a policy μ is S-regular if the VI iteration corresponding to μ, $J_{k+1} = T_\mu J_k$, represents a dynamic system that has J_μ as its unique equilibrium within S, and is asymptotically stable in the sense that the iteration converges to J_μ, starting from any $J \in S$ (see Fig. 3.1.1).

For orientation purposes, we note the distinction between the set S and the problem data: *S is an analytical device*, and is not part of the problem's definition. Its choice, however, can enable analysis and clarify properties of J_μ and J^*. For example, we will later prove local fixed point statements such as

"J^* is the unique fixed point of T within S"

or local region of attraction assertions such as

"the VI sequence $\{T^k J\}$ converges to J^* starting from any $J \in S$."

Results of this type and their proofs depend on the choice of S: they may hold for some choices but not for others.

Generally, with our selection of S we will aim to differentiate between S-regular and S-irregular policies in a manner that produces useful results for the given problem and does not necessitate restrictive assumptions. Examples of sets S that we will use are $R(X)$, $B(X)$, and subsets of $R(X)$, $B(X)$, and $E(X)$ involving functions J satisfying $J \geq J^*$ or $J \geq \bar{J}$. However, there is a diverse range of other possibilities, so it makes sense to

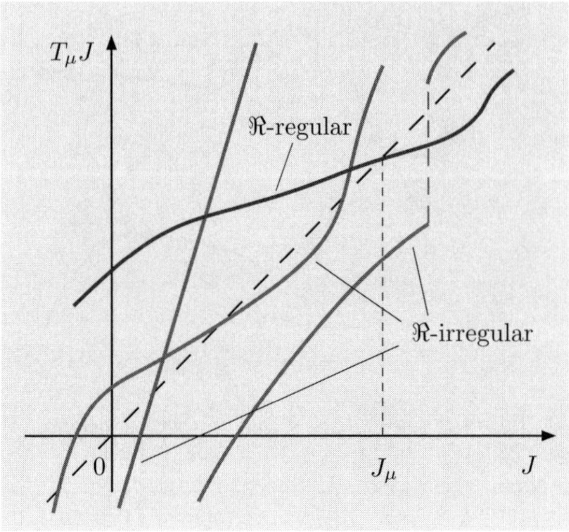

Figure 3.1.2. Illustration of S-regular and S-irregular policies for the case where there is only one state and $S = \Re$. There are three mappings T_μ corresponding to S-irregular policies: one crosses the 45-degree line at multiple points, another crosses at a single point but at an angle greater than 45 degrees, and the third is discontinuous and does not cross at all. The mapping T_μ of the $\Re$-regular policy has J_μ as its unique fixed point and satisfies $T_\mu^k J \to J_\mu$ for all $J \in \Re$.

postpone making the choice of S more specific. Figure 3.1.2 illustrates the mappings T_μ of some S-regular and S-irregular policies for the case where there is a single state and $S = \Re$. Figure 3.1.3 illustrates the mapping T_μ of an S-regular policy μ, where T_μ has multiple fixed points, and upon changing S, the policy may become S-irregular.

3.1.1 Fixed Points, Optimality Conditions, and Algorithmic Results

We will now introduce an analytical framework where S-regular policies are central. Our focus is reflected by our first assumption in the following proposition, which is that optimal policies can be found among the S-regular policies, i.e., that for some S-regular μ^* we have $J^* = J_{\mu^*}$. This assumption implies that

$$J^* = J_{\mu^*} = T_{\mu^*} J_{\mu^*} \geq T J_{\mu^*} = T J^*,$$

where the second equality follows from the S-regularity of μ^*. Thus the Bellman equation $J^* = TJ^*$ follows if μ^* attains the infimum in the relation $TJ^* = \inf_{\mu \in \mathcal{M}} T_\mu J^*$, which is our second assumption. In addition to existence of solution of the Bellman equation, the regularity of μ^* implies a uniqueness assertion and a convergence result for the VI algorithm, as shown in the following proposition.

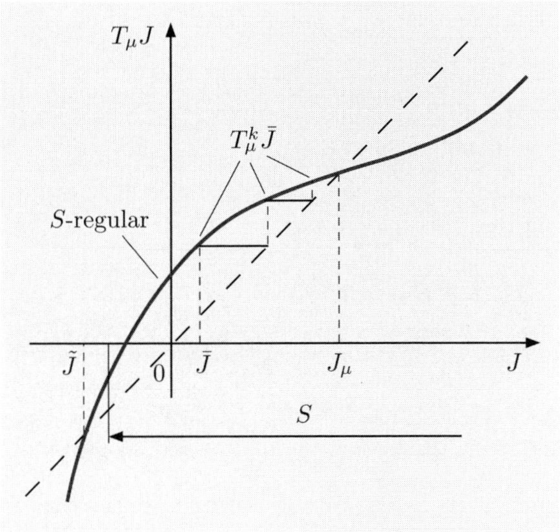

Figure 3.1.3. Illustration of a mapping T_μ where there is only one state and S is a subset of the real line. Here T_μ has two fixed points, J_μ and $\tilde{J}$. If S is as shown, μ is S-regular. If S is enlarged to include $\tilde{J}$, μ becomes S-irregular.

Proposition 3.1.1: Let S be a given subset of $E(X)$. Assume that:

(1) There exists an S-regular policy μ^* that is optimal, i.e., $J_{\mu^*} = J^*$.

(2) The policy μ^* satisfies $T_{\mu^*} J^* = TJ^*$.

Then the following hold:

(a) The optimal cost function J^* is the unique fixed point of T within the set $\{J \in S \mid J \geq J^*\}$.

(b) We have $T^k J \to J^*$ for every $J \in S$ with $J \geq J^*$.

(c) An S-regular policy μ that satisfies $T_\mu J^* = TJ^*$ is optimal. Conversely if μ is an S-regular optimal policy, it satisfies $T_\mu J^* = TJ^*$.

Proof: (a) The proof uses a more refined version of the argument preceding the statement of the proposition. We first show that any fixed point J of T that lies in S satisfies $J \leq J^*$. Indeed, if $J = TJ$, then for the optimal S-regular policy μ^*, we have $J \leq T_{\mu^*} J$, so in view of the monotonicity of T_{μ^*} and the S-regularity of μ^*,

$$J \leq \lim_{k \to \infty} T_{\mu^*}^k J = J_{\mu^*} = J^*.$$

Thus the only function within $\{J \in S \mid J \geq J^*\}$ that can be a fixed point of T is J^*. Using the optimality and S-regularity of μ^*, and condition (2), we have

$$J^* = J_{\mu^*} = T_{\mu^*} J_{\mu^*} = T_{\mu^*} J^* = TJ^*,$$

so J^* is a fixed point of T. Finally, $J^* \in S$ since $J^* = J_{\mu^*}$ and μ^* is S-regular, so J^* is the unique fixed point of T within $\{J \in S \mid J \geq J^*\}$.

(b) For the optimal S-regular policy μ^* and any $J \in S$ with $J \geq J^*$, we have

$$T_{\mu^*}^k J \geq T^k J \geq T^k J^* = J^*, \qquad k = 0, 1, \ldots.$$

Taking the limit as $k \to \infty$, and using the fact

$$\lim_{k \to \infty} T_{\mu^*}^k J = J_{\mu^*} = J^*,$$

which holds since μ^* is S-regular and optimal, we see that $T^k J \to J^*$.

(c) If μ satisfies $T_\mu J^* = TJ^*$, then using part (a), we have $T_\mu J^* = J^*$ and hence $\lim_{k\to\infty} T_\mu^k J^* = J^*$. If μ is in addition S-regular, then $J_\mu = \lim_{k\to\infty} T_\mu^k J^* = J^*$ and μ is optimal. Conversely, if μ is optimal and S-regular, then $J_\mu = J^*$ and $J_\mu = T_\mu J_\mu$, which combined with $J^* = TJ^*$ [cf. part (a)], yields $T_\mu J^* = TJ^*$. **Q.E.D.**

Note that given condition (1) of the proposition, condition (2) is equivalent to the seemingly weaker assumption that *some* S-regular μ satisfies $T_\mu J^* = TJ^*$. To see this note that if this latter condition holds together with condition (1), we have

$$J_{\mu^*} = T_{\mu^*} J_{\mu^*} = T_{\mu^*} J^* \geq TJ^* = T_\mu J^* = T_\mu J_{\mu^*} \geq \lim_{k\to\infty} T_\mu^k J_{\mu^*} = J_\mu,$$

where the first two equalities follow from the S-regularity and optimality of μ^*, the second inequality follows from the monotonicity of T_μ, and the last equality follows from the S-regularity of μ. Since μ^* is optimal, it follows that μ is also optimal, so equality holds in the above relation, and we have $T_{\mu^*} J^* = TJ^*$, implying condition (2) as stated in the proposition.

Let us also show an equivalent variation of the preceding proposition, for problems where the validity of Bellman's equation $J^* = TJ^*$ can be independently verified. We will later encounter models where this can be done (e.g., the perturbation model of Section 3.2.2, and the monotone increasing and monotone decreasing models of Section 4.3).

Proposition 3.1.2: Let S be a given subset of $E(X)$. Assume that:

(1) There exists an S-regular policy μ^* that is optimal, i.e., $J_{\mu^*} = J^*$.

(2) We have $J^* = TJ^*$.

Then the assumptions and the conclusions of Prop. 3.1.1 hold.

Proof: We have

$$J^* = J_{\mu^*} = T_{\mu^*} J_{\mu^*} = T_{\mu^*} J^*,$$

so, using also the assumption $J^* = TJ^*$, we obtain $T_{\mu^*} J^* = TJ^*$. Hence condition (2) of Prop. 3.1.1 holds. **Q.E.D.**

The following proposition is a special case of Prop. 3.1.1. It applies when functions in S are real-valued, and through its condition (1), it requires that S-irregular policies have a certain "infinite cost-type" property. Conditions of this type will appear prominently in Section 3.2 [see Assumptions 3.2.1(c) and 3.2.3(b)].

Proposition 3.1.3: Let S be a given subset of $R(X)$. Assume that:

(1) There exists an optimal S-regular policy, and for every S-irregular policy μ, there is at least one state $x \in X$ such that

$$\limsup_{k \to \infty} (T_\mu^k J^*)(x) = \infty.$$

(2) There exists a policy μ such that $T_\mu J^* = TJ^*$.

Then the assumptions and the conclusions of Prop. 3.1.1 hold.

Proof: In view of the remark following the proof of Prop. 3.1.1, it will suffice to show that the policy μ of condition (2) is S-regular. Let μ satisfy $T_\mu J^* = TJ^*$, and let μ^* be an optimal S-regular policy. Then for all $k \geq 1$,

$$J_{\mu^*} = T_{\mu^*} J_{\mu^*} \geq TJ_{\mu^*} = T_\mu J_{\mu^*} \geq T_\mu^k J_{\mu^*},$$

where the first equality follows from the definition of an S-regular policy, and the second inequality follows from the monotonicity of T_μ. If μ is S-irregular, by taking the limit as $k \to \infty$ in the preceding relation, the right-hand side tends to ∞ for some $x \in X$, while the left-hand side is finite since $J_{\mu^*} \in S \subset R(X)$ - a contradiction. Thus μ is S-regular. **Q.E.D.**

The examples of Fig. 3.1.2 show how Bellman's equation may fail in the absence of existence of an optimal S-regular policy [cf. condition (1) of Props. 3.1.1-3.1.3]. Consider for instance a problem where there is only one policy μ that is S-irregular and T_μ has no fixed point.

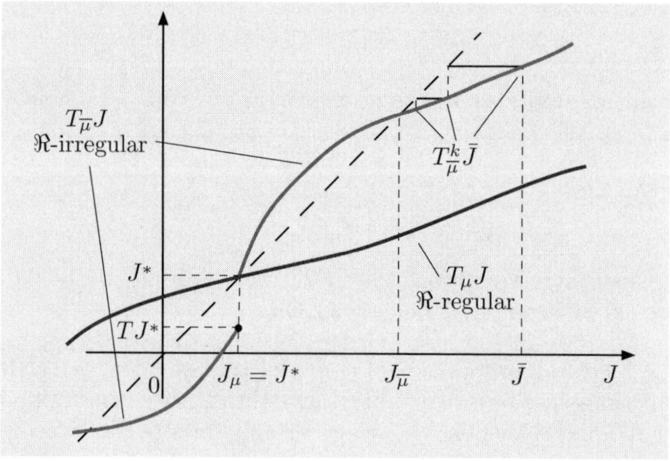

Figure 3.1.4. Illustration of why condition (2) is essential in Prop. 3.1.1. Here there is only one state and $S = \Re$. There are two stationary policies: μ for which T_μ is a contraction, so μ is $\Re$-regular, and $\overline{\mu}$ for which $T_{\overline{\mu}}$ has multiple fixed points, so $\overline{\mu}$ is $\Re$-irregular. Moreover, $T_{\overline{\mu}}$ is discontinuous from above at J_μ as shown. Here, it can be verified that $T_{\mu_0} \cdots T_{\mu_k} \bar{J} \geq J_\mu$ for all $\mu_0, \ldots, \mu_k$ and k, so that $J_\pi \geq J_\mu$ for all π and the S-regular policy μ is optimal. However, μ does not satisfy $T_\mu J^* = TJ^*$ [cf. condition (2) of Prop. 3.1.1] and we have $J^* \neq TJ^*$. Here the conclusions (a) and (c) of Prop. 3.1.1 are violated.

Another example that illustrates the need for existence of an optimal S-regular policy is the classical blackmailer problem, described in Exercise 3.1. This is a one-state problem, where T_μ is a contraction for all μ, so all policies are $\Re$-regular, but we have $J^* = -\infty$, so there is no optimal stationary policy. Here Bellman's equation, $J = TJ$, has no solution within $\Re$ (although we do have $J^* = TJ^*$). Moreover, it can be shown that there exists a nonstationary optimal policy for this problem; see [Ber12a] (Example 3.2.1).

Figure 3.1.4 shows what may happen if condition (2) of Prop. 3.1.1 is violated. The figure shows how we can then have $J^* \neq TJ^*$, and underscores the importance of existence of an S-regular μ satisfying the optimality equation $T_\mu J^* = TJ^*$ for a strong connection of our framework with fixed point theory. This condition will be assumed either directly or indirectly, via other conditions, throughout our analysis of semicontractive models.

The two conditions of Props. 3.1.1-3.1.3 may not be easily verified in a given problem. However, they can often be guaranteed through other reasonable conditions, in which case Props. 3.1.1-3.1.3 can be brought to bear on the analysis. We will encounter several such instances in Sections 3.2, 4.4, and 4.5.

Regardless of their assumptions, some of the conclusions (a)-(c) of Props. 3.1.1-3.1.3 are not as strong as one would like. In particular, part (a)

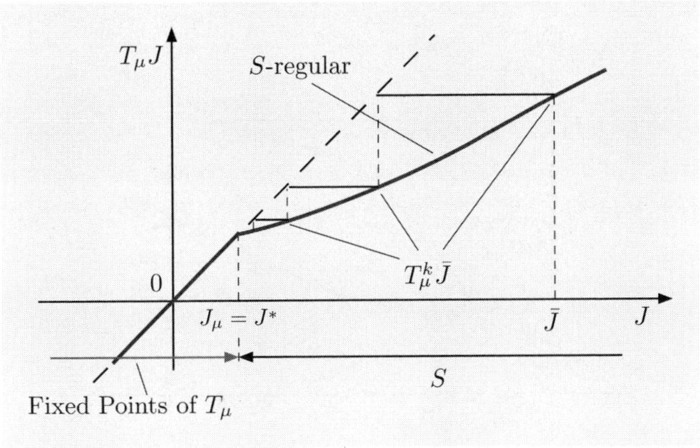

Figure 3.1.5. Illustration of multiplicity of fixed points J satisfying $J \le J^*$, under the assumptions of Props. 3.1.1-3.1.2. Here there is only one state, so S is a subset of the real line, and there is only one policy μ (so $J_\mu = J^*$), which is S-regular for $S = \{J \mid J \ge J_\mu\}$.

asserts uniqueness of the fixed point of T only within the set $\{J \in S \mid J \ge J^*\}$. One may hope that there would be a unique fixed point, at least within S. Similarly, part (b) asserts the convergence of $T^k J$ to J^* only for J in the set $\{J \in S \mid J \ge J^*\}$, and one would like to assert convergence starting anywhere within S. These results cannot be improved in the absence of additional conditions, as can be illustrated with simple examples involving a single policy; see Fig. 3.1.5. The deterministic shortest path problem with zero length cycles provides an interesting practical context where there may exist additional fixed points J of T that do not satisfy $J \ge J^*$ (see the next subsection). However, with additional conditions, one may be able to show uniqueness of the fixed point of T within S, and demonstrate an enlarged region of initial conditions J from which $T^k J$ converges to J^* (see for example Sections 3.2.1 and 4.4.1).

We finally note a subtle point in part (c) of Props. 3.1.1-3.1.2, which leaves open the possibility that the optimality condition $T_\mu J^* = T J^*$ is satisfied by a nonoptimal S-irregular μ. Indeed this can happen as can be shown with simple examples; see Fig. 3.1.6.†

---

† In the important case where $\bar J \le J^*$, we can show that the condition $T_\mu J^* = T J^*$ implies that μ is optimal, regardless of whether it is S-regular or not. The reason is that in this case we have

$$T_\mu^k \bar J \le T_\mu^k J^* = T^k J^* = J^*,$$

and taking the lim sup as $k \to \infty$, we obtain $J_\mu \le J^*$, so μ is optimal. Note that the condition $\bar J \le J^*$ holds for the monotone increasing models of Section 4.3.

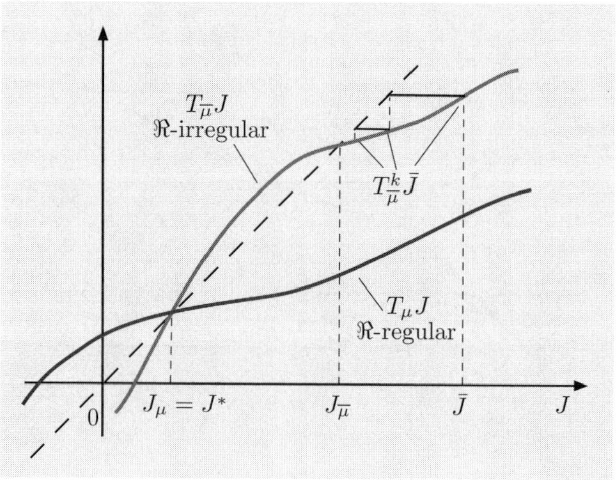

Figure 3.1.6. Illustration of a nonoptimal S-irregular policy $\overline{\mu}$ that satisfies the optimality condition $T_{\overline{\mu}}J^* = TJ^*$. Here there is only one state and $S = \Re$. There are two policies: μ for which T_μ is a contraction, so μ is $\Re$-regular, and $\overline{\mu}$ for which $T_{\overline{\mu}}$ has two fixed points, so $\overline{\mu}$ is $\Re$-irregular. For $\bar{J}$ as shown in the figure, $\overline{\mu}$ is nonoptimal, yet it satisfies $T_{\overline{\mu}}J^* = TJ^*$.

Policy Iteration

We established in Chapter 2 the significance of PI and its variations as a major class of computational methods for abstract DP. However, for semicontractive models, the convergence properties of PI are complicated, and under the conditions of Props. 3.1.1-3.1.2, the sequence of generated policies may not converge to an optimal policy.

What can be proved is that if μ and $\overline{\mu}$ are S-regular policies that satisfy the policy improvement equation $T_{\overline{\mu}}J_\mu = TJ_\mu$, then $J_{\overline{\mu}} \leq J_\mu$. To see this note that by using the S-regularity of μ, we have

$$J_\mu = T_\mu J_\mu \geq TJ_\mu = T_{\bar{\mu}} J_\mu \geq T_{\bar{\mu}}^k J_\mu, \qquad k \geq 1,$$

where the last inequality holds by the monotonicity of $T_{\bar{\mu}}$. By taking the limit as $k \to \infty$ in the preceding relation and using the S-regularity of $\overline{\mu}$, we obtain $J_\mu \geq J_{\bar{\mu}}$.

The policy improvement relation $J_\mu \geq J_{\bar{\mu}}$ shows that the PI algorithm, when restricted to S-regular policies, generates a nonincreasing sequence $\{J_{\mu^k}\}$, but this does not guarantee that $J_{\mu^k} \downarrow J^*$. Moreover, guaranteeing that the policies μ^k are S-regular may not be easy since the equation $T_{\overline{\mu}}J_\mu = TJ_\mu$ may be satisfied by an S-irregular $\overline{\mu}$, in which case there is no guarantee that $J_{\overline{\mu}} \leq J_\mu$, and an oscillation between policies may occur. This can be seen from the example of Fig. 3.1.7, where there

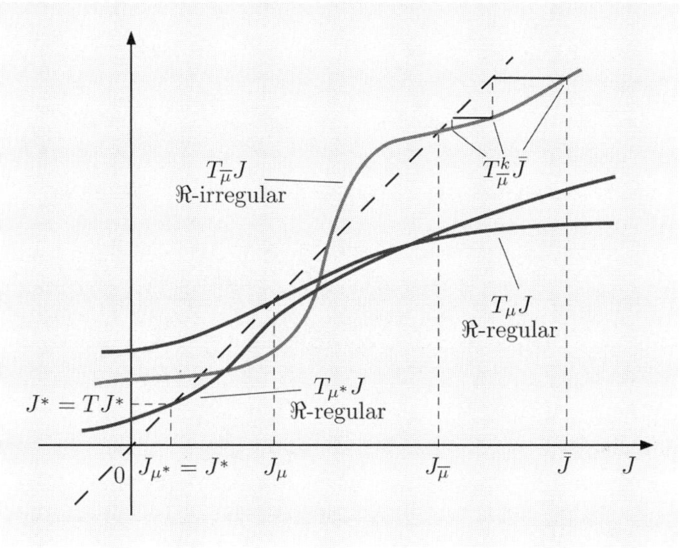

Figure 3.1.7. Oscillation of PI between two nonoptimal policies: an S-regular policy μ and an S-irregular policy $\overline{\mu}$ satisfying

$$T_{\overline{\mu}}J_\mu = TJ_\mu, \qquad T_\mu J_{\overline{\mu}} = TJ_{\overline{\mu}}.$$

Here there is only one state and $S = \Re$. In addition to μ and $\overline{\mu}$, there is a third policy μ^*, which is S-regular and optimal. In this example all the assumptions and conclusions of Props. 3.1.1-3.1.2 are satisfied.

is oscillation between two nonoptimal policies: an $\Re$-regular policy μ and an $\Re$-irregular policy $\overline{\mu}$ satisfying

$$T_{\overline{\mu}}J_\mu = TJ_\mu, \qquad T_\mu J_{\overline{\mu}} = TJ_{\overline{\mu}}.$$

A similar example of PI oscillation will be given for deterministic shortest path problems with zero length cycles in the next subsection. Thus additional assumptions or modifications of the PI algorithm are needed to improve its reliability. We will address this issue in Section 3.3.2, as well as in Sections 4.4 and 4.5 of the next chapter.

3.1.2 Illustrative Example: Deterministic Shortest Path Problems

In this section, we will highlight some of the analytical issues raised in the preceding subsection through the classical deterministic shortest path problem described in Example 1.2.7. We have a graph of n nodes $x = 1,\ldots,n$, plus the destination 0, and an arc length a_{xy} for each directed arc (x, y). Here $X = \{1,\ldots,n\}$. A policy chooses at state/node $x \in X$

an outgoing arc from x. Thus the controls available at x can be identified with the outgoing neighbors of x [the nodes u such that (x, u) is an arc]. The corresponding mapping H is given by

$$H(x, u, J) = \begin{cases} a_{xu} + J(u) & \text{if } u \neq 0, \\ a_{x0} & \text{if } u = 0, \end{cases}$$

and $\bar{J} = 0$.

We will consider S-regularity with $S = \Re^n$. A policy μ defines a graph whose arcs are $\big(x, \mu(x)\big)$, $x = 1, \ldots, n$. If this graph contains a cycle with m arcs, $x_1 \to x_2 \to \cdots \to x_m \to x_1$, with length $L = a_{x_1 x_2} + \cdots + a_{x_{m-1} x_m} + a_{x_m x_1}$, then it can be seen that for all $k \geq 1$, we have

$$(T_\mu^{km} J)(x_1) = kL + J(x_1).$$

Thus such a policy cannot be $\Re^n$-regular (and if $L \neq 0$, its cost function J_μ has some infinite entries, so it is outside $\Re^n$). By contrast if a policy defines a graph that is acyclic, it can be verified to be $\Re^n$-regular.

Let us assume now that all cycles have positive cost ($L > 0$ above), and that every node is connected to the destination with some path (this is a common assumption in deterministic shortest path problems, which will be revisited and generalized considerably in Section 3.2.1). Then every $\Re^n$-irregular policy has infinite cost starting from some node/state, and it can be shown that there exists an optimal $\Re^n$-regular policy. Thus Prop. 3.1.3 applies, and guarantees that J^* is the unique fixed point of T within the set $\{J \mid J \geq J^*\}$, and that the VI algorithm converges to J^* starting only from within that set. Actually the uniqueness of the fixed point and the convergence of VI can be shown within the entire space $\Re^n$. This is well-known in shortest path theory, and will be covered by results to be given in Section 3.2.1.

In the other extreme case where there is a cycle of negative cost, there are $\Re^n$-irregular policies that are optimal and no $\Re^n$-regular policy can be optimal. Thus Props. 3.1.1-3.1.3 do not apply in this case.

The case where there is a cycle with zero cost exhibits the most complex behavior and will be illustrated for the example of Fig. 3.1.8. Here

$$X = \{1, 2\}, \qquad U(1) = \{0, 2\}, \qquad U(2) = \{1\}, \qquad \bar{J}(1) = \bar{J}(2) = 0.$$

There are two policies:

μ : where $\mu(1) = 0$, corresponding to the path $2 \to 1 \to 0$,

$\overline{\mu}$: where $\overline{\mu}(1) = 2$, corresponding to the cycle $1 \to 2 \to 1$,

and the corresponding mapping H is

$$H(x, u, J) = \begin{cases} b & \text{if } x = 1,\ u = 0, \\ a + J(2) & \text{if } x = 1,\ u = 2, \\ a + J(1) & \text{if } x = 2,\ u = 1. \end{cases} \tag{3.1}$$

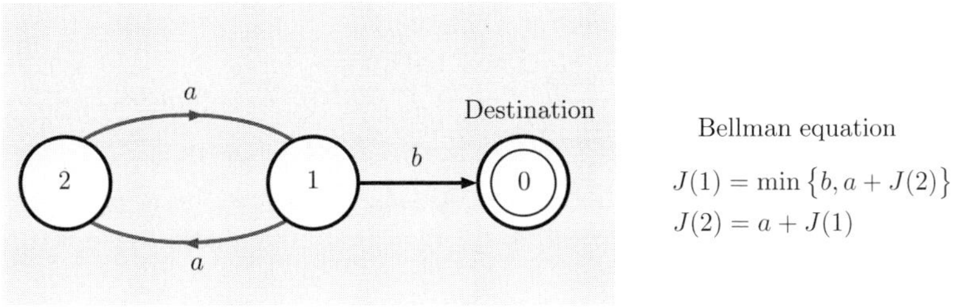

Figure 3.1.8. A deterministic shortest path problem with nodes 1, 2, and destination 0. Arc lengths are shown next to the arcs.

The Bellman equation is given by

$$J(1) = \min\big\{b, a + J(2)\big\}, \qquad J(2) = a + J(1), \tag{3.2}$$

while the VI algorithm takes the form

$$J_{k+1}(1) = \min\big\{b, a + J_k(2)\big\}, \qquad J_{k+1}(2) = a + J_k(1). \tag{3.3}$$

Here the policy μ is $\Re^2$-regular [the VI for μ is $J_{k+1}(1) = b$, $J_{k+1}(2) = a + J_k(1)$], while the policy $\overline{\mu}$ is $\Re^2$-irregular [the VI for $\overline{\mu}$ is $J_{k+1}(1) = a + J_k(2)$, $J_{k+1}(2) = a + J_k(1)$].

In the case where the cycle has zero length, so $a = 0$, there are two possibilities, $b \leq 0$ and $b > 0$, which we will consider separately:

(a) $a = 0$, $b \leq 0$: Here the $\Re^2$-regular policy is optimal, and Prop. 3.1.1 applies. Bellman's equation (3.2) has the unique solution

$$J^*(1) = b, \qquad J^*(2) = b,$$

within the set $\Re^2$, and the VI algorithm (3.3) converges to J^* from any starting $J_0 \geq J^*$. However, it can be verified that Bellman's equation has multiple solutions: the set of solutions is

$$\big\{J \mid J(1) = J(2),\ J \leq J^*\big\},$$

and VI starting from one of these solutions, will keep generating that solution. Moreover we can verify that PI may oscillate between the optimal $\Re^2$-regular policy and the $\Re^2$-irregular policy (which is nonoptimal if $b < 0$). Indeed, the $\Re^2$-irregular policy $\overline{\mu}$ is evaluated as $J_{\overline{\mu}}(1) = J_{\overline{\mu}}(2) = 0$, while the $\Re^2$-regular policy μ is evaluated as $J_\mu(1) = J_\mu(2) = b$, so in the policy improvement phase of the algorithm, we have

$$\mu(1) \in \arg\min\big\{b,\ J_{\overline{\mu}}(2)\big\}, \qquad \overline{\mu}(1) \in \arg\min\big\{b,\ J_\mu(2)\big\}.$$

Thus policy improvement starting with $\overline{\mu}$ yields μ, and starting with μ may yield $\overline{\mu}$, with the oscillatory sequence $\{\mu, \overline{\mu}, \mu, \overline{\mu}, \ldots\}$ resulting. Note that here we have $T_{\overline{\mu}}J^* = TJ^*$, so the optimality condition of Prop. 3.1.1(b) is attained by $\overline{\mu}$, which is nonoptimal when $b < 0$.

(b) $a = 0$, $b > 0$: Here the unique optimal policy is the $\Re^2$-irregular $\overline{\mu}$, and Props. 3.1.1-3.1.3 do not apply. The policy generates a sequence of cycles $1 \to 2 \to 1$, rather than a path that leads to the destination. In this case, the abstract DP model based on the mapping H of Eq. (3.1) cannot be used to model the shortest path problem (its optimal solution does not yield paths from nodes 1 and 2 to the destination). However, we may still be interested in finding an optimal policy within the class of $\Re^2$-regular policies. It turns out that we may address this problem by using a perturbation approach, which is described in Section 3.2.2. In particular, we will add a small amount $\delta > 0$ to the length of each arc. This has a strong effect on the problem: the cost function of the $\Re^2$-irregular policy becomes infinite, while the cost function of the $\Re^2$-regular policy changes by an $O(\delta)$ amount. Thus with $\delta > 0$, we obtain the acyclic $\Re^2$-regular policy μ.

3.2 IRREGULAR POLICIES AND A PERTURBATION APPROACH

In this section we will use the model and the results of the preceding section as a starting point and motivation for the analysis of various special cases. In particular, we will introduce various analytical techniques and alternative conditions, in order to strengthen the results of Props. 3.1.1-3.1.3, and to extend the existing theory of the SSP problem of Example 1.2.6.

3.2.1 The Case Where Irregular Policies Have Infinite Cost

A weakness of Props. 3.1.1-3.1.3 is that it is sometimes difficult to verify their assumptions, particularly the existence of an optimal S-regular policy. In this section we will use the following assumption that combines elements of the assumptions of these propositions, indirectly guarantees the existence of an optimal S-regular policy, and yields stronger results.

Assumption 3.2.1: We are given a subset $S \subset R(X)$ such that the following hold:

(a) S contains $\bar{J}$, and has the property that if J_1, J_2 are two functions in S, then S contains all functions J with $J_1 \leq J \leq J_2$.

(b) The function $\hat{J}$ given by

$$\hat{J}(x) = \inf_{\mu:\, S\text{-regular}} J_\mu(x), \qquad x \in X,$$

belongs to S.

(c) For each S-irregular policy μ and each $J \in S$, there is at least one state $x \in X$ such that

$$\limsup_{k \to \infty} (T_\mu^k J)(x) = \infty. \tag{3.4}$$

(d) The control set U is a metric space, and the set

$$\{u \in U(x) \mid H(x, u, J) \leq \lambda\}$$

is compact for every $J \in S$, $x \in X$, and $\lambda \in \Re$.

(e) For each sequence $\{J_m\} \subset S$ with $J_m \uparrow J$ for some $J \in S$ we have

$$\lim_{m \to \infty} H(x, u, J_m) = H(x, u, J), \qquad \forall\, x \in X,\ u \in U(x).$$

(f) For each function $J \in S$, there exists a function $J' \in S$ such that $J' \leq J$ and $J' \leq TJ'$.

Note that the preceding assumption requires that S is a set of *real-valued* functions; this is similar to Prop. 3.1.3, and it allows us to make use of Eq. (3.4) in the subsequent analysis. Part (a) holds for some common choices of S, such as when $S = R(X)$ or $S = B(X)$, or when S is a subset of $R(X)$ or $B(X)$ of the form $S = \{J \in R(X) \mid J \geq J'\}$ or $S = \{J \in B(X) \mid J \geq J'\}$ for a given function J' in $R(X)$ or $B(X)$, respectively. For a finite number n of states, $R(X)$ and $B(X)$ can both be identified with $\Re^n$, while otherwise $R(X)$ may be simpler as it does not require the use of a norm. On the other hand, for an infinite number of states, the choice between $R(X)$ and $B(X)$ may have a substantial impact on whether a policy μ is S-regular or not. In particular, $T_\mu^k J$ may converge to J_μ for all $J \in B(X)$ but not for all $J \in R(X)$, because $T_\mu J \in B(X)$ for $J \in B(X)$ while $T_\mu J \notin R(X)$ for some $J \in R(X)$. This can happen even if T_μ is a contraction mapping with respect to the norm of $B(X)$. Thus some care is needed in deciding whether S should be a subset of $R(X)$ or a subset of $B(X)$.

Since part (b) requires that $\hat{J}$ belongs to S, and is therefore real-valued, it also implies that *there exists at least one S-regular policy* [otherwise the infimum in part (b) is taken over the empty set, and $\hat{J}(x) = \infty$ for all x]. If S satisfies part (a), then part (b) holds if and only if there exists at least one S-regular policy, and also there exists a function in S that is a lower bound to the cost function of all S-regular policies. The existence of such a lower bound is essential, as can be shown by the blackmailer problem of Exercise 3.1.

Part (c) asserts among others that an S-irregular policy cannot be optimal, and is consistent with our analytical approach for semicontractive models, which relies on the dominance of S-regular policies (cf. Prop. 3.1.3). Part (e) is a mild technical continuity assumption that is needed for the subsequent analysis. Part (f) is also of technical nature, but it may not be satisfied in some problems of interest, a notable case being multiplicative models discussed in Example 1.2.8, where

$$H(x, u, J) = \sum_{y \in X} p_{xy}(u) g(x, u, y) J(y),$$

S contains only strictly positive functions, and the function g may take values less than 1; see also the affine monotonic and exponential cost SSP models of Section 4.5.

The compactness part (d) of the semicontraction Assumption 3.2.1 plays a key role for asserting the existence of an optimal S-regular policy, as well as for various proof arguments (see Exercise 3.1 for counterexamples). It implies that *for every $J \in S$, the infimum in the equation*

$$(TJ)(x) = \inf_{u \in U(x)} H(x, u, J), \tag{3.5}$$

is attained for all $x \in X$, and it also implies that *for every $J \in S$, there exists a policy μ such that $T_\mu J = TJ$.* This will be shown as part of the proof of the following proposition.

The compactness condition of Assumption 3.2.1(d) can be verified in a few interesting cases involving both finite and infinite state and control spaces:

(1) The case where U is a finite set.

(2) Cases where for each x, $H(x, u, J)$ depends on J only through its values $J(y)$ for y in a finite set Y_x. For an illustration, consider a mapping like the one of the SSP Example 1.2.6:

$$H(x, u, J) = g(x, u) + \sum_{y \in Y_x} p_{xy}(u) J(y).$$

Then the infimum in Eq. (3.5) is attained if $U(x)$ is compact, $g(x, \cdot)$ is lower semicontinuous, and $p_{xy}(\cdot)$ is continuous for each $y \in Y_x$, since then $H(x, \cdot, J)$ is lower semicontinuous as a function of u. This covers important cases of finite-state and countable-state MDP with compact control spaces (see [BeT91]).

(3) Cases of stochastic optimal control problems such as those of Example 1.2.1, under conditions involving a continuous state space, a compact constraint set $U(x)$, and a problem structure implying that $H(x, \cdot, J)$ is continuous. However, in such cases one must often require that policies obey additional measurability restrictions, and to this end a more complex mathematical formulation is needed to address these restrictions. Such a formulation and corresponding analysis is given for abstract contractive DP models in Chapter 5; see also [BeS78], Ch. 6, and [JaC06] for SSP problems. The extension to the semicontractive models of this section, while in principle straightforward, has not been worked out.

We will show the following proposition, which is the main result of this section.

Proposition 3.2.1: Let Assumption 3.2.1 hold. Then:

(a) The optimal cost function J^* is the unique fixed point of T within the set S.

(b) We have $T^k J \to J^*$ for all $J \in S$. Moreover, there exists an optimal S-regular policy.

(c) A policy μ is optimal if and only if $T_\mu J^* = TJ^*$.

(d) For any $J \in S$, if $J \leq TJ$ we have $J \leq J^*$, and if $J \geq TJ$ we have $J \geq J^*$.

In comparing this proposition with Props. 3.1.1-3.1.3 of Section 3.1, we see that it requires more conditions (cf. Assumption 3.2.1). However, the two assumptions of Props. 3.1.1-3.1.3 require some prior analysis for verification. Assumption 3.2.1 provides a reasonably convenient way to verify these two assumptions in the case where S consists of real-valued functions, but goes further with additional technical conditions, and in doing so it leads to stronger conclusions. These are the uniqueness of the fixed point of T within S (not just within the set $\{J \in S \mid J \geq J^*\}$), and the convergence of the VI sequence $\{T^k J\}$ starting from any $J \in S$ (not just starting from $J \in S$ with $J \geq J^*$).

The proof of Prop. 3.2.1 is long and is developed through several lemmas. These lemmas will also help to illuminate the implications of the various parts of Assumption 3.2.1, and to identify the roles of these parts in the major steps of the proof. The lemmas culminate with showing that the function $\hat{J}$ of Assumption 3.2.1(b) is the unique fixed point of T, and that any policy μ satisfying $T_\mu \hat{J} = T\hat{J}$ is optimal within the set of S-regular policies. Then the proposition is proved by first showing that $T^k J \to \hat{J}$ for all $J \in S$, and then by using this to prove that $\hat{J} = J^*$ and that there exists an optimal S-regular policy.

Lemma 3.2.1: Let Assumption 3.2.1(d) hold. For every $J \in S$, there exists a policy μ such that $T_\mu J = TJ$.

Proof: Since H is in general extended real-valued, for a given $x \in X$, we need to consider separately the cases $(TJ)(x) < \infty$ and $(TJ)(x) = \infty$. Consider any $x \in X$ with $(TJ)(x) < \infty$, and let $\{\lambda_m(x)\}$ be a decreasing scalar sequence with

$$\lambda_m(x) \downarrow \inf_{u \in U(x)} H(x, u, J).$$

The set

$$U_m(x) = \{u \in U(x) \mid H(x, u, J) \leq \lambda_m(x)\},$$

is nonempty, and by Assumption 3.2.1(d), it is compact. The set of points attaining the infimum of $H(x, u, J)$ over $U(x)$ is $\cap_{m=0}^{\infty} U_m(x)$, and is therefore nonempty. Let u_x be a point in this intersection. Then we have

$$H(x, u_x, J) \leq \lambda_m(x), \qquad \forall\, m \geq 0. \tag{3.6}$$

Consider the policy μ formed by the point u_x, for x with $(TJ)(x) < \infty$, and by any point $u_x \in U(x)$ for x with $(TJ)(x) = \infty$. Taking the limit in Eq. (3.6) as $m \to \infty$ shows that μ satisfies $(T_\mu J)(x) = (TJ)(x)$ for x with $(TJ)(x) < \infty$. For x with $(TJ)(x) = \infty$, we also have trivially $(T_\mu J)(x) = (TJ)(x)$, so $T_\mu J = TJ$. **Q.E.D.**

Lemma 3.2.2: Let Assumption 3.2.1(c) hold. A policy μ that satisfies $T_\mu J \leq J$ for some $J \in S$ is S-regular.

Proof: By the monotonicity of T_μ, we have $T_\mu^k J \leq J$, for all $k \geq 1$. Thus $\limsup_{k \to \infty} T_\mu^k J \leq J$ and since J is real-valued, from Assumption 3.2.1(c) it follows that μ cannot be S-irregular. **Q.E.D.**

Lemma 3.2.3: Let Assumption 3.2.1(a),(d),(e) hold. Then if $J' \in S$ and $T^k J' \uparrow J$ for some $J \in S$, we have $J = TJ$.

Proof: We first note that since $J' \in S$ and $J \in S$, from Assumption 3.2.1(a) it follows that $T^k J' \in S$. We fix $x \in X$, and consider the sets

$$U_k(x) = \big\{u \in U(x) \mid H(x, u, T^k J') \le J(x)\big\}, \qquad k = 0, 1, \ldots, \tag{3.7}$$

which are compact by Assumption 3.2.1(d). Let $u_k \in U(x)$ be such that

$$H(x, u_k, T^k J') = \inf_{u \in U(x)} H(x, u, T^k J') = (T^{k+1} J')(x) \le J(x);$$

(such a point exists by Lemma 3.2.1). Then $u_k \in U_k(x)$.

For every k, consider the sequence $\{u_i\}_{i=k}^\infty$. Since $T^k J' \uparrow J$, it follows using the monotonicity of H, that for all $i \ge k$,

$$H(x, u_i, T^k J') \le H(x, u_i, T^i J') \le J(x).$$

Therefore from the definition (3.7), we have $\{u_i\}_{i=k}^\infty \subset U_k(x)$. Since $U_k(x)$ is compact, all the limit points of $\{u_i\}_{i=k}^\infty$ belong to $U_k(x)$ and at least one limit point exists. Hence the same is true for the limit points of the whole sequence $\{u_i\}$. Thus if $\tilde{u}$ is a limit point of $\{u_i\}$, we have

$$\tilde{u} \in \cap_{k=0}^\infty U_k(x).$$

By Eq. (3.7), this implies that

$$H\big(x, \tilde{u}, T^k J'\big) \le J(x), \qquad k = 0, 1, \ldots.$$

Taking the limit as $k \to \infty$ and using Assumption 3.2.1(e), we obtain

$$(TJ)(x) \le H(x, \tilde{u}, J) \le J(x).$$

Thus, since x was chosen arbitrarily within X, we have $TJ \le J$. To show the reverse inequality, we write $T^k J' \le J$, apply T to this inequality, and take the limit as $k \to \infty$, so that $J = \lim_{k\to\infty} T^{k+1} J' \le TJ$. It follows that $J = TJ$. **Q.E.D.**

Lemma 3.2.4: Let Assumption 3.2.1(b),(c),(d) hold. Then:

(a) The function $\hat{J}$ of Assumption 3.2.1(b),

$$\hat{J}(x) = \inf_{\mu:\, S\text{-regular}} J_\mu(x), \qquad x \in X,$$

is the unique fixed point of T within S.

(b) Every policy μ satisfying $T_\mu \hat{J} = T\hat{J}$ is optimal within the set of S-regular policies, i.e., μ is S-regular and $J_\mu = \hat{J}$. Moreover, there exists at least one such policy.

Proof: For all S-regular policies μ, we have $J_\mu \geq \hat{J}$, and by applying T_μ to this relation, we have

$$J_\mu = T_\mu J_\mu \geq T_\mu \hat{J} \geq T\hat{J},$$

where the first equality follows from the S-regularity of μ. Taking the infimum in this relation over all S-regular policies μ and using the definition of $\hat{J}$, we obtain $\hat{J} \geq T\hat{J}$.

To prove the reverse relation, let μ be any policy such that $T_\mu \hat{J} = T\hat{J}$ (there exists one by Lemma 3.2.1). In view of the inequality $\hat{J} \geq T\hat{J}$ just shown, we have $\hat{J} \geq T_\mu \hat{J}$, so μ is S-regular by Lemma 3.2.2. Thus we have, using also the monotonicity of T_μ,

$$\hat{J} \geq T\hat{J} = T_\mu \hat{J} \geq \lim_{k\to\infty} T_\mu^k \hat{J} = J_\mu.$$

From the definition of $\hat{J}$, it follows that equality holds throughout in the preceding relation, so μ is optimal within the class of S-regular policies, and $\hat{J}$ is a fixed point of T.

Next we show that $\hat{J}$ is the unique fixed point of T within S. Indeed if $J' \in S$ is another fixed point, we choose an S-regular μ such that $J_\mu = \hat{J}$ (there exists one by the preceding argument), and we have

$$J' = TJ' \leq T_\mu J' \leq \lim_{k\to\infty} T_\mu^k J' = J_\mu = \hat{J}.$$

Let μ' be such that $J' = TJ' = T_{\mu'}J'$ (cf. Lemma 3.2.1). Then μ' is S-regular (cf. Lemma 3.2.2), and we have

$$J' = \lim_{k\to\infty} T_{\mu'}^k J' = J_{\mu'}.$$

Combining the preceding two relations, we have $J' = J_{\mu'} \leq \hat{J}$, which in view of the definition of $\hat{J}$, implies that $J' = \hat{J}$. **Q.E.D.**

Proof of Prop. 3.2.1: (a), (b) We will first prove that $T^k J \to \hat{J}$ for all $J \in S$, and we will use this to prove that $\hat{J} = J^*$ and that there exists an optimal S-regular policy. Thus both parts (a) and (b) will be shown simultaneously.

We fix $J \in S$, and choose $J' \in S$ such that $J' \leq J$ and $J' \leq TJ'$ [cf. Assumption 3.2.1(f)]. By the monotonicity of T, we have $T^k J' \uparrow \tilde{J}$ for some $\tilde{J} \in E(X)$. Let μ be an S-regular policy such that $J_\mu = \hat{J}$ [cf. Lemma 3.2.4(b)]. Then we have, using again the monotonicity of T,

$$\tilde{J} = \lim_{k\to\infty} T^k J' \leq \liminf_{k\to\infty} T^k J \leq \limsup_{k\to\infty} T^k J \leq \lim_{k\to\infty} T_\mu^k J = J_\mu = \hat{J}. \quad (3.8)$$

Since J' and $\hat{J}$ belong to S, and $J' \leq \tilde{J} \leq \hat{J}$, Assumption 3.2.1(a) implies that $\tilde{J} \in S$. From Lemma 3.2.3, it then follows that $\tilde{J} = T\tilde{J}$. Since $\hat{J}$

is the unique fixed point of T within S [cf. Lemma 3.2.4(a)], it follows that $\tilde{J} = \hat{J}$. Thus equality holds throughout in Eq. (3.8), proving that $\lim_{k\to\infty} T^k J = \hat{J}$.

There remains to show that $\hat{J} = J^*$ and that there exists an optimal S-regular policy. To this end, we note that by the monotonicity Assumption 3.1.1, for any policy $\pi = \{\mu_0, \mu_1, \ldots\}$, we have

$$T_{\mu_0} \cdots T_{\mu_{k-1}} \bar{J} \geq T^k \bar{J}.$$

Taking the limit of both sides as $k \to \infty$, we obtain

$$J_\pi \geq \lim_{k\to\infty} T^k \bar{J} = \hat{J},$$

where the equality follows since $T^k J \to \hat{J}$ for all $J \in S$ (as shown earlier), and $\bar{J} \in S$ [cf. Assumption 3.2.1(a)]. Thus for all $\pi \in \Pi$, $J_\pi \geq \hat{J} = J_\mu$, implying that the policy μ that is optimal within the class of S-regular policies is optimal over all policies, and that $\hat{J} = J^*$.

(c) If μ is optimal, then $J_\mu = J^* \in S$, so by Assumption 3.2.1(c), μ is S-regular and therefore $T_\mu J_\mu = J_\mu$. Hence, $T_\mu J^* = T_\mu J_\mu = J_\mu = J^* = TJ^*$. Conversely, if $J^* = TJ^* = T_\mu J^*$, μ is S-regular (cf. Lemma 3.2.2), so $J^* = \lim_{k\to\infty} T_\mu^k J^* = J_\mu$. Therefore, μ is optimal.

(d) If $J \in S$ and $J \leq TJ$, by repeatedly applying T to both sides and using the monotonicity of T, we obtain $J \leq T^k J$ for all k. Taking the limit as $k \to \infty$ and using the fact $T^k J \to J^*$ [cf. part (b)], we obtain $J \leq J^*$. The proof that $J \geq TJ$ implies $J \geq J^*$ is similar. **Q.E.D.**

3.2.2 The Case Where Irregular Policies Have Finite Cost - Perturbations

In this section, we consider problems where some S-irregular policies may have finite cost for all states, so Prop. 3.2.1 does not apply. An example is SSP problems where all one-stage costs are nonpositive and $J^*(x) > -\infty$ for all x. The following example describes a classical problem of this type.

Example 3.2.1 (Search Problem)

Consider a situation where the objective is to move within a finite set of states searching for a state to stop while minimizing the expected cost. We formulate this as a DP problem with finite state space X, and two controls at each $x \in X$: *stop*, which yields an immediate cost $s(x)$, and *continue*, in which case we move to a state $f(x, w)$ at cost $g(x, w)$, where w is a random variable with given distribution that may depend on x. The mapping H has the form

$$H(x, u, J) = \begin{cases} s(x) & \text{if } u = \text{stop}, \\ E\big\{g(x, w) + J\big(f(x, w)\big)\big\} & \text{if } u = \text{continue}, \end{cases}$$

and the function $\bar{J}$ is identically 0.

Letting $S = R(X)$, we note that the policy $\overline{\mu}$ that stops nowhere is S-irregular, since $T_{\overline{\mu}}$ cannot have a unique fixed point (adding any unit function multiple to J adds to $T_{\overline{\mu}}J$ the same multiple). This policy may violate Assumption 3.2.1(c) of the preceding subsection, because its cost may be finite for all states. A special case where this occurs is when $g(x, w) \equiv 0$ for all x. Then the cost function of $\overline{\mu}$ is identically 0.

Note that case (a) of the three-node shortest path problem given in Section 3.1.2, which involves a zero length cycle, is a special case of the search problem just described. Therefore, the anomalous behavior we saw there (nonconvergence of VI starting from $J_0 < J^*$ and oscillation of PI) may also arise in the context of the present example.

In this section, we show that the results of Props. 3.1.1-3.1.3 (uniqueness of fixed point of T within the set $\{J \in S \mid J \geq J^*\}$ and convergence of VI starting from within that set) hold, provided that there exists an optimal S-regular policy, and the assumptions are suitably modified by introducing a positive perturbation into T_μ. The idea is that with a perturbation, the cost functions of S-irregular policies may increase disproportionately relative to the cost functions of the S-regular policies, thereby making the problem more amenable to analysis.

In particular, for each $\delta \geq 0$ and policy μ, we consider the mappings $T_{\mu,\delta}$ and T_δ given by

$$(T_{\mu,\delta}J)(x) = H\big(x, \mu(x), J\big) + \delta, \quad x \in X, \qquad T_\delta J = \inf_{\mu \in \mathcal{M}} T_{\mu,\delta}J.$$

We define the corresponding cost functions of policies $\pi = \{\mu_0, \mu_1, \ldots\} \in \Pi$ and $\mu \in \mathcal{M}$, and optimal cost function J_δ^* by

$$J_{\pi,\delta}(x) = \limsup_{k \to \infty} T_{\mu_0,\delta} \cdots T_{\mu_k,\delta}\bar{J}, \qquad J_{\mu,\delta}(x) = \limsup_{k \to \infty} T_{\mu,\delta}^k \bar{J},$$

$$J_\delta^* = \inf_{\pi \in \Pi} J_{\pi,\delta}.$$

We refer to the problem associated with the mappings $T_{\mu,\delta}$ as the *δ-perturbed problem.*

The following proposition shows that if the δ-perturbed problem is "well-behaved" with respect to the S-regular policies, then its cost function J_δ^* can be used to approximate the optimal cost function *over the S-regular policies only.*

Proposition 3.2.2: Given a set $S \subset E(X)$, assume that:

(1) For every $\delta > 0$, there exists an optimal S-regular policy for the δ-perturbed problem.

(2) If μ is an S-regular policy, we have

$$J_{\mu,\delta} \leq J_\mu + w_\mu(\delta), \qquad \forall\, \delta > 0,$$

where w_μ is a function such that $\lim_{\delta\downarrow 0} w_\mu(\delta) = 0$.

Then

$$\lim_{\delta\downarrow 0} J_\delta^* = \inf_{\mu:\, S\text{-regular}} J_\mu,$$

where J_δ^* is the optimal cost function of the δ-perturbed problem.

Proof: For all $\delta > 0$, we have by using condition (2),

$$\inf_{\mu:\, S\text{-regular}} J_\mu \le J_{\mu_\delta^*} \le J_{\mu_\delta^*,\delta} = J_\delta^* \le J_{\mu',\delta} \le J_{\mu'} + w_{\mu'}(\delta), \quad \forall\ \mu' : S\text{-regular},$$

where μ_δ^* is an optimal S-regular policy of the δ-perturbed problem [cf. condition (1)]. By taking the limit as $\delta \downarrow 0$ and then the infimum over all μ' that are S-regular, it follows that

$$\inf_{\mu:\, S\text{-regular}} J_\mu \le \lim_{\delta\downarrow 0} J_\delta^* \le \inf_{\mu:\, S\text{-regular}} J_\mu.$$

Q.E.D.

The preceding proposition does not require that existence of an optimal S-regular policy for the original problem. It applies even if the optimal cost function J^* does not belong to S and we may have $\lim_{\delta\downarrow 0} J_\delta^*(x) > J^*(x)$ for some $x \in X$. This is illustrated by the following example.

Example 3.2.2

Consider the case of a single state where $\bar{J} = 0$, and there are two policies, μ^* and μ, with

$$T_{\mu^*} J = J, \qquad T_\mu J = 1, \qquad \forall\ J \in \Re.$$

Here we have $J_{\mu^*} = 0$ and $J_\mu = 1$. Moreover, it can be verified that for any set $S \subset \Re$ that contains the point 1, the optimal policy μ^* is not S-regular while the suboptimal policy μ is S-regular. For $\delta > 0$, the δ-perturbed problem has optimal cost $J_\delta^* = 1 + \delta$, the unique solution of the Bellman equation

$$J = T_\delta J = \min\{1, J\} + \delta,$$

and its optimal policy is the S-regular policy μ (see Fig. 3.2.1). We also have

$$\lim_{\delta\downarrow 0} J_\delta^* = J_\mu = 1 > 0 = J^*,$$

consistent with Prop. 3.2.2.

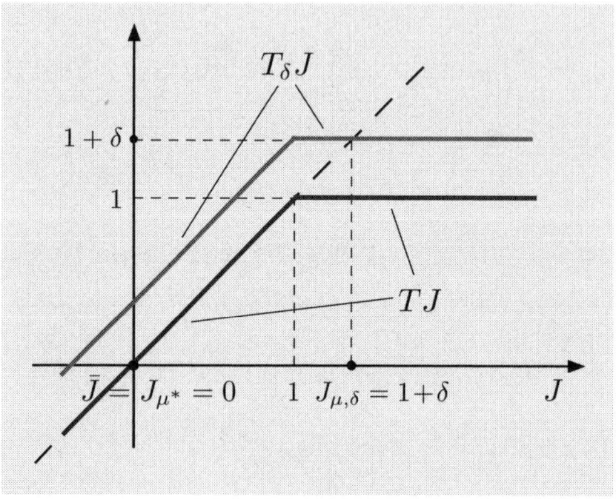

Figure 3.2.1: The mapping T and its perturbed version T_δ in Example 3.2.2.

A simple way to guarantee that $\lim_{\delta \downarrow 0} J_\delta^* = J^*$ is to assume that there exists an optimal S-regular policy for the unperturbed problem. This will also guarantee Bellman's equation $J^* = TJ^*$, under some additional conditions which are collected in the following assumption.

Assumption 3.2.2: We are given a set $S \subset E(X)$ such that the following hold:

(a) There exists an S-regular policy μ^* that is optimal, i.e., $J_{\mu^*} = J^*$, and satisfies

$$J_{\mu^*,\delta} \leq J_{\mu^*} + w(\delta), \qquad \forall\, \delta > 0,$$

where w is a function such that $\lim_{\delta \downarrow 0} w(\delta) = 0$.

(b) The optimal cost function J_δ^* of the δ-perturbed problem belongs to S and satisfies the Bellman equation $J_\delta^* = T_\delta J_\delta^*$ for each $\delta > 0$.

(c) For each sequence $\{J_m\} \subset S$ with $J_m \downarrow J$ for some $J \geq J^*$, we have

$$T_\mu J_m \downarrow T_\mu J, \qquad \forall\, \mu \in \mathcal{M}.$$

Under the preceding assumption we will show that $J^* = TJ^*$. This will allow us to use Prop. 3.1.2 and yield the results of Props. 3.1.1-3.1.3.

Proposition 3.2.3: Let Assumption 3.2.2 hold. Then:

(a) The optimal cost function J^* is the unique fixed point of T within the set $\{J \in S \mid J \geq J^*\}$.

(b) We have $T^k J \to J^*$ for every $J \in S$ with $J \geq J^*$.

(c) An S-regular policy μ that satisfies $T_\mu J^* = TJ^*$ is optimal. Conversely if μ is an S-regular optimal policy, it satisfies $T_\mu J^* = TJ^*$.

Proof: By the monotonicity of T_μ, we clearly have $J^* \leq J_\delta^*$, so using Assumption 3.2.2(a), we obtain for all $\delta > 0$,

$$J^* \leq J_\delta^* \leq J_{\mu^*,\delta} \leq J_{\mu^*} + w(\delta) = J^* + w(\delta),$$

and $\lim_{\delta \downarrow 0} J_\delta^* = J^*$. The Bellman equation $J_\delta^* = T_\delta J_\delta^*$ is written as

$$J_\delta^* = \inf_{\mu \in \mathcal{M}} T_\mu J_\delta^* + \delta\, e. \tag{3.9}$$

From this relation, the fact $\lim_{\delta \downarrow 0} J_\delta^* = J^*$ just shown, and Assumption 3.2.2(c), we have

$$J^* = \lim_{\delta \downarrow 0} \inf_{\mu \in \mathcal{M}} T_\mu J_\delta^* \leq \inf_{\mu \in \mathcal{M}} \lim_{\delta \downarrow 0} T_\mu J_\delta^* = \inf_{\mu \in \mathcal{M}} T_\mu J^* = TJ^*. \tag{3.10}$$

We also have

$$TJ^* \leq TJ_\delta^* = \inf_{\mu \in \mathcal{M}} T_\mu J_\delta^* = J_\delta^* - \delta\, e, \qquad \forall\, \delta > 0,$$

where the last equality follows from Eq. (3.9). By taking the limit as $\delta \downarrow 0$, we obtain $TJ^* \leq J^*$, which combined with Eq. (3.10), shows that $J^* = TJ^*$. Thus the assumptions of Prop. 3.1.2 are satisfied and the conclusions follow from this proposition. **Q.E.D.**

The following example illustrates the preceding line of analysis. For another application, see Section 4.5.3 on exponential cost models.

Example 3.2.3 (Search Problem Continued)

Consider the search problem of Example 3.2.1, assuming that the expected costs for not stopping are nonnegative, $E\big\{g(x,w)\big\} \geq 0$ for all x. Then for all policies μ that don't stop with probability 1 starting from state x we have $J_{\mu,\delta}(x) = \infty$ for all $\delta > 0$, since an expected cost of at least δ is incurred at each transition in the δ-perturbed problem.

If the costs $s(x)$ for stopping are nonpositive for all x, then from known results on SSP problems (cf. Example 1.2.6 and [BeT91]), it follows that there exists an optimal $R(X)$-regular policy, which stops with probability 1 starting from every state. In this case, Assumption 3.2.2 holds, and Prop. 3.2.3 applies. If some stopping costs $s(x)$ are positive, it may happen that each optimal policy is S-irregular, and there is no optimal $R(X)$-regular policy. In this case, however, there is an optimal $R(X)$-regular policy for the δ-perturbed problem, for all $\delta > 0$, and Prop. 3.2.2 applies. Thus $\lim_{\delta \downarrow 0} J_\delta^*$ yields the best that can be achieved when restricted to policies that stop with probability 1.

An Alternative Line of Analysis

A weakness of Assumption 3.2.2(b) is that it requires the verification of Bellman's equation $J_\delta^* = T_\delta J_\delta^*$ for the δ-perturbed problem. An alternative line of analysis makes instead regularity assumptions on the policies of this problem, and is based on the following definition.

Definition 3.2.1: Given a set $S \subset E(X)$ and a scalar $\delta \geq 0$, we say that a stationary policy μ is *δ-S-regular* if $J_{\mu,\delta}$ is the unique fixed point of $T_{\mu,\delta}$ within S, and

$$T_{\mu,\delta}^k J \to J_{\mu,\delta}, \qquad \forall\ J \in S.$$

A policy that is not δ-S-regular is called *δ-S-irregular*.

Thus μ is δ-S-regular if and only if it is 0-S-regular for the δ-perturbed problem. Our earlier notions of S-regular and S-irregular policies are equivalent to 0-S-regular and 0-S-irregular policies, respectively. To illustrate, consider the case where T_μ is a weighted sup-norm contraction (e.g., a proper μ in a finite-state SSP problem). Then assuming also that $T_{\mu,\delta}$ maps $B(X)$ into $B(X)$ [e.g., when $e \in B(X)$], $T_{\mu,\delta}$ is a weighted sup-norm contraction for all $\delta \geq 0$, μ is δ-$B(X)$-regular for all $\delta \geq 0$.

Note that δ-S-regularity for all $\delta > 0$ does not imply 0-S-regularity, nor does it imply that $J_{\mu,\delta} \downarrow J_\mu$ as $\delta \downarrow 0$. This can be illustrated by a single-state example, a variation of Example 3.2.2, where $\bar{J} = 0$, and there is a single policy μ with $T_\mu J = \min\{1, J\}$. Here for $S = \Re$, μ is δ-S-regular for all $\delta > 0$, but it is not 0-S-regular, and in fact it can be verified that $J_\mu = 0$ while $J_{\mu,\delta} = 1 + \delta$ (cf. Fig. 3.2.1).

We introduce the following assumption, whose conditions resemble the ones of Prop. 3.1.3. In particular, parts (a)-(c) of the assumption are patterned after conditions (1) and (2) of Prop. 3.1.3.

Assumption 3.2.3: We are given a set $S \subset R(X)$ that contains the function $\bar{J}$, and is such that the following hold:

(a) There exists an S-regular policy μ^* that is optimal, i.e., $J_{\mu^*} = J^*$.

(b) Each S-regular policy is δ-S-regular for every $\delta > 0$. Moreover, if μ is a δ-S-irregular policy for a given $\delta > 0$, then there is at least one state $x \in X$ such that

$$\limsup_{k \to \infty} (T_{\mu,\delta}^k J_{\mu^*,\delta})(x) = \infty, \tag{3.11}$$

where μ^* is the optimal S-regular policy of (a).

(c) For each $\delta > 0$, there exists a policy μ such that $T_\mu J_{\mu^*,\delta} = TJ_{\mu^*,\delta}$, where μ^* is the optimal S-regular policy of (a).

(d) For each sequence $\{J_{\mu^k,\delta_k}\}$, where for all k, μ^k is S-regular, $\delta_k > 0$, $\delta_k \downarrow 0$, and $J_{\mu^k,\delta_k} \downarrow J$,

$$\lim_{m\to\infty} H(x,u,J_{\mu^k,\delta_k}) = H(x,u,J), \qquad \forall\, x \in X,\ u \in U(x).$$

Note that similar to Assumption 3.2.1, the preceding assumption requires that S is a set of *real-valued* functions; this allows us to take advantage of Eq. (3.11). We first show a preliminary lemma.

Lemma 3.2.5: Let Assumption 3.2.3 hold. Then:

(a) If $0 \le \delta \le \delta'$, then for all policies μ, $k \ge 1$, and functions $J, J' \in E(X)$, with $J \le J'$, we have $T^k_{\mu,\delta} J \le T^k_{\mu,\delta'} J'$.

(b) A policy that is δ-S-irregular for some $\delta > 0$ is δ'-S-irregular for all $\delta' \in (\delta,\infty)$.

(c) A policy that is δ-S-regular for some $\delta > 0$ is δ'-S-regular for all $\delta' \in (0,\delta)$.

(d) For every S-regular policy μ and sequence $\{\delta_k\}$ with $\delta_k > 0$ for all k, $\delta_k \downarrow 0$, we have $J_{\mu,\delta_k} \downarrow J_\mu$.

(e) Let $\overline{\mu}$ be a policy that satisfies $T_{\overline{\mu}} J_{\mu,\delta} = TJ_{\mu,\delta}$, where $\delta > 0$ and μ is a δ-S-regular policy. Then

$$T_{\overline{\mu},\delta} J_{\mu,\delta} = T_{\overline{\mu}} J_{\mu,\delta} + \delta\, e = TJ_{\mu,\delta} + \delta\, e \le T_\mu J_{\mu,\delta} + \delta\, e = J_{\mu,\delta}.$$

Proof: (a) For $k = 1$, we have $T_{\mu,\delta} J \le T_{\mu,\delta'} J \le T_{\mu,\delta'} J'$. The proof is completed by induction.

(b) Assume, to arrive at a contradiction, that μ is δ-S-irregular for some $\delta > 0$, and is δ'-S-regular for some $\delta' > \delta$. Then, if μ^* is the optimal S-regular policy of Assumption 3.2.3(a), by the δ-S-irregularity of μ and Assumption 3.2.3(b), there exists $x \in X$ such that

$$J_{\mu,\delta'}(x) = \lim_{k\to\infty} (T^k_{\mu,\delta'} J_{\mu^*,\delta})(x) \ge \limsup_{k\to\infty} (T^k_{\mu,\delta} J_{\mu^*,\delta})(x) = \infty,$$

where the first equality holds because μ is δ'-S-regular and $J_{\mu^*,\delta} \in S$, and the inequality uses part (a). This contradicts the δ'-S-regularity of μ, which implies that $J_{\mu,\delta'}$ belongs to S and is therefore real-valued.

(c) Follows from part (b).

(d) Since μ is an S-regular policy, it is δ-S-regular for all $\delta > 0$ by Assumption 3.2.3(b). The sequence $\{J_{\mu,\delta_k}\}$ is monotonically nonincreasing, belongs to S, and is bounded below by J_μ, so $J_{\mu,\delta_k} \downarrow J^+$ for some $J^+ \geq J_\mu \geq J^*$. Hence, by Assumption 3.2.3(d), we have $J^+ \in S$ and for all $x \in X$,

$$H\big(x, \mu(x), J^+\big) = \lim_{k\to\infty} H\big(x, \mu(x), J_{\mu,\delta_k}\big) = \lim_{k\to\infty} \big(J_{\mu,\delta_k}(x) - \delta_k\big) = J^+(x),$$

where the second equality follows from the definition of J_{μ,δ_k} as the fixed point of T_{μ,δ_k}. Thus J^+ satisfies $T_\mu J^+ = J^+$ and is therefore equal to J_μ, since μ is S-regular. Hence $J_{\mu,\delta_k} \downarrow J_\mu$.

(e) In the desired relation, repeated below for convenience,

$$T_{\overline{\mu},\delta} J_{\mu,\delta} = T_{\overline{\mu}} J_{\mu,\delta} + \delta\, e = T J_{\mu,\delta} + \delta\, e \leq T_\mu J_{\mu,\delta} + \delta\, e = J_{\mu,\delta},$$

the inequality is evident, the second equality is an assumption, and the other equalities follow from the definitions of $T_{\overline{\mu},\delta}$ and $T_{\mu,\delta}$, and the fixed point property $J_{\mu,\delta} = T_{\mu,\delta} J_{\mu,\delta}$. **Q.E.D.**

We have the following proposition, whose conclusions are identical to the ones of the earlier Prop. 3.2.3.

Proposition 3.2.4: Under Assumption 3.2.3 the conclusions of Prop. 3.2.3 hold.

Proof: We will show that $J^* = TJ^*$. The proof will then follow from Prop. 3.1.2. Let μ^* be the optimal S-regular policy of Assumption 3.2.3(a), and let $\{\delta_k\}$ be a positive sequence such that $\delta_k \downarrow 0$. Using Assumption 3.2.3(c), we may choose a policy μ^k such that

$$T_{\mu^k} J_{\mu^*,\delta_k} = T J_{\mu^*,\delta_k}.$$

Using Lemma 3.2.5(e) with $\mu = \mu^*$, which applies since μ^* is δ-S-regular for all $\delta > 0$ [cf. Assumption 3.2.3(b)], we have for all $m \geq 1$,

$$T^m_{\mu^k,\delta_k} J_{\mu^*,\delta_k} \leq T_{\mu^k,\delta_k} J_{\mu^*,\delta_k} \leq T J_{\mu^*,\delta_k} + \delta_k\, e \leq J_{\mu^*,\delta_k},$$

where the first inequality follows from the monotonicity of T_{μ^k,δ_k}. Taking the limit as $m \to \infty$, and using Assumption 3.2.3(b) [cf. Eq. (3.11)], it follows that μ^k is δ^k-S-regular, and we have

$$J_{\mu^*} \leq J_{\mu^k} \leq J_{\mu^k,\delta_k} \leq T J_{\mu^*,\delta_k} + \delta_k\, e \leq J_{\mu^*,\delta_k}, \tag{3.12}$$

where the second inequality follows from Lemma 3.2.5(a). Since $J_{\mu^*,\delta_k} \downarrow J_{\mu^*}$ [cf. Lemma 3.2.5(d)], by taking the limit as $k \to \infty$ in Eq. (3.12), we obtain

$$J_{\mu^*} = \lim_{k\to\infty} TJ_{\mu^*,\delta_k}. \tag{3.13}$$

We thus obtain

$$\begin{aligned}(T_{\mu^*}J_{\mu^*})(x) &= J_{\mu^*}(x)\\ &= \lim_{k\to\infty}\inf_{u\in U(x)} H(x,u,J_{\mu^*,\delta_k})\\ &\le \inf_{u\in U(x)}\lim_{k\to\infty} H(x,u,J_{\mu^*,\delta_k})\\ &= \inf_{u\in U(x)} H(x,u,J_{\mu^*})\\ &= (TJ_{\mu^*})(x)\\ &\le (T_{\mu^*}J_{\mu^*})(x),\end{aligned}$$

where the first equality is the Bellman equation for the S-regular policy μ^*, the second equality is Eq. (3.13), and the third equality follows from Assumption 3.2.3(d) and the fact $J_{\mu^k,\delta_k} \downarrow J_{\mu^*}$. Thus equality holds throughout above and we obtain $J_{\mu^*} = TJ_{\mu^*}$. Since μ^* is optimal, we obtain $J^* = TJ^*$, and the conclusions follow from Prop. 3.1.2. **Q.E.D.**

To see what may happen if there is no optimal S-regular policy, even though there exists a δ-S-regular policy for all $\delta > 0$, consider the example given following the Definition 3.2.1 of a δ-S-regular policy. Here there is a single state, $\bar{J} = 0$, and there is a single policy μ with

$$T_\mu J = TJ = \min\{1, J\},$$

and $J_\mu = J^* = 0$. Then for $S = \Re$, μ is S-irregular, and Assumptions 3.2.3(a) and 3.2.3(b) are violated. As a result, contrary to the assertion of Prop. 3.2.4, the set of fixed points of T is $\{J \mid -\infty < J \le 1\}$ and contains $J < J^* = 0$, while VI starting from every $J \neq 0$ does not converge to J^*.

The following example addresses a class of SSP problems where the perturbation approach applies and yields interesting results.

Example 3.2.4 (Stochastic Shortest Problems with an Optimal Proper Policy)

Consider the finite-spaces SSP problem of Example 1.2.6, and let $S = R(X)$. We assume that there exists an optimal proper policy, and we will show that Assumption 3.2.3 is satisfied, so that Prop. 3.2.4 applies.

Indeed, according to known results for SSP problems discussed in Example 1.2.6 (e.g., [BeT96], Prop. 2.2, [Ber12a], Prop. 3.3.1), a policy μ is proper (stops with probability 1 starting from any $x \in X$) if and only if T_μ is a contraction with respect to a weighted sup-norm. It follows that for a proper policy μ, $T_{\mu,\delta}$ is a weighted sup-norm contraction for all $\delta \geq 0$, so μ is δ-S-regular and $J_{\mu,\delta} \in R(X)$. Moreover for an improper policy μ we have $J_\mu(x) > -\infty$ for all x (since there exists an optimal policy that is proper and hence its cost function is real-valued). Thus if $\delta > 0$, we obtain

$$\limsup_{k\to\infty} (T_{\mu,\delta}^k J)(x) = \infty, \qquad \forall\ J \in R(X);$$

this is because an additional cost of δ is incurred each time that the policy does not stop. Since for the optimal proper policy μ^*, we have $J_{\mu^*,\delta} \in R(X)$, Assumption 3.2.3(b) holds. In addition the conditions (c) and (d) of Assumption 3.2.3 are clearly satisfied.

Thus if there exists an optimal proper policy, Assumption 3.2.3 holds, and the results of Prop. 3.2.4 apply. In particular, J^* is the unique fixed point of T within the set $\big\{J \in R(X) \mid J \geq J^*\big\}$, and the VI algorithm converges to J^* starting from any function J within this set. These results also apply to the search problem of Example 3.2.1, assuming that there exists an optimal policy that stops with probability 1.

We finally note that similar to the search problem, if we just assume that there exists at least one proper policy, while $J^*(x) > -\infty$ for all $x \in X$, Prop. 3.2.2 applies and shows that $\lim_{\delta\downarrow 0} J_\delta^*$ yields the best that can be achieved when restricted to proper policies only.

The results for the preceding SSP example cannot be improved, in the sense that uniqueness of the fixed point of T within $R(X)$ cannot be shown. This can be verified using case (a) of the shortest path example of Section 3.1.2. Moreover, as shown by the same example, the PI algorithm may oscillate between an optimal and a nonoptimal policy. This motivates modifications of the PI framework, which we will discuss in Section 3.3.3.

3.3 ALGORITHMS

In this section, we will discuss VI and PI algorithms for finding J^* and an optimal policy under the assumptions of the preceding section. We have already shown that the VI algorithm converges to the optimal cost function J^* for any starting function $J \in S$ in the case of Assumption 3.2.1 (cf. Prop. 3.2.1), and also for any starting function $J \in S$ with $J \geq J^*$ in the case of Assumption 3.2.3 (cf. Prop. 3.2.4). We will discuss asynchronous versions of VI under these two assumptions in Section 3.3.1, and will prove satisfactory convergence properties.

In Section 3.3.2, we will show that there is a valid version of the PI algorithm, which starting from an S-regular μ^0, generates a sequence of S-regular policies $\{\mu^k\}$ such that $J_{\mu^k} \to J^*$. We will briefly discuss this algorithm, and then focus on a modified version of PI that is unaffected by the presence of S-irregular policies. This algorithm is similar to the PI algorithm of Section 2.6.3, and can also be implemented in a distributed asynchronous environment. Finally, we will discuss in Section 3.3.3 a version of PI that is based on the perturbation approach of Section 3.2.2.

3.3.1 Asynchronous Value Iteration

Let us consider the model of Section 2.6.1 for asynchronous distributed computation of the fixed point of a mapping T, and the asynchronous distributed VI method described there. The model involves a partition of X into disjoint nonempty subsets $X_1, \ldots, X_m$, and a corresponding partition of J as $J = (J_1, \ldots, J_m)$, where J_ℓ is the restriction of J on the set X_ℓ.

We consider a network of m processors, each updating asynchronously corresponding components of J. In particular, we assume that J_ℓ is updated only by processor ℓ, and only for times t in a selected subset $\mathcal{R}_\ell$ of iterations. Moreover, as in Section 2.6.1, processor ℓ uses components J_j supplied by other processors $j \neq \ell$ with communication "delays" $t - \tau_{\ell j}(t) \geq 0$:

$$J_\ell^{t+1}(x) = \begin{cases} T\left(J_1^{\tau_{\ell 1}(t)}, \ldots, J_m^{\tau_{\ell m}(t)}\right)(x) & \text{if } t \in \mathcal{R}_\ell,\ x \in X_\ell, \\ J_\ell^t(x) & \text{if } t \notin \mathcal{R}_\ell,\ x \in X_\ell. \end{cases} \tag{3.14}$$

Under the assumptions of Section 3.2, we can prove convergence by using the asynchronous convergence theorem (cf. Prop. 2.6.1), and the fact that T is monotone and has J^* as its unique fixed point within the appropriate set. We will consider two types of conditions, corresponding to the Assumptions of Sections 3.2.1 and 3.2.2, respectively. In the first case, we will choose $S = B(X)$, while in the second case we will choose $S = \big\{J \in B(X) \mid J \geq J^*\big\}$. The reason for using $B(X)$ instead of $R(X)$ is that it may make it easier for policies to be S-regular, since we allow an infinite state space (cf. the remarks following Assumption 3.2.1).

Consider first the case where Assumption 3.2.1 holds with $S = B(X)$, and assume that the continuous updating and information renewal Assumption 2.6.1. Assume further that we have two functions $\underline{V}, \overline{V} \in S$ such that

$$\underline{V} \leq T\underline{V} \leq T\overline{V} \leq \overline{V}, \tag{3.15}$$

so that, by Prop. 3.2.1, $T^k\underline{V} \leq J^* \leq T^k\overline{V}$ for all k, and

$$T^k\underline{V} \uparrow J^*, \qquad T^k\overline{V} \downarrow J^*.$$

Then we can show asynchronous convergence of the VI algorithm (3.14), starting from any function J^0 with $\underline{V} \leq J^0 \leq \overline{V}$.

Indeed, let us apply Prop. 2.6.1 with the sets $S(k)$ given by

$$S(k) = \big\{J \in S \mid T^k\underline{V} \leq J \leq T^k\overline{V}\big\}, \qquad k = 0, 1, \ldots.$$

The sets $S(k)$ satisfy $S(k+1) \subset S(k)$ in view of Eq. (3.15) and the monotonicity of T. Using Prop. 3.2.1, we also see that $S(k)$ satisfy the synchronous convergence and box conditions of Prop. 2.6.1. Thus, together with Assumption 2.6.1, all the conditions of Prop. 2.6.1 are satisfied, and the convergence of the algorithm follows starting from any $J^0 \in S(0)$.

Consider next the case where Assumption 3.2.3 holds with $S = \{J \in B(X) \mid J \geq J^*\}$. In this case we use the sets $S(k)$ given by

$$S(k) = \{J \in S \mid J^* \leq J \leq T^k \overline{V}\}, \qquad k = 0, 1, \ldots,$$

where $\overline{V}$ is a function in S with $J^* \leq T\overline{V} \leq \overline{V}$. These sets satisfy the synchronous convergence and box conditions of Prop. 2.6.1, and we can similarly show asynchronous convergence to J^* of the generated sequence $\{J^t\}$ starting from any $J^0 \in S(0)$.

3.3.2 Asynchronous Policy Iteration

In this section, we focus on PI methods, under Assumption 3.2.1 and some additional assumptions to be introduced shortly. We first discuss briefly a natural form of PI algorithm, which generates S-regular policies exclusively. Let μ^0 be an initial S-regular policy [there exists one by Assumption 3.2.1(b)]. At the typical iteration k, we have an S-regular policy μ^k, and we compute a policy μ^{k+1} such that $T_{\mu^{k+1}} J_{\mu^k} = T J_{\mu^k}$ (this is possible by Lemma 3.2.1). Then μ^{k+1} is S-regular, by Lemma 3.2.2, and we have

$$J_{\mu^k} = T_{\mu^k} J_{\mu^k} \geq T J_{\mu^k} = T_{\mu^{k+1}} J_{\mu^k} \geq \lim_{m \to \infty} T^k_{\mu^{k+1}} J_{\mu^k} = J_{\mu^{k+1}}. \qquad (3.16)$$

We can thus construct a sequence of S-regular policies $\{\mu^k\}$ and a corresponding nonincreasing sequence $\{J_{\mu^k}\}$. Under some additional mild conditions it is then possible to show that $J_{\mu^k} \downarrow J^*$ (see Exercise 3.6).

Unfortunately, when there are S-irregular policies, the preceding PI algorithm is somewhat limited, because an initial S-regular policy may not be known, and also because when asynchronous versions of the algorithm are implemented, it is difficult to guarantee that all the generated policies are S-regular. In what follows in this section, we will discuss a PI algorithm that works in the presence of S-irregular policies, and can operate in a distributed asynchronous environment. We will need a few assumptions that are in addition to the ones of Section 3.2.1. For analytical simplicity, we include in these assumptions finiteness of the state and control spaces.

Assumption 3.3.1: The set S is equal to $R(X)$, and Assumption 3.2.1 holds with this choice of S. Furthermore, the following hold:

(a) $H(x, u, J)$ is real-valued for all $J \in S$, $x \in X$, and $u \in U(x)$.

(b) X and U are finite sets.

(c) For all scalars $r > 0$ and functions $J \in S$, we have

$$H(x, u, J + r\, e) \leq H(x, u, J) + r\, e, \qquad \forall\, x \in X,\ u \in U(x), \qquad (3.17)$$

where e is the unit function.

In view of the requirement that $S = R(X)$ with X being a finite set, part (c) of the preceding assumption is a nonexpansiveness condition for $H(x, u, \cdot)$, which also implies continuity of $H(x, u, \cdot)$.

Similar to Section 2.6.3, we introduce a new mapping that is parametrized by μ and can be shown to have a common fixed point for all μ. It operates on a pair (V, Q) where:

- V is a function with a component $V(x)$ for each x.
- Q is a function with a component $Q(x, u)$ for each pair (x, u) with $u \in U(x)$.

The mapping produces a pair

$$\big(MF_\mu(V, Q), F_\mu(V, Q)\big),$$

where

- $F_\mu(V, Q)$ is a function with a component $F_\mu(V, Q)(x, u)$ for each (x, u), defined by
$$F_\mu(V, Q)(x, u) = H\big(x, u, \min\{V, Q_\mu\}\big), \tag{3.18}$$
where for any Q and μ, we denote by Q_μ the function of x defined by
$$Q_\mu(x) = Q\big(x, \mu(x)\big), \qquad x \in X,$$
and for any two functions V_1 and V_2, we denote by $\min\{V_1, V_2\}$ the function of x given by
$$\min\{V_1, V_2\}(x) = \min\big\{V_1(x), V_2(x)\big\}, \qquad x \in X.$$
- $MF_\mu(V, Q)$ is a function with a component $\big(MF_\mu(V, Q)\big)(x)$ for each x, where M is the operator of pointwise minimization over u:
$$(MQ)(x) = \min_{u \in U(x)} Q(x, u),$$
so that
$$\big(MF_\mu(V, Q)\big)(x) = \min_{u \in U(x)} F_\mu(V, Q)(x, u).$$

We consider an algorithm that is similar to the asynchronous PI algorithm given in Section 2.6.3 for contractive models. It applies asynchronously the mapping $MF_\mu(V, Q)$ for local policy improvement and update of V and μ, and the mapping $F_\mu(V, Q)$ for local policy evaluation and update of Q. The algorithm involves a partition of the state space into sets $X_1, \ldots, X_m$, and assignment of each subset X_ℓ to a processor $\ell \in \{1, \ldots, m\}$. For each ℓ, there are two infinite disjoint subsets of times

$\mathcal{R}_\ell, \overline{\mathcal{R}}_\ell \subset \{0,1,\ldots\}$, corresponding to policy improvement and policy evaluation iterations, respectively. At time t, each processor ℓ operates on $V^t(x)$, $Q^t(x,u)$, and $\mu^t(x)$, only for x in its "local" state space X_ℓ. In particular, at each time t, each processor ℓ does one of the following:

(a) *Local policy improvement*: If $t \in \mathcal{R}_\ell$, processor ℓ sets for all $x \in X_\ell$,

$$V^{t+1}(x) = \min_{u \in U(x)} H\big(x,u,\min\{V^t, Q^t_{\mu^t}\}\big) = \big(MF_{\mu^t}(V^t,Q^t)\big)(x), \tag{3.19}$$

sets $\mu^{t+1}(x)$ to a u that attains the minimum, and leaves Q unchanged, i.e., $Q^{t+1}(x,u) = Q^t(x,u)$ for all $x \in X_\ell$ and $u \in U(x)$.

(b) *Local policy evaluation*: If $t \in \overline{\mathcal{R}}_\ell$, processor ℓ sets for all $x \in X_\ell$ and $u \in U(x)$,

$$Q^{t+1}(x,u) = H\big(x,u,\min\{V^t, Q^t_{\mu^t}\}\big) = F_{\mu^t}(V^t,Q^t)(x,u), \tag{3.20}$$

and leaves V and μ unchanged, i.e., $V^{t+1}(x) = V^t(x)$ and $\mu^{t+1}(x) = \mu^t(x)$ for all $x \in X_\ell$.

(c) *No local change*: If $t \notin \mathcal{R}_\ell \cup \overline{\mathcal{R}}_\ell$, processor ℓ leaves Q, V, and μ unchanged, i.e., $Q^{t+1}(x,u) = Q^t(x,u)$ for all $x \in X_\ell$ and $u \in U(x)$, $V^{t+1}(x) = V^t(x)$, and $\mu^{t+1}(x) = \mu^t(x)$ for all $x \in X_\ell$.

Under Assumption 3.3.1, we will show convergence of the algorithm to (J^*, Q^*), where Q^* is defined by

$$Q^*(x,u) = H(x,u,J^*), \qquad x \in X,\ u \in U(x). \tag{3.21}$$

To this end, we first show that Q^* is the unique fixed point of the mapping F defined by s

$$(FQ)(x,u) = H\big(x,u,MQ\big), \qquad x \in X,\ u \in U(x).$$

Indeed, under our assumption, Prop. 3.2.1 applies, so J^* is the unique fixed point of T, and we have $MQ^* = TJ^* = J^*$. Thus, from the definition (3.21), Q^* is a fixed point of F. To show uniqueness of the fixed point of F, note that if $\overline{Q}$ is a fixed point of F, then $\overline{Q}(x,u) = H(x,u,M\overline{Q})$ for all $x \in X$, $u \in U(x)$, and by minimization over $u \in U(x)$, we have $M\overline{Q} = T(M\overline{Q})$. Hence $M\overline{Q}$ is equal to the unique fixed point J^* of T, so that the equation $\overline{Q} = F\overline{Q}$ yields $\overline{Q}(x,u) = H(x,u,M\overline{Q}) = H(x,u,J^*)$, for all (x,u). From the definition (3.21) of Q^*, it then follows that $\overline{Q} = Q^*$.

We introduce the μ-dependent mapping

$$L_\mu(V,Q) = \big(MQ, F_\mu(V,Q)\big), \tag{3.22}$$

where $F_\mu(V,Q)$ is given by Eq. (3.18). Note that the policy evaluation part of the algorithm [cf. Eq. (3.20)] amounts to applying the second component of L_μ, while the policy improvement part of the algorithm [cf. Eq. (3.19)] amounts to applying the second component of L_μ, *and* then applying the first component of L_μ. The following proposition shows that (J^*, Q^*) is the common fixed point of the mappings L_μ, for all μ.

Proposition 3.3.1: Let Assumption 3.3.1 hold. Then for all $\mu \in \mathcal{M}$, the mapping L_μ of Eq. (3.22) is monotone and has (J^*, Q^*) as its unique fixed point.

Proof: Monotonicity of L_μ follows from the monotonicity of the operators M and F_μ. To show that L_μ has (J^*, Q^*) as its unique fixed point, we first note that $J^* = MQ^*$ and $Q^* = FQ^*$, as shown earlier. Then, using also the definition of F_μ, we have

$$J^* = MQ^*, \qquad Q^* = FQ^* = F_\mu(J^*, Q^*),$$

which shows that (J^*, Q^*) is a fixed point of L_μ. To show uniqueness, let $(\overline{V}, \overline{Q})$ be a fixed point of L_μ, i.e., $\overline{V} = M\overline{Q}$ and $\overline{Q} = F_\mu(\overline{V}, \overline{Q})$. Then

$$\overline{Q} = F_\mu(\overline{V}, \overline{Q}) = F\overline{Q},$$

where the last equality follows from $\overline{V} = M\overline{Q}$. Thus $\overline{Q}$ is a fixed point of F, and since Q^* is the unique fixed point of F, as shown earlier, we have $\overline{Q} = Q^*$. It follows that $\overline{V} = MQ^* = J^*$, so (J^*, Q^*) is the unique fixed point of L_μ. **Q.E.D.**

The uniform fixed point property of L_μ just shown is, however, insufficient for the convergence proof of the asynchronous algorithm, in the absence of a contraction property. For this reason, we introduce two mappings $\underline{L}$ and $\overline{L}$ that are associated with the mappings L_μ and satisfy

$$\underline{L}(V, Q) \le L_\mu(V, Q) \le \overline{L}(V, Q), \qquad \forall\, \mu \in \mathcal{M}. \tag{3.23}$$

These are the mappings defined by

$$\underline{L}(V, Q) = \Big(MQ, \min_{\mu \in \mathcal{M}} F_\mu(V, Q)\Big), \quad \overline{L}(V, Q) = \Big(MQ, \max_{\mu \in \mathcal{M}} F_\mu(V, Q)\Big), \tag{3.24}$$

where the min and max over μ are attained in view of the finiteness of $\mathcal{M}$ [cf. Assumption 3.3.1(b)]. We will show that $\underline{L}$ and $\overline{L}$ also have (J^*, Q^*) as their unique fixed point. Note that there exists $\bar{\mu}$ that attains the maximum in Eq. (3.24), uniformly for all V and (x, u), namely a policy $\bar{\mu}$ for which

$$Q\big(x, \bar{\mu}(x)\big) = \max_{u \in U(x)} Q(x, u), \qquad \forall\, x \in X,$$

[cf. Eq. (3.18)]. Similarly, there exists $\underline{\mu}$ that attains the minimum in Eq. (3.24), uniformly for all V and (x,u). Thus for any given (V,Q), we have

$$\underline{L}(V,Q) = L_{\underline{\mu}}(V,Q), \qquad \overline{L}(V,Q) = L_{\bar{\mu}}(V,Q), \tag{3.25}$$

where $\underline{\mu}$ and $\bar{\mu}$ are some policies. The following proposition shows that (J^*,Q^*), the common fixed point of the mappings L_μ, for all μ, is also the unique fixed point of $\underline{L}$ and $\overline{L}$.

> **Proposition 3.3.2:** Let Assumption 3.3.1 hold. Then the mappings $\underline{L}$ and $\overline{L}$ of Eq. (3.24) are monotone, and have (J^*,Q^*) as their unique fixed point.

Proof: Monotonicity is clear from the monotonicity of the operators M and F_μ. Since (J^*,Q^*) is the common fixed point of L_μ for all μ (cf. Prop. 3.3.1), and there exists $\underline{\mu}$ such that $\underline{L}(J^*,Q^*) = L_{\underline{\mu}}(J^*,Q^*)$ [cf. Eq. (3.25)], it follows that (J^*,Q^*) is a fixed point of $\underline{L}$. To show uniqueness, suppose that (V,Q) is a fixed point, so $(V,Q) = \underline{L}(V,Q)$. Then by Eq. (3.25), we have

$$(V,Q) = \underline{L}(V,Q) = L_{\underline{\mu}}(V,Q)$$

for some $\underline{\mu} \in \mathcal{M}$. Since by Prop. 3.3.1, (J^*,Q^*) is the only fixed point of $L_{\underline{\mu}}$, it follows that $(V,Q) = (J^*,Q^*)$, so (J^*,Q^*) is the only fixed point of $\underline{L}$. Similarly, we show that (J^*,Q^*) is the unique fixed point of $\overline{L}$. **Q.E.D.**

We are now ready to construct a sequence of sets needed to apply Prop. 2.6.1 and prove convergence. For a scalar $c \geq 0$, we denote

$$J_c^- = J^* - c\,e, \qquad Q_c^- = Q^* - c\,e_Q,$$

$$J_c^+ = J^* + c\,e, \qquad Q_c^+ = Q^* + c\,e_Q,$$

with e and e_Q are the unit functions in the spaces of J and Q, respectively.

> **Proposition 3.3.3:** Let Assumption 3.3.1 hold. Then for all $c > 0$,
>
> $$\underline{L}^k(J_c^-,Q_c^-) \uparrow (J^*,Q^*), \qquad \overline{L}^k(J_c^+,Q_c^+) \downarrow (J^*,Q^*), \tag{3.26}$$
>
> where $\underline{L}^k$ (or $\overline{L}^k$) denotes the k-fold composition of $\underline{L}$ (or $\overline{L}$, respectively).

Proof: For any μ, using the assumption (3.17), we have for all (x,u),

$$\begin{aligned} F_\mu(J_c^+,Q_c^+)(x,u) &= H\big(x,u,\min\{J_c^+,Q_c^+\}\big) \\ &= H\big(x,u,\min\{J^*,Q^*\}+c\,e\big) \\ &\le H\big(x,u,\min\{J^*,Q^*\}\big)+c \\ &= Q^*(x,u)+c \\ &= Q_c^+(x,u), \end{aligned}$$

and similarly

$$Q_c^-(x,u) \le F_\mu(J_c^-,Q_c^-)(x,u).$$

We also have $MQ_c^+ = J_c^+$ and $MQ_c^- = J_c^-$. From these relations, the definition of L_μ, and the fact $L_\mu(J^*,Q^*) = (J^*,Q^*)$ (cf. Prop. 3.3.1),

$$(J_c^-,Q_c^-) \le L_\mu(J_c^-,Q_c^-) \le (J^*,Q^*) \le L_\mu(J_c^+,Q_c^+) \le (J_c^+,Q_c^+).$$

Using this relation and Eqs. (3.23) and (3.25), we obtain

$$(J_c^-,Q_c^-) \le \underline{L}(J_c^-,Q_c^-) \le (J^*,Q^*) \le \overline{L}(J_c^+,Q_c^+) \le (J_c^+,Q_c^+). \tag{3.27}$$

Denote for $k=0,1,\ldots,$

$$(\overline{V}_k,\overline{Q}_k) = \overline{L}^k(J_c^+,Q_c^+), \qquad (\underline{V}_k,\underline{Q}_k) = \underline{L}^k(J_c^-,Q_c^-).$$

From the monotonicity of $\overline{L}$ and $\underline{L}$ and Eq. (3.27), we have that $(\overline{V}_k,\overline{Q}_k)$ converges monotonically from above to some $(\overline{V},\overline{Q}) \ge (J^*,Q^*)$, while $(\underline{V}_k,\underline{Q}_k)$ converges monotonically from below to some $(\underline{V},\underline{Q}) \le (J^*,Q^*)$. By taking the limit in the equation

$$(\overline{V}_{k+1},\overline{Q}_{k+1}) = \overline{L}(\overline{V}_k,\overline{Q}_k),$$

and using the continuity property of $\overline{L}$, implied by Eq. (3.17) and the finiteness of the control constraint set, it follows that $(\overline{V},\overline{Q}) = \overline{L}(\overline{V},\overline{Q})$, so $(\overline{V},\overline{Q})$ must be equal to (J^*,Q^*), the unique fixed point of $\overline{L}$. Thus, $\overline{L}^k(J_c^+,Q_c^+) \downarrow (J^*,Q^*)$. Similarly, $\underline{L}^k(J_c^-,Q_c^-) \uparrow (J^*,Q^*)$. **Q.E.D.**

To show asynchronous convergence of the algorithm (3.19)-(3.20), consider the sets

$$S(k) = \big\{(V,Q) \mid \underline{L}^k(J_c^-,Q_c^-) \le (V,Q) \le \overline{L}^k(J_c^+,Q_c^+)\big\}, \qquad k=0,1,\ldots,$$

whose intersection is (J^*,Q^*) [cf. Eq. (3.26)]. By Prop. 3.3.3 and Eq. (3.23), this set sequence together with the mappings L_μ satisfy the synchronous convergence and box conditions of the asynchronous convergence theorem of Prop. 2.6.1 (more precisely, its time-varying version of Exercise 2.2). This proves the convergence of the algorithm (3.19)-(3.20) for starting points $(V,Q) \in S(0)$. Since c can be chosen arbitrarily large, it follows that the algorithm is convergent from an arbitrary starting point.

Finally, let us note some variations of the asynchronous PI algorithm. One such variation is to allow "communication delays" $t-\tau_{\ell j}(t)$. Another variation, for the case where we want to calculate just J^*, is to use a reduced space implementation similar to the one discussed in Section 2.6.3. There is also a variant with interpolation, cf. Section 2.6.3.

3.3.3 Policy Iteration With Perturbations

Let us now consider PI for problems where there exists an optimal S-regular policy, but S-irregular policies may have real-valued cost functions, and the perturbation approach of Section 3.2.2 applies. We will develop an algorithm that generates a sequence of policies $\{\mu^k\}$ such that $J_{\mu^k} \to J^*$, under the following assumption, which among others, is satisfied in the SSP problem of Example 3.2.4.

Assumption 3.3.2: Assumption 3.2.3 holds, and in addition:

(a) For every $\delta > 0$ and δ-S-regular policy μ, there exists a policy $\overline{\mu}$ such that $T_{\overline{\mu}} J_{\mu,\delta} = T J_{\mu,\delta}$.

(b) For every $\delta > 0$ and δ-S-irregular policy μ, and for every $J \in S$, there exists at least one state $x \in X$ such that

$$\limsup_{k \to \infty} (T^k_{\mu,\delta} J)(x) = \infty.$$

We generate a sequence $\{\mu^k\}$ with a perturbed version of PI as follows. Let $\{\delta_k\}$ be a positive sequence with $\delta_k \downarrow 0$, and let μ^0 be any δ_0-S-regular policy. At the typical iteration k, we have a δ_k-S-regular policy μ^k, and we generate μ^{k+1} according to

$$T_{\mu^{k+1}} J_{\mu^k,\delta_k} = T J_{\mu^k,\delta_k}. \tag{3.28}$$

Such μ^{k+1} exists by Assumption 3.3.2(a), and we claim that μ^{k+1} is δ_{k+1}-S-regular. To see this, note that from Lemma 3.2.5(e), we have

$$T_{\mu^{k+1},\delta_k} J_{\mu^k,\delta_k} = T J_{\mu^k,\delta_k} + \delta_k\, e \le T_{\mu^k} J_{\mu^k,\delta_k} + \delta_k\, e = J_{\mu^k,\delta_k},$$

so that

$$T^m_{\mu^{k+1},\delta_k} J_{\mu^k,\delta_k} \le T_{\mu^{k+1},\delta_k} J_{\mu^k,\delta_k} = T J_{\mu^k,\delta_k} + \delta_k\, e \le J_{\mu^k,\delta_k}, \qquad \forall\ m \ge 1. \tag{3.29}$$

Since $J_{\mu^k,\delta_k} \in R(X)$, from Assumption 3.3.2(b) it follows that μ^{k+1} is δ_k-S-regular, and hence also δ_{k+1}-S-regular, by Lemma 3.2.5(c). Thus the sequence $\{\mu^k\}$ generated by the perturbed PI algorithm (3.28) is well-defined and consists of δ_k-S-regular policies. We have the following proposition.

Proposition 3.3.4: Let Assumption 3.3.2 hold. Then the sequence $\{J_{\mu^k}\}$ generated by the algorithm (3.28) satisfies $J_{\mu^k} \to J^*$.

Proof: Using Eq. (3.29), we have

$$J_{\mu^{k+1},\delta_{k+1}} \leq J_{\mu^{k+1},\delta_k} = \lim_{m\to\infty} T^m_{\mu^{k+1},\delta_k} J_{\mu^k,\delta_k} \leq TJ_{\mu^k,\delta_k} + \delta_k\, e \leq J_{\mu^k,\delta_k},$$

where the equality holds because μ^{k+1} is δ_k-S-regular, as shown earlier. Taking the limit as $k \to \infty$, and noting that $J_{\mu^{k+1},\delta_{k+1}} \geq J^*$, we see that $J_{\mu^k,\delta_k} \downarrow J^+$ for some $J^+ \geq J^*$, and we obtain

$$J^* \leq J^+ = \lim_{k\to\infty} TJ_{\mu^k,\delta_k}. \tag{3.30}$$

We also have

$$\begin{aligned} \inf_{u\in U(x)} H(x,u,J^+) &\leq \lim_{k\to\infty} \inf_{u\in U(x)} H(x,u,J_{\mu^k,\delta_k}) \\ &\leq \inf_{u\in U(x)} \lim_{k\to\infty} H(x,u,J_{\mu^k,\delta_k}) \\ &= \inf_{u\in U(x)} H(x,u,J^+), \end{aligned}$$

where the equality follows from Assumption 3.2.3(d). It follows that equality holds throughout above, so that

$$\lim_{k\to\infty} TJ_{\mu^k,\delta_k} = TJ^+. \tag{3.31}$$

Combining Eqs. (3.30) and (3.31), we obtain $J^* \leq J^+ = TJ^+$. Since by Prop. 3.2.4, J^* is the unique fixed point of T within $\{J \in S \mid J \geq J^*\}$, it follows that $J^+ = J^*$. Thus $J_{\mu^k,\delta_k} \downarrow J^*$, and since $J_{\mu^k,\delta_k} \geq J_{\mu^k} \geq J^*$, we have $J_{\mu^k} \to J^*$. **Q.E.D.**

Note that when X and U are finite sets, as in the SSP problem of Example 3.2.4, Prop. 3.3.4 implies that the generated policies μ^k will be optimal for all k sufficiently large. The reason is that in this case, the set of policies is finite and there exists a sufficiently small $\epsilon > 0$, such that for all nonoptimal μ there is some state x such that $J_\mu(x) \geq J^*(x) + \epsilon$.

In the absence of finiteness of X and U, Prop. 3.3.4 guarantees the monotonic pointwise convergence of $\{J_{\mu^k,\delta_k}\}$ to J^* (see the preceding proof) and the (possibly nonmonotonic) pointwise convergence of $\{J_{\mu^k}\}$ to J^*. This convergence behavior should be contrasted with the behavior of PI without perturbations, which may lead to oscillation between two nonoptimal policies, as noted earlier.

3.4 NOTES, SOURCES, AND EXERCISES

The semicontractive model framework of this chapter and the material of Section 3.1 are new. The framework is inspired from the analysis of the SSP problem of Example 1.2.6, which involves finite state and control spaces, as well as a termination state. In the absence of a termination state, a key idea has been to generalize the notion of a proper policy from one that leads to termination with probability 1, to one that is S-regular for an appropriate set of functions S.

The line of proof of Prop. 3.1.1 dates back to an analysis of SSP problems with finite state and control spaces, given in the author's [Ber87], Section 6.4, which assumes existence of an optimal proper policy and non-negativity of the one-stage cost. Proposition 3.2.1 is patterned after a similar result in Bertsekas and Tsitsiklis [BeT91] for SSP problems with finite state space and compact control constraint sets. The proof given there contains an intricate part (Lemma 3 of [BeT91]) to show a lower bound on the cost functions of proper policies, which is assumed here in part (b) of the semicontraction Assumption 3.2.1.

The perturbation analysis of Section 3.2.2, including the PI algorithm of Section 3.3.3, are new and are based on unpublished collaboration of the author with H. Yu. The results for SSP problems using this analysis (cf. Prop. 3.2.4) strengthen the results of [Ber87] (Section 6.4) and [BeT91] (Prop. 3), in that the one-stage cost need not be assumed nonnegative. We have given two different perturbation approaches in Section 3.2.2. The first approach places assumptions on the optimal cost function J_δ^* of the δ-perturbed problem (cf. Prop. 3.2.2 and Assumption 3.2.2), while the second places assumptions on policies (cf. Assumption 3.2.3) and separates them into δ-S-regular and δ-S-irregular. The first approach is simpler analytically, and at least in part, does not require existence of an S-regular policy (cf. Prop. 3.2.2). The second approach allows the development of a perturbed PI algorithm and the corresponding analysis of Section 3.3.3 (under the extra conditions of Assumption 3.3.2).

The asynchronous PI algorithm of Section 3.3.2 is essentially the same as one of the optimistic PI algorithms of Yu and Bertsekas [YuB11a] for the SSP problem of Example 1.2.6. This paper also analyzed asynchronous stochastic iterative versions of the algorithms, and proved convergence results that parallel those for classical Q-learning for SSP, given in Tsitsiklis [Tsi94] and Yu and Bertsekas [YuB11b]. We follow the line of analysis of that paper. A related paper, which deals with a slightly different asynchronous PI algorithm in an abstract setting and without a contraction structure, is Bertsekas and Yu [BeY10b].

By allowing an infinite state space, the analysis of the present chapter applies among others to SSP problems with a countable state space. Such problems often arise in queueing control problems where the termination state corresponds to an empty queue. The problem then is to empty the system with minimum expected cost. Generalized forms of SSP problems, which involve an infinite (uncountable) number of states, in addition to the termination state, are analyzed by Pliska [Pli78], Hernandez-Lerma et al. [HCP99], and James and Collins [JaC06]. The latter paper allows improper policies, assumes that J^* is bounded below, and generalizes the results of [BeT91] to infinite (Borel) state spaces, using a similar line of proof.

An important case of an SSP problem where the state space is infinite arises under imperfect state information. There the problem is converted to a perfect state information problem whose states are the belief states, i.e., the posterior probability distributions of the original state given the observations thus far. Patek [Pat07] proves results that are similar to the ones for SSP problems with perfect state information. These results can also be derived from the analysis of this chapter. In particular, the critical condition that the cost functions of proper policies are bounded below by some real-valued function [cf. Assumption 3.2.1(b)] is proved as Lemma 5 in [Pat07], using the fact that the cost functions of the proper policies are bounded below by the optimal cost function of a corresponding perfect state information problem.

EXERCISES

3.1 (Blackmailer's Dilemma)

Consider an SSP problem where there is only one state $x = 1$, in addition to the termination state 0. At state 1, we can choose a control u with $0 < u \leq 1$, while incurring a cost $-u$; we then move to state 0 with probability u^2, and stay in state 1 with probability $1 - u^2$. We may regard u as a demand made by a blackmailer, and state 1 as the situation where the victim complies. State 0 is the situation where the victim (permanently) refuses to yield to the blackmailer's demand. The problem then can be seen as one whereby the blackmailer tries to maximize his total gain by balancing his desire for increased demands with keeping his victim compliant. In terms of abstract DP we have

$$X = \{1\}, \qquad U(1) = (0, 1], \qquad \bar{J}(1) = 0, \qquad H(1, u, J) = -u + (1 - u^2)J(1).$$

(a) Verify that T_μ is a sup-norm contraction for each μ. In addition, show that $J_\mu(1) = -\frac{1}{\mu(1)}$, so that $J^*(1) = -\infty$, that there is no optimal policy, and that T has no fixed points within $\Re$. Which parts of Assumption 3.2.1 with $S = \Re$ are violated?

(b) Consider a variant of the problem where at state 1, we terminate at no cost with probability u, and stay in state 1 at a cost $-u$ with probability $1 - u$. Here we have

$$H(1, u, J) = (1 - u)(-u) + (1 - u)J(1).$$

Verify that $J^*(1) = -1$, that there is no optimal policy, and that T has multiple fixed points within $\Re$. Which parts of Assumption 3.2.1 with $S = \Re$ are violated?

(c) Repeat part (b) for the case where at state 1, we may also choose $u = 0$ at a cost c. Show that the policy $\overline{\mu}$ that chooses $\overline{\mu}(1) = 0$ is $\Re$-irregular. What are the optimal policies and the fixed points of T in the three cases where $c > 0$, $c = 0$, and $c < 0$. Which parts of Assumption 3.2.1 with $S = \Re$ are violated in each of these three cases?

3.2 (Equivalent Semicontractive Conditions)

Let S be a given subset of $E(X)$. Show that the assumptions of Prop. 3.1.1 hold if and only if $J^* \in S$, $TJ^* \leq J^*$, and there exists an S-regular policy μ such that $T_\mu J^* = TJ^*$.

3.3

Consider the three-node shortest path example of Section 3.1.2. Try to apply Prop. 3.1.1 with $S = [-\infty, \infty) \times [-\infty, \infty)$. What conclusions can you obtain for various values of a and b, and how do they compare with those for $S = \Re^2$?

3.4 (Changing $\bar{J}$)

Let the assumptions of Prop. 3.1.1 hold, and let J^* be the optimal cost function. Suppose that $\bar{J}$ is changed to some function $J \in S$.

(a) Show that following the change, J^* continues to be the optimal cost function over just the S-regular policies.

(b) Consider the three-node shortest path problem of Section 3.1.2 for the case where $a = 0$, $b < 0$. Change $\bar{J}$ from $\bar{J} = 0$ to $\bar{J} = r\,e$ where $r \in \Re$. Verify the result of part (a) for this example. For which values of r is the $\Re^2$-irregular policy optimal?

3.5 (Alternative Semicontractive Conditions)

The purpose of this exercise and the next one is to provide conditions that imply the results of Prop. 3.1.1. Let S be a given subset of $E(X)$. Assume that:

(1) There exists an optimal S-regular policy.

(2) For every S-irregular policy $\overline{\mu}$, we have $T_{\overline{\mu}} J^* \geq J^*$.

Then the assumptions and the conclusions of Prop. 3.1.1 hold.

3.6 (Convergence of PI)

Let Assumption 3.2.1 hold, and let $\{\mu^k\}$ be the sequence generated by the PI algorithm described at the start of Section 3.3.2 [cf. Eq. (3.16)]. Let also $J_\infty = \lim_{k\to\infty} J_{\mu^k}$, and assume that $H(x, u, J_{\mu^k}) \to H(x, u, J_\infty)$ for all $x \in X$ and $u \in U(x)$. Show that $J_\infty = J^*$.

4

Noncontractive Models

Contents

In this chapter, we consider abstract DP models similar to the ones of the earlier chapters, but without assuming any contraction-like property. We will discuss both finite and infinite horizon models, and introduce just enough assumptions (including monotonicity) to obtain some minimal results, which we will strengthen as we go along.

In Section 4.2, we discuss a general type of finite horizon problem. We show under some reasonable assumptions the standard results that one may expect in an abstract setting.

In Section 4.3, we consider an infinite horizon problem that is motivated by the well-known *positive* and *negative* DP models (see [Ber12a], Chapter 4). These are the special cases of the infinite horizon stochastic optimal control problem of Example 1.2.1, where the cost per stage g is uniformly nonpositive or uniformly nonnegative. For these models there is interesting theory (the validity of Bellman's equation and the availability of optimality conditions in a DP context), which we discuss in Section 4.3.1. There are also interesting computational methods, patterned after the value and policy iteration methods, which we discuss in Sections 4.3.2 and 4.3.3. However, the performance guarantees for these methods are not as powerful as in the contractive case, and their validity hinges upon certain additional assumptions.

In Section 4.4, we discuss a semicontractive model, which combines elements of the monotonic noncontractive models of Section 4.3 and the semicontractive models of Chapter 3.

Finally, in Section 4.5 we apply the semicontractive analysis of Chapter 3 and Section 4.4 to the class of monotonic affine models, which includes the multiplicative and exponential cost/risk-sensitive models of Example 1.2.8.

4.1 NONCONTRACTIVE MODELS

Throughout this chapter we will continue to use the model of Chapter 3, which involves the set of extended real numbers

$$\Re^* = \Re \cup \{\infty, -\infty\}$$

and the set $E(X)$ the set of all extended real-valued functions $J : X \mapsto \Re^*$. We denote by $R(X)$ the set of real-valued functions $J : X \mapsto \Re$, and by $B(X)$ the set of real-valued functions $J : X \mapsto \Re$ that are bounded with respect to a given weighted sup-norm. The operations with ∞ and $-\infty$ are summarized in Appendix A. In particular, we adopt standard conventions regarding ordering, addition, and multiplication in $\Re^*$, except that we take $\infty - \infty = -\infty + \infty = \infty$, and we take the product of 0 and ∞ or $-\infty$ to be 0, so that the sum and product of two extended real numbers are well-defined (see Appendix A for details).

To repeat some of the basic definitions, we have a set X of states and a set U of controls, and for each $x \in X$, the nonempty control constraint set $U(x) \subset U$. We denote by $\mathcal{M}$ the set of all functions $\mu : X \mapsto U$ with $\mu(x) \in U(x)$, for all $x \in X$, and by Π the set of "nonstationary policies" $\pi = \{\mu_0, \mu_1, \ldots\}$, with $\mu_k \in \mathcal{M}$ for all k. We refer to a stationary policy $\{\mu, \mu, \ldots\}$ simply as μ.

We introduce a mapping $H : X \times U \times E(X) \mapsto \Re^*$, and we define the mapping $T : E(X) \mapsto E(X)$ by

$$(TJ)(x) = \inf_{u \in U(x)} H(x, u, J), \qquad \forall\, x \in X,\ J \in E(X),$$

and for each $\mu \in \mathcal{M}$ the mapping $T_\mu : E(X) \mapsto E(X)$ by

$$(T_\mu J)(x) = H\big(x, \mu(x), J\big), \qquad \forall\, x \in X,\ J \in E(X).$$

We continue to use the following assumption throughout this chapter, without mentioning it explicitly in various propositions.

Assumption 4.1.1: (Monotonicity) If $J, J' \in E(X)$ and $J \leq J'$, then

$$H(x, u, J) \leq H(x, u, J'), \qquad \forall\, x \in X,\ u \in U(x).$$

A fact that we will be using frequently is that for each $J \in E(X)$ and scalar $\epsilon > 0$, there exists a $\mu_\epsilon \in \mathcal{M}$ such that for all $x \in X$,

$$(T_{\mu_\epsilon} J)(x) \leq \begin{cases} (TJ)(x) + \epsilon & \text{if } (TJ)(x) > -\infty, \\ -(1/\epsilon) & \text{if } (TJ)(x) = -\infty. \end{cases}$$

In particular, if J is such that $(TJ)(x) > -\infty$ for all $x \in X$, then for each $\epsilon > 0$, there exists a $\mu_\epsilon \in \mathcal{M}$ such that

$$(T_{\mu_\epsilon} J)(x) \leq (TJ)(x) + \epsilon, \qquad \forall\, x \in X.$$

We will often use in our analysis the unit function e, defined by $e(x) \equiv 1$, so for example, we will write the above relation in shorthand as

$$T_{\mu_\epsilon} J \leq TJ + \epsilon\, e.$$

We define cost functions for policies consistently with Chapters 2 and 3. In particular, we are given a function $\bar{J} \in E(X)$, and we consider for every policy $\pi = \{\mu_0, \mu_1, \ldots\} \in \Pi$ and positive integer N the function $J_{N,\pi} \in E(X)$ defined by

$$J_{N,\pi}(x) = (T_{\mu_0} \cdots T_{\mu_{N-1}} \bar{J})(x), \qquad \forall\, x \in X,$$

and the function $J_\pi \in E(X)$ defined by

$$J_\pi(x) = \limsup_{k\to\infty} (T_{\mu_0}\cdots T_{\mu_k}\bar J)(x), \qquad \forall\, x \in X.$$

We refer to $J_{N,\pi}$ as the N-stage cost function of π and to J_π as the infinite horizon cost function of π (or just "cost function" if the length of the horizon is clearly implied by the context). For a stationary policy $\pi = \{\mu, \mu, \ldots\}$ we also write J_π as J_μ.

In Section 4.2, we consider the N-stage optimization problem

$$\begin{aligned} &\text{minimize} \quad J_{N,\pi}(x) \\ &\text{subject to} \quad \pi \in \Pi, \end{aligned} \tag{4.1}$$

while in Section 4.3 we discuss its infinite horizon version

$$\begin{aligned} &\text{minimize} \quad J_{\pi}(x) \\ &\text{subject to} \quad \pi \in \Pi. \end{aligned} \tag{4.2}$$

For a fixed $x \in X$, we denote by $J_N^*(x)$ and $J^*(x)$ the optimal costs for these problems, i.e.,

$$J_N^*(x) = \inf_{\pi\in\Pi} J_{N,\pi}(x), \qquad J^*(x) = \inf_{\pi\in\Pi} J_\pi(x), \qquad \forall\, x \in X.$$

We say that a policy $\pi^* \in \Pi$ is *N-stage optimal* if

$$J_{N,\pi^*}(x) = J_N^*(x), \qquad \forall\, x \in X,$$

and (infinite horizon) *optimal* if

$$J_{\pi^*}(x) = J^*(x), \qquad \forall\, x \in X.$$

For a given $\epsilon > 0$, we say that π_ϵ is *N-stage ϵ-optimal* if

$$(J_{\pi_\epsilon} J)(x) \le \begin{cases} J_N^*(x) + \epsilon & \text{if } J_N^*(x) > -\infty, \\ -(1/\epsilon) & \text{if } J_N^*(x) = -\infty, \end{cases}$$

and we say that π_ϵ is *ϵ-optimal* if

$$(J_{\pi_\epsilon} J)(x) \le \begin{cases} J^*(x) + \epsilon & \text{if } J^*(x) > -\infty, \\ -(1/\epsilon) & \text{if } J^*(x) = -\infty. \end{cases}$$

4.2 FINITE HORIZON PROBLEMS

Consider the N-stage problem (4.1), where the cost function $J_{N,\pi}$ is defined by

$$J_{N,\pi}(x) = (T_{\mu_0} \cdots T_{\mu_{N-1}} \bar{J})(x), \qquad \forall\, x \in X.$$

Based on the theory of finite horizon DP, we expect that (at least under some conditions) the optimal cost function J_N^* is obtained by N successive applications of the DP mapping T on the initial function $\bar{J}$, i.e.,

$$J_N^* = \inf_{\pi \in \Pi} J_{N,\pi} = T^N \bar{J}.$$

This is the analog of Bellman's equation for the finite horizon problem in a DP context.

The Case Where Uniformly N-Stage Optimal Policies Exist

A favorable case where the analysis is simplified and we can easily show that $J_N^* = T^N \bar{J}$ is when the finite horizon DP algorithm yields an optimal policy during its execution. By this we mean that the algorithm that starts with $\bar{J}$, and sequentially computes $T\bar{J}, T^2\bar{J}, \ldots, T^N\bar{J}$, also yields corresponding $\mu_{N-1}^*, \mu_{N-2}^*, \ldots, \mu_0^* \in \mathcal{M}$ such that

$$T_{\mu_k^*} T^{N-k-1} \bar{J} = T^{N-k} \bar{J}, \qquad k = 0, \ldots, N-1. \tag{4.3}$$

While $\mu_{N-1}^*, \ldots, \mu_0^* \in \mathcal{M}$ satisfying this relation need not exist (because the corresponding infimum in the definition of T is not attained), if they do exist, they both form an optimal policy and also guarantee that

$$J_N^* = T^N \bar{J}.$$

The proof is simple: we have for every $\pi = \{\mu_0, \mu_1, \ldots\} \in \Pi$

$$J_{N,\pi} = T_{\mu_0} \cdots T_{\mu_{N-1}} \bar{J} \geq T^N \bar{J} = T_{\mu_0^*} \cdots T_{\mu_{N-1}^*} \bar{J},$$

where the inequality follows from the monotonicity assumption and the definition of T, and the last equality follows from Eq. (4.3). Thus $\{\mu_0^*, \mu_1^*, \ldots\}$ has no worse N-stage cost function than every other policy, so it is N-stage optimal and $J_N^* = T_{\mu_0^*} \cdots T_{\mu_{N-1}^*} \bar{J}$. By taking the infimum of the left-hand side over $\pi \in \Pi$, we obtain $J_N^* = T^N \bar{J}$.

The preceding argument can also be used to show that $\{\mu_k^*, \mu_{k+1}^*, \ldots\}$ is $(N-k)$-stage optimal for all $k = 0, \ldots, N-1$. Such a policy is called *uniformly N-stage optimal*. The fact that the finite horizon DP algorithm provides an optimal solution of *all* the k-stage problems for $k = 1, \ldots, N$, rather than just the last one, is a manifestation of the classical principle of optimality, expounded by Bellman in the early days of DP (the tail portion of an optimal policy obtained by DP minimizes the corresponding tail portion of the finite horizon cost). Note, however, that there may exist an N-stage optimal policy that is not k-stage optimal for some $k < N$.

We state the result just derived as a proposition.

Proposition 4.2.1: Suppose that a policy $\{\mu_0^*, \mu_1^*, \ldots\}$ satisfies the condition (4.3). Then this policy is uniformly N-stage optimal, and we have $J_N^* = T^N \bar{J}$.

While the preceding result is theoretically limited, it is very useful in practice, because the existence of a policy satisfying the condition (4.3) can often be simply established. For example, this condition is trivially satisfied if the control space is finite. The following proposition provides a generalization.

Proposition 4.2.2: Let the control space U be a metric space, and assume that for each $x \in X$, $\lambda \in \Re$, and $k = 0, 1, \ldots, N-1$, the set

$$U_k(x, \lambda) = \big\{u \in U(x) \mid H(x, u, T^k \bar{J}) \leq \lambda\big\}$$

is compact. Then there exists a uniformly N-stage optimal policy.

Proof: We will show that the infimum in the relation

$$(T^{k+1}\bar{J})(x) = \inf_{u \in U(x)} H\big(x, u, T^k \bar{J}\big)$$

is attained for all $x \in X$ and k. Indeed if $H\big(x, u, T^k \bar{J}\big) = \infty$ for all $u \in U(x)$, then every $u \in U(x)$ attains the infimum. If for a given $x \in X$,

$$\inf_{u \in U(x)} H\big(x, u, T^k \bar{J}\big) < \infty,$$

the corresponding part of the proof of Prop. 3.2.1 (cf. Lemma 3.2.1) applies and shows that the above infimum is attained. **Q.E.D.**

The General Case

We now consider the case where there is no uniformly N-stage optimal policy. By using the definitions of J_N^* and $T^N \bar{J}$, the equation $J_N^* = T^N \bar{J}$ can be equivalently written as

$$\inf_{\mu_0, \ldots, \mu_{N-1} \in \mathcal{M}} T_{\mu_0} \cdots T_{\mu_{N-1}} \bar{J} = \inf_{\mu_0 \in \mathcal{M}} T_{\mu_0} \left(\inf_{\mu_1 \in \mathcal{M}} T_{\mu_1} \left(\cdots \inf_{\mu_{N-1} \in \mathcal{M}} T_{\mu_{N-1}} \bar{J} \right)\right).$$

Thus we have $J_N^* = T^N \bar{J}$ if the operations inf and T_μ can be interchanged in the preceding equation. We will introduce two alternative assumptions, which guarantee that this interchange is valid. Our first assumption is a form of continuity from above of H with respect to J.

Assumption 4.2.1: For each sequence $\{J_m\} \subset E(X)$ with $J_m \downarrow J$ and $H(x, u, J_0) < \infty$ for all $x \in X$ and $u \in U(x)$, we have

$$\lim_{m\to\infty} H(x, u, J_m) = H(x, u, J), \qquad \forall\, x \in X,\ u \in U(x). \tag{4.4}$$

Note that if $\{J_m\}$ and $\{T_\mu J_m\}$ are monotonically nonincreasing, then

$$\inf_m J_m = \lim_{m\to\infty} J_m, \qquad \inf_m (T_\mu J_m) = \lim_{m\to\infty} (T_\mu J_m),$$

so for all $\mu \in \mathcal{M}$, Eq. (4.4) implies that

$$\inf_m (T_\mu J_m) = \lim_{m\to\infty} (T_\mu J_m) = T_\mu \left(\lim_{m\to\infty} J_m \right) = T_\mu \left(\inf_m J_m \right).$$

This equality can be extended for any $\mu_1, \ldots, \mu_k \in \mathcal{M}$ as follows:

$$\begin{aligned} \inf_m (T_{\mu_1} \cdots T_{\mu_k} J_m) &= T_{\mu_1} \left(\inf_m (T_{\mu_1} \cdots T_{\mu_k} J_m) \right) \\ &= \cdots \\ &= T_{\mu_1} T_{\mu_1} \cdots T_{\mu_{k-1}} \left(\inf_m (T_{\mu_k} J_m) \right) \\ &= T_{\mu_1} \cdots T_{\mu_k} \left(\inf_m J_m \right). \end{aligned} \tag{4.5}$$

We use this relation to prove the following proposition.

Proposition 4.2.3: Let Assumption 4.2.1 hold, and assume further that $J_{k,\pi}(x) < \infty$, for all $x \in X$, $\pi \in \Pi$, and $k \geq 1$. Then $J_N^* = T^N \bar{J}$.

Proof: We select for each $k = 0, \ldots, N-1$, a sequence $\{\mu_k^m\} \subset \mathcal{M}$ such that

$$\lim_{m\to\infty} T_{\mu_k^m}(T^{N-k-1} \bar{J}) \downarrow T^{N-k} \bar{J}.$$

Since $J_N^* \leq T_{\mu_0} \cdots T_{\mu_{N-1}} \bar{J}$ for all $\mu_0, \ldots, \mu_{N-1} \in \mathcal{M}$, we have using also Eq. (4.5) and the assumption $J_{k,\pi}(x) < \infty$, for all k, π, and x,

$$
\begin{aligned}
J_N^* &\leq \inf_{m_0} \cdots \inf_{m_{N-1}} T_{\mu_0^{m_0}} \cdots T_{\mu_{N-1}^{m_{N-1}}} \bar{J} \\
&= \inf_{m_0} \cdots \inf_{m_{N-2}} T_{\mu_0^{m_0}} \cdots T_{\mu_{N-2}^{m_{N-2}}} \left(\inf_{m_{N-1}} T_{\mu_{N-1}^{m_{N-1}}} \bar{J} \right) \\
&= \inf_{m_0} \cdots \inf_{m_{N-2}} T_{\mu_0^{m_0}} \cdots T_{\mu_{N-2}^{m_{N-2}}} T \bar{J} \\
&\ \ \vdots \\
&= \inf_{m_0} T_{\mu_0^{m_0}} (T^{N-1} \bar{J}) \\
&= T^N \bar{J}.
\end{aligned}
$$

On the other hand, it is clear from the definitions that $T^N \bar{J} \leq J_{N,\pi}$ for all N and $\pi \in \Pi$, so that $T^N \bar{J} \leq J_N^*$. Thus, $J_N^* = T^N \bar{J}$. **Q.E.D.**

We now introduce an alternative assumption, which in addition to $J_N^* = T^N \bar{J}$, guarantees the existence of an ϵ-optimal policy.

Assumption 4.2.2: We have

$$J_k^*(x) > -\infty, \qquad \forall\, x \in X,\ k = 1, \ldots, N.$$

Moreover, there exists a scalar $\alpha \in (0, \infty)$ such that for all scalars $r \in (0, \infty)$ and functions $J \in E(X)$, we have

$$H(x, u, J + r\, e) \leq H(x, u, J) + \alpha\, r, \qquad \forall\, x \in X,\ u \in U(x). \tag{4.6}$$

Proposition 4.2.4: Let Assumption 4.2.2 hold. Then $J_N^* = T^N \bar{J}$, and for every $\epsilon > 0$, there exists an ϵ-optimal policy.

Proof: Note that since by assumption, $J_N^*(x) > -\infty$ for all $x \in X$, an N-stage ϵ-optimal policy $\pi_\epsilon \in \Pi$ is one for which

$$J_N^* \leq J_{N,\pi_\epsilon} \leq J_N^* + \epsilon\, e.$$

We use induction. The result clearly holds for $N = 1$. Assume that it holds for $N = k$, i.e., $J_k^* = T^k \bar{J}$ and for a given $\epsilon > 0$, there is a $\pi_\epsilon \in \Pi$

with $J_{k,\pi_\epsilon} \leq J_k^* + \epsilon\, e$. Using Eq. (4.6), we have for all $\mu \in \mathcal{M}$,

$$J_{k+1}^* \leq T_\mu J_{k,\pi_\epsilon} \leq T_\mu J_k^* + \alpha\epsilon\, e.$$

Taking the infimum over μ and then the limit as $\epsilon \to 0$, we obtain $J_{k+1}^* \leq TJ_k^*$. By using the induction hypothesis $J_k^* = T^k\bar{J}$, it follows that $J_{k+1}^* \leq T^{k+1}\bar{J}$. On the other hand, we have clearly $T^{k+1}\bar{J} \leq J_{k+1,\pi}$ for all $\pi \in \Pi$, so that $T^{k+1}\bar{J} \leq J_{k+1}^*$, and hence $T^{k+1}\bar{J} = J_{k+1}^*$.

We now turn to the existence of an ϵ-optimal policy part of the induction argument. Using the assumption $J_k^*(x) > -\infty$ for all $x \in x \in X$, for any $\bar{\epsilon} > 0$, we can choose $\bar{\pi} = \{\bar{\mu}_0, \bar{\mu}_1, \ldots\}$ such that

$$J_{k,\bar{\pi}} \leq J_k^* + \frac{\bar{\epsilon}}{2\alpha}\, e, \tag{4.7}$$

and $\bar{\mu} \in \mathcal{M}$ such that

$$T_{\bar{\mu}} J_k^* \leq TJ_k^* + \frac{\bar{\epsilon}}{2}\, e.$$

Let $\bar{\pi}_{\bar{\epsilon}} = \{\bar{\mu}, \bar{\mu}_0, \bar{\mu}_1, \ldots\}$. Then

$$J_{k+1,\bar{\pi}_{\bar{\epsilon}}} = T_{\bar{\mu}} J_{k,\bar{\pi}} \leq T_{\bar{\mu}} J_k^* + \frac{\bar{\epsilon}}{2}\, e \leq TJ_k^* + \bar{\epsilon}\, e = J_{k+1}^* + \bar{\epsilon}\, e,$$

where the first inequality is obtained by applying $T_{\bar{\mu}}$ to Eq. (4.7) and using Eq. (4.6). The induction is complete. **Q.E.D.**

We now provide some counterexamples showing that the conditions of the preceding propositions are necessary, and that for exceptional (but otherwise very simple) problems, the Bellman equation $J_N^* = T^N\bar{J}$ may not hold and/or there may not exist an ϵ-optimal policy.

Example 4.2.1 (Counterexample to Bellman's Equation I)

Let

$$X = \{0\}, \qquad U(0) = (-1, 0], \qquad \bar{J}(0) = 0,$$

$$H(0, u, J) = \begin{cases} u & \text{if } -1 < J(0), \\ J(0) + u & \text{if } J(0) \leq -1. \end{cases}$$

Then

$$(T_{\mu_0} \cdots T_{\mu_{N-1}} \bar{J})(0) = \mu_0(0),$$

and $J_N^*(0) = -1$, while $(T^N\bar{J})(0) = -N$ for every N. Here Assumption 4.2.1, and the condition (4.6) (cf. Assumption 4.2.2) are violated, even though the condition $J_k^*(x) > -\infty$ for all $x \in X$ (cf. Assumption 4.2.2) is satisfied.

Example 4.2.2 (Counterexample to Bellman's Equation II)

Let

$$X = \{0,1\}, \qquad U(0) = U(1) = (-\infty, 0], \qquad \bar{J}(0) = \bar{J}(1) = 0,$$

$$H(0,u,J) = \begin{cases} u & \text{if } J(1) = -\infty, \\ 0 & \text{if } J(1) > -\infty, \end{cases} \qquad H(1,u,J) = u.$$

Then

$$(T_{\mu_0} \cdots T_{\mu_{N-1}} \bar{J})(0) = 0, \quad (T_{\mu_0} \cdots T_{\mu_{N-1}} \bar{J})(1) = \mu_0(1), \qquad \forall\, N \geq 1.$$

It can be seen that for $N \geq 2$, we have $J_N^*(0) = 0$ and $J_N^*(1) = -\infty$, but $(T^N \bar{J})(0) = (T^N \bar{J})(1) = -\infty$. Here Assumption 4.2.1, and the condition $J_k^*(x) > -\infty$ for all $x \in X$ (cf. Assumption 4.2.2) are violated, even though the condition (4.6) of Assumption 4.2.2 is satisfied.

In the preceding two examples, the anomalies are due to discontinuity of the mapping H with respect to J. In classical finite horizon DP, the mapping H is generally continuous when it takes finite values, but counterexamples arise in unusual problems where infinite values occur. The next example is a simple stochastic optimal control problem, which involves some infinite expected values of random variables and we have $J_2^* \neq T^2 \bar{J}$.

Example 4.2.3 (Counterexample to Bellman's Equation III)

Let

$$X = \{0,1\}, \qquad U(0) = U(1) = \Re, \qquad \bar{J}(0) = \bar{J}(1) = 0,$$

let w be a real-valued random variable with $E\{w\} = \infty$, and let

$$H(x,u,J) = \begin{cases} E\big\{w + J(1)\big\} & \text{if } x = 0, \\ u + J(1) & \text{if } x = 1, \end{cases} \qquad \forall\, x \in X,\ u \in U(x).$$

Then if J_m is real-valued for all m, and $J_m(1) \downarrow J(1) = -\infty$, we have

$$\lim_{m\to\infty} H(0,u,J_m) = \lim_{m\to\infty} E\big\{w + J_m(1)\big\} = \infty,$$

while

$$H\Big(0,u, \lim_{m\to\infty} J_m\Big) = E\big\{w + J(1)\big\} = -\infty,$$

so Assumption 4.2.1 is violated. Indeed, the reader may verify with a straightforward calculation that $J_2^*(0) = \infty$, $J_2^*(1) = -\infty$, while $(T^2\bar{J})(0) = -\infty$, $(T^2\bar{J})(1) = -\infty$, so $J_2^* \neq T^2\bar{J}$. Note that Assumption 4.2.2 is also violated because $J_2^*(1) = -\infty$.

In the next counterexample, Bellman's equation holds, but there is no ϵ-optimal policy. This is an undiscounted deterministic optimal control problem of the type discussed in Section 1.1, where $J_k^*(x) = -\infty$ for some x and k, so Assumption 4.2.2 is violated. We use the notation introduced there.

Example 4.2.4 (Counterexample to Existence of an ϵ-Optimal Policy)

Let $\alpha = 1$ and

$$N = 2, \qquad X = \{0, 1, \ldots\}, \qquad U(x) = (0, \infty), \qquad \bar{J}(x) = 0, \quad \forall\, x \in X,$$

$$f(x, u) = 0, \qquad \forall\, x \in X,\ u \in U(x),$$

$$g(x, u) = \begin{cases} -u & \text{if } x = 0, \\ x & \text{if } x \neq 0, \end{cases} \qquad \forall\, u \in U(x),$$

so that

$$H(x, u, J) = g(x, u) + J(0).$$

Then for $\pi \in \Pi$ and $x \neq 0$, we have $J_{2,\pi}(x) = x - \mu_1(0)$, so that $J_2^*(x) = -\infty$ for all $x \in X$. Here Assumption 4.2.1, as well as Eq. (4.6) (cf. Assumption 4.2.2) are satisfied, and indeed we have $J_2^*(x) = (T^2\bar{J})(x) = -\infty$ for all $x \in X$. However, the condition $J_k^*(x) > -\infty$ for all x and k (cf. Assumption 4.2.2) is violated, and it is seen that there does not exist a two-stage ϵ-optimal policy for any $\epsilon > 0$, since an ϵ-optimal policy $\pi = \{\mu_0, \mu_1\}$ must satisfy

$$J_{2,\pi}(x) = x - \mu_1(0) \leq -\frac{1}{\epsilon}, \qquad \forall\, x \in X,$$

[in view of $J_2^*(x) = -\infty$ for all $x \in X$], which is impossible.

4.3 INFINITE HORIZON PROBLEMS

Consider the infinite horizon problem (4.2), where the cost function of a policy $\pi = \{\mu_0, \mu_1, \ldots\}$ is

$$J_\pi(x) = \limsup_{k \to \infty} (T_{\mu_0} \cdots T_{\mu_k} \bar{J})(x), \qquad \forall\, x \in X.$$

In this section one of the following two assumptions will be in effect.

Assumption I: (Monotone Increase)

(a) We have

$$-\infty < \bar{J}(x) \leq H(x, u, \bar{J}), \qquad \forall\, x \in X,\ u \in U(x).$$

(b) For each sequence $\{J_m\} \subset E(X)$ with $J_m \uparrow J$ and $\bar{J} \leq J_m$ for all $m \geq 0$, we have

$$\lim_{m \to \infty} H(x, u, J_m) = H(x, u, J), \qquad \forall\, x \in X,\ u \in U(x).$$

(c) There exists a scalar $\alpha \in (0, \infty)$ such that for all scalars $r \in (0, \infty)$ and functions $J \in E(X)$ with $\bar{J} \leq J$, we have

$$H(x, u, J + r\,e) \leq H(x, u, J) + \alpha\, r, \qquad \forall\, x \in X,\ u \in U(x).$$

Assumption D: (Monotone Decrease)

(a) We have

$$\bar{J}(x) \geq H(x, u, \bar{J}), \qquad \forall\, x \in X,\ u \in U(x).$$

(b) For each sequence $\{J_m\} \subset E(X)$ with $J_m \downarrow J$ and $J_m \leq \bar{J}$ for all $m \geq 0$, we have

$$\lim_{m \to \infty} H(x, u, J_m) = H\left(x, u, J\right), \qquad \forall\, x \in X,\ u \in U(x).$$

Assumptions I and D apply to the classes of the negative and positive DP models, respectively (see [Ber12a], Chapter 4). These are the special cases of the infinite horizon stochastic optimal control problem of Example 1.2.1, where $\bar{J}(x) \equiv 0$ and the cost per stage g is uniformly nonnegative or uniformly nonpositive, respectively. The latter occurs often when we want to maximize positive rewards.

It is important to note that Assumptions I and D allow J_π to be defined as a limit rather than as a lim sup. In particular, part (a) of the assumptions and the monotonicity of H imply that

$$\bar{J} \leq T_{\mu_0}\bar{J} \leq T_{\mu_0}T_{\mu_1}\bar{J} \leq \cdots \leq T_{\mu_0}\cdots T_{\mu_k}\bar{J} \leq \cdots$$

under Assumption I, and

$$\bar{J} \geq T_{\mu_0}\bar{J} \geq T_{\mu_0}T_{\mu_1}\bar{J} \geq \cdots \geq T_{\mu_0}\cdots T_{\mu_k}\bar{J} \geq \cdots$$

under Assumption D. Thus we have

$$J_\pi(x) = \lim_{k \to \infty} (T_{\mu_0}\cdots T_{\mu_k}\bar{J})(x), \qquad \forall\, x \in X,$$

with the limit being a real number or ∞ or $-\infty$.

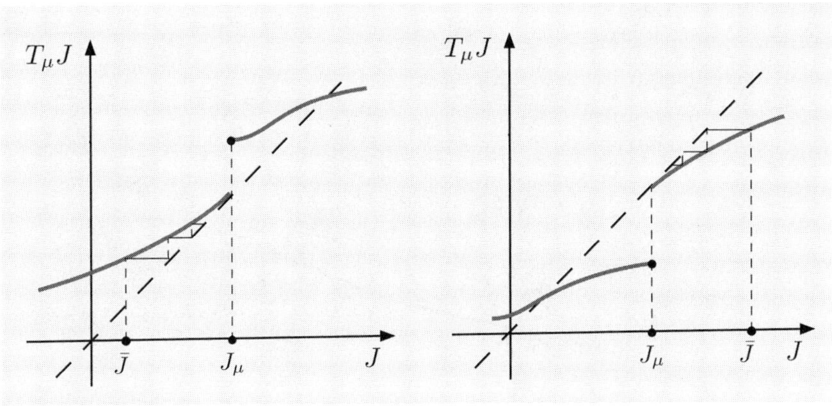

Figure 4.3.1. Illustration of the consequences of lack of continuity of T_μ from below or from above [cf. part (b) of Assumption I or D, respectively]. In the figure on the left, we have $\bar J \le T_\mu \bar J$ but T_μ is discontinuous from below at J_μ, so Assumption I does not hold, and J_μ is not a fixed point of T_μ. In the figure on the right, we have $\bar J \ge T_\mu \bar J$ but T_μ is discontinuous from above at J_μ, so Assumption D does not hold, and J_μ is not a fixed point of T_μ.

The conditions of part (b) of Assumptions I and D are continuity assumptions designed to preclude some of the anomalies of the type encountered also in Chapter 3, and addressed with the use of S-regular policies. In particular, these conditions are essential for making a connection with fixed point theory: they ensure that J_μ is a fixed point of T_μ, as shown in the following proposition.

Proposition 4.3.1: Let Assumption I or Assumption D hold. Then for every policy $\mu \in \mathcal{M}$, we have

$$J_\mu = T_\mu J_\mu.$$

Proof: Let Assumption I hold. Then for all $k \ge 0$,

$$(T_\mu^{k+1} \bar J)(x) = H\big(x, \mu(x), T_\mu^k \bar J\big), \qquad x \in X,$$

and by taking the limit as $k \to \infty$, and using part (b) of Assumption I, and the fact $T_\mu^k \bar J \uparrow J_\mu$, we have for all $x \in X$,

$$J_\mu(x) = \lim_{k\to\infty} H\big(x, \mu(x), T_\mu^k \bar J\big) = H\big(x, \mu(x), \lim_{k\to\infty} T_\mu^k \bar J\big) = H\big(x, \mu(x), J_\mu\big),$$

or equivalently $J_\mu = T_\mu J_\mu$. The proof for the case of Assumption D is similar. **Q.E.D.**

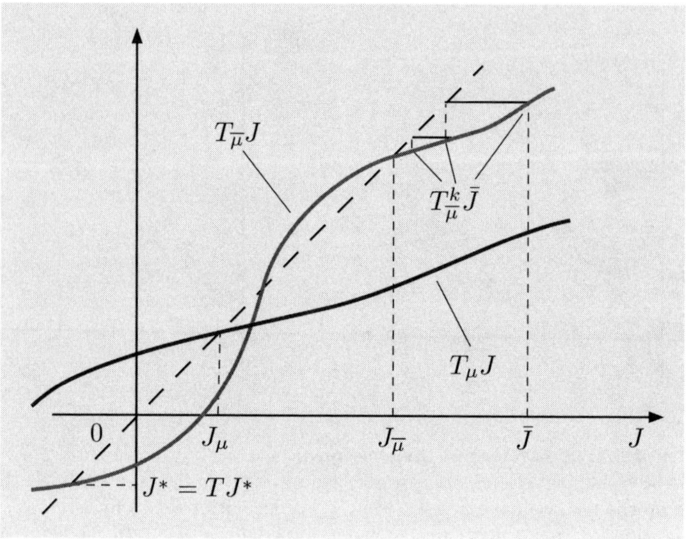

Figure 4.3.2. An example where nonstationary policies are dominant under Assumption D. Here there is only one state and $S = \Re$. There are two stationary policies μ and $\overline{\mu}$ with cost functions J_μ and $J_{\overline{\mu}}$ as shown. However, by considering a nonstationary policy of the form $\pi_k = \{\overline{\mu}, \ldots, \overline{\mu}, \mu, \mu, \ldots\}$, with a number k of policies $\overline{\mu}$, we can obtain a sequence $\{J_{\pi_k}\}$ that converges to the value J^* shown. Note that here there is no optimal policy, stationary or not.

Figure 4.3.1 illustrates how J_μ may fail to be a fixed point of T_μ if part (b) of Assumption I or D is violated. Note also that continuity of T_μ does not imply continuity of T, and for example, under Assumption I, T may be discontinuous from below. We will see later that as a result, the value iteration sequence $\{T^k \bar{J}\}$ may fail to converge to J^* in the absence of additional conditions (see Section 4.3.2). Part (c) of Assumption I is a technical condition that facilitates the analysis, and assures the existence of ϵ-optimal policies.

Despite the similarities between Assumptions I and D, the corresponding results that one may obtain involve some substantial differences. In particular, Fig. 4.3.2 shows that nonstationary policies may become important, and may dominate all stationary policies under Assumption D. It turns out that this cannot happen under Assumption I. An important fact, which breaks the symmetry between the two cases, is that J^* is approached by J_μ from above, but it is approached by $T^k \bar{J}$ from below in the case of Assumption I and from above in the case of Assumption D. Another important fact about Assumption I is that since we assume

$$\bar{J}(x) > -\infty, \qquad \forall\, x \in X,$$

all the functions J encountered in the analysis under this assumption (such as $T^k\bar{J}$, J_π, and J^*) also satisfy

$$J(x) > -\infty, \qquad \forall\, x \in X.$$

In particular, if $J \geq \bar{J}$, we have $(TJ)(x) \geq (T\bar{J})(x) > -\infty$ for all $x \in X$, and for every $\epsilon > 0$ there exists $\mu_\epsilon \in \mathcal{M}$ such that

$$T_{\mu_\epsilon} J \leq TJ + \epsilon\, e.$$

This property is not available under Assumption D and accounts in part for the different character of the results that can be obtained under the two assumptions.

4.3.1 Fixed Point Properties and Optimality Conditions

We first consider the question whether the optimal cost function J^* is a fixed point of T. This is indeed true, but the lines of proof are different under the Assumptions I and D. We begin with the proof under Assumption I, and as a preliminary step we show the following result, which is of independent interest.

> **Proposition 4.3.2:** Let Assumption I hold. Then given any $\epsilon > 0$, there exists a policy $\pi_\epsilon \in \Pi$ such that
>
> $$J^* \leq J_{\pi_\epsilon} \leq J^* + \epsilon\, e.$$
>
> Furthermore, if the scalar α in part (c) of Assumption I satisfies $\alpha < 1$, the policy π_ϵ can be taken to be stationary.

Proof: Let $\{\epsilon_k\}$ be a sequence such that $\epsilon_k > 0$ for all k and

$$\sum_{k=0}^{\infty} \alpha^k \epsilon_k = \epsilon. \tag{4.8}$$

For each $x \in X$, consider a sequence of policies $\big\{\pi_k[x]\big\} \subset \Pi$ of the form

$$\pi_k[x] = \big\{\mu_0^k[x], \mu_1^k[x], \ldots\big\}, \tag{4.9}$$

such that for $k = 0, 1, \ldots,$

$$J_{\pi_k[x]} \leq J^* + \epsilon_k\, e. \tag{4.10}$$

Such a sequence exists, since we have assumed that $\bar{J}(x) > -\infty$, and therefore $J^*(x) > -\infty$, for all $x \in X$.

The preceding notation should be interpreted as follows. The policy $\pi_k[x]$ of Eq. (4.9) is associated with x. Thus $\mu_i^k[x]$ denotes for each x and k, a function in $\mathcal{M}$, while $\mu_i^k[x](z)$ denotes the value of $\mu_i^k[x]$ at an element $z \in X$. In particular, $\mu_i^k[x](x)$ denotes the value of $\mu_i^k[x]$ at $x \in X$.

Consider the functions $\overline{\mu}_k$ defined by

$$\overline{\mu}_k(x) = \mu_0^k[x](x), \qquad \forall\, x \in X, \tag{4.11}$$

and the functions $\bar{J}_k$ defined by

$$\bar{J}_k(x) = H\left(x, \overline{\mu}_k(x), \lim_{m\to\infty} T_{\mu_1^k[x]} \cdots T_{\mu_m^k[x]} \bar{J}\right), \qquad \forall\, x \in X,\ k = 0, 1, \ldots. \tag{4.12}$$

By using Eqs. (4.10), (4.11), and part (b) of Assumption I, we obtain for all $x \in X$ and $k = 0, 1, \ldots$

$$\begin{aligned} \bar{J}_k(x) &= \lim_{m\to\infty} \big(T_{\mu_0^k[x]} \cdots T_{\mu_m^k[x]} \bar{J}\big)(x) \\ &= J_{\pi_k[x]}(x) \\ &\le J^*(x) + \epsilon_k. \end{aligned} \tag{4.13}$$

From Eqs. (4.12), (4.13), and part (c) of Assumption I, we have for all $x \in X$ and $k = 1, 2, \ldots,$

$$\begin{aligned} (T_{\overline{\mu}_{k-1}} \bar{J}_k)(x) &= H\big(x, \overline{\mu}_{k-1}(x), \bar{J}_k\big) \\ &\le H\big(x, \overline{\mu}_{k-1}(x), J^* + \epsilon_k\, e\big) \\ &\le H\big(x, \overline{\mu}_{k-1}(x), J^*\big) + \alpha\epsilon_k \\ &\le H\left(x, \overline{\mu}_{k-1}(x), \lim_{m\to\infty} T_{\mu_1^{k-1}[x]} \cdots T_{\mu_m^{k-1}[x]} \bar{J}\right) + \alpha\epsilon_k \\ &= \bar{J}_{k-1}(x) + \alpha\epsilon_k, \end{aligned}$$

and finally

$$T_{\overline{\mu}_{k-1}} \bar{J}_k \le \bar{J}_{k-1} + \alpha\epsilon_k\, e, \qquad k = 1, 2, \ldots.$$

Using this inequality and part (c) of Assumption I, we obtain

$$\begin{aligned} T_{\overline{\mu}_{k-2}} T_{\overline{\mu}_{k-1}} \bar{J}_k &\le T_{\overline{\mu}_{k-2}} (\bar{J}_{k-1} + \alpha\epsilon_k\, e) \\ &\le T_{\overline{\mu}_{k-2}} \bar{J}_{k-1} + \alpha^2\epsilon_k\, e \\ &\le \bar{J}_{k-2} + (\alpha\epsilon_{k-1} + \alpha^2\epsilon_k)\, e. \end{aligned}$$

Continuing in the same manner, we have for $k = 1, 2, \ldots,$

$$T_{\overline{\mu}_0} \cdots T_{\overline{\mu}_{k-1}} \bar{J}_k \le \bar{J}_0 + (\alpha\epsilon_1 + \cdots + \alpha^k\epsilon_k)\, e \le J^* + \left(\sum_{i=0}^{k} \alpha^i \epsilon_i\right) e.$$

Since $\bar{J} \le \bar{J}_k$, it follows that

$$T_{\overline{\mu}_0} \cdots T_{\overline{\mu}_{k-1}} \bar{J} \le J^* + \left(\sum_{i=0}^{k} \alpha^i \epsilon_i \right) e.$$

Denote $\pi_\epsilon = \{\overline{\mu}_0, \overline{\mu}_1, \ldots\}$. Then by taking the limit in the preceding inequality and using Eq. (4.8), we obtain

$$J_{\pi_\epsilon} \le J^* + \epsilon\, e.$$

If $\alpha < 1$, we take $\epsilon_k = \epsilon(1-\alpha)$ for all k, and $\pi_k[x] = \{\mu_0[x], \mu_1[x], \ldots\}$ in Eq. (4.10). The stationary policy $\pi_\epsilon = \{\overline{\mu}, \overline{\mu}, \ldots\}$, where $\overline{\mu}(x) = \mu_0[x](x)$ for all $x \in X$, satisfies $J_{\pi_\epsilon} \le J^* + \epsilon\, e$. **Q.E.D.**

Note that the assumption $\alpha < 1$ is essential in order to be able to take π_ϵ stationary in the preceding proposition. As an example, let $X = \{0\}$, $U(0) = (0, \infty)$, $\bar{J}(0) = 0$, $H(0, u, J) = u + J(0)$. Then $J^*(0) = 0$, but for any $\mu \in \mathcal{M}$, we have $J_\mu(0) = \infty$.

By using Prop. 4.3.2 we can prove the following.

Proposition 4.3.3: Let Assumption I hold. Then

$$J^* = TJ^*.$$

Furthermore, if $J' \in E(X)$ is such that $J' \ge \bar{J}$ and $J' \ge TJ'$, then $J' \ge J^*$.

Proof: For every $\pi = \{\mu_0, \mu_1, \ldots\} \in \Pi$ and $x \in X$, we have using part (b) of Assumption I,

$$\begin{aligned} J_\pi(x) &= \lim_{k\to\infty} (T_{\mu_0} T_{\mu_1} \cdots T_{\mu_k} \bar{J})(x) \\ &= T_{\mu_0} \left(\lim_{k\to\infty} T_{\mu_1} \cdots T_{\mu_k} \bar{J} \right)(x) \\ &\ge (T_{\mu_0} J^*)(x) \\ &\ge (TJ^*)(x). \end{aligned}$$

By taking the infimum of the left-hand side over $\pi \in \Pi$, we obtain

$$J^* \ge TJ^*.$$

To prove the reverse inequality, let ϵ_1 and ϵ_2 be any positive scalars, and let $\overline{\pi} = \{\overline{\mu}_0, \overline{\mu}_1, \ldots\}$ be such that

$$T_{\overline{\mu}_0} J^* \le TJ^* + \epsilon_1\, e, \qquad J_{\pi_1} \le J^* + \epsilon_2\, e,$$

where $\pi_1 = \{\overline{\mu}_1, \overline{\mu}_2, \ldots\}$ (such a policy exists by Prop. 4.3.2). The sequence $\{T_{\overline{\mu}_1} \cdots T_{\overline{\mu}_k} \bar{J}\}$ is monotonically nondecreasing, so by using the preceding relations and part (c) of Assumption I, we have

$$\begin{aligned} T_{\overline{\mu}_0} T_{\overline{\mu}_1} \cdots T_{\overline{\mu}_k} \bar{J} &\leq T_{\overline{\mu}_0} \left(\lim_{k \to \infty} T_{\overline{\mu}_1} \cdots T_{\overline{\mu}_k} \bar{J} \right) \\ &= T_{\overline{\mu}_0} J_{\pi_1} \\ &\leq T_{\overline{\mu}_0} J^* + \alpha \epsilon_2 \, e \\ &\leq TJ^* + (\epsilon_1 + \alpha \epsilon_2) \, e. \end{aligned}$$

Taking the limit as $k \to \infty$, we obtain

$$J^* \leq J_{\overline{\pi}} = \lim_{k \to \infty} T_{\overline{\mu}_0} T_{\overline{\mu}_1} \cdots T_{\overline{\mu}_k} \bar{J} \leq TJ^* + (\epsilon_1 + \alpha \epsilon_2) \, e.$$

Since ϵ_1 and ϵ_2 can be taken arbitrarily small, it follows that

$$J^* \leq TJ^*.$$

Hence $J^* = TJ^*$.

Assume that $J' \in E(X)$ satisfies $J' \geq \bar{J}$ and $J' \geq TJ'$. Let $\{\epsilon_k\}$ be any sequence with $\epsilon_k > 0$ for all k, and consider a policy $\overline{\pi} = \{\overline{\mu}_0, \overline{\mu}_1, \ldots\} \in \Pi$ such that

$$T_{\overline{\mu}_k} J' \leq TJ' + \epsilon_k \, e, \qquad k = 0, 1, \ldots.$$

We have from part (c) of Assumption I

$$\begin{aligned} J^* &= \inf_{\pi \in \Pi} \lim_{k \to \infty} T_{\mu_0} \cdots T_{\mu_k} \bar{J} \\ &\leq \inf_{\pi \in \Pi} \liminf_{k \to \infty} T_{\mu_0} \cdots T_{\mu_k} J' \\ &\leq \liminf_{k \to \infty} T_{\overline{\mu}_0} \cdots T_{\overline{\mu}_k} J' \\ &\leq \liminf_{k \to \infty} T_{\overline{\mu}_0} \cdots T_{\overline{\mu}_{k-1}} (TJ' + \epsilon_k \, e) \\ &\leq \liminf_{k \to \infty} T_{\overline{\mu}_0} \cdots T_{\overline{\mu}_{k-1}} (J' + \epsilon_k \, e) \\ &\leq \liminf_{k \to \infty} (T_{\overline{\mu}_0} \cdots T_{\overline{\mu}_{k-1}} J' + \alpha^k \epsilon_k \, e) \\ &\;\vdots \\ &\leq \lim_{k \to \infty} \left(TJ' + \left(\sum_{i=0}^{k} \alpha^i \epsilon_i \right) e \right) \\ &\leq J' + \left(\sum_{i=0}^{k} \alpha^i \epsilon_i \right) e. \end{aligned}$$

Since we may choose $\sum_{i=0}^{k} \alpha^i \epsilon_i$ as small as desired, it follows that $J^* \leq J'$. **Q.E.D.**

The following counterexamples show that parts (b) and (c) of Assumption I are essential for the preceding proposition to hold.

Example 4.3.1 (Counterexample to Bellman's Equation I)

Let

$$X = \{0, 1\}, \qquad U(0) = U(1) = (-1, 0], \qquad \bar{J}(0) = \bar{J}(1) = -1,$$

$$H(0, u, J) = \begin{cases} u & \text{if } J(1) \leq -1, \\ 0 & \text{if } J(1) > -1, \end{cases} \qquad H(1, u, J) = u.$$

Then for $N \geq 1$,

$$(T_{\mu_0} \cdots T_{\mu_{N-1}} \bar{J})(0) = 0, \qquad (T_{\mu_0} \cdots T_{\mu_{N-1}} \bar{J})(1) = \mu_0(1).$$

Thus

$$J^*(0) = 0, \qquad J^*(1) = -1, \qquad (TJ^*)(0) = -1, \qquad (TJ^*)(1) = -1,$$

and hence $J^* \neq TJ^*$. Notice also that $\bar{J}$ is a fixed point of T, while $\bar{J} \leq J^*$ and $\bar{J} \neq J^*$, so the second part of Prop. 4.3.3 fails when $\bar{J} = J'$. Here parts (a) and (b) of Assumption I are satisfied, but part (c) is violated, since $H(0, u, \cdot)$ is discontinuous at $J = -1$ when $u < 0$.

Example 4.3.2 (Counterexample to Bellman's Equation II)

Let

$$X = \{0, 1\}, \qquad U(0) = U(1) = \{0\}, \qquad \bar{J}(0) = \bar{J}(1) = 0,$$

$$H(0, 0, J) = \begin{cases} 0 & \text{if } J(1) < \infty, \\ \infty & \text{if } J(1) = \infty, \end{cases} \qquad H(1, 0, J) = J(1) + 1.$$

Here there is only one policy, which we denote by μ. For all $N \geq 1$, we have

$$(T_\mu^N \bar{J})(0) = 0, \qquad (T_\mu^N \bar{J})(1) = N,$$

so $J^*(0) = 0$, $J^*(1) = \infty$. On the other hand, we have $(TJ^*)(0) = (TJ^*)(1) = \infty$ and $J^* \neq TJ^*$. Here parts (a) and (c) of Assumption I are satisfied, but part (b) is violated.

As a corollary to Prop. 4.3.3 we obtain the following.

Proposition 4.3.4: Let Assumption I hold. Then for every $\mu \in \mathcal{M}$, we have

$$J_\mu = T_\mu J_\mu.$$

Furthermore, if $J' \in E(X)$ is such that $J' \geq \bar{J}$ and $J' \geq T_\mu J'$, then $J' \geq J_\mu$.

Proof: Consider the variant of the infinite horizon problem where the control constraint set is $U_\mu(x) = \{\mu(x)\}$ rather than $U(x)$ for all $x \in X$. Application of Prop. 4.3.3 yields the result. **Q.E.D.**

We now provide the counterpart of Prop. 4.3.3 under Assumption D. We first prove a preliminary result regarding the convergence of the value iteration method, which is of independent interest (we will see later that this result need not hold under Assumption I).

Proposition 4.3.5: Let Assumption D hold. Then $T^N \bar{J} = J_N^*$, where J_N^* is the optimal cost function for the N-stage problem. Moreover

$$J^* = \lim_{N\to\infty} J_N^*.$$

Proof: By repeating the proof of Prop. 4.2.3, we have $T^N \bar{J} = J_N^*$ [part (b) of Assumption D is essentially identical to the assumption of that proposition]. Clearly we have $J^* \le J_N^*$ for all N, and hence $J^* \le \lim_{N\to\infty} J_N^*$. Also for all $\pi = \{\mu_0, \mu_1, \ldots\} \in \Pi$, we have

$$T_{\mu_0} \cdots T_{\mu_{N-1}} \bar{J} \ge J_N^*,$$

so by taking the limit of both sides as $N \to \infty$, we obtain $J_\pi \ge \lim_{N\to\infty} J_N^*$, and by taking infimum over π, $J^* \ge \lim_{N\to\infty} J_N^*$. Thus $J^* = \lim_{N\to\infty} J_N^*$. **Q.E.D.**

Proposition 4.3.6: Let Assumption D hold. Then

$$J^* = TJ^*.$$

Furthermore, if $J' \in E(X)$ is such that $J' \le \bar{J}$ and $J' \le TJ'$, then $J' \le J^*$.

Proof: For any $\pi = \{\mu_0, \mu_1, \ldots\} \in \Pi$, we have

$$J_\pi = \lim_{k\to\infty} T_{\mu_0} T_{\mu_1} \cdots T_{\mu_k} \bar{J} \ge \lim_{k\to\infty} T_{\mu_0} T^k \bar{J} \ge T_{\mu_0} J^*,$$

where the last inequality follows from the fact $T^k \bar{J} \downarrow J^*$ (cf. Prop. 4.3.5). Taking the infimum of both sides over $\pi \in \Pi$, we obtain $J^* \ge TJ^*$.

To prove the reverse inequality, we select any $\mu \in \mathcal{M}$, and we apply T_μ to both sides of the equation $J^* = \lim_{N\to\infty} T^N \bar{J}$ (cf. Prop. 4.3.5). By using part (b) of assumption D, we obtain

$$T_\mu J^* = T_\mu \left(\lim_{N\to\infty} T^N \bar{J} \right) = \lim_{N\to\infty} T_\mu T^N \bar{J} \geq \lim_{N\to\infty} T^{N+1} \bar{J} = J^*.$$

Taking the infimum of the left-hand side over $\mu \in \mathcal{M}$, we obtain $TJ^* \geq J^*$, showing that $TJ^* = J^*$.

To complete the proof, let $J' \in E(X)$ be such that $J' \leq \bar{J}$ and $J' \leq TJ'$. Then we have

$$\begin{aligned} J^* &= \inf_{\pi\in\Pi} \lim_{N\to\infty} T_{\mu_0} \cdots T_{\mu_{N-1}} \bar{J} \\ &\geq \lim_{N\to\infty} \inf_{\pi\in\Pi} T_{\mu_0} \cdots T_{\mu_{N-1}} \bar{J} \\ &\geq \lim_{N\to\infty} \inf_{\pi\in\Pi} T_{\mu_0} \cdots T_{\mu_{N-1}} J' \\ &\geq \lim_{N\to\infty} T^N J' \\ &\geq J', \end{aligned}$$

where the last inequality follows from the hypothesis $J' \leq TJ'$. Thus $J^* \geq J'$. **Q.E.D.**

Counterexamples to Bellman's equation can be readily constructed if part (b) of Assumption D (continuity from above) is violated. In particular, in Examples 4.2.1 and 4.2.2, part (a) of Assumption D is satisfied but part (b) is not. In both cases we have $J^* \neq TJ^*$, as the reader can verify with a straightforward calculation.

Similar to Prop. 4.3.4, we obtain the following.

Proposition 4.3.7: Let Assumption D hold. Then for every $\mu \in \mathcal{M}$, we have

$$J_\mu = T_\mu J_\mu.$$

Furthermore, if $J' \in E(X)$ is such that $J' \leq \bar{J}$ and $J' \leq T_\mu J'$, then $J' \leq J_\mu$.

Proof: Consider the variation of our problem where the control constraint set is $U_\mu(x) = \{\mu(x)\}$ rather than $U(x)$ for all $x \in X$. Application of Prop. 4.3.6 yields the result. **Q.E.D.**

An examination of the proof of Prop. 4.3.6 shows that the only point where we need part (b) of Assumption D was in establishing the relations

$$\lim_{N\to\infty} TJ_N^* = T\left(\lim_{N\to\infty} J_N^* \right)$$

and $J_N^* = T^N \bar{J}$. If these relations can be established independently, then the result of Prop. 4.3.6 follows. In this manner we obtain the following proposition.

Proposition 4.3.8: Let part (a) of Assumption D hold, assume that X is a finite set, and that $J^*(x) > -\infty$ for all $x \in X$. Assume further that there exists a scalar $\alpha \in (0, \infty)$ such that for all scalars $r \in (0, \infty)$ and functions $J \in E(X)$ with $J \le \bar{J}$, we have

$$H(x, u, J) - \alpha r \le H(x, u, J - r e), \qquad \forall\, x \in X,\ u \in U(x). \quad (4.14)$$

Then

$$J^* = TJ^*.$$

Furthermore, if $J' \in E(X)$ is such that $J' \le \bar{J}$ and $J' \le TJ'$, then $J' \le J^*$.

Proof: A nearly verbatim repetition of Prop. 4.2.4 shows that under our assumptions we have $J_N^* = T^N \bar{J}$ for all N. We will show that

$$\lim_{N\to\infty} H(x, u, J_N^*) \le H\left(x, u, \lim_{N\to\infty} J_N^*\right), \qquad \forall\, x \in X,\ u \in U(x).$$

Then the result follows as in the proof of Prop. 4.3.6.

Assume the contrary, i.e., that for some $\tilde{x} \in X$, $\tilde{u} \in U(\tilde{x})$, and $\epsilon > 0$, there holds

$$H(\tilde{x}, \tilde{u}, J_k^*) - \epsilon > H\left(\tilde{x}, \tilde{u}, \lim_{N\to\infty} J_N^*\right), \qquad k = 1, 2, \ldots.$$

From the finiteness of X and the fact $J^*(x) = \lim_{N\to\infty} J_N^*(x) > -\infty$ for all x, we know that for some integer $\overline{k} > 0$

$$J_k^* - (\epsilon/\alpha)e \le \lim_{N\to\infty} J_N^*, \qquad \forall\, k \ge \overline{k}.$$

By using the condition (4.14), we obtain for all $k \ge \overline{k}$

$$H(\tilde{x}, \tilde{u}, J_k^*) - \epsilon \le H\big(\tilde{x}, \tilde{u}, J_k^* - (\epsilon/\alpha)\, e\big) \le H\left(\tilde{x}, \tilde{u}, \lim_{N\to\infty} J_N^*\right),$$

which contradicts the earlier inequality. **Q.E.D.**

Characterization of Optimal Policies

We now provide necessary and sufficient conditions for optimality of a stationary policy. These conditions are markedly different under Assumptions I and D.

Proposition 4.3.9: Let Assumption I hold. Then a stationary policy μ is optimal if and only if

$$T_\mu J^* = TJ^*.$$

Proof: If μ is optimal, then $J_\mu = J^*$ so that the equation $J^* = TJ^*$ (cf. Prop. 4.3.3) implies that $J_\mu = TJ_\mu$. Since $J_\mu = T_\mu J_\mu$ (cf. Prop. 4.3.4), it follows that $T_\mu J^* = TJ^*$.

Conversely, if $T_\mu J^* = TJ^*$, then since $J^* = TJ^*$, it follows that $T_\mu J^* = J^*$. By Prop. 4.3.4, it follows that $J_\mu \leq J^*$, so μ is optimal. **Q.E.D.**

Proposition 4.3.10: Let Assumption D hold. Then a stationary policy μ is optimal if and only if

$$T_\mu J_\mu = TJ_\mu.$$

Proof: If μ is optimal, then $J_\mu = J^*$, so that the equation $J^* = TJ^*$ (cf. Prop. 4.3.6) can be written as $J_\mu = TJ_\mu$. Since $J_\mu = T_\mu J_\mu$ (cf. Prop. 4.3.4), it follows that $T_\mu J_\mu = TJ_\mu$.

Conversely, if $T_\mu J_\mu = TJ_\mu$, then since $J_\mu = T_\mu J_\mu$, it follows that $J_\mu = TJ_\mu$. By Prop. 4.3.7, it follows that $J_\mu \leq J^*$, so μ is optimal. **Q.E.D.**

An example showing that under Assumption I, the condition $T_\mu J_\mu = TJ_\mu$ does not guarantee optimality of μ is given in Exercise 4.3. Under Assumption D, we note that by Prop. 4.3.1 or 4.3.7, we have $J_\mu = T_\mu J_\mu$ for all μ, so if μ is a stationary optimal policy, the fixed point equation

$$J^*(x) = \inf_{u \in U(x)} H(x, u, J^*), \qquad \forall\, x \in X, \tag{4.15}$$

and the optimality condition of Prop. 4.3.10, yield

$$TJ^* = J^* = J_\mu = T_\mu J_\mu = T_\mu J^*.$$

Thus under D, a stationary optimal policy attains the infimum in the fixed point Eq. (4.15) for all x. However, there may exist nonoptimal stationary policies also attaining the infimum for all x, as shown by Fig. 4.3.2, and by case (a) of the three-node shortest path example of Section 3.1.2. Moreover, it is possible that this infimum is attained but no optimal policy exists, as shown by Fig. 4.3.2 (see also Exercise 4.7).

Proposition 4.3.9 shows that under Assumption I, there exists a stationary optimal policy if and only if the infimum in the optimality equation

$$J^*(x) = \inf_{u \in U(x)} H(x, u, J^*)$$

is attained for every $x \in X$. When the infimum is not attained for some $x \in X$, this optimality equation can still be used to yield an ϵ-optimal policy, which can be taken to be stationary whenever the scalar α in Assumption I(c) is strictly less than 1. This is shown in the following proposition.

Proposition 4.3.11: Let Assumption I hold. Then:

(a) If $\epsilon > 0$, the sequence $\{\epsilon_k\}$ satisfies $\sum_{k=0}^{\infty} \alpha^k \epsilon_k = \epsilon$, and $\epsilon_k > 0$ for all k, and the policy $\pi^* = \{\mu_0^*, \mu_1^*, \ldots\} \in \Pi$ is such that

$$T_{\mu_k^*} J^* \le TJ^* + \epsilon_k \, e, \qquad \forall \; k = 0, 1, \ldots,$$

then

$$J^* \le J_{\pi^*} \le J^* + \epsilon \, e.$$

(b) If $\epsilon > 0$, the scalar α in part (c) of Assumption I is strictly less than 1, and $\mu^* \in \mathcal{M}$ is such that

$$T_{\mu^*} J^* \le TJ^* + \epsilon(1 - \alpha) \, e,$$

then

$$J^* \le J_{\mu^*} \le J^* + \epsilon \, e.$$

Proof: (a) Since $TJ^* = J^*$, we have

$$T_{\mu_k^*} J^* \le J^* + \epsilon_k \, e,$$

and applying $T_{\mu_{k-1}^*}$ to both sides, we obtain

$$T_{\mu_{k-1}^*} T_{\mu_k^*} J^* \le T_{\mu_{k-1}^*} J^* + \alpha \epsilon_k \, e \le J^* + (\epsilon_{k-1} + \alpha \epsilon_k) \, e.$$

Applying $T_{\mu_{k-2}^*}$ throughout and repeating the process, we obtain for every $k = 1, 2, \ldots$,

$$T_{\mu_0^*} \cdots T_{\mu_k^*} J^* \leq J^* + \left(\sum_{i=0}^{k} \alpha^i \epsilon_i \right) e, \qquad k = 1, 2, \ldots.$$

Since $\bar{J} \leq J^*$, it follows that

$$T_{\mu_0^*} \cdots T_{\mu_k^*} \bar{J} \leq J^* + \left(\sum_{i=0}^{k} \alpha^i \epsilon_i \right) e, \qquad k = 1, 2, \ldots.$$

By taking the limit as $k \to \infty$, we obtain $J_{\pi^*} \leq J^* + \epsilon\, e$.

(b) This part is proved by taking $\epsilon_k = \epsilon(1 - \alpha)$ and $\mu_k^* = \mu^*$ for all k in the preceding argument. **Q.E.D.**

Under Assumption D, the existence of an ϵ-optimal policy is harder to establish, and requires some restrictive conditions.

Proposition 4.3.12: Let Assumption D hold, and let the additional assumptions of Prop. 4.3.8 hold. Then for any $\epsilon > 0$, there exists an ϵ-optimal policy.

Proof: For each N, denote

$$\epsilon_N = \frac{\epsilon}{2(1 + \alpha + \cdots + \alpha^{N-1})},$$

and let

$$\pi_N = \{\mu_0^N, \mu_1^N, \ldots, \mu_{N-1}^N, \mu, \mu \ldots\}$$

be such that $\mu \in \mathcal{M}$, and for $k = 0, \ldots, N-1$, $\mu_k^N \in \mathcal{M}$ and

$$T_{\mu_k^N} T^{N-k-1} \bar{J} = T^{N-k} \bar{J} + \epsilon_N\, e.$$

We have $T_{\mu_{N-1}}^N \bar{J} \leq T\bar{J} + \epsilon_N\, e$, and applying $T_{\mu_{N-2}}^N$ to both sides, we obtain

$$T_{\mu_{N-2}}^N T_{\mu_{N-1}}^N \bar{J} \leq T_{\mu_{N-2}}^N T\bar{J} + \alpha\epsilon_N\, e \leq T^2\bar{J} + (1 + \alpha)\epsilon_N\, e.$$

Continuing in the same manner, we have

$$T_{\mu_0}^N \cdots T_{\mu_{N-1}}^N \bar{J} \leq T^N \bar{J} + (1 + \alpha + \cdots + \alpha^{N-1})\epsilon_N\, e,$$

from which we obtain for $N = 0, 1, \ldots$,

$$J_{\pi_N} \leq T^N \bar{J} + (\epsilon/2)\, e.$$

By Prop. 4.3.5, we have $J^* = \lim_{N\to\infty} T^N \bar{J}$, so let $\bar{N}$ be such that

$$T^{\bar{N}} \bar{J} \leq J^* + (\epsilon/2)\, e$$

[such a $\bar{N}$ exists using the assumptions of finiteness of X and $J^*(x) > -\infty$ for all $x \in X$]. Then we obtain $J_{\pi_{\bar{N}}} \leq J^* + \epsilon\, e$, and $\pi_{\bar{N}}$ is the desired policy. **Q.E.D.**

4.3.2 Value Iteration

We will now discuss algorithms for abstract DP under Assumptions I and and D. We first consider value iteration (VI for short), which consists of successively generating $T\bar{J}, T^2\bar{J}, \ldots$. Note that because T need not be a contraction, it may have multiple fixed points J all of which satisfy $J \geq J^*$ under Assumption I (cf. Prop. 4.3.3) or $J \leq J^*$ under Assumption D (cf. Prop. 4.3.6). Thus, in the absence of additional conditions, it is essential to start VI with $\bar{J}$ or an initial J_0 such that $\bar{J} \leq J_0 \leq J^*$ under Assumption I or $\bar{J} \geq J_0 \geq J^*$ under Assumption D. In the next two propositions, we show that for such initial conditions, we have convergence of VI to J^* under Assumption D, and with an additional compactness condition, under Assumption I.

Proposition 4.3.13: Let Assumption D hold, and assume that $J_0 \in E(X)$ is such that $\bar{J} \geq J_0 \geq J^*$. Then

$$\lim_{k\to\infty} T^k J_0 = J^*.$$

Proof: The condition $\bar{J} \geq J_0 \geq J^*$ implies that $T^k\bar{J} \geq T^k J_0 \geq J^*$ for all k. By Prop. 4.3.5, $T^k\bar{J} \to J^*$, and the result follows. **Q.E.D.**

The convergence of VI under I requires an additional compactness condition, which is satisfied in particular if $U(x)$ is a finite set for all $x \in X$.

Proposition 4.3.14: Let Assumption I hold, let U be a metric space, and assume that the sets

$$U_k(x,\lambda) = \big\{u \in U(x) \,\big|\, H(x,u,T^k\bar{J}) \leq \lambda\big\} \tag{4.16}$$

are compact for every $x \in X$, $\lambda \in \Re$, and for all k greater than some integer $\bar{k}$. Assume that $J_0 \in E(X)$ is such that $\bar{J} \leq J_0 \leq J^*$. Then

$$\lim_{k\to\infty} T^k J_0 = J^*.$$

Furthermore, there exists a stationary optimal policy.

Proof: Similar to the proof of Prop. 4.3.13, it will suffice to show that $T^k\bar{J} \to J^*$. Since $\bar{J} \leq J^*$, we have $T^k\bar{J} \leq T^k J^* = J^*$, so that

$$\bar{J} \leq T\bar{J} \leq \cdots \leq T^k\bar{J} \leq \cdots \leq J^*.$$

Thus we have $T^k \bar{J} \uparrow J_\infty$ for some $J_\infty \in E(X)$ satisfying $T^k \bar{J} \leq J_\infty \leq J^*$ for all k. Applying T to this relation, we obtain

$$(T^{k+1}\bar{J})(x) = \min_{u \in U(x)} H(x, u, T^k \bar{J}) \leq (TJ_\infty)(x),$$

and by taking the limit as $k \to \infty$, it follows that

$$J_\infty \leq TJ_\infty.$$

Assume to arrive at a contradiction that there exists a state $\tilde{x} \in X$ such that

$$J_\infty(\tilde{x}) < (TJ_\infty)(\tilde{x}). \tag{4.17}$$

Similar to Lemma 3.2.1, there exists a point u_k attaining the minimum in

$$(T^{k+1}\bar{J})(\tilde{x}) = \inf_{u \in U(\tilde{x})} H(\tilde{x}, u, T^k \bar{J});$$

i.e., u_k is such that

$$(T^{k+1}\bar{J})(\tilde{x}) = H(\tilde{x}, u_k, T^k \bar{J}).$$

Clearly, by Eq. (4.17), we must have $J_\infty(\tilde{x}) < \infty$. For every k, consider the set

$$U_k\big(\tilde{x}, J_\infty(\tilde{x})\big) = \Big\{u \in U(\tilde{x}) \mid H(\tilde{x}, u_k, T^k \bar{J}) \leq J_\infty(\tilde{x})\Big\},$$

and the sequence $\{u_i\}_{i=k}^\infty$. Since $T^k \bar{J} \uparrow J_\infty$, it follows that for all $i \geq k$,

$$H(\tilde{x}, u_i, T^k \bar{J}) \leq H(\tilde{x}, u_i, T^i \bar{J}) \leq J_\infty(\tilde{x}).$$

Therefore $\{u_i\}_{i=k}^\infty \subset U_k\big(\tilde{x}, J_\infty(\tilde{x})\big)$, and since $U_k\big(\tilde{x}, J_\infty(\tilde{x})\big)$ is compact, all the limit points of $\{u_i\}_{i=k}^\infty$ belong to $U_k\big(\tilde{x}, J_\infty(\tilde{x})\big)$ and at least one such limit point exists. Hence the same is true of the limit points of the whole sequence $\{u_i\}$. It follows that if $\tilde{u}$ is a limit point of $\{u_i\}$ then

$$\tilde{u} \in \cap_{k=0}^\infty U_k\big(\tilde{x}, J_\infty(\tilde{x})\big).$$

By Eq. (4.16), this implies that for all $k \geq \overline{k}$

$$J_\infty(\tilde{x}) \geq H(\tilde{x}, \tilde{u}, T^k \bar{J}) \geq (T^{k+1}\bar{J})(\tilde{x}).$$

Taking the limit as $k \to \infty$, and using part (b) of Assumption I, we obtain

$$J_\infty(\tilde{x}) \geq H(\tilde{x}, \tilde{u}, J_\infty) \geq (TJ_\infty)(\tilde{x}). \tag{4.18}$$

which contradicts Eq. (4.17). Hence $J_\infty = TJ_\infty$, which implies that $J_\infty \geq J^*$ in view of Prop. 4.3.3. Combined with the inequality $J_\infty \leq J^*$, which was shown earlier, we have $J_\infty = J^*$.

To show that there exists an optimal stationary policy, observe that the relation $J^* = J_\infty = TJ_\infty$ and Eq. (4.18) [whose proof is valid for all $\tilde{x} \in X$ such that $J^*(\tilde{x}) < \infty$] imply that $\tilde{u}$ attains the infimum in

$$J^*(\tilde{x}) = \inf_{u \in U(\tilde{x})} H(\tilde{x}, u, J^*)$$

for all $\tilde{x} \in X$ with $J^*(\tilde{x}) < \infty$. For $\tilde{x} \in X$ such that $J^*(\tilde{x}) = \infty$, every $u \in U(\tilde{x})$ attains the preceding minimum. Hence by Prop. 4.3.9 an optimal stationary policy exists. **Q.E.D.**

The reader may verify by inspection of the preceding proof that if $\mu_k(\tilde{x})$, $k = 0, 1, \ldots$, attains the infimum in the relation

$$(T^{k+1}\bar{J})(\tilde{x}) = \inf_{u \in U(x)} H(\tilde{x}, u, T^k\bar{J}),$$

and $\mu^*(\tilde{x})$ is a limit point of $\{\mu_k(\tilde{x})\}$, for every $\tilde{x} \in X$, then the stationary policy μ^* is optimal. Furthermore, $\{\mu_k(\tilde{x})\}$ has at least one limit point for every $\tilde{x} \in X$ for which $J^*(\tilde{x}) < \infty$. Thus *the VI algorithm under the assumption of Prop. 4.3.14 yields in the limit not only the optimal cost function J^* but also an optimal stationary policy.*

On the other hand, under Assumption I but in the absence of the compactness condition (4.16), $T^k\bar{J}$ need not converge to J^*. What is happening here is that while the mappings T_μ are continuous from below as required by Assumption I(b), T may not be, and a phenomenon like the one illustrated in the left-hand side of Fig. 4.3.1 may occur, whereby

$$\lim_{k \to \infty} T^k\bar{J} \leq T\left(\lim_{k \to \infty} T^k\bar{J}\right),$$

with strict inequality for some $x \in X$. This can happen even in simple deterministic optimal control problems, as shown by the following example.

Example 4.3.3 (Counterexample to Convergence of VI)

Let

$$X = [0, \infty), \qquad U(x) = (0, \infty), \quad \bar{J}(x) = 0, \quad \forall\, x \in X,$$

and

$$H(x, u, J) = \min\big\{1,\ x + J(2x + u)\big\}, \qquad \forall\, x \in X,\ u \in U(x).$$

Then it can be verified that for all $x \in X$ and policies μ, we have $J_\mu(x) = 1$, as well as $J^*(x) = 1$, while it can be seen by induction that starting with $\bar{J}$, the VI algorithm yields

$$(T^k\bar{J})(x) = \min\big\{1,\ (1 + 2^{k-1})x\big\}, \qquad \forall\, x \in X,\ k = 1, 2 \ldots.$$

Thus we have $0 = \lim_{k\to\infty} (T^k \bar{J})(0) \neq J^*(0) = 1$.

The range of convergence of VI may be expanded under additional assumptions. In particular, in Chapter 3, under various conditions involving the existence of optimal S-regular policies, we showed that VI converges to J^* assuming that the initial condition J_0 satisfies $J_0 \geq J^*$. Thus if the assumptions of Prop. 4.3.14 hold in addition, we are guaranteed convergence of VI starting from any J satisfying $J \geq \bar{J}$. Results of this type will be obtained in the Section 4.4.1, where semicontractive models satisfying Assumption I will be discussed.

Asynchronous Value Iteration

The concepts of asynchronous VI that we developed in Section 2.6.1 apply also under the Assumptions I and D of this section. Under Assumption I, if J^* is real-valued, we may apply Prop. 2.6.1 with the sets $S(k)$ defined by

$$S(k) = \{J \mid T^k\bar{J} \leq J \leq J^*\}, \qquad k = 0, 1, \ldots.$$

Assuming that $T^k\bar{J} \to J^*$ (cf. Prop. 4.3.14), it follows that the asynchronous form of VI converges pointwise to J^* starting from any function in $S(0)$. This result can also be shown for the case where J^* is not real-valued, by using a simple extension of Prop. 2.6.1, where the set of real-valued functions $R(X)$ is replaced by the set of all $J \in E(X)$ with $\bar{J} \leq J \leq J^*$.

Under Assumption D similar conclusions hold for the asynchronous version of VI that starts with a function J with $J^* \leq J \leq \bar{J}$. Asynchronous pointwise convergence to J^* can be shown, based on an extension of the asynchronous convergence theorem (Prop. 2.6.1), where $R(X)$ is replaced by the set of all $J \in E(X)$ with $J^* \leq J \leq \bar{J}$.

4.3.3 Policy Iteration

Unfortunately, in the absence of further conditions, policy iteration (PI for short) is not guaranteed to yield the optimal cost function and/or an optimal policy under either Assumption I or D. However, there are convergence results for nonoptimistic and optimistic variants of PI under some conditions. These results have a different character than the ones we have seen so far in Chapters 2 and 3. One major difference is that *they guarantee convergence to J^*, but not to an optimal policy* (in fact in the case of Assumption D, there need not exist an optimal policy).

In what follows in this section we will provide an analysis of various types of PI, mainly under Assumption D. The analysis of PI under Assumption I will be given primarily in the next section, as it requires different assumptions and methods of proof, and will be coupled with ideas relating to the semicontractive models of Chapter 3.

Optimistic Policy Iteration Under D

A surprising fact under Assumption D is that nonoptimistic/exact PI may generate a policy that is strictly inferior over the preceding one. Moreover there may be an oscillation between nonoptimal policies even when the state and control spaces are finite. This is illustrated by the example of Fig. 3.1.7, and by case (a) of the three-node shortest path example of Section 3.1.2, where it can be verified that exact PI may oscillate between the policy that moves to the destination from node 1 and the policy that does not (see also Exercises 4.7 and 4.8). A related difficulty is that, under Assumption D, we may have $T_\mu J^* = TJ^*$ without μ being optimal, so starting from an optimal policy, we may obtain a nonoptimal policy by PI.

On the other hand optimistic PI under Assumption D has much better convergence properties, because it embodies the mechanism of VI, which is convergent to J^* as we saw in the preceding subsection. Indeed, let us consider an optimistic PI algorithm that generates a sequence $\{J_k, \mu^k\}$ according to†

$$T_{\mu^k} J_k = TJ_k, \qquad J_{k+1} = T_{\mu^k}^{m_k} J_k, \tag{4.19}$$

where m_k is a positive integer. We assume that the algorithm starts with a function $J_0 \in E(X)$ that satisfies $\bar{J} \geq J_0 \geq TJ_0$ and $J_0 \geq J^*$. For example, we may choose $J_0 = \bar{J}$. We have the following proposition.

Proposition 4.3.15: Let Assumption D hold and let $\{J_k, \mu^k\}$ be a sequence generated by the optimistic PI algorithm (4.19), assuming that $\bar{J} \geq J_0 \geq J^*$ and $J_0 \geq TJ_0$. Then $J_k \downarrow J^*$.

Proof: We have

$$J_0 \geq T_{\mu^0} J_0 \geq T_{\mu^0}^{m_0} J_0 = J_1 \geq T_{\mu^0}^{m_0+1} J_0 = T_{\mu^0} J_1 \geq TJ_1 = T_{\mu^1} J_1 \geq \cdots \geq J_2,$$

where the first, second, and third inequalities hold because the assumption $J_0 \geq TJ_0 = T_{\mu^0} J_0$ implies that $T_{\mu^0}^{\ell} J_0 \geq T_{\mu^0}^{\ell+1} J_0$ for all $\ell \geq 0$. Continuing similarly we obtain

$$J_k \geq TJ_k \geq J_{k+1}, \qquad \forall\, k \geq 0. \tag{4.20}$$

Moreover, we can show by induction that $J_k \geq J^*$. Indeed this is true for $k = 0$ by assumption. If $J_k \geq J^*$, we have

$$J_{k+1} = T_{\mu^k}^{m_k} J_k \geq T^{m_k} J_k \geq T^{m_k} J^* = J^*, \tag{4.21}$$

† As with all PI algorithms in this book, we assume that the policy improvement operation is well-defined, in the sense that there exists μ^k such that $T_{\mu^k} J_k = TJ_k$ for all k.

where the last equality follows from the fact $TJ^* = J^*$ (cf. Prop. 4.3.6), thus completing the induction. Thus, by combining the preceding two relations, we have

$$J_k \geq TJ_k \geq J_{k+1} \geq J^*, \qquad \forall\, k \geq 0. \tag{4.22}$$

We will now show by induction that

$$T^k J_0 \geq J_k \geq J^*, \qquad \forall\, k \geq 0. \tag{4.23}$$

Indeed this relation holds by assumption for $k = 0$, and assuming that it holds for some $k \geq 0$, we have by applying T to it and by using Eq. (4.22),

$$T^{k+1} J_0 \geq TJ_k \geq J_{k+1} \geq J^*,$$

thus completing the induction. By applying Prop. 4.3.13 to Eq. (4.23), we obtain $J_k \downarrow J^*$. **Q.E.D.**

For an illustration of the convergence of optimistic PI in an example where nonoptimistic PI oscillates between nonoptimal policies, the reader may trace the generated sequence $\{J_k\}$ in the example of Fig. 3.1.7, and verify that $J_k \downarrow J^*$. Note that the preceding proposition makes no assertion about obtaining an optimal policy or about convergence of J_{μ^k} to J^*. Indeed in the example of Fig. 3.1.7 the two available policies are both nonoptimal, so J_{μ^k} does not converge to J^* (in this example, J^* is approached by the cost functions of nonstationary policies). Note also that we have $J_{\mu^k} \to J^*$, even if $J^*(x) = -\infty$ for some x; for an example, see the blackmailer's problem of Exercise 4.6. The reason why optimistic PI can deal with the absence of an optimal policy is that it acts as a form of VI, which is convergent to J^* under Assumption D (cf. Prop. 4.3.13). However, optimistic PI tends to be more computationally efficient than VI, as experience has shown, so it is usually preferable in practice.

λ-Policy Iteration Under D

We now consider an alternative optimistic PI algorithm, which for undiscounted finite-state MDP, can be implemented by using matrix inversion, just like nonoptimistic PI for discounted finite-state MDP. This is the λ-PI algorithm, which is defined by

$$T_{\mu^k} J_k = TJ_k, \qquad J_{k+1} = T^{(\lambda)}_{\mu^k} J_k, \tag{4.24}$$

where for any policy μ and scalar $\lambda \in (0, 1)$, $T^{(\lambda)}_\mu$ is the mapping defined by

$$T^{(\lambda)}_\mu J = (1 - \lambda) \sum_{\ell=0}^{\infty} \lambda^\ell T^{\ell+1}_\mu J.$$

Here we assume that T_μ maps $R(X)$ to $R(X)$, and that for all $\mu \in \mathcal{M}$ and $J \in R(X)$, the limit of the series above is well-defined as a function in $R(X)$.

We also assume a linearity property for T_μ, whereby we have

$$T_\mu\big(T_\mu^{(\lambda)} J\big) = T_\mu^{(\lambda)}(T_\mu J), \qquad \forall\ \mu \in \mathcal{M},\ J \in R(X). \tag{4.25}$$

This assumption is commonly satisfied in DP problems where T_μ is linear, such as the stochastic optimal control problem of Example 1.2.1.

To compare the λ-PI method (4.24) with the optimistic PI method (4.19), we note that both mappings $T_{\mu^k}^{(\lambda)}$ and $T_{\mu^k}^{m_k}$ appearing in Eqs. (4.24) and (4.19), respectively, involve multiple applications of the VI mapping T_{μ^k}: a fixed number m_k in the latter case, and a geometrically weighted number in the former case. Thus λ-PI and optimistic PI are similar: they just use the mapping T_{μ^k} to apply VI in different ways.

Since λ-PI is a form of optimistic PI, it is not surprising that it has the same type of convergence properties as the earlier optimistic PI method (4.19). Similar to Prop. 4.3.15, we have the following.

Proposition 4.3.16: Let Assumption D hold and let $\{J_k, \mu^k\}$ be a sequence generated by the λ-PI algorithm (4.24), assuming Eq. (4.25), and that $\bar{J} \geq J_0 \geq J^*$ and $J_0 \geq TJ_0$. Then $J_k \downarrow J^*$.

Proof: As in the proof of Prop. 4.3.15, by using Assumption D, the monotonicity of T_μ, and the hypothesis $J_0 \geq TJ_0$, we have

$$J_0 \geq TJ_0 = T_{\mu^0}J_0 \geq T_{\mu^0}^{(\lambda)} J_0 = J_1 \geq T_{\mu^0}J_1 \geq TJ_1 = T_{\mu^1}J_1 \geq T_{\mu^1}^{(\lambda)} J_0 = J_2,$$

where for the third inequality, we use the relation $J_0 \geq T_{\mu^0}J_0$, the definition of J_1, and the assumption (4.25). Continuing in the same manner,

$$J_k \geq TJ_k \geq J_{k+1}, \qquad \forall\ k \geq 0.$$

Similar to the proof of Prop. 4.3.15, we show by induction that $J_k \geq J^*$, using the fact that if $J_k \geq J^*$, then

$$J_{k+1} = T_{\mu^k}^{(\lambda)} J_k \geq T_{\mu^k}^{(\lambda)} J^* = (1-\lambda)\sum_{\ell=0}^{\infty} \lambda^\ell T^{\ell+1} J^* = J^*,$$

[cf. the induction step of Eq. (4.21)]. By combining the preceding two relations, we obtain Eq. (4.22), and the proof is completed by using the argument following that equation. **Q.E.D.**

The λ-PI algorithm has a useful property, which involves the mapping $W_k : R(X) \mapsto R(X)$ given by

$$W_k J = (1-\lambda) T_{\mu^k} J_k + \lambda\, T_{\mu^k} J. \tag{4.26}$$

In particular J_{k+1} *is a fixed point of* W_k. Indeed, using the definition $J_{k+1} = T_{\mu^k}^{(\lambda)} J_k$ [cf. Eq. (4.24)], and the linearity assumption (4.25), we have

$$\begin{aligned} W_k J_{k+1} &= (1-\lambda) T_{\mu^k} J_k + \lambda T_{\mu^k} \left(T_{\mu^k}^{(\lambda)} J_k \right) \\ &= (1-\lambda) T_{\mu^k} J_k + \lambda\, T_{\mu^k}^{(\lambda)} (T_{\mu^k} J_k) \\ &= T_{\mu^k}^{(\lambda)} J_k \\ &= J_{k+1}. \end{aligned}$$

Thus J_{k+1} can be calculated as a fixed point of W_k.

Consider now the case where T_{μ^k} is nonexpansive with respect to some norm. Then from Eq. (4.26), it is seen that W_k is a contraction of modulus λ with respect to that norm, so J_{k+1} is the unique fixed point of W_k. Moreover, if the norm is a weighted sup-norm, J_{k+1} can be found using the methods of Chapter 2 for contractive models. The following example applies this idea to finite-state SSP, where contrary to the models of Section 3.2, we do not assume that an optimal proper policy exists.

Example 4.3.4 (Stochastic Shortest Path Problems with Nonpositive Costs)

Consider the SSP problem of Example 1.2.6 with states $1, \ldots, n$, plus the termination state 0. For all $u \in U(x)$, the state following x is y with probability $p_{xy}(u)$ and the expected cost incurred is nonpositive. This problem arises when we wish to maximize nonnegative rewards up to termination. It includes the classical search problem of Section 3.2.2, where the aim, roughly speaking, is to move through the state space looking for states with favorable termination rewards. We have noted earlier the difficulties regarding PI for this type of problem. In particular, case (a) of the three-node shortest path problem of Section 3.1.2 provided an example where nonoptimistic PI oscillates between an optimal and a nonoptimal policy (see also Exercise 4.8). The PI method with perturbations of Section 3.3.3 applies only under the conditions of that section. Here we will consider instead the λ-PI method, which applies under the different conditions of Assumption D.

We view the problem within our abstract framework with $\bar{J}(x) \equiv 0$ and

$$T_\mu J = g_\mu + P_\mu J, \tag{4.27}$$

with $g_\mu \in \Re^n$ being the corresponding nonpositive one-stage cost vector, and P_μ being an $n \times n$ substochastic matrix. The components of P_μ are the probabilities $p_{xy}\big(\mu(x)\big)$, $x, y = 1, \ldots, n$. Clearly Assumption D holds.

Consider the λ-PI method (4.24), with J_{k+1} computed by solving the fixed point equation $J = W_k J$, cf. Eq. (4.26). This is a nonsingular n-dimensional system of linear equations, and can be solved by matrix inversion, just like in exact PI for discounted n-state MDP. In particular, using Eqs. (4.26) and (4.27), we have

$$J_{k+1} = (I - \lambda P_{\mu^k})^{-1} \big(g_{\mu^k} + (1-\lambda) P_{\mu^k} J_k\big), \tag{4.28}$$

For a small number of states n, this matrix inversion-based policy evaluation may be simpler than the optimistic PI policy evaluation equation

$$J_{k+1} = T_{\mu^k}^{m_k} J_k$$

[cf. Eq. (4.19)], which points to an advantage of λ-PI.

Note that as $\lambda \to 1$, the policy evaluation Eq. (4.28) resembles the policy evaluation equation

$$J_{\mu^k} = (I - \lambda P_{\mu^k})^{-1} g_{\mu^k}$$

for λ-discounted n-state MDP. An important difference, however, is that for a discounted finite-state MDP, exact PI will find an optimal policy in a finite number of iterations, while this is not guaranteed for λ-PI. Indeed λ-PI does not require that there exists an optimal policy or even that $J^*(x)$ is finite for all x. Note also that the λ-PI method applies even to SSP problems with nonpositive costs where there is an optimal improper policy and no optimal proper policy. This is true for the optimistic PI method (4.19) as well.

Policy Iteration Under I

Contrary to the case of Assumption D, the important cost improvement property of PI holds under Assumption I. Thus, if μ is a policy and $\bar{\mu}$ satisfies the policy improvement equation $T_{\bar{\mu}} J_\mu = T J_\mu$, we have

$$J_\mu = T_\mu J_\mu \geq T J_\mu = T_{\bar{\mu}} J_\mu,$$

from which we obtain $J_\mu \geq \lim_{k\to\infty} T_{\bar{\mu}}^k J_\mu$. Since $J_\mu \geq \bar{J}$ and $J_{\bar{\mu}} = \lim_{k\to\infty} T_{\bar{\mu}}^k \bar{J}$, it follows that

$$J_\mu \geq T J_\mu \geq J_{\bar{\mu}}. \tag{4.29}$$

However, this cost improvement property is not sufficient by itself to guarantee the validity of PI under Assumption I. For example, it is not clear that strict inequality holds in Eq. (4.29) for at least one state $x \in X$ when μ is not optimal. As Exercise 4.3 shows, there may exist a nonoptimal policy μ such that $T_\mu J_\mu = T J_\mu$, and PI will stop when started with such a policy. Thus additional conditions are needed to obtain solid convergence guarantees. The next section provides a semicontractive framework for this purpose, which bears a connection with the corresponding framework of Chapter 3.

4.4 SEMICONTRACTIVE-MONOTONE INCREASING MODELS

In this section we combine Assumption I with the semicontractive abstract DP framework involving S-regular policies, as per Chapter 3. To this end, we introduce a special set of functions S that satisfies

$$S \subset \{J \in E(X) \mid J \geq \bar{J}\}, \qquad \bar{J} \in S. \tag{4.30}$$

The further specification of S will be left open for the moment, but we will see that its choice is important for the application of the following analysis in specific contexts. We will use the notion of S-regularity as defined in Section 3.1.1 (cf. Def. 3.1.1), i.e., μ is called S-regular if J_μ is the unique fixed point of T_μ within S, and

$$T_\mu^k J \to J_\mu, \qquad \forall\ J \in S. \tag{4.31}$$

Our analysis bears similarity to the one of semicontractive models in Chapter 3, but also takes advantage of Assumption I, thereby bringing to bear the results of Section 4.3. For example, we typically assume that there exists an S-regular optimal policy, but this is not a severe restriction, since under Assumption I, optimal stationary policies usually exist (any μ such that $T_\mu J^* = TJ^*$ is an optimal stationary policy, cf. Prop. 4.3.9), and the verification that these policies are S-regular is often simple.

4.4.1 Value and Policy Iteration Algorithms

The following proposition addresses the issue of uniqueness of solution of the fixed point equation $J = TJ$, and the convergence of the VI algorithm.

Proposition 4.4.1: (Fixed Point Properties and Convergence of Value Iteration) Let Assumption I hold, and assume that there exists an optimal S-regular policy, where S satisfies Eq. (4.30). Then:

(a) The optimal cost function J^* is the unique fixed point of T within S.

(b) We have $T^k J \to J^*$ for every $J \in S$ with $J \geq J^*$.

(c) If $\lim_{k\to\infty} T^k \bar{J} = J^*$ (as it is true under the assumptions of Prop. 4.3.14), then we have $T^k J \to J^*$ for every $J \in S$.

Proof: (a), (b) In view of the existence of an optimal S-regular policy and the fixed point property $J^* = TJ^*$ (cf. Prop. 4.3.3), Prop. 3.1.2 applies, and part (b) follows. Also by Prop. 3.1.2, J^* is the unique fixed point of T in the set $\{J \mid J \geq J^*\}$, while by Prop. 4.3.3, there are no fixed points of T that belong to S and are outside this set. This proves part (a).

(c) Let μ^* be an optimal S-regular policy. For any $J \in S$, we have

$$T_{\mu^*}^k J \geq T^k J \geq T^k \bar{J},$$

where the second inequality holds since $J \geq \bar{J}$ for all $J \in S$. Taking the limit in the preceding relation, and using the fact $\lim_{k\to\infty} T_{\mu^*}^k J = J_{\mu^*} = J^*$ (which holds by the regularity and optimality of μ^*), and $\lim_{k\to\infty} T^k \bar{J} = J^*$ (which holds by assumption), we obtain $\lim_{k\to\infty} T^k J = J^*$. **Q.E.D.**

Policy Iteration

We now consider a PI algorithm that starts with a policy μ^0 and generates a sequence $\{\mu^k\}$ of policies according to

$$T_{\mu^{k+1}} J_{\mu^k} = T J_{\mu^k}. \tag{4.32}$$

Thanks to the cost improvement property [cf. Eq. (4.29)], the sequence $\{\mu^k\}$ (regardless of whether it consists of S-regular policies) satisfies

$$J_{\mu^k} \geq T J_{\mu^k} \geq J_{\mu^{k+1}}, \qquad k = 0, 1, \ldots, \tag{4.33}$$

and it follows that $J_{\mu^k} \downarrow J_\infty$ for some $J_\infty \geq J^*$. The following proposition gives conditions for $J_\infty = J^*$.

Proposition 4.4.2: (Convergence of PI) Let Assumption I hold, and assume that:

(1) There exists an optimal S-regular policy, where S satisfies Eq. (4.30).

(2) For each sequence $\{J_m\} \subset S$ with $J_m \downarrow J$ we have

$$\lim_{m\to\infty} H(x, u, J_m) = H(x, u, J), \quad \forall\, x \in X,\ u \in U(x). \tag{4.34}$$

(3) For some initial $\mu^0 \in \mathcal{M}$, the monotonically nonincreasing sequence $\{J_{\mu^k}\}$ generated by the PI algorithm (4.32) belongs to S and its limit J_∞ also belongs to S.

Then $J_\infty = J^*$.

Proof: From Eq. (4.33), we have $J_{\mu^k} \geq T J_{\mu^k}$ for all k, and by taking the limit as $k \to \infty$,

$$J_\infty \geq \lim_{k\to\infty} T J_{\mu^k} \geq T J_\infty, \tag{4.35}$$

where the second inequality follows from the fact $J_{\mu^k} \geq J_\infty$. We also have for all $x \in X$ and $u \in U(x)$,

$$H(x, u, J_\infty) = \lim_{k\to\infty} H(x, u, J_{\mu^k}) \geq \lim_{k\to\infty} (TJ_{\mu^k})(x) = J_\infty(x),$$

where the first equality follows from Eq. (4.34) and the second equality follows from Eq. (4.33). By taking the infimum of the left-hand side over $u \in U(x)$, we obtain $TJ_\infty \geq J_\infty$, which combined with Eq. (4.35), yields $J_\infty = TJ_\infty$. Since there exists an optimal S-regular policy and $J_\infty \in S$, we have $J_\infty = J^*$ in view of the uniqueness property shown in Prop. 4.4.1(a). **Q.E.D.**

The condition (3) regarding PI convergence in the preceding proposition automatically holds if we can choose

$$S = \big\{J \in R(X) \mid J \geq \bar{J}\big\} \quad \text{or} \quad S = \big\{J \in B(X) \mid J \geq \bar{J}\big\}$$

without affecting other assumptions, where $R(X)$ [or $B(X)$] are the sets of functions on X that are real-valued (or bounded with respect to a weighted sup-norm, respectively). Note that this condition requires that the PI algorithm works as described for *some* initial policy μ^0 (not all initial policies). This provides flexibility in selecting a suitable μ^0.

Optimistic Policy Iteration

We have discussed so far the VI algorithm in Prop. 4.4.1(b), and the PI algorithm in Prop. 4.4.2. There is a variant of Prop. 4.4.2, which relates to optimistic PI, where policies are evaluated inexactly, with a finite number of VIs. In particular, this algorithm starts with $J_0 \in S$ such that $J_0 \geq TJ_0$, and generates $\{J_k, \mu^k\}$ according to

$$T_{\mu^k} J_k = TJ_k, \qquad J_{k+1} = T_{\mu^k}^{m_k} J_k, \qquad k = 0, 1, \ldots, \tag{4.36}$$

where m_k is a positive integer for each k. Then we have

$$J_0 \geq T_{\mu^0} J_0 \geq T_{\mu^0}^{m_0} J_0 \geq J_1 \geq T_{\mu^0}^{m_0+1} J_0 = T_{\mu^0} J_1 \geq TJ_1 = T_{\mu^1} J_1 \geq \cdots \geq J_2,$$

and continuing similarly, we have

$$J_k \geq TJ_k \geq J_{k+1}, \qquad k = 0, 1, \ldots. \tag{4.37}$$

Thus $\{J_k\}$ is monotonically nonincreasing and converges to a limit J_∞. The following proposition gives conditions for $J_\infty = J^*$.

Proposition 4.4.3: (Convergence of Optimistic PI) Let Assumption I hold, and assume that:

(1) There exists an optimal S-regular policy, where S satisfies Eq. (4.30).

(2) For each sequence $\{J_m\} \subset S$ with $J_m \downarrow J$ we have

$$\lim_{m\to\infty} H(x,u,J_m) = H\left(x,u,J\right), \quad \forall\, x \in X,\ u \in U(x).$$

(3) For some initial $J_0 \in S$ such that $J_0 \geq TJ_0$, the monotonically nonincreasing sequence $\{J_{\mu^k}\}$ generated by the optimistic PI algorithm (4.36) belongs to S and its limit J_∞ also belongs to S.

Then $J_\infty = J^*$.

Proof: We have shown that $J_k \geq TJ_k$ for all $k \geq 0$ [cf. Eq. (4.37)]. The result follows by taking the limit in this equation to obtain

$$J_\infty \geq \lim_{k\to\infty} TJ_k \geq TJ_\infty,$$

[cf. Eq. (4.35)], and then by repeating the corresponding part of the proof of Prop. 4.4.2. **Q.E.D.**

Note that a similar result may be shown when the λ-PI method is used in place of the optimistic PI method (4.36); cf. Prop. 4.3.16.

4.4.2 Some Applications

The key to applying Props. 4.4.1 and 4.4.2 is to choose the set S in a way that there exists an optimal S-regular policy, and the other required assumptions are satisfied. We describe a few applications.

Example 4.4.1 (Stochastic Shortest Path Problems with Countable State Space and Nonnegative Costs)

A context where the preceding analysis applies is SSP problems with countable state space, and nonnegative cost per stage, where with the choice $\bar J(x) \equiv 0$, the monotone increase condition

$$\bar J(x) \leq H(x,u,\bar J), \qquad \forall\, x \in X,\ u \in U(x),$$

is satisfied. Then to obtain strong results it is not necessary that all S-irregular or δ-S-irregular policies have infinite cost from some initial state, as in Section 3.2.1. Instead we may choose

$$S = \big\{J \in R(X) \mid J \geq \bar J\big\} \quad \text{or} \quad S = \big\{J \in B(X) \mid J \geq \bar J\big\}.$$

where $B(X)$ is the space of bounded functions with respect to a weighted sup-norm, and apply Props. 4.4.1 and 4.4.2, assuming the conditions of these propositions are satisfied. Then:

(a) J^* is the unique fixed point of T within S [cf. Prop. 4.4.1(a)].

(b) The VI algorithm converges to J^* if started with any $J \geq J^*$ [cf. Prop. 4.4.1(b)].

(c) If the control space is finite, the VI algorithm converges to J^* if started with any $J \geq 0$ [cf. Prop. 4.4.1(c), which applies because $T^k \bar{J} \to J^*$ in view of the finiteness of the control space, as shown in Prop. 4.3.14].

(d) The PI algorithm, started with any policy μ^0, generates a cost function sequence that converges to J^* (cf. Prop. 4.4.2).

Except for (d), these results are well-known for the case of finite-state problems; see [Ber87] (Section 6.4) and [BeT91] (Prop. 3).

Here is another example involving a discounted stochastic optimal control problem where T_μ need not be a contraction for all μ.

Example 4.4.2 (Discounted Semicontractive Optimal Control Problems)

Consider the stochastic optimal control problem of Example 1.2.1, where

$$H(x, u, J) = E\big\{g(x, u, w) + \alpha J\big(f(x, u, w)\big)\big\}, \tag{4.38}$$

$\alpha \in (0, 1)$, and $\bar{J}(x) \equiv 0$. Let

$$S = \big\{J \in B(X) \mid J \geq \bar{J}\big\}.$$

Note that X need not be a finite set, and that the functions in S need not have finite unweighted sup-norm. Assume that there is a set of policies $\overline{\mathcal{M}} \subset \mathcal{M}$ such that:

(a) The function $E\big\{g\big(x, \mu(x), w\big)\big\}$ belongs to S for all $\mu \in \overline{\mathcal{M}}$.

(b) The function $E\big\{J\big(f(x, \mu(x), w)\big)\big\}$ belongs to S for all $\mu \in \overline{\mathcal{M}}$ and $J \in S$.

(c) For each $J \in S$ there exists $\mu \in \overline{\mathcal{M}}$ such that $T_\mu J = TJ$.

(d) There exists an optimal policy within $\overline{\mathcal{M}}$.

It can be seen that S is a closed subset of $B(X)$, and that T_μ maps S into S and is a contraction with modulus α within S for all $\mu \in \overline{\mathcal{M}}$.† This

---

† To see this note that by Eq. (4.38), we have for all $J, J' \in B(X)$ and $x \in X$,

$$\frac{(T_\mu J)(x) - (T_\mu J')(x)}{v(x)} \leq \alpha \sup_{y \in X} \frac{\big|J(y) - J'(y)\big|}{v(y)} = \alpha \|J - J'\|,$$

implies that all policies in $\overline{\mathcal{M}}$ are S-regular, since J_μ is the unique fixed point of T_μ within S, and $T_\mu^k J$ converges to the fixed point J_μ for all $J \in S$.

In view of property (c) above, there exists $\mu \in \overline{\mathcal{M}}$ such that $T_\mu J^* = TJ^*$, which by Prop. 4.3.9, is optimal. Thus there exists an optimal S-regular policy, and it may be verified that Prop. 4.4.1 applies. It follows from Prop. 4.4.1(a) that J^* is the unique fixed point of T within S. By Prop. 4.4.1(b), J^* can be obtained in the limit by the VI algorithm starting with $J \in S$ such that $J \geq J^*$ [also starting with $J \in S$ such that $J \geq \bar{J}$, if we can show that $T^k \bar{J} \to J^*$ (e.g., if the control space is finite); cf. Prop. 4.4.1(c)]. By Prop. 4.4.2, J^* can be obtained in the limit by the PI algorithm, which starts from a policy $\mu^0 \in \overline{\mathcal{M}}$ and generates exclusively policies in $\overline{\mathcal{M}}$ [this is possible in view of property (c) above], provided condition (2) of the proposition can be verified.

4.4.3 Linear-Quadratic Problems

In this subsection, we consider a classical problem from control theory, where an effective PI algorithm can be developed. Here introducing contraction mappings is difficult because the optimal cost function is quadratic and unbounded above. However, it is possible to use a semicontractive framework with an appropriate set S, such that S-regular policies can be related to policies that are stable in traditional control theoretic terms.

Consider the linear system

$$x_{k+1} = Ax_k + Bu_k + w_k, \qquad k = 0, 1, \ldots,$$

where $x_k \in \Re^n$, $u_k \in \Re^m$ for all k, and A and B are given matrices. We assume that the random disturbances w_k are independent identically distributed with zero mean and finite second moment. The cost function of a policy $\pi = \{\mu_0, \mu_1, \ldots\}$ has the form

$$J_\pi(x_0) = \lim_{N \to \infty} E\left\{ \sum_{k=0}^{N-1} \alpha^k \big(x_k' Q x_k + \mu_k(x_k)' R \mu_k(x_k) \big) \right\},$$

where x' denotes the transpose of a column vector x, $\alpha \in (0, 1)$, Q is a positive semidefinite symmetric $n \times n$ matrix, and R is a positive definite

---

where v is the weight function of the sup-norm of $B(X)$. Interchanging J and J', we obtain

$$\frac{\big|(T_\mu J)(x) - (T_\mu J')(x)\big|}{v(x)} \leq \alpha \sup_{y \in X} \frac{\big|J(y) - J'(y)\big|}{v(y)} = \alpha \|J - J'\|,$$

and by taking supremum over $x \in X$, we see that T_μ is a contraction with modulus α.

symmetric $m \times m$ matrix. This is a special case of the stochastic optimal control problem of Example 1.2.1.

To convert the problem to the abstract format of this section, we let

$$X = \Re^n, \qquad U(x) = \Re^m, \quad \forall\, x \in X,$$

$$H(x, u, J) = x'Qx + u'Ru + \alpha E\big\{J(Ax + Bu + w)\big\},$$

$$\bar{J}(x) = 0, \qquad \forall\, x \in X.$$

Clearly Assumption I is satisfied.

The theory of this problem is well-known and is discussed in various forms in many sources, including [Ber12a] (Section 4.2) whose notation and presentation we follow. In summary, the optimal cost function J^* is quadratic of the form

$$J^*(x) = x'Kx + c,$$

where K is a positive definite symmetric $n \times n$ matrix and c is a nonnegative constant. The matrix K is the unique solution of the equation

$$K = A'\big(\alpha K - \alpha^2 KB(\alpha B'KB + R)^{-1}B'K\big)A + Q, \tag{4.39}$$

within the class of nonnegative definite matrices, and

$$c = \frac{\alpha}{1 - \alpha} E\{w'Kw\}.$$

The optimal policy is linear of the form

$$\mu^*(x) = -\alpha(\alpha B'KB + R)^{-1}B'KAx, \qquad x \in \Re^n.$$

The results just stated require that the pairs (A, B) and (A, C), where $Q = C'C$, are controllable and observable, respectively (see [Ber12a] for a definition of these terms and corresponding proofs).

We now discuss how the problem can be solved by PI based on the theory of this section. We define S to be the set of positive definite quadratic functions plus a nonnegative constant,

$$S = \big\{J(x) = x'Wx + \gamma \mid W : \text{positive definite symmetric}, \ \gamma \geq 0\big\}$$

It is easily seen that the continuity condition (4.34) of Prop. 4.4.2 is satisfied.

Consider the set $\overline{\mathcal{M}} \subset \mathcal{M}$ of all *linear* controllers μ that stabilize the system, i.e,

$$\mu(x) = Lx, \qquad \forall\, x \in \Re^n,$$

where L is an $m \times n$ matrix such that the matrix

$$A + BL$$

has eigenvalues strictly within the unit circle. We call such a controller *linear-stable*. It is well-known that under the controllability and observability assumption noted earlier, there exists a linear-stable controller that is optimal (see e.g., [Ber12a]). Moreover, from the definition of regularity (4.31), it can be seen that a linear-stable controller μ is S-regular.

Consider now the PI algorithm of this section, starting with a linear-stable controller $\mu^0(x) = L_0 x$. Then the cost corresponding to μ^0 has the form

$$J_{\mu^0}(x) = x' K_0 x + \text{nonnegative constant},$$

where K_0 is a positive definite symmetric matrix satisfying the (linear) equation

$$K_0 = \alpha(A + BL_0)' K_0 (A + BL_0) + Q + L_0' R L_0.$$

Let $\mu^1(x)$ attain the minimum for each x in the expression

$$\min_u \big\{ u' R u + \alpha(Ax + Bu)' K_0 (Ax + Bu) \big\}.$$

Then it can be seen that

$$J_{\mu^1}(x) = x' K_1 x + \text{constant} \ \leq J_{\mu^0}(x), \qquad \forall\, x \in X,$$

where K_1 is some positive semidefinite symmetric matrix, and we have $J_{\mu^1} \in S$ (see e.g., [Ber12a]). Continuing similarly, the PI algorithm yields a sequence of linear-stable controllers and corresponding sequence of matrices $\{K_k\}$ such that

$$K_k \to K_\infty,$$

where K_∞ is a positive definite symmetric matrix. The corresponding sequence $\{J_{\mu^k}\}$ as well as its limit belong to S. By Prop. 4.4.2, K_∞ is equal to K, the optimal cost matrix of the problem. Thus the problem can be solved by PI, which generates a sequence of linear-stable controllers of the form

$$\mu_k(x) = L_k x.$$

The cost function of each of these controllers is quadratic with positive semidefinite matrices K_k that can be obtained by solving the linear matrix equation

$$K_k = \alpha(A + BL_k)' K_k (A + BL_k) + Q,$$

as can be verified from Eq. (4.39). This equation can be solved with efficient specialized methods, for which we refer to the literature.

4.5 AFFINE MONOTONIC MODELS

In this section, we consider the case where

$$T_\mu J = A_\mu J + b_\mu, \tag{4.40}$$

where b_μ is a function in $R(X)$, and $A_\mu : R(X) \mapsto R(X)$ is a linear mapping such that

$$(A_\mu J)(x) \geq 0, \qquad \forall\, x \in X,\ \mu \in \mathcal{M},\ J \geq 0, \tag{4.41}$$

$$b_\mu(x) \geq 0, \qquad \forall\, x \in X,\ \mu \in \mathcal{M}. \tag{4.42}$$

To avoid some technical issues that relate to infinite spaces and thus simplify the analysis, *we assume that X and U are finite sets*, so $\{A_\mu \mid \mu \in \mathcal{M}\}$ and $\{b_\mu \mid \mu \in \mathcal{M}\}$ can be viewed as finite collections of matrices and vectors, respectively. This allows us to extend the definition (4.40) of T_μ over $E(X)$, the set of the extended real-valued functions, using also our convention that $+\infty - \infty = +\infty$. With this convention, it can be verified, using the nonnegativity conditions (4.41) and (4.42), that the mapping T_μ is a monotone mapping from $E(X)$ to $E(X)$, and the monotonicity Assumption 4.1.1 holds. Finally, we assume that

$$\bar{J} \in R(X), \qquad \bar{J}(x) \geq 0, \quad \forall\, x \in X. \tag{4.43}$$

We refer to the model (4.40)-(4.43) as an *affine monotonic* model.

A prominent case of this model is when A_μ is a transition probability matrix and $\bar{J}(x) \equiv 0$. Then we obtain the finite-spaces case of the negative DP model of [Str66], which is fully covered by the theory of Section 4.3, under Assumption I. A similar case is obtained when A_μ is a substochastic matrix and $\bar{J}(x) \equiv 0$.

Another important special case is the multiplicative model of Example 1.2.8, where X and U are finite sets, $\bar{J}$ is the unit function ($\bar{J} = e$), and for transition probabilities $p_{xy}(u)$ and real-valued function $g(x,u,y) \geq 0$, we have

$$H(x,u,J) = \sum_{y \in X} p_{xy}(u) g(x,u,y) J(y).$$

Thus with $b_\mu = 0$ and A_μ having components

$$A_\mu(x,y) = p_{xy}\big(\mu(x)\big) g\big(x,\mu(x),y\big),$$

we obtain an affine monotonic model.

In a variant of the multiplicative model that involves a cost-free and absorbing termination state 0, similar to SSP problems, H may contain a "constant" term, i.e., have the form

$$H(x,u,J) = p_{x0}(u) g(x,u,0) + \sum_{y \in X} p_{xy}(u) g(x,u,y) J(y), \tag{4.44}$$

in which case

$$b_\mu(x) = p_{x0}\big(\mu(x)\big)g\big(x, \mu(x), 0\big).$$

A special case of this model is the risk-sensitive SSP problem with exponential cost function, which will be discussed later in Section 4.5.3.

Note that the nonnegativity conditions (4.41)-(4.42) do not guarantee that the monotone increase Assumption I holds because we may not have $T\bar{J} \geq \bar{J}$. However, when the condition $T\bar{J} \geq \bar{J}$ holds, it automatically implies Assumption I, because by the finiteness of X and U, it can be seen that the remaining two conditions of Assumption I are satisfied. We will consider separately the two cases where the monotone increase condition $T\bar{J} \geq \bar{J}$ is satisfied and where it is not. Once this is done, we will discuss a risk-sensitive SSP model.

4.5.1 Increasing Affine Monotonic Models

The affine monotonic model admits a straightforward analysis in the case where $T\bar{J} \geq \bar{J}$ and

$$S = \big\{J \in R(X) \mid J \geq \bar{J}\big\}. \tag{4.45}$$

These assumptions bring to bear the theory of Section 4.4.1 and the parts of Section 4.3 that relate to the monotone increase Assumption I. In particular, we have the following proposition.

Proposition 4.5.1: Consider the affine monotonic model and the set S of Eq. (4.45). Assume that there exists an optimal S-regular policy and that $T\bar{J} \geq \bar{J}$. Then:

(a) The optimal cost function J^* is the unique fixed point of T within S.

(b) A policy μ is optimal if and only if $T_\mu J^* = TJ^*$.

(c) We have $T^k J \to J^*$ for every $J \geq \bar{J}$ with $J \in S$.

(d) The PI convergence results of Props. 4.4.2 and 4.4.3 apply.

Proof: (a) Follows from Prop. 4.4.1(a).

(b) Follows from Prop. 4.3.9.

(c) Follows from Prop. 4.4.1(c) and the assumed finiteness of the control space U.

(d) It is clear that the assumptions of Props. 4.4.2 and 4.4.3 hold. **Q.E.D.**

The preceding proposition relies strongly on the monotone increase condition $T\bar{J} \geq \bar{J}$, and cannot be shown without it. Of course the analysis of Chapters 2 and 3 may apply in some special cases. A particularly favorable case is when there is a weighted sup-norm for which A_μ is a contraction for all μ, and with the same modulus. Then we are essentially faced with a contractive model that can be addressed with the methodology of Chapter 2. We will next deal with another case where the condition $T\bar{J} \geq \bar{J}$ need not hold, but there is additional compensating structure.

4.5.2 Nonincreasing Affine Monotonic Models

In this subsection, we consider the affine monotonic model, without a guarantee that the monotone increase condition $T\bar{J} \geq \bar{J}$ holds. We use

$$S = \left\{ J \in R(X) \;\Big|\; J(x) > 0, \ \forall\, x \in X \right\}. \tag{4.46}$$

We will assume in the following proposition that $b_\mu(x) > 0$ for all x and μ, together with an additional condition guaranteeing that S-irregular policies cannot be optimal (this condition resembles corresponding assumptions in Props. 3.1.3, 3.2.1, and 3.2.4). We will use a scaling argument to modify $\bar{J}$ so that the condition $T\bar{J} \geq \bar{J}$ holds, and then we will apply the results of the preceding subsection.

Proposition 4.5.2: Consider the affine monotonic model and the set S of Eq. (4.46). Assume that

$$\bar{J}(x) > 0, \qquad b_\mu(x) > 0, \qquad \forall\, x \in X,\ \mu \in \mathcal{M}, \tag{4.47}$$

and that the following hold:

(1) There exists an optimal S-regular policy.

(2) If μ is an S-irregular policy, then for some $x \in X$, we have

$$\sum_{m=0}^{\infty} (A_\mu^m e)(x) = \infty. \tag{4.48}$$

Then:

(a) The optimal cost function J^* is the unique fixed point of T within S.

(b) We have $T^k J \to J^*$ for every $J \geq \bar{J}$ with $J \in S$.

(c) A policy μ is optimal if and only if $T_\mu J^* = TJ^*$.

(d) All the optimal policies are S-regular.

Proof: (a)-(c) The cost function of a policy μ is given by

$$J_\mu(x) = \limsup_{k\to\infty} (A_\mu^k \bar{J})(x) + \sum_{m=0}^{\infty} (A_\mu^m b_\mu)(x), \tag{4.49}$$

as can be verified using the form of T_μ and the definition $J_\mu = \lim_{k\to\infty} T_\mu^k \bar{J}$. Suppose that $\bar{J}$ is replaced by $\hat{J}$ of the form

$$\hat{J} = \epsilon\, e, \tag{4.50}$$

where ϵ is a positive scalar. Then the cost function of μ will change to

$$\hat{J}_\mu(x) = \limsup_{k\to\infty} (A_\mu^k \hat{J})(x) + \sum_{m=0}^{\infty} (A_\mu^m b_\mu)(x). \tag{4.51}$$

If μ is S-regular, from the requirement that $J_\mu = \lim_{k\to\infty} T_\mu^k J$ for all $J \in S$ and the form (4.46) of S, it follows that

$$J_\mu = \sum_{m=0}^{\infty} A_\mu^m b_\mu, \qquad A_\mu^k J \to 0, \quad \forall\ J \in S,$$

so from Eqs. (4.49), (4.51), after the change from $\bar{J}$ to $\hat{J}$, μ will continue to be S-regular, and $\hat{J}_\mu = J_\mu$.

We will now show that $\hat{J}_\mu = J_\mu$ when μ is S-irregular as well. Indeed for an S-irregular μ and for each $x \in X$, there are two possibilities. The first is that

$$\sum_{m=0}^{\infty} (A_\mu^m e)(x) = \infty,$$

in which case from Eqs. (4.47), (4.49), (4.51), we obtain $\hat{J}_\mu(x) = J_\mu(x) = \infty$. The second possibility is that

$$\sum_{m=0}^{\infty} (A_\mu^m e)(x) < \infty.$$

Then we have $(A_\mu^k e)(x) \to 0$, which (in view of the fact that $\bar{J}$ and $\hat{J}$ are bounded above by a positive multiple of e) implies that

$$\limsup_{k\to\infty} (A_\mu^k \bar{J})(x) = \limsup_{k\to\infty} (A_\mu^k \hat{J})(x) = 0.$$

Thus from Eqs. (4.49), (4.51), we again obtain $\hat{J}_\mu(x) = J_\mu(x)$.

Suppose now that we change $\bar{J}$ to $\hat{J} = \epsilon\, e$ [cf. Eq. (4.50)] with ϵ satisfying

$$0 < \epsilon \le \min_{x\in X,\, \mu\in\mathcal{M}} b_\mu(x).$$

Then clearly $T\hat{J} \geq \hat{J}$, while the cost functions of all stationary policies will remain unchanged as shown above. Also in view of the assumed finiteness of the control constraint set, the infimum over μ in the equation

$$TJ^* = \inf_{\mu \in \mathcal{M}} T_\mu J^*$$

is attained, and by Prop. 4.3.9, an optimal stationary policy exists. Thus the optimal S-regular policy of condition (1) is also an optimal $\{J \in R(X) \mid J \geq \hat{J}\}$-regular policy for the problem with $\bar{J}$ replaced by $\hat{J} = \epsilon\, e$. It follows that the assumptions of Prop. 4.5.1 are satisfied, implying the conclusions (a)-(c). These conclusions hold with $\bar{J}$ replaced by $\hat{J}$, but they depend only on J^* and the optimal policies, which remain unchanged after $\bar{J}$ is replaced by $\hat{J}$. Thus they hold as stated in the proposition.

(d) Let μ be an S-irregular policy. Then from Eq. (4.48) and the fact $\bar{J} \in S$, we have $J_\mu(x) = \infty$ for some $x \in X$, and since J^* is real-valued being the cost function of an S-regular policy, μ cannot be optimal. **Q.E.D.**

4.5.3 Exponential Cost Stochastic Shortest Path Problems

We will now apply the analysis of the affine monotonic model to SSP problems with an exponential cost function, which is introduced to incorporate risk sensitivity in the control selection process.

Consider an SSP problem with transition probabilities $p_{xy}(u)$, and real-valued transition costs $h(x,u,y)$. State 0 is a termination state, which is cost-free and absorbing. Instead of the standard additive cost function (cf. Example 1.2.6), we consider an exponential cost function of the form

$$J_\mu(x) = \lim_{k\to\infty} E\left\{\exp\left(\sum_{m=0}^{k-1} h\big(x_m,\mu(x_m),x_{m+1}\big)\right) \;\Big|\; x_0 = x\right\}, \qquad x \in X,$$

where $\{x_0, x_1, \ldots\}$ denotes the trajectory produced by the Markov chain under policy μ. We assume that X and U are finite sets. This is an affine monotonic model with mapping T_μ given by

$$(T_\mu J)(x) = \sum_{y\in X} p_{xy}\big(\mu(x)\big)\exp\big(h(x,\mu(x),y)\big)J(y) + p_{x0}\big(\mu(x)\big)\exp\big(h(x,\mu(x),0)\big), \qquad x \in X, \tag{4.52}$$

[cf. Eq. (4.44)]. Here A_μ and b_μ have components

$$A_\mu(x,y) = p_{xy}\big(\mu(x)\big)\exp\big(h(x,\mu(x),y)\big), \tag{4.53}$$

$$b_\mu(x) = p_{x0}\big(\mu(x)\big)\exp\big(h(x,\mu(x),0)\big). \tag{4.54}$$

As noted earlier, the analysis separates naturally into the two cases where the condition $T\bar{J} \geq \bar{J}$ holds (cf. Section 4.5.1 - the "easy" case) and where it does not (cf. Section 4.5.2). Consider first the case where $T\bar{J} \geq \bar{J}$, an example of which is when

$$h(x, u, y) \geq 0, \qquad \forall\, x,\, y \in X,\ u \in U(x),$$

so that from Eq. (4.52), we have $\exp\big(h(x, u, y)\big) \geq 1$ and for $\bar{J} = e$, we have

$$T_\mu \bar{J} = A_\mu \bar{J} + b_\mu \geq \bar{J}, \qquad \forall\, \mu \in \mathcal{M}.$$

As in Section 4.5.1, by letting

$$S = \big\{J \in R(X) \mid J \geq \bar{J}\big\},$$

and by assuming the existence of an optimal S-regular policy, we can apply Prop. 4.5.1 to obtain the conclusions (a)-(d) of that proposition. In particular, J^* is the unique fixed point of T within S [cf. Eq. (4.45)], all optimal policies are S-regular and satisfy the optimality condition $T_\mu J^* = TJ^*$, and VI and PI yield J^* in the limit, when initialized appropriately.

On the other hand, there are interesting applications where the condition $T\bar{J} \geq \bar{J}$ does not hold. The following is an example.

Example 4.5.1 (Optimal Stopping with Risk-Sensitive Cost)

Consider an SSP problem where there are two controls at each x: *stop*, in which case we move to the termination state 0 with a cost $s(x)$, and *continue*, in which case we move to a state y, with given transition probabilities p_{xy} [at no cost if $y \neq 0$ and a cost $\bar{s}(x)$ if $y = 0$]. The mapping H has the form

$$H(x, u, J) = \begin{cases} \exp\big(s(x)\big) & \text{if } u = \text{stop}, \\ \sum_{y \in X} p_{xy} J(y) + p_{x0} \exp\big(\bar{s}(x)\big) & \text{if } u = \text{continue}, \end{cases}$$

and $\bar{J}$ is the unit function e. Here the stopping cost $s(x)$ will often naturally be negative for some x (this is true for example in search problems of the type discussed in Example 3.2.1), so the condition $T\bar{J} \geq \bar{J}$ can be written as

$$\min \left\{ \exp\big(s(x)\big),\ \sum_{y \in X} p_{xy} + p_{x0} \exp\big(\bar{s}(x)\big) \right\} \geq 1, \qquad \forall\, x \in X,$$

and is violated.

When the condition $T\bar{J} \geq \bar{J}$ does not hold, we may use the analysis of Section 4.5.2, under the condition

$$b_\mu(x) > 0, \qquad \forall\, x \in X,\ \mu \in \mathcal{M}, \tag{4.55}$$

[cf. Eq. (4.47)], and with

$$S = \left\{ J \in R(X) \;\middle|\; J(x) > 0,\ \forall\, x \in X \right\},$$

[cf. Eq. (4.46)]. Then Prop. 4.5.2 applies under the corresponding assumptions, namely that there exists an optimal S-regular policy, and for every S-irregular policy μ, there exists $x \in X$ such that

$$\sum_{m=0}^{\infty} (A_\mu^m e)(x) = \infty,$$

[cf. Eq. (4.48)], where A_μ is given by Eq. (4.53).

Still, however, the condition (4.55) may be too restrictive in the present context [cf. Eq. (4.54)]. In this case we may use the perturbation approach of Section 3.2.2, which also allows a countable state space X. In particular, we introduce an additive perturbation δ to b_μ. We assume that the optimal cost function J_δ^* of the δ-perturbed problem is a fixed point of the mapping T_δ given by

$$(T_\delta J)(x) = \min_{u \in U(x)} \left\{ \sum_{y \in X} p_{xy}(u) \mathrm{exp}\big(h(x,u,y)\big) J(y) + p_{x0}(u) \mathrm{exp}\big(h(x,u,0)\big) \right\} + \delta, \qquad x \in X,$$

and we assume existence of an optimal S-regular policy with

$$S = \big\{ B(X) \mid J(x) > 0,\ \forall\, x \in X \big\},$$

where $B(X)$ is the space of bounded functions with respect to some weighted sup-norm. The remaining conditions of Assumption 3.2.2 are relatively mild and we assume that they hold. Then Prop. 3.2.4 applies and shows that J^* is equal to $\lim_{\delta \downarrow 0} J_\delta^*$ and is the unique fixed point of T within the set $\{J \in S \mid J \geq J^*\}$, and that the VI sequence $\{T^k J\}$ converges to J^* starting from a function $J \in S$ with $J \geq J^*$.

Note here that there may exist improper policies that never terminate, but are S-regular because they can generate some negative transition costs $h(x,u,y)$ that make A_μ contractive [cf. Eq. (4.52)]. Similarly, there may exist proper policies that terminate with probability one, but are S-irregular because for the corresponding mapping A_μ we have $(A_\mu^k e)(x) \to \infty$ for some x. It may also happen that for some $x \in X$, $J^*(x)$ is strictly smaller than $\lim_{\delta \downarrow 0} J_\delta^*(x)$, the optimal cost over all S-regular policies, while there may exist S-irregular policies that are optimal and attain J^*, in which case Prop. 3.2.2 applies.

Example 4.5.2 (Shortest Paths with Risk-Sensitive Cost)

As an illustration of the preceding remarks, consider the context of the three-node shortest path problem of Section 3.1.2, but with the exponential cost function of the present subsection. There are two policies denoted μ and $\overline{\mu}$: the 1st policy is $2 \to 1 \to 0$, while the 2nd policy is $2 \to 1 \to 2$. The corresponding mappings T_μ and $T_{\overline{\mu}}$ are given by

$$(T_\mu J)(1) = \exp(b), \qquad (T_\mu J)(2) = \exp(a)J(1),$$
$$(T_{\overline{\mu}} J)(1) = \exp(a)J(2), \qquad (T_{\overline{\mu}} J)(2) = \exp(a)J(1).$$

Here we have $b_\mu(2) = b_{\overline{\mu}}(1) = b_{\overline{\mu}}(2) = 0$, so it is essential to use the perturbation approach of Section 3.2.2.

The cost functions of μ and $\overline{\mu}$, with $\bar{J} = e$, are

$$J_\mu(1) = \exp(b), \qquad J_\mu(2) = \exp(a + b),$$

$$J_{\overline{\mu}}(1) = J_{\overline{\mu}}(2) = \lim_{k\to\infty} \exp\left(\sum_{m=0}^{k-1} a\right) = \lim_{k\to\infty} \big(\exp(a)\big)^k.$$

Policy μ is proper and S-regular (S is equal to $\Re^2$ here), while policy $\overline{\mu}$ is improper and S-irregular. If $a > 0$, $\overline{\mu}$ is inferior to μ. If $a = 0$, $\overline{\mu}$ is superior to μ if and only if $b > 0$. Consistent with Prop. 3.2.2, $\lim_{\delta\downarrow 0} J_\delta^*$ is the optimal cost over the S-regular policies only, which is J_μ if $a \geq 0$. In particular, if $a = 0$ and $b > 0$, we have

$$J_\mu(1) = \exp(b) = \lim_{\delta\downarrow 0} J_\delta^*(x) > J^*(x) = 1, \qquad x = 1, 2.$$

In the case where $a < 0$, $\overline{\mu}$ is optimal and S-irregular (since its cost function is $J_{\overline{\mu}} = 0$ and does not belong to S). Then it can be seen that $J_\delta^* = \delta/\big(1 - \exp(a)\big)$, so it is not true that $\lim_{\delta\downarrow 0} J_\delta^*$, which is 0, is equal to the optimal cost function over the S-regular policies only, which is still consistent with Prop. 3.2.3 because the S-regular policy is not optimal for the δ-perturbed problem for every $\delta > 0$.

Finally, let us consider the fixed points of the mapping T:

$$(TJ)(1) = \min\big\{\exp(b),\ \exp(a)J(2)\big\}, \qquad (TJ)(2) = \exp(a)J(1).$$

In the case $a = 0$ and $b = 0$, T takes the form

$$(TJ)(1) = \min\big\{1,\ J(2)\big\}, \qquad (TJ)(2) = J(1).$$

The set of its fixed points is

$$\big\{J \in R(X) \mid J = \epsilon\, e,\ \epsilon \leq 1\big\},$$

so it contains the optimal cost function, which is $J^* = e$. Indeed, J^* is the unique fixed point of T within the set $\big\{J \in S \mid J \geq J^*\big\}$, consistently with Prop. 3.2.2(a). However, J^* is not the unique fixed point within S, as would have been asserted by Prop. 4.5.2(a) if the condition (4.55) were true.

Let us finally mention another interesting case, which arises when A_μ is a contraction with respect to the same weighted sup-norm for all μ; this may happen for example if $h(x, u, y) < 0$ for all (x, u, y). Then we have a contractive model for which the strong results of Chapter 2 apply.

4.6 AN OVERVIEW OF SEMICONTRACTIVE MODELS AND RESULTS

Several semicontractive models and results have been discussed in this chapter and in Chapter 3, under several different assumptions, and it may be worth summarizing them. Three types of models have been considered:

(a) Models where the set S may include extended real-valued functions, an optimal S-regular policy is assumed to exist, and no other conditions are placed on S-irregular policies. These models are covered by Props. 3.1.1, 3.1.2, and 4.4.1, and they may require substantial analysis to verify the corresponding assumptions. Note here that the existence of an optimal stationary policy (regular or irregular) may not be easily verified. However, in the special case where Assumption I and the compactness assumption of Prop. 4.3.14 holds, existence of an optimal stationary policy is guaranteed, and then requiring the existence of an optimal S-regular policy may not be restrictive.

(b) Models where S consists of real-valued functions, and conditions are placed on S-irregular policies, which roughly imply that their cost is infinite from some states. There are two propositions that apply to such models: Prop. 3.1.3, which assumes also that an optimal S-regular policy exists, and Prop. 3.2.1, which indirectly guarantees the existence of an optimal S-regular policy through other assumptions.

(c) Perturbation models, where S-irregular policies cannot be adequately differentiated from S-regular ones on the basis of their cost functions, but they become differentiated once a positive additive perturbation is added to their associated mapping. These models include the ones of Sections 3.2.2 and are covered by Props. 3.2.2-3.2.4.

Variants of these models may also include special structure that enhances the power of the analysis, as for example in SSP problems, linear quadratic problems, and affine monotonic and exponential cost models.

The two significant issues in the analysis of semicontractive models are how to select the set S so that an optimal S-regular policy exists, and how to verify the existence of such a policy. There seems to be no universal approach for addressing these issues, as can be evidenced by the variety of alternative sets of assumptions that we have introduced, and by the variety of special cases that we have analyzed. Thus the analysis of the special structure of the given model becomes important. This analysis may be guided by the general ideas and results of the semicontractive theory that we have developed.

4.7 NOTES, SOURCES, AND EXERCISES

The analysis of noncontractive abstract DP models of Sections 4.3.1 and 4.3.2 dates to the author's paper [Ber77]. This analysis and its finite horizon counterpart of Section 4.2 were also presented in the monograph by Bertsekas and Shreve [BeS78].

Important examples of noncontractive infinite horizon examples are the classical positive DP problems, analyzed by Blackwell [Bla65], and by Dubins and Savage [DuS65], and the negative DP problems analyzed in Strauch [Str66] (and also in Strauch's Ph.D. thesis, written under the supervision of Blackwell). The monograph by Bertsekas and Shreve [BeS78] provides a detailed treatment of these two models, which also resolves the associated measurability questions. A simpler textbook treatment, which bypasses the measurability questions, is given in [Ber12a], Chapter 4.

The compactness condition that guarantees convergence of VI to J^* under Assumption I (cf. Prop. 4.3.14) has been discussed by the author in [Ber73] for reachability problems (see Exercise 4.9), and in [Ber77] for negative DP models; also by Schal [Sch75] and Whittle [Whi80] for negative DP models. A more refined analysis of the question of convergence of VI to J^* is possible. This analysis provides a necessary and sufficient condition for convergence and improves over the compactness condition of Prop. 4.3.14. In particular, the following characterization is shown in [Ber77], Prop. 11 (see also [BeS78], Prop. 5.9):

For every set $C \subset X \times U \times \Re$, let $\Pi(C)$ denote the projection of C onto $X \times \Re$:

$$\Pi(C) = \big\{(x, \lambda) \mid (x, u, \lambda) \in C \text{ for some } u \in U(x)\big\},$$

and denote also

$$\overline{\Pi(C)} = \big\{(x, \lambda) \mid \lambda_m \to \lambda \text{ for some sequence } \{\lambda_m\} \text{ with } \{(x, \lambda_m)\} \subset C\big\}.$$

Consider the sets $C_k \subset X \times U \times \Re$ given by

$$C_k = \big\{(x, u, \lambda) \mid H(x, u, T^k \bar{J}) \leq \lambda,\ x \in X,\ u \in U(x)\big\}, \qquad k = 0, 1, \ldots.$$

Then under Assumption I we have $T^k \bar{J} \to J^*$ if and only if

$$\overline{\Pi\big(\cap_{k=0}^{\infty} C_k\big)} = \cap_{k=0}^{\infty} \overline{\Pi(C_k)}.$$

Moreover we have $T^k \bar{J} \to J^*$ and in addition there exists an optimal stationary policy if and only if

$$\Pi\big(\cap_{k=0}^{\infty} C_k\big) = \cap_{k=0}^{\infty} \overline{\Pi(C_k)}. \tag{4.56}$$

For a connection with Prop. 4.3.14, it can be shown that compactness of the sets

$$U_k(x, \lambda) = \big\{u \in U(x) \big| \ H(x, u, T^k \bar{J}) \leq \lambda\big\}$$

implies Eq. (4.56) (see [Ber77], Prop. 12, or [BeS78], Prop. 5.10).

Optimistic PI and λ-PI have not been considered earlier under Assumption D, and the corresponding analysis of Section 4.3.3 is new. See [BeI96], [ThS10a], [ThS10b], [Ber11b], [Sch11] for analyses of λ-PI for discounted and SSP problems. A related extension, called Λ-PI, is discussed in Yu and Bertsekas [YuB12], Section 5.

The connection of the monotone increasing model with the semicontractive model, discussed in Section 4.4, and the corresponding PI algorithms are also new. Some finite-state SSP problems with nonpositive costs may be related to average cost MDP, with possibly multichain policies, for which there are special PI methods (see [Put94], Section 10.4). However, these PI methods are more complicated than the ones discussed here. Linear-quadratic problems have been exhaustively analyzed in the literature, and the convergence of PI for these problems was first shown by Kleinman [Kle68].

The monotonic affine models of Sections 4.5.1 and 4.5.2 have not been considered earlier, to the author's knowledge. The analysis of the SSP model with exponential cost of Section 4.5.3 is based on unpublished collaboration with H. Yu. Two prominent papers for the latter model are by Denardo and Rothblum [DeR79], and by Patek [Pat01]. The paper [DeR79] assumes that the state and control spaces are finite, that there exists at least one S-regular policy (a transient policy in the terminology of [DeR79]), and that every improper policy is S-irregular. The paper [Pat01] assumes that the state space is finite, that the control constraint set is compact, and that the expected one-stage cost is strictly positive for all state-control pairs.

E X E R C I S E S

4.1 (Example of Nonexistence of an Optimal Policy Under D)

This is an example of a deterministic stopping problem where Assumption D holds, and an optimal policy does not exist, even though only two controls are available at each state (stop and continue). The state space is $X = \{1, 2, \ldots\}$. Continuation from state x leads to state $x+1$ with certainty and no cost, while the stopping cost is $-1 + (1/x)$, so that there is an incentive to delay stopping at every state. Here for all x, $\bar{J}(x) = 0$, and

$$H(x, u, J) = \begin{cases} J(x+1) & \text{if } u = \text{continue}, \\ -1 + (1/x) & \text{if } u = \text{stop}. \end{cases}$$

Show that $J^*(x) = -1$ for all x, but there is no policy (stationary or not) that attains the optimal cost starting from x.

4.2 (Counterexample for Optimality Condition Under D)

For the problem of Exercise 4.1, show that the policy μ that never stops is nonoptimal and satisfies $T_\mu J^* = TJ^*$.

4.3 (Counterexample for Optimality Condition Under I)

Let

$$X = \Re, \qquad U(x) \equiv (0, 1], \qquad \bar{J}(x) \equiv 0,$$

$$H(x, u, J) = |x| + J(ux), \qquad \forall\, x \in X,\ u \in U(x).$$

Let $\mu(x) = 1$ for all $x \in X$. Then $J_\mu(x) = \infty$ if $x \neq 0$ and $J_\mu(0) = 0$. Verify that $T_\mu J_\mu = TJ_\mu$. Verify also that $J^*(x) = |x|$, and hence μ is not optimal.

4.4 (Solution by Mathematical Programming)

This exercise shows that under Assumptions I and D, it is possible to devise a computational method based on mathematical programming when $X = \{1, \ldots, n\}$.

(a) Under Assumption I, show that J^* is the unique solution of the following optimization problem in $z = (z_1, \ldots, z_n)$:

$$\text{minimize} \ \sum_{i=1}^{n} z_i$$
$$\text{subject to} \ \ z_i \geq \bar{J}(i), \quad z_i \geq \inf_{u \in U(i)} H(i, u, z), \qquad i = 1, \ldots, n.$$

(b) Under Assumption D, show that J^* is the unique solution of the following optimization problem in $z = (z_1, \ldots, z_n)$:

$$\text{maximize} \ \sum_{i=1}^{n} z_i$$
$$\text{subject to} \ \ z_i \leq \bar{J}(i), \quad z_i \leq H(i, u, z), \qquad i = 1, \ldots, n, \quad u \in U(i).$$

Note: Generally, these programs may not be linear or even convex.

4.5 (Semicontractive Discounted Problems with Unbounded Cost per Stage)

This exercise applies the theory of semicontractive models under Assumption I (cf. Section 4.4.1) to a broad class of discounted problems. It is related to Example 4.4.2. Consider a countable-state MDP where $X = \{1, 2, \ldots\}$, the discount factor is $\alpha \in (0, 1)$, the transition probabilities are denoted $p_{xy}(u)$ for $x, y \in X$

and $u \in U(x)$, and the expected cost per stage is denoted by $g(x,u)$, $x \in X$, $u \in U(x)$. We assume that

$$g(x,u) \geq 0, \qquad \forall\, x \in X,\ u \in U(x).$$

For a positive weight sequence $v = \{v(1), v(2), \ldots\}$, we consider the space $B(X)$ of sequences $J = \{J(1), J(2), \ldots\}$ such that $\|J\| < \infty$, where $\|\cdot\|$ is the corresponding weighted sup-norm. Let

$$S = \{J \in B(x) \mid J(x) \geq 0\},$$

and consider the monotone mappings T_μ and T, given by

$$(T_\mu J)(x) = g\big(x, \mu(x)\big) + \alpha \sum_{y \in X} p_{xy}\big(\mu(x)\big) J(y), \qquad x \in X,$$

$$(TJ)(x) = \inf_{u \in U(x)} \left[g(x,u) + \alpha \sum_{y \in X} p_{xy}(u) J(y) \right], \qquad x \in X.$$

(a) Assume that there exists a subset $\overline{\mathcal{M}}$ of policies such that for all $\mu \in \overline{\mathcal{M}}$:

(1) The sequence $G = \{G_1, G_2, \ldots\}$, where

$$G_x = g\big(x, \mu(x)\big), \qquad x \in X,$$

belongs to S.

(2) The sequence $V = \{V_1, V_2, \ldots\}$, where

$$V_x = \sum_{y \in X} p_{xy}\big(\mu(x)\big)\, v(y), \qquad x \in X,$$

belongs to S.

(3) We have

$$\frac{\sum_{y \in X} p_{xy}\big(\mu(x)\big) v(y)}{v(x)} \leq 1, \qquad x \in X.$$

Show that for all $\mu \in \overline{\mathcal{M}}$, T_μ maps S into S, and is a contraction mapping with modulus α. In particular, all policies in $\overline{\mathcal{M}}$ are S-regular.

(b) Assume further that for each $J \in S$ there exists $\mu \in \overline{\mathcal{M}}$ such that $T_\mu J = TJ$, and that there exists an optimal policy within $\overline{\mathcal{M}}$. Show that Props. 4.4.1 and 4.4.2 apply, so that J^* is the unique fixed point of T within S, and it can be obtained as the limit of cost functions generated by the PI algorithm, starting from a policy $\mu^0 \in \overline{\mathcal{M}}$.

4.6 (Blackmailer's Dilemma)

Consider the blackmailer's dilemma (cf. Exercise 3.1), where

$$X = \{1\}, \qquad U(1) = (0, 1], \qquad \bar{J}(1) = 0,$$

and

$$H(1, u, J) = -u + (1 - u^2)J(1).$$

From Exercise 3.1 we have $J^*(1) = -\infty$ and that there is no optimal stationary policy. Show that:

(a) The PI algorithm generates a sequence $\{\mu^k\}$ of policies according to

$$J_{\mu^k}(1) = -\frac{1}{\mu^k(1)}, \qquad \mu^{k+1}(1) = -\frac{1}{2J_{\mu^k}(1)},$$

so that $J_{\mu^{k+1}} = 2J_{\mu^k}$, and $J_{\mu^k} \downarrow J^* = -\infty$ since $J_{\mu^0} < 0$.

(b) The optimistic PI and λ-PI algorithms starting from $J_0 = \bar{J} = 0$ generate sequences $\{J_k\}$ with $J_k \downarrow J^*$.

4.7 (Counterexample for Policy Improvement Under D - Infinite State Space)

Consider the deterministic stopping problem of Exercise 4.1. Let μ be the policy that stops at every state.

(a) Show that the next policy $\overline{\mu}$ generated by nonoptimistic PI is to continue at every state, and that we have

$$J_{\overline{\mu}}(x) = 0 > -1 + \frac{1}{x} = J_\mu(x), \qquad x \in X.$$

Moreover, the method oscillates between the policies μ and $\overline{\mu}$, none of which is optimal.

(b) The optimistic PI and λ-PI algorithms starting from $J_0 = \bar{J} = 0$ generate sequences $\{J_k\}$ with $J_k \downarrow J^*$.

4.8 (Counterexample for Policy Improvement Under D - Finite State Space)

Consider a finite-state version of the problem of Exercises 4.1 and 4.7, where the state space is $X = \{1, \ldots, n\}$ and there are two controls: stop and continue. Continuation from states $x = 1, \ldots, n-1$ leads to state $x + 1$ at no cost, while continuation at state $x = n$ keeps the state at n with no cost. The stopping cost is $-1 + (1/x)$ for all $x > 0$. Here $\bar{J}(x) \equiv 0$, and

$$H(x, u, J) = \begin{cases} J(x+1) & \text{if } x = 1, \ldots, n-1, \text{ and } u = \text{continue}, \\ J(x) & \text{if } x = n, \text{ and } u = \text{continue}, \\ -1 + (1/x) & \text{if } x = 1, \ldots, n, \text{ and } u = \text{stop}. \end{cases}$$

(a) Show that the pathology of Exercise 4.7(a) still can occur: nonoptimistic PI can oscillate between the policy μ that stops at every state and the policy $\overline{\mu}$ that continues at every state, and that none of these two policies is optimal (at any state except $x = n$). *Note*: This can be viewed as an example of a finite-state SSP problem where there exists an optimal proper policy, and all improper policies are not optimal (but have finite cost for all initial states). The latter fact invalidates Assumption 3.2.1 of Chapter 3, and as a result the proof of Prop. 3.2.1 breaks down.

(b) Show that the pathology of part (a) still occurs if μ is replaced by the optimal policy, which is to stop at $x = n$ and to continue at $x \neq n$. *Note*: Here we have $T_{\overline{\mu}} J^* = TJ^*$ even though $\overline{\mu}$ is not optimal.

4.9 (Infinite Time Reachability [Ber72])

This exercise provides an instance of an interesting problem where the mapping H is naturally extended real-valued. Consider a dynamic system

$$x_{k+1} = f(x_k, u_k, w_k),$$

where w_k is viewed as an uncertain disturbance that may be any point in a set $W(x_k, u_k)$ (this is known in the literature as an "unknown but bounded" disturbance, and is the basis for a worst case/minimax treatment of uncertainty in the control of uncertain dynamic systems). We introduce an abstract DP model where the objective is to find a policy that keeps the state x_k of the system within a given set X at all times, for all possible values of the sequence $\{w_k\}$. This is a common objective, which arises in a variety of control theory contexts, including model predictive control.

Let

$$\bar{J}(x) = \begin{cases} 0 & \text{if } x \in X, \\ \infty & \text{otherwise,} \end{cases}$$

and

$$H(x, u, J) = \begin{cases} 0 & \text{if } J(x) = 0,\ u \in U(x), \text{ and } J\big(f(x, u, w)\big) = 0,\ \forall\ w \in W(x, u), \\ \infty & \text{otherwise.} \end{cases}$$

(a) Show that Assumption I holds, and that the optimal cost function has the form

$$J^*(x) = \begin{cases} 0 & \text{if } x \in X^*, \\ \infty & \text{otherwise,} \end{cases}$$

where X^* is some subset of X.

(b) Consider the sequence of sets $\{X_k\}$, where

$$X_k = \big\{ x \in X \mid (T^k \bar{J})(x) = 0 \big\}.$$

Show that $X_{k+1} \subset X_k$ for all k, and that $X^* \subset \cap_{k=0}^{\infty} X_k$. Show also that convergence of VI (i.e., $T^k \bar{J} \to J^*$) is equivalent to $X^* = \cap_{k=0}^{\infty} X_k$.

(c) Show that $X^* = \cap_{k=0}^{\infty} X_k$ and there exists an optimal stationary policy if the sets X_k are compact for all k greater than some index $\bar{k}$. *Hint*: Use Prop. 4.3.14.

5

Models with Restricted Policies

Contents

In this chapter, we discuss variants of some of the models of the preceding chapters, where there are restrictions on the set of policies. In particular, policies may be selected from a strict subset $\overline{\mathcal{M}}$ of the set of functions $\mu : X \mapsto U$ with $\mu(x) \in U(x)$ for all $x \in X$. One potential use of such a restriction arises when $\overline{\mathcal{M}}$ consists of specially structured policies that result in convenient characterization and computation. Classical examples of situations of this type are linear policies in linear-quadratic optimal control problems, (s, S) policies in inventory control, and various threshold policies in queueing and scheduling problems (see e.g., [Ber05a], [Ber12a], [Put94]). In this context, the main focus of the analysis is to show that attention can be confined to the policies $\mu \in \overline{\mathcal{M}}$ and their associated mappings T_μ. If this can be shown, then the analytical solution of Bellman's equation may be enhanced, and the computational solution using for example policy iteration that is restricted within $\overline{\mathcal{M}}$ may be facilitated (cf. Section 4.4.3, which deals with linear-quadratic optimal control).

Another major use arises in mathematically rigorous probabilistic treatments of stochastic optimal control problems, and relates to the need for μ to be measurable in an appropriate sense. We take this as the starting point and motivation for the development of a general theory of restricted models in the next section, and we develop this theory in subsequent sections for finite horizon and for contractive models. In the last section of this chapter, we return to the treatment of measurability issues using the theory developed in the earlier sections.

5.1 A FRAMEWORK FOR RESTRICTED POLICIES

As a motivating example, let us consider the mapping H of the stochastic optimal control Example 1.2.1,

$$H(x, u, J) = E\big\{g(x, u, w) + \alpha J\big(f(x, u, w)\big)\big\}. \tag{5.1}$$

We have considered so far the case where w is a discrete random variable, taking a finite or a countably infinite set of values, so that the mapping T_μ is defined for all $\mu \in \mathcal{M}$ in terms of a summation. In the general case, however, where w is a continuous random variable, H is well-defined only if the expected value over w is well-defined. For this it is necessary to introduce an appropriate probability space for w, and for g and f to be appropriately measurable.

Most importantly, we cannot simply take J to belong to $E(X)$, the space of extended real-valued functions over X. We must restrict J to a subset $\overline{E}(X) \subset E(X)$, consisting of appropriately measurable functions. In addition, to define T_μ as a function from $\overline{E}(X)$ to $\overline{E}(X)$ by

$$(T_\mu J)(x) = H\big(x, \mu(x), J\big)$$

or equivalently

$$(T_\mu J)(x) = E\big\{g(x,\mu(x),w) + \alpha J\big(f(x,\mu(x),w)\big)\big\},$$

μ must belong to a subclass $\overline{\mathcal{M}}$ of appropriately measurable functions from $\mathcal{M}$. Appendix C provides a further illustration of the measurability issues through a simple two-stage example, and also introduces some of the terminology and background on measure theoretic issues, based on Borel measurability, which we will use in this chapter (the monograph [BeS78] contains an extensive account of this material).

The preceding discussion indicates that to define a restricted policies model, we need at least two basic subsets of functions and policies:

(a) A *restricted set of functions* $\overline{E}(X) \subset E(X)$.

(b) A *restricted set of policies* $\overline{\mathcal{M}} \subset \mathcal{M}$, such that

$$T_\mu J \in \overline{E}(X), \qquad \forall\ J \in \overline{E}(X),\ \mu \in \overline{\mathcal{M}},$$

where T_μ is given by

$$(T_\mu J)(x) = H\big(x,\mu(x),J\big), \qquad \forall\ x \in X.$$

To conduct an analysis similar to the one of earlier chapters, we also need to concern ourselves with the corresponding mapping T. To this end, we assume, without loss of generality, that

$$U(x) = \big\{\mu(x) \mid \mu \in \overline{\mathcal{M}}\big\}, \qquad \forall\ x \in X,$$

so that the mapping T can be interchangeably defined as

$$(TJ)(x) = \inf_{\mu \in \overline{\mathcal{M}}} (T_\mu J)(x), \qquad \forall\ J \in \overline{E}(X),\ x \in X,$$

or as

$$(TJ)(x) = \inf_{u \in U(x)} H(x,u,J), \qquad \forall\ J \in \overline{E}(X),\ x \in X. \tag{5.2}$$

An issue to contend with here is whether the infimum in the definition of TJ is attained, exactly or within a small tolerance $\epsilon > 0$, by a policy in $\overline{\mathcal{M}}$ (simultaneously for all x), i.e., whether there exists $\mu \in \overline{\mathcal{M}}$ such that $(T_\mu J)(x)$ is close to $(TJ)(x)$ uniformly for all $x \in X$. This issue turns out to be quite delicate in the context of stochastic optimal control problems, as we will discuss shortly. We first consider the case where the infimum is exactly attained, and then address the more complex case where it is not.

Models Admitting Exact Selection

Let us assume that $\overline{E}(X)$ and $\overline{\mathcal{M}}$ have been defined as described above. Consider the case where there exists $\mu \in \overline{\mathcal{M}}$ such that the infimum in Eq. (5.2) is attained at $\mu(x)$ for all $x \in X$, i.e., for all $J \in \overline{E}(X)$ there exists a $\mu \in \overline{\mathcal{M}}$ such that

$$T_\mu J = TJ. \tag{5.3}$$

Otherwise stated, *for all $J \in \overline{E}(X)$, the minimization in Eq. (5.2) admits an exact selector μ from within $\overline{\mathcal{M}}$.* Then assuming also that T and T_μ, $\mu \in \overline{\mathcal{M}}$, preserve membership in $\overline{E}(X)$, i.e.,

$$T_\mu J \in \overline{E}(X), \quad TJ \in \overline{E}(X), \qquad \forall\ J \in \overline{E}(X),\ \mu \in \overline{\mathcal{M}}, \tag{5.4}$$

a large portion of the analysis of the preceding chapters carries through verbatim, and much of the remainder can be extended with minimal modifications.

In particular, in the finite horizon problems of Chapter 4, under this condition, the condition $\bar{J} \in \overline{E}(X)$, and the monotonicity assumption

$$H(x,u,J) \leq H(x,u,J'), \qquad \forall\ J,J' \in \overline{E}(X),\ x \in X,\ u \in U(x), \tag{5.5}$$

we have $J_N^* = T^N \bar{J}$ and that there exists an N-stage optimal policy. Such a policy can be obtained via the DP algorithm that starts with the terminal cost function $\bar{J}$, and sequentially computes $T\bar{J}, T^2\bar{J}, \ldots, T^N\bar{J}$, and corresponding $\mu_{N-1}^*, \mu_{N-2}^*, \ldots, \mu_0^* \in \overline{\mathcal{M}}$ such that

$$T_{\mu_k^*} T^{N-k-1}\bar{J} = T^{N-k}\bar{J}, \qquad k = 0,\ldots,N-1, \tag{5.6}$$

(cf. the discussion in the early part of Section 4.2).

To extend the analysis of the contractive models of Chapter 2, under Eqs. (5.3) and (5.4), we need to assume that $\overline{E}(X)$ is a *closed* subset of $B(X)$, the space of functions $J : X \mapsto \Re$ that are bounded with respect to a weighted sup-norm. This is necessary so that the fixed point theorems of Appendix B apply. We also need to assume that the mappings T_μ are contractions for all $\mu \in \overline{\mathcal{M}}$ with respect to a common weighted sup-norm. Then the relevant portion of the analysis of Chapter 2 carries through with hardly any change. The analysis of the semicontractive and infinite horizon noncontractive models of Chapters 3 and 4, also admit a similar treatment, under the exact selection assumption (5.3) and Eq. (5.4).

Generally, when the exact selection property (5.3) holds in the context of the stochastic optimal control example where H is defined by Eq. (5.1), there are few complications in providing a rigorous mathematical treatment, even when w is a continuous random variable. Typically X, U, and W are taken to be Borel spaces, $\overline{E}(X)$ and $\overline{\mathcal{M}}$ are chosen to be the spaces of Borel measurable functions from X to $\Re^*$, and from X to U, respectively. Also g, f, and the probability space of w must satisfy certain Borel measurability conditions (see Appendix C).

Models Without Exact Selection

When the exact selection property (5.3) may not hold, to conduct any kind of meaningful analysis, it is necessary to adopt a restriction framework for policies and functions, which guarantees that TJ can be approximated by $T_\mu J$, with appropriate choice of μ. To this end, a seemingly natural assumption would be that given $J \in \overline{E}(X)$ and $\epsilon > 0$, *there exists an ϵ-optimal selector*, that is, a $\mu_\epsilon \in \overline{\mathcal{M}}$ such that

$$(T_{\mu_\epsilon} J)(x) \leq \begin{cases} (TJ)(x) + \epsilon & \text{if } (TJ)(x) > -\infty, \\ -(1/\epsilon) & \text{if } (TJ)(x) = -\infty, \end{cases} \qquad \forall\, x \in X. \tag{5.7}$$

However, in the Borel space model noted earlier and described in Appendix C, there is a serious difficulty: *if $\overline{E}(X)$ and $\overline{\mathcal{M}}$ are the spaces of Borel measurable functions from X to $\Re^*$, and from X to U, respectively, there need not exist an ϵ-optimal selector*. For this reason, Borel measurability of cost functions and policies is not the most appropriate probabilistic framework for stochastic optimal control problems.† Instead, in the most general framework for bypassing this difficulty, it is necessary to consider a different kind of measurability, which is described in Appendix C. In this framework:

(a) $\overline{E}(X)$ is taken to be the class of universally measurable functions from X to $\Re^*$.

(b) $\overline{\mathcal{M}}$ is taken to be the class of universally measurable functions from X to U.

(c) g, f, and the probability space of w must satisfy certain Borel measurability conditions.

A key fact is that an ϵ-selection property holds, whereby there exists a $\mu_\epsilon \in \overline{\mathcal{M}}$ such that

$$(T_{\mu_\epsilon} J)(x) \leq \begin{cases} (TJ)(x) + \epsilon & \text{if } (TJ)(x) > -\infty, \\ -(1/\epsilon) & \text{if } (TJ)(x) = -\infty, \end{cases} \qquad \forall\, x \in X, \tag{5.8}$$

---

† There have been efforts to address the lack of an ϵ-optimal selector within the Borel measurability framework using the concept of a "p-ϵ-optimal selector," whereby the concept of ϵ-optimal selection is modified to hold over a set for states that has p-measure 1, with p being any chosen probability measure over X (see [Str66], [Str75], [DyY79]). This leads to a theory based on p-ϵ-optimal and p-optimal policies, i.e., policies that depend on the choice of p and are optimal only for states in a subset of X that has p-measure 1 (rather than over all states as in our case). It seems difficult to extend the abstract framework of this book based on this inherently probabilistic viewpoint. For a related discussion and a comparison of the p-ϵ-optimal approach with ours, we refer to [BeS78].

for each J in the class $\hat{E}(X)$ of *lower semianalytic* functions from X to $\Re^*$; this is a strict subset of $\overline{E}(X)$, the set of universally measurable functions (see Appendix C).

Because of the difficulty with ϵ-selection within a Borel measurability framework, to construct a more generally applicable restricted policies model, it is necessary to introduce the set of lower semianalytic functions $\hat{E}(X)$ within the Borel space framework, as a *third subset*, additional to $\overline{E}(X)$ and $\overline{\mathcal{M}}$. In summary:

(a) We take $\overline{E}(X)$ to be the class of universally measurable functions from X to $\Re^*$, and $\overline{\mathcal{M}}$ to be the class of universally measurable functions from X to U. Then, $T_\mu J \in \overline{E}(X)$ for all $\mu \in \overline{\mathcal{M}}$ and $J \in \overline{E}(X)$, so the cost function of a policy lies in $\overline{E}(X)$.

(b) We take $\hat{E}(X)$ to be the set of lower semianalytic functions from X to $\Re^*$. Then we have $TJ \in \hat{E}(X)$ for all $J \in \hat{E}(X)$, and the ϵ-selection property (5.8) holds. As a result, the VI algorithm produces functions in $\hat{E}(X)$, if started within in $\hat{E}(X)$, and J^* can be proved to lie in $\hat{E}(X)$.

Motivated by the preceding discussion, we will now introduce a model that involves a set of policies $\overline{\mathcal{M}}$, and two sets of functions $\overline{E}(X)$ and $\hat{E}(X)$ with properties that are analogous to the ones just discussed for Borel space models for stochastic optimal control, along with some additional technical assumptions. We will use this model for the analysis of abstract finite and infinite horizon problems, and we will review later its use within the Borel measurability framework.

5.1.1 General Assumptions

As in Section 4.1, we have the sets X and U, and we introduce a set $\overline{\mathcal{M}}$ of functions $\mu : X \mapsto U$, which we view as a restricted set of stationary policies. We define

$$U(x) = \big\{\mu(x) \mid \mu \in \overline{\mathcal{M}}\big\}, \qquad \forall\, x \in X, \tag{5.9}$$

and we assume that $U(x)$ is nonempty for all $x \in X$. The corresponding set of (nonstationary) policies $\pi = \{\mu_0, \mu_1, \ldots\}$ with $\mu_k \in \overline{\mathcal{M}}$, $k = 0, 1, \ldots$, is denoted by $\overline{\Pi}$. We introduce two subsets $\hat{E}(X)$ and $\overline{E}(X)$ of $E(X)$ (the set of extended real-valued functions on X), such that

$$\hat{E}(X) \subset \overline{E}(X),$$

and the following assumption is satisfied.

Assumption 5.1.1:

(a) For each sequence $\{J_m\} \subset \overline{E}(X)$ with $J_m \to J$, we have $J \in \overline{E}(X)$, and for each sequence $\{J_m\} \subset \hat{E}(X)$ with $J_m \to J$, we have $J \in \hat{E}(X)$.

(b) For all $r \in \Re$, we have

$$J \in \overline{E}(X) \quad \Rightarrow \quad J + r\,e \in \overline{E}(X),$$

and

$$J \in \hat{E}(X) \quad \Rightarrow \quad J + r\,e \in \hat{E}(X),$$

where e is the unit function, $e(x) \equiv 1$.

We also introduce a mapping $H : X \times U \times \overline{E}(X) \mapsto \Re^*$ satisfying the monotonicity assumption.

Assumption 5.1.2: (Monotonicity) If $J, J' \in \overline{E}(X)$ and $J \leq J'$, then

$$H(x, u, J) \leq H(x, u, J'), \qquad \forall\, x \in X,\ u \in U(x).$$

We define the mapping $T : \overline{E}(X) \mapsto \Re^*$ by

$$(TJ)(x) = \inf_{u \in U(x)} H(x, u, J), \qquad \forall\, x \in X,\ J \in \overline{E}(X),$$

and for each $\mu \in \overline{\mathcal{M}}$, the mapping $T_\mu : \overline{E}(X) \mapsto \Re^*$ by

$$(T_\mu J)(x) = H\big(x, \mu(x), J\big), \qquad \forall\, x \in X,\ J \in \overline{E}(X).$$

Note that in view of the definition (5.9) of $U(x)$, we also have

$$(TJ)(x) = \inf_{\mu \in \overline{\mathcal{M}}} (T_\mu J)(x), \qquad \forall\, x \in X,\ J \in \overline{E}(X),$$

or in shorthand

$$TJ = \inf_{\mu \in \overline{\mathcal{M}}} T_\mu J.$$

The sets $\overline{\mathcal{M}}$, $\overline{E}(X)$, and $\hat{E}(X)$, and the mappings T_μ and T are assumed to satisfy the following.

Assumption 5.1.3:

(a) For all $\mu \in \overline{\mathcal{M}}$, we have

$$J \in \overline{E}(X) \qquad \Rightarrow \qquad T_\mu J \in \overline{E}(X).$$

(b) We have

$$J \in \hat{E}(X) \qquad \Rightarrow \qquad TJ \in \hat{E}(X).$$

Finally, we require that $\hat{E}(X)$ has the following critical ϵ-selection property.

Assumption 5.1.4: (ϵ-Selection) For each $J \in \hat{E}(X)$ and $\epsilon > 0$, there exists a $\mu_\epsilon \in \overline{\mathcal{M}}$ such that

$$(T_{\mu_\epsilon} J)(x) \leq \begin{cases} (TJ)(x) + \epsilon & \text{if } (TJ)(x) > -\infty, \\ -(1/\epsilon) & \text{if } (TJ)(x) = -\infty, \end{cases} \qquad \forall\, x \in X. \tag{5.10}$$

The relevant selection theorem, which guarantees that the Assumption 5.1.4 holds in the stochastic optimal control context is given as Prop. C.5 in Appendix C. Note that Assumption 5.1.3 does not guarantee that $T_\mu J \in \hat{E}(X)$ for $J \in \hat{E}(X)$. As a result, the function $T_{\mu_\epsilon} J$ of Assumption 5.1.4 is only guaranteed to belong to the larger set $\overline{E}(X)$.

Problem Formulation

We are given a function $\bar{J} \in \hat{E}(X)$ satisfying

$$\bar{J}(x) > -\infty, \qquad \forall\, x \in X, \tag{5.11}$$

and we consider for every policy $\pi = \{\mu_0, \mu_1, \ldots\} \in \overline{\Pi}$ and positive integer N the function $J_{N,\pi} \in \overline{E}(X)$ defined by

$$J_{N,\pi}(x) = (T_{\mu_0} \cdots T_{\mu_{N-1}} \bar{J})(x), \qquad \forall\, x \in X,$$

and the function J_π defined by

$$J_\pi(x) = \limsup_{k \to \infty} (T_{\mu_0} \cdots T_{\mu_k} \bar{J})(x), \qquad \forall\, x \in X.$$

For a stationary policy $\pi = \{\mu, \mu, \ldots\}$ we also write J_μ in place of J_π.

As earlier, we consider the N-stage optimization problem

$$\begin{aligned} &\text{minimize} \quad J_{N,\pi}(x) \\ &\text{subject to} \quad \pi \in \overline{\Pi}, \end{aligned} \tag{5.12}$$

and its infinite horizon version

$$\begin{aligned} &\text{minimize} \quad J_{\pi}(x) \\ &\text{subject to} \quad \pi \in \overline{\Pi}. \end{aligned} \tag{5.13}$$

For a fixed $x \in X$, we denote by $J_N^*(x)$ and $J^*(x)$ the optimal costs for these problems, i.e.,

$$J_N^*(x) = \inf_{\pi \in \overline{\Pi}} J_{N,\pi}(x), \qquad J^*(x) = \inf_{\pi \in \overline{\Pi}} J_{\pi}(x), \qquad \forall\, x \in X.$$

We say that a policy $\pi^* \in \overline{\Pi}$ is *N-stage optimal* if

$$J_{N,\pi^*}(x) = J_N^*(x), \qquad \forall\, x \in X,$$

and (infinite horizon) *optimal* if

$$J_{\pi^*}(x) = J^*(x), \qquad \forall\, x \in X.$$

For a given $\epsilon > 0$, we say that $\pi_\epsilon \in \overline{\Pi}$ is *N-stage ϵ-optimal* if

$$J_{\pi_\epsilon}(x) \le \begin{cases} J_N^*(x) + \epsilon & \text{if } J_N^*(x) > -\infty, \\ -(1/\epsilon) & \text{if } J_N^*(x) = -\infty, \end{cases}$$

and we say that π_ϵ is (infinite horizon) *ϵ-optimal* if

$$J_{\pi_\epsilon}(x) \le \begin{cases} J^*(x) + \epsilon & \text{if } J^*(x) > -\infty, \\ -(1/\epsilon) & \text{if } J^*(x) = -\infty. \end{cases}$$

Note that since $\bar{J} \in \hat{E}(X)$, the function $T^k \bar{J}$ belongs to $\hat{E}(X)$ for all k [cf. Assumption 5.1.3(b)]. Similar to Chapter 4, we will aim to show under various assumptions that $J_N^* = T^N \bar{J}$, and that $J^* \in \hat{E}(X)$ and $J^* = TJ^*$.

5.2 FINITE HORIZON PROBLEMS

To show that $J_N^* = T^N \bar{J}$, we use an analysis that is similar to the one of Section 4.2. In particular, we introduce the following assumption, which is analogous to Assumption 4.2.1.

Assumption 5.2.1: For each sequence $\{J_m\} \subset \overline{E}(X)$ with $J_m \downarrow J$ for some $J \in \overline{E}(X)$, we have

$$\lim_{m\to\infty} H(x,u,J_m) \le H(x,u,J), \qquad \forall\, x \in X,\ u \in U(x). \tag{5.14}$$

Note that Assumption 5.1.1 implies that if $\{J_m\} \subset \overline{E}(X)$ and $J_m \downarrow J \in \overline{E}(X)$, we have

$$J = \lim_{m\to\infty} J_m = \inf_{m=0,1,\ldots} J_m \in \overline{E}(X),$$

so for all $\mu \in \overline{\mathcal{M}}$, by Assumption 5.2.1,

$$\inf_m (T_\mu J_m) = T_\mu \left(\inf_m J_m\right).$$

This inequality can be extended for any $\mu_1,\ldots,\mu_k \in \overline{\mathcal{M}}$ as follows:

$$\begin{aligned} \inf_m (T_{\mu_1}\cdots T_{\mu_k} J_m) &= T_{\mu_1}\left(\inf_m (T_{\mu_1}\cdots T_{\mu_k} J_m)\right) \\ &= \cdots \\ &= T_{\mu_1}\cdots T_{\mu_k}\left(\inf_m J_m\right). \end{aligned} \tag{5.15}$$

We have the following proposition, which extends Prop. 4.2.3 to the restricted policies framework.

Proposition 5.2.1: Let Assumptions 5.1.1-5.1.4 and 5.2.1 hold. Then

$$J_N^* = T^N \bar{J}.$$

Proof: We select for each $k = 0,\ldots,N-1$, a sequence $\{\mu_k^m\} \subset \overline{\mathcal{M}}$ such that

$$\lim_{m\to\infty} T_{\mu_k^m}(T^{N-k-1}\bar{J}) \downarrow T^{N-k}\bar{J}.$$

This is possible in view of the ϵ-selection property of Assumption 5.1.4, since $T^{N-k}\bar{J} \in \hat{E}(X)$ [cf. Assumption 5.1.3(b)]. Using Eq. (5.15), we have

$$
\begin{aligned}
J_N^* &\leq \inf_{m_0} \cdots \inf_{m_{N-1}} T_{\mu_0}^{m_0} \cdots T_{\mu_{N-1}}^{m_{N-1}} \bar{J} \\
&= \inf_{m_0} \cdots \inf_{m_{N-2}} T_{\mu_0}^{m_0} \cdots T_{\mu_{N-2}}^{m_{N-2}} \left(\inf_{m_{N-1}} T_{\mu_{N-1}}^{m_{N-1}} \bar{J} \right) \\
&= \inf_{m_0} \cdots \inf_{m_{N-2}} T_{\mu_0}^{m_0} \cdots T_{\mu_{N-2}}^{m_{N-2}} T\bar{J} \\
&= \cdots \\
&= T^N \bar{J},
\end{aligned}
$$

where the last equality is obtained by repeating the process used to obtain the previous equalities. On the other hand, it is clear from the definitions that $T^N\bar{J} \leq J_{N,\pi}$ for all N and $\pi \in \Pi$, so that $T^N\bar{J} \leq J_N^*$. Thus, $J_N^* = T^N\bar{J}$. **Q.E.D.**

We also introduce the following alternative assumption, which parallels Assumption 4.2.2.

Assumption 5.2.2: The k-stages optimal cost function J_k^* satisfies

$$J_k^*(x) > -\infty, \qquad \forall\, x \in X,\ k = 1, \ldots, N.$$

Moreover, there exists a scalar $\alpha \in (0, \infty)$ such that for all scalars $r \in (0, \infty)$ and functions $J \in \overline{E}(X)$, we have

$$H(x,u,J) \leq H(x,u,J+r\,e) \leq H(x,u,J)+\alpha\, r, \qquad \forall\, x \in X,\ u \in U(x). \tag{5.16}$$

We have the following proposition whose statement and proof parallel the ones of Prop. 4.2.4.

Proposition 5.2.2: Let Assumptions 5.1.1-5.1.4, and 5.2.2 hold. Then $J_N^* = T^N\bar{J}$, and for every $\epsilon > 0$, there exists an ϵ-optimal policy.

Proof: Note that since by assumption, $J_N^*(x) > -\infty$ for all $x \in X$, an N-stage ϵ-optimal policy $\pi_\epsilon \in \overline{\Pi}$ is one for which

$$J_N^* \leq J_{N,\pi_\epsilon} \leq J_N^* + \epsilon\, e.$$

We use induction. The result clearly holds for $N = 1$. Assume that it holds for $N = k$, i.e., $J_k^* = T^k\bar{J} \in \hat{E}(X)$ and for a given $\epsilon > 0$, there is a

$\pi_e \in \overline{\Pi}$ with $J_{k,\pi_\epsilon} \le J_k^* + \epsilon\, e$. Using Eq. (5.16), we have for all $\mu \in \overline{\mathcal{M}}$,

$$J_{k+1}^* \le T_\mu J_{k,\pi_\epsilon} \le T_\mu J_k^* + \alpha\epsilon\, e.$$

Taking the infimum over μ and then the limit as $\epsilon \to 0$, we obtain $J_{k+1}^* \le TJ_k^*$. By using the induction hypothesis, it follows that $J_{k+1}^* \le T^{k+1}\bar{J}$. On the other hand, we have clearly $T^{k+1}\bar{J} \le J_{k+1}^*$, and hence $T^{k+1}\bar{J} = J_{k+1}^*$.

Using the assumption $J_k^*(x) > -\infty$ for all $x \in X$, for any $\bar{\epsilon} > 0$, we can choose $\bar{\pi} = \{\bar{\mu}_0, \bar{\mu}_1, \ldots\} \in \overline{\Pi}$ such that

$$J_{k,\bar{\pi}} \le J_k^* + \frac{\bar{\epsilon}}{2\alpha}\, e,$$

and $\bar{\mu} \in \overline{\mathcal{M}}$ such that

$$T_{\bar{\mu}} J_k^* \le TJ_k^* + \frac{\bar{\epsilon}}{2}\, e.$$

Let $\bar{\pi}_{\bar{\epsilon}} = \{\bar{\mu}, \bar{\mu}_0, \bar{\mu}_1, \ldots\}$. Then

$$J_{k+1,\bar{\pi}_{\bar{\epsilon}}} = T_{\bar{\mu}} J_{k,\bar{\pi}} \le T_{\bar{\mu}} J_k^* + \frac{\bar{\epsilon}}{2}\, e \le TJ_k^* + \bar{\epsilon}\, e = J_{k+1}^* + \bar{\epsilon}\, e,$$

where the first inequality is obtained by using Eq. (5.16). The induction is complete. **Q.E.D.**

5.3 CONTRACTIVE MODELS

In this section, we will discuss briefly the infinite horizon problem

$$\begin{aligned} &\text{minimize} \quad J_\pi(x) \\ &\text{subject to} \quad \pi \in \overline{\Pi}, \end{aligned} \tag{5.17}$$

where for a policy $\{\mu_0, \mu_1, \ldots\} \in \overline{\Pi}$, $J_\pi \in \overline{E}(X)$ is defined by

$$J_\pi(x) = \limsup_{k\to\infty} (T_{\mu_0} \cdots T_{\mu_k} \bar{J})(x), \qquad \forall\, x \in X.$$

We analyze this problem under a contraction assumption, similar to Chapter 2. To this end, we introduce a function $v : X \mapsto \Re$ with

$$v(x) > 0, \qquad \forall\, x \in X,$$

and we consider the weighted sup-norm

$$\|J\| = \sup_{x\in X} \frac{\big|J(x)\big|}{v(x)}$$

on $B(X)$, the space of real-valued functions J on X such that $J(x)/v(x)$ is bounded over $x \in X$.

In addition to the Assumptions 5.1.1-5.1.4, we assume the following.

Assumption 5.3.1: (Contraction)

(a) The sets $\overline{E}(X)$ and $\hat{E}(X)$ are closed subsets of $B(X)$.

(b) For some $\alpha \in (0,1)$, we have

$$\|T_\mu J - T_\mu J'\| \leq \alpha \|J - J'\|, \qquad \forall\, J, J' \in \overline{E}(X),\ \mu \in \overline{\mathcal{M}}. \tag{5.18}$$

The analysis of Chapter 2 carries through with few modifications. In particular the following analog of the major analytical result of Chapter 2, can be proved with an essentially identical proof. The key fact here is that $\overline{E}(X)$ and $\hat{E}(X)$ are closed subsets of $B(X)$, so the Contraction Mapping Theorem (Prop. B.1) applies.

Proposition 5.3.1: Let Assumptions 5.1.1-5.1.4 and the contraction Assumption 5.3.1 hold. Then:

(a) For all $\mu \in \overline{\mathcal{M}}$, the mapping T_μ is a contraction mapping with modulus α over $\overline{E}(X)$, and its unique fixed point within $\overline{E}(X)$ is J_μ.

(b) The mapping T is a contraction mapping with modulus α over $\hat{E}(X)$, and its unique fixed point within $\hat{E}(X)$ is equal to J^*.

(c) For any $J \in \overline{E}(X)$ and $\mu \in \overline{\mathcal{M}}$, we have

$$\lim_{k\to\infty} T_\mu^k J = J_\mu.$$

(d) For any $J \in \hat{E}(X)$, we have

$$\lim_{k\to\infty} T^k J = J^*.$$

(e) We have $T_\mu J^* = TJ^*$ if and only if $J_\mu = J^*$.

(f) For every $\epsilon > 0$ there exists an ϵ-optimal policy within $\overline{\mathcal{M}}$.

Proof: As in Section 1.2, T_μ is a contraction with modulus α over $\overline{E}(X)$. Similarly, T is a contraction with modulus α over $\hat{E}(X)$. Parts (a), (b), (c), and (d) follow from Prop. B.1 of Appendix B.

To show part (e), note that if $T_\mu J^* = TJ^*$, then in view of $TJ^* = J^*$, we have $T_\mu J^* = J^*$, which implies that $J^* = J_\mu$, since J_μ is the unique fixed point of T_μ. Conversely, if $J_\mu = J^*$, we have

$$T_\mu J^* = T_\mu J_\mu = J_\mu = J^* = TJ^*.$$

Part (f) follows similarly, using the proof of Prop. 2.1.2. **Q.E.D.**

5.4 BOREL SPACE MODELS

We will now apply the preceding analysis to models where the set of policies is restricted in order to address measurability issues. The Borel space model is the most general such model, and we will focus on it. Appendix C provides a motivation and an outline of the model for finite horizon problems, including the associated mathematical definitions, some basic results, and a two-stage example. In this section we will provide a brief discussion of an infinite horizon contractive model.

We consider the mapping H defined by

$$H(x, u, J) = g(x, u) + \alpha \int J(y)\, p(dy \mid x, u). \tag{5.19}$$

Here X and U are Borel spaces, α is a scalar in $(0, 1]$, J is an extended real-valued functions on X, and $p(dy \mid x, u)$ is a transition probability measure for each x and $u \in U(x)$. To make mathematical sense of the expression in the right-hand side of Eq. (5.19), J must satisfy certain measurability restrictions, so we assume that g is Borel measurable and that $p(dy \mid x, u)$ is a Borel measurable stochastic kernel. We let

$$\overline{E}(X) = \text{ the subset of universally measurable functions from } E(X).$$

Then the integral in Eq. (5.19) is well-defined as an extended real number for every (x, u) for all $J \in \overline{E}(X)$ (recall that in our integration framework we allow the sum $\infty - \infty$ to appear and interpret it as ∞).

A requirement of the framework of this chapter is that $T_\mu J$ must belong to $\overline{E}(X)$ for each $J \in \overline{E}(X)$. For this it is sufficient that g be Borel measurable as a function of (x, u), and the policy μ be a universally measurable function of x. However, as noted earlier, universal measurability of H [as a function of (x, u) for fixed J] is insufficient to guarantee that $TJ \in \overline{E}(X)$. We thus let

$$\hat{E}(X) = \text{ the subset of lower semianalytic functions from } \overline{E}(X).$$

Then assuming that $J \in \hat{E}(X)$, that $g(x,u)$ and $p(dy \mid x,u)$ are Borel measurable, and that the set

$$\big\{(x,u) \mid u \in U(x)\big\}$$

is Borel measurable, we have that the function $H(\cdot,\cdot,J)$ is lower semianalytic and $TJ \in \hat{E}(X)$, as discussed in Appendix C (cf. Prop. C.4).

Note that our framework requires that ϵ-optimal selection is possible, i.e., that for every $\epsilon > 0$, there exists a universally measurable μ such that the conditions of Assumption 5.1.4 are satisfied. This is ensured under our assumptions by the selection theorem of Prop. C.5 in Appendix C.

We now consider a contractive infinite horizon problem, which is based on the mapping H defined by Eq. (5.19), where $\alpha \in (0,1)$ is a discount factor, and the preceding conditions hold. In addition g is assumed to be not only Borel measurable, but also bounded above and below, in which case we obtain a contractive model in the space of bounded functions $B(X)$ with respect to the unweighted sup-norm. It is important to note that $\overline{E}(X)$ and $\hat{E}(X)$ are closed subsets of $B(X)$, since the pointwise limit of universally measurable and lower semianalytic functions are universally measurable and lower semianalytic, respectively (see [BeS78]).

Thus Prop. 5.3.1 applies and provides the basic analytical results for contractive Borel space models, which are:

(a) J^* is the unique fixed point of T within $\hat{E}(X)$.

(b) For every $J \in \hat{E}(X)$, $T^kJ \in \hat{E}(X)$ for all k, and we have $T^kJ \to J^*$.

(c) There exists a universally measurable optimal policy if and only if the infimum of $H(x,u,J^*)$ over u is attained for each $x \in X$.

(d) For any $\epsilon > 0$, there exists an ϵ-optimal universally measurable policy.

For a detailed discussion and proofs of these results, we refer to [BeS78].

5.5 NOTES, SOURCES, AND EXERCISES

The restricted model framework of this chapter was treated briefly in the book [BeS78] (Chapter 6). This book focused far more extensively on the classical type of stochastic optimal control problems (cf. Example 1.2.1), rather than the more general abstract restricted model case.

The restricted policies framework may also be applied to the so-called *semicontinuous models* similar to how it was applied to Borel models in Section 5.4. The semicontinuous models provide more powerful results regarding the character of the cost functions, but require additional assumptions, which may be restrictive, namely that the cost function g and the stochastic kernel p in Eq. (5.19) have certain upper or lower semicontinuity properties. The relevant mathematical background is given in Section 7.5 of [BeS78], and the critical selection theorems (with Borel measurable selection) are given in Props. 7.33 and 7.34 of that reference. Detailed related references to the literature may also be found in [BeS78].

APPENDIX A:

Notation and Mathematical Conventions

In this appendix we collect our notation, and some related mathematical facts and conventions.

A.1 SET NOTATION AND CONVENTIONS

If X is a set and x is an element of X, we write $x \in X$. A set can be specified in the form $X = \{x \mid x \text{ satisfies } P\}$, as the set of all elements satisfying property P. The union of two sets X_1 and X_2 is denoted by $X_1 \cup X_2$, and their intersection by $X_1 \cap X_2$. The empty set is denoted by $\emptyset$. The symbol $\forall$ means "for all."

The set of real numbers (also referred to as scalars) is denoted by $\Re$. The set of extended real numbers is denoted by $\Re^*$:

$$\Re^* = \Re \cup \{\infty, -\infty\}.$$

We write $-\infty < x < \infty$ for all real numbers x, and $-\infty \le x \le \infty$ for all extended real numbers x. We denote by $[a, b]$ the set of (possibly extended) real numbers x satisfying $a \le x \le b$. A rounded, instead of square, bracket denotes strict inequality in the definition. Thus $(a, b]$, $[a, b)$, and (a, b) denote the set of all x satisfying $a < x \le b$, $a \le x < b$, and $a < x < b$, respectively.

Generally, we adopt standard conventions regarding addition and multiplication in $\Re^*$, except that we take

$$\infty - \infty = -\infty + \infty = \infty,$$

and we take the product of 0 and ∞ or $-\infty$ to be 0. In this way the sum and product of two extended real numbers is well-defined. Division by 0 or ∞ does not appear in our analysis. In particular, we adopt the following rules in calculations involving ∞ and $-\infty$:

$$\alpha + \infty = \infty + \alpha = \infty, \qquad \forall\, \alpha \in \Re^*,$$

$$\alpha - \infty = -\infty + \alpha = -\infty, \qquad \forall\, \alpha \in [-\infty, \infty),$$

$$\alpha \cdot \infty = \infty, \qquad \alpha \cdot (-\infty) = \infty, \qquad \forall\, \alpha \in (0, \infty],$$

$$\alpha \cdot \infty = -\infty, \qquad \alpha \cdot (-\infty) = -\infty, \qquad \forall\, \alpha \in [-\infty, 0),$$

$$0 \cdot \infty = \infty \cdot 0 = 0 = 0 \cdot (-\infty) = (-\infty) \cdot 0, \qquad -(-\infty) = \infty.$$

Under these rules, the following laws of arithmetic are still valid within $\Re^*$:

$$\alpha_1 + \alpha_2 = \alpha_2 + \alpha_1, \qquad (\alpha_1 + \alpha_2) + \alpha_3 = \alpha_1 + (\alpha_2 + \alpha_3),$$

$$\alpha_1\alpha_2 = \alpha_2\alpha_1, \qquad (\alpha_1\alpha_2)\alpha_3 = \alpha_1(\alpha_2\alpha_3).$$

We also have

$$\alpha(\alpha_1 + \alpha_2) = \alpha\alpha_1 + \alpha\alpha_2$$

if either $\alpha \geq 0$ or else $(\alpha_1 + \alpha_2)$ is not of the form $\infty - \infty$.

Inf and Sup Notation

The *supremum* of a nonempty set $X \subset \Re^*$, denoted by $\sup X$, is defined as the smallest $y \in \Re^*$ such that $y \geq x$ for all $x \in X$. Similarly, the *infimum* of X, denoted by $\inf X$, is defined as the largest $y \in \Re^*$ such that $y \leq x$ for all $x \in X$. For the empty set, we use the convention

$$\sup \emptyset = -\infty, \qquad \inf \emptyset = \infty.$$

If $\sup X$ is equal to an $\overline{x} \in \Re^*$ that belongs to the set X, we say that $\overline{x}$ is the *maximum point* of X and we write $\overline{x} = \max X$. Similarly, if $\inf X$ is equal to an $\overline{x} \in \Re^*$ that belongs to the set X, we say that $\overline{x}$ is the *minimum point* of X and we write $\overline{x} = \min X$. Thus, when we write $\max X$ (or $\min X$) in place of $\sup X$ (or $\inf X$, respectively), we do so just for emphasis: we indicate that it is either evident, or it is known through earlier analysis, or it is about to be shown that the maximum (or minimum, respectively) of the set X is attained at one of its points.

A.2 FUNCTIONS

If f is a function, we use the notation $f : X \mapsto Y$ to indicate the fact that f is defined on a nonempty set X (its *domain*) and takes values in a set Y (its *range*). Thus when using the notation $f : X \mapsto Y$, we implicitly assume that X is nonempty. We will often use the *unit function* $e : X \mapsto \Re$, defined by

$$e(x) = 1, \qquad \forall\, x \in X.$$

Given a set X, we denote by $R(X)$ the set of real-valued functions $J : X \mapsto \Re$, and by $E(X)$ the set of all extended real-valued functions $J : X \mapsto \Re^*$. For any collection $\{J_\gamma \mid \gamma \in \Gamma\} \subset E(X)$, parameterized by the elements of a set Γ, we denote by $\inf_{\gamma\in\Gamma} J_\gamma$ the function taking the value $\inf_{\gamma\in\Gamma} J_\gamma(x)$ at each $x \in X$.

For two functions $J_1, J_2 \in E(X)$, we use the shorthand notation $J_1 \le J_2$ to indicate the pointwise inequality

$$J_1(x) \le J_2(x), \qquad \forall\, x \in X.$$

We use the shorthand notation $\inf_{i\in I} J_i$ to denote the function obtained by pointwise infimum of a collection $\{J_i \mid i \in I\} \subset E(X)$, i.e.,

$$\left(\inf_{i\in I} J_i\right)(x) = \inf_{i\in I} J_i(x), \qquad \forall\, x \in X.$$

We use similar notation for sup.

Given subsets $S_1, S_2, S_3 \subset E(X)$ and mappings $T_1 : S_1 \mapsto S_3$ and $T_2 : S_2 \mapsto S_1$, the *composition* of T_1 and T_2 is the mapping $T_1T_2 : S_2 \mapsto S_3$ defined by

$$(T_1T_2J)(x) = \big(T_1(T_2J)\big)(x), \qquad \forall\, J \in S_2,\ x \in X.$$

In particular, given a subset $S \subset E(X)$ and mappings $T_1 : S \mapsto S$ and $T_2 : S \mapsto S$, the composition of T_1 and T_2 is the mapping $T_1T_2 : S \mapsto S$ defined by

$$(T_1T_2J)(x) = \big(T_1(T_2J)\big)(x), \qquad \forall\, J \in S,\ x \in X.$$

Similarly, given mappings $T_k : S \mapsto S$, $k = 1, \ldots, N$, their composition is the mapping $(T_1 \cdots T_N) : S \mapsto S$ defined by

$$(T_1T_2 \cdots T_NJ)(x) = \big(T_1(T_2(\cdots(T_NJ)))\big)(x), \qquad \forall\, J \in S,\ x \in X.$$

In our notation involving compositions we minimize the use of parentheses, as long as clarity is not compromised. In particular, we write T_1T_2J instead of (T_1T_2J) or $(T_1T_2)J$ or $T_1(T_2J)$, but we write $(T_1T_2J)(x)$ to indicate the value of T_1T_2J at $x \in X$.

If X and Y are nonempty sets, a mapping $T : S_1 \mapsto S_2$, where $S_1 \subset E(X)$ and $S_2 \subset E(Y)$, is said to be *monotone* if for all $J, J' \in S_1$,

$$J \le J' \qquad \Rightarrow \qquad TJ \le TJ'.$$

Sequences of Functions

For a sequence of functions $\{J_k\} \subset E(X)$ that converges pointwise, we denote by $\lim_{k\to\infty} J_k$ the pointwise limit of $\{J_k\}$. We denote by $\limsup_{k\to\infty} J_k$ (or $\liminf_{k\to\infty} J_k$) the pointwise limit superior (or inferior, respectively) of $\{J_k\}$. If $\{J_k\} \subset E(X)$ converges pointwise to J, we write $J_k \to J$. Note that we reserve this notation for pointwise convergence. To denote convergence with respect to a norm $\|\cdot\|$, we write $\|J_k - J\| \to 0$.

A sequence of functions $\{J_k\} \subset E(X)$ is said to be *monotonically nonincreasing* (or *monotonically nondecreasing*) if $J_{k+1} \leq J_k$ for all k (or $J_{k+1} \geq J_k$ for all k, respectively). Such a sequence always has a (pointwise) limit within $E(X)$. We write $J_k \downarrow J$ (or $J_k \uparrow J$) to indicate that $\{J_k\}$ is monotonically nonincreasing (or monotonically nonincreasing, respectively) and that its limit is J.

Let $\{J_{mn}\} \subset E(X)$ be a double indexed sequence, which is monotonically nonincreasing separately for each index in the sense that

$$J_{(m+1)n} \leq J_{mn}, \qquad J_{m(n+1)} \leq J_{mn}, \qquad \forall\, m, n = 0, 1, \ldots.$$

For such sequences, a useful fact is that

$$\lim_{m\to\infty} \left(\lim_{n\to\infty} J_{mn} \right) = \lim_{m\to\infty} J_{mm}.$$

There is a similar fact for monotonically nondecreasing sequences.

Expected Values

Given a random variable w defined over a probability space Ω, the expected value of w is defined by

$$E\{w\} = E\{w^+\} + E\{w^-\},$$

where w^+ and w^- are the positive and negative parts of w,

$$w^+(\omega) = \max\big\{0, w(\omega)\big\}, \qquad w^-(\omega) = \min\big\{0, w(\omega)\big\}.$$

In this way, taking also into account the rule $\infty - \infty = \infty$, the expected value $E\{w\}$ is well-defined if Ω is finite or countably infinite. In more general cases, $E\{w\}$ is similarly defined by the appropriate form of integration, as will be discussed in more detail at specific points as needed.

APPENDIX B:

Contraction Mappings

B.1 CONTRACTION MAPPING FIXED POINT THEOREMS

The purpose of this appendix is to provide some background on contraction mappings and their properties. Let Y be a real vector space with a norm $\|\cdot\|$, i.e., a real-valued function satisfying for all $y \in Y$, $\|y\| \geq 0$, $\|y\| = 0$ if and only if $y = 0$, and

$$\|ay\| = |a|\|y\|, \quad \forall\, a \in \Re, \qquad \|y+z\| \leq \|y\| + \|z\|, \quad \forall\, y, z \in Y.$$

Let $\bar{Y}$ be a closed subset of Y. A function $F : \bar{Y} \mapsto \bar{Y}$ is said to be a *contraction mapping* if for some $\rho \in (0,1)$, we have

$$\|Fy - Fz\| \leq \rho \|y - z\|, \qquad \forall\, y, z \in \bar{Y}.$$

The scalar ρ is called the *modulus of contraction* of F.

Example B.1 (Linear Contraction Mappings in $\Re^n$)

Consider the case of a linear mapping $F : \Re^n \mapsto \Re^n$ of the form

$$Fy = b + Ay,$$

where A is an $n \times n$ matrix and b is a vector in $\Re^n$. Let $\sigma(A)$ denote the spectral radius of A (the largest modulus among the moduli of the eigenvalues of A). Then it can be shown that *A is a contraction mapping with respect to some norm if and only if $\sigma(A) < 1$.*

Specifically, given $\epsilon > 0$, there exists a norm $\|\cdot\|_s$ such that

$$\|Ay\|_s \leq \big(\sigma(A) + \epsilon\big)\|y\|_s, \qquad \forall\, y \in \Re^n. \tag{B.1}$$

Thus, if $\sigma(A) < 1$ we may select $\epsilon > 0$ such that $\rho = \sigma(A) + \epsilon < 1$, and obtain the contraction relation

$$\|Fy - Fz\|_s = \big\|A(y-z)\big\|_s \leq \rho \|y - z\|_s, \qquad \forall\, y, z \in \Re^n. \tag{B.2}$$

The norm $\|\cdot\|_s$ can be taken to be a weighted Euclidean norm, i.e., it may have the form $\|y\|_s = \|My\|$, where M is a square invertible matrix, and $\|\cdot\|$ is the standard Euclidean norm, i.e., $\|x\| = \sqrt{x'x}$.†

Conversely, if Eq. (B.2) holds for some norm $\|\cdot\|_s$ and all real vectors y, z, it also holds for all complex vectors y, z with the squared norm $\|c\|_s^2$ of a complex vector c defined as the sum of the squares of the norms of the real and the imaginary components. Thus from Eq. (B.2), by taking $y - z = u$, where u is an eigenvector corresponding to an eigenvalue λ with $|\lambda| = \sigma(A)$, we have $\sigma(A)\|u\|_s = \|Au\|_s \leq \rho\|u\|_s$. Hence $\sigma(A) \leq \rho$, and it follows that if F is a contraction with respect to a given norm, we must have $\sigma(A) < 1$.

A sequence $\{y_k\} \subset Y$ is said to be a *Cauchy sequence* if $\|y_m - y_n\| \to 0$ as $m, n \to \infty$, i.e., given any $\epsilon > 0$, there exists N such that $\|y_m - y_n\| \leq \epsilon$ for all $m, n \geq N$. The space Y is said to be *complete* under the norm $\|\cdot\|$ if every Cauchy sequence $\{y_k\} \subset Y$ is convergent, in the sense that for some $\bar{y} \in Y$, we have $\|y_k - \bar{y}\| \to 0$. Note that a Cauchy sequence is always bounded. Also, a Cauchy sequence of real numbers is convergent, implying that the real line is a complete space and so is every real finite-dimensional vector space. On the other hand, an infinite dimensional space may not be complete under some norms, while it may be complete under other norms.

When Y is complete and $\bar{Y}$ is a closed subset of Y, an important property of a contraction mapping $F : \bar{Y} \mapsto \bar{Y}$ is that it has a unique fixed point within $\bar{Y}$, i.e., the equation

$$y = Fy$$

has a unique solution $y^* \in \bar{Y}$, called the *fixed point of* F. Furthermore, the sequence $\{y_k\}$ generated by the iteration

$$y_{k+1} = Fy_k$$

---

† We may show Eq. (B.1) by using the Jordan canonical form of A, which is denoted by J. In particular, if P is a nonsingular matrix such that $P^{-1}AP = J$ and D is the diagonal matrix with $1, \delta, \ldots, \delta^{n-1}$ along the diagonal, where $\delta > 0$, it is straightforward to verify that $D^{-1}P^{-1}APD = \hat{J}$, where $\hat{J}$ is the matrix that is identical to J except that each nonzero off-diagonal term is replaced by δ. Defining $\hat{P} = PD$, we have $A = \hat{P}\hat{J}\hat{P}^{-1}$. Now if $\|\cdot\|$ is the standard Euclidean norm, we note that for some $\beta > 0$, we have $\|\hat{J}z\| \leq \big(\sigma(A) + \beta\delta\big)\|z\|$ for all $z \in \Re^n$ and $\delta \in (0, 1]$. For a given $\delta \in (0, 1]$, consider the weighted Euclidean norm $\|\cdot\|_s$ defined by $\|y\|_s = \|\hat{P}^{-1}y\|$. Then we have for all $y \in \Re^n$,

$$\|Ay\|_s = \|\hat{P}^{-1}Ay\| = \|\hat{P}^{-1}\hat{P}\hat{J}\hat{P}^{-1}y\| = \|\hat{J}\hat{P}^{-1}y\| \leq \big(\sigma(A) + \beta\delta\big)\|\hat{P}^{-1}y\|,$$

so that $\|Ay\|_s \leq \big(\sigma(A) + \beta\delta\big)\|y\|_s$, for all $y \in \Re^n$. For a given $\epsilon > 0$, we choose $\delta = \epsilon/\beta$, so the preceding relation yields Eq. (B.1).

converges to y^*, starting from an arbitrary initial point y_0.

Proposition B.1: (Contraction Mapping Fixed-Point Theorem) Let Y be a complete vector space and let $\bar{Y}$ be a closed subset of Y. Then if $F : \bar{Y} \mapsto \bar{Y}$ is a contraction mapping with modulus $\rho \in (0,1)$, there exists a unique $y^* \in \bar{Y}$ such that

$$y^* = Fy^*.$$

Furthermore, the sequence $\{F^k y\}$ converges to y^* for any $y \in \bar{Y}$, and we have

$$\|F^k y - y^*\| \leq \rho^k \|y - y^*\|, \qquad k = 1, 2, \ldots.$$

Proof: Let $y \in \bar{Y}$ and consider the iteration $y_{k+1} = Fy_k$ starting with $y_0 = y$. By the contraction property of F,

$$\|y_{k+1} - y_k\| \leq \rho\|y_k - y_{k-1}\|, \qquad k = 1, 2, \ldots,$$

which implies that

$$\|y_{k+1} - y_k\| \leq \rho^k\|y_1 - y_0\|, \qquad k = 1, 2, \ldots.$$

It follows that for every $k \geq 0$ and $m \geq 1$, we have

$$\begin{aligned} \|y_{k+m} - y_k\| &\leq \sum_{i=1}^{m} \|y_{k+i} - y_{k+i-1}\| \\ &\leq \rho^k(1 + \rho + \cdots + \rho^{m-1})\|y_1 - y_0\| \\ &\leq \frac{\rho^k}{1-\rho}\|y_1 - y_0\|. \end{aligned}$$

Therefore, $\{y_k\}$ is a Cauchy sequence in $\bar{Y}$ and must converge to a limit $y^* \in \bar{Y}$, since Y is complete and $\bar{Y}$ is closed. We have for all $k \geq 1$,

$$\|Fy^* - y^*\| \leq \|Fy^* - y_k\| + \|y_k - y^*\| \leq \rho\|y^* - y_{k-1}\| + \|y_k - y^*\|$$

and since y_k converges to y^*, we obtain $Fy^* = y^*$. Thus, the limit y^* of y_k is a fixed point of F. It is a unique fixed point because if $\tilde{y}$ were another fixed point, we would have

$$\|y^* - \tilde{y}\| = \|Fy^* - F\tilde{y}\| \leq \rho\|y^* - \tilde{y}\|,$$

which implies that $y^* = \tilde{y}$.

To show the convergence rate bound of the last part, note that

$$\|F^k y - y^*\| = \|F^k y - F y^*\| \le \rho \|F^{k-1} y - y^*\|.$$

Repeating this process for a total of k times, we obtain the desired result. **Q.E.D.**

The convergence rate exhibited by $F^k y$ in the preceding proposition is said to be *geometric*, and $F^k y$ is said to converge to its limit y^* *geometrically*. This is in reference to the fact that the error $\|F^k y - y^*\|$ converges to 0 faster than some geometric progression ($\rho^k \|y - y^*\|$ in this case).

In some contexts of interest to us one may encounter mappings that are not contractions, but become contractions when iterated a finite number of times. In this case, one may use a slightly different version of the contraction mapping fixed point theorem, which we now present.

We say that a function $F : \bar{Y} \mapsto \bar{Y}$ is an *m-stage contraction mapping* if there exists a positive integer m and some $\rho < 1$ such that

$$\|F^m y - F^m y'\| \le \rho \|y - y'\|, \qquad \forall\, y, y' \in \bar{Y},$$

where F^m denotes the composition of F with itself m times. Thus, F is an m-stage contraction if F^m is a contraction. Again, the scalar ρ is called the modulus of contraction. We have the following generalization of Prop. B.1.

Proposition B.2: (m-Stage Contraction Mapping Fixed-Point Theorem) Let Y be a complete vector space and let $\bar{Y}$ be a closed subset of Y. Then if $F : \bar{Y} \mapsto \bar{Y}$ is an m-stage contraction mapping with modulus $\rho \in (0, 1)$, there exists a unique $y^* \in \bar{Y}$ such that

$$y^* = F y^*.$$

Furthermore, $\{F^k y\}$ converges to y^* for any $y \in \bar{Y}$.

Proof: Since F^m maps $\bar{Y}$ into $\bar{Y}$ and is a contraction mapping, by Prop. B.1, it has a unique fixed point in $\bar{Y}$, denoted y^*. Applying F to both sides of the relation $y^* = F^m y^*$, we see that $F y^*$ is also a fixed point of F^m, so by the uniqueness of the fixed point, we have $y^* = F y^*$. Therefore y^* is a fixed point of F. If F had another fixed point, say $\tilde{y}$, then we would have $\tilde{y} = F^m \tilde{y}$, which by the uniqueness of the fixed point of F^m implies that $\tilde{y} = y^*$. Thus, y^* is the unique fixed point of F.

To show the convergence of $\{F^k y\}$, note that by Prop. B.1, we have for all $y \in \bar{Y}$,

$$\lim_{k \to \infty} \|F^{mk} y - y^*\| = 0.$$

Using $F^\ell y$ in place of y, we obtain

$$\lim_{k\to\infty} \|F^{mk+\ell}y - y^*\| = 0, \qquad \ell = 0, 1, \ldots, m-1,$$

which proves the desired result. **Q.E.D.**

B.2 WEIGHTED SUP-NORM CONTRACTIONS

In this section, we will focus on contraction mappings within a specialized context that is particularly important in DP. Let X be a set (typically the state space in DP), and let $v : X \mapsto \Re$ be a positive-valued function,

$$v(x) > 0, \qquad \forall\, x \in X.$$

Let $B(X)$ denote the set of all functions $J : X \mapsto \Re$ such that $J(x)/v(x)$ is bounded as x ranges over X. We define a norm on $B(X)$, called the *weighted sup-norm*, by

$$\|J\| = \sup_{x\in X} \frac{|J(x)|}{v(x)}. \tag{B.3}$$

It is easily verified that $\|\cdot\|$ thus defined has the required properties for being a norm. Furthermore, $B(X)$ *is complete under this norm.* To see this, consider a Cauchy sequence $\{J_k\} \subset B(X)$, and note that $\|J_m - J_n\| \to 0$ as $m, n \to \infty$ implies that for all $x \in X$, $\{J_k(x)\}$ is a Cauchy sequence of real numbers, so it converges to some $J^*(x)$. We will show that $J^* \in B(X)$ and that $\|J_k - J^*\| \to 0$. To this end, it will be sufficient to show that given any $\epsilon > 0$, there exists a K such that

$$\frac{|J_k(x) - J^*(x)|}{v(x)} \le \epsilon, \qquad \forall\, x \in X,\ k \ge K.$$

This will imply that

$$\sup_{x\in X} \frac{|J^*(x)|}{v(x)} \le \epsilon + \|J_k\|, \qquad \forall\, k \ge K,$$

so that $J^* \in B(X)$, and will also imply that $\|J_k - J^*\| \le \epsilon$, so that $\|J_k - J^*\| \to 0$. Assume the contrary, i.e., that there exists an $\epsilon > 0$ and a subsequence $\{x_{m_1}, x_{m_2}, \ldots\} \subset X$ such that $m_i < m_{i+1}$ and

$$\epsilon < \frac{\big|J_{m_i}(x_{m_i}) - J^*(x_{m_i})\big|}{v(x_{m_i})}, \qquad \forall\, i \ge 1.$$

The right-hand side above is less or equal to

$$\frac{\big|J_{m_i}(x_{m_i}) - J_n(x_{m_i})\big|}{v(x_{m_i})} + \frac{\big|J_n(x_{m_i}) - J^*(x_{m_i})\big|}{v(x_{m_i})}, \qquad \forall\, n \ge 1,\ i \ge 1.$$

The first term in the above sum is less than $\epsilon/2$ for i and n larger than some threshold; fixing i and letting n be sufficiently large, the second term can also be made less than $\epsilon/2$, so the sum is made less than ϵ - a contradiction. In conclusion, the space $B(X)$ is complete, so the fixed point results of Props. B.1 and B.2 apply.

In our discussions, we will always assume that $B(X)$ is equipped with the weighted sup-norm above, where the weight function v will be clear from the context. There will be frequent occasions where the norm will be unweighted, i.e., $v(x) \equiv 1$ and $\|J\| = \sup_{x\in X} \big|J(x)\big|$, in which case we will explicitly state so.

Finite-Dimensional Cases

Let us now focus on the finite-dimensional case $X = \{1, \ldots, n\}$, in which case $R(X)$ and $B(X)$ can be identified with $\Re^n$. Consider a linear mapping $F : \Re^n \mapsto \Re^n$ of the form

$$Fy = b + Ay,$$

where A is an $n \times n$ matrix with components a_{ij}, and b is a vector in $\Re^n$ (cf. Example B.1). Then it can be shown (see the following proposition) that F *is a contraction with respect to the weighted sup-norm* $\|y\| = \max_{i=1,\ldots,n} |y_i|/v(i)$ *if and only if*

$$\frac{\sum_{j=1}^n |a_{ij}|\, v(j)}{v(i)} < 1, \qquad i = 1, \ldots, n.$$

Let us also denote by $|A|$ the matrix whose components are the absolute values of the components of A and let $\sigma\big(|A|\big)$ denote the spectral radius of $|A|$. Then it can be shown that F *is a contraction with respect to some weighted sup-norm if and only if* $\sigma\big(|A|\big) < 1$. A proof of this may be found in [BeT89], Ch. 2, Cor. 6.2. Thus any substochastic matrix P ($p_{ij} \geq 0$ for all i, j, and $\sum_{j=1}^n p_{ij} \leq 1$, for all i) is a contraction with respect to some weighted sup-norm if and only if $\sigma(P) < 1$.

Finally, let us consider a nonlinear mapping $F : \Re^n \mapsto \Re^n$ that has the property

$$|Fy - Fz| \leq P\,|y - z|, \qquad \forall\ y, z \in \Re^n,$$

for some matrix P with nonnegative components and $\sigma(P) < 1$. Here, we generically denote by $|w|$ the vector whose components are the absolute values of the components of w, and the inequality is componentwise. Then we claim that F is a contraction with respect to some weighted sup-norm. To see this note that by the preceding discussion, P is a contraction with respect to some weighted sup-norm $\|y\| = \max_{i=1,\ldots,n} |y_i|/v(i)$, and we have

$$\frac{\big(|Fy - Fz|\big)(i)}{v(i)} \leq \frac{\big(P\,|y - z|\big)(i)}{v(i)} \leq \alpha\, \|y - z\|, \qquad \forall\ i = 1, \ldots, n,$$

for some $\alpha \in (0,1)$, where $\big(|Fy - Fz|\big)(i)$ and $\big(P\,|y - z|\big)(i)$ are the ith components of the vectors $|Fy - Fz|$ and $P\,|y - z|$, respectively. Thus, F is a contraction with respect to $\|\cdot\|$. For additional discussion of linear and nonlinear contraction mapping properties and characterizations such as the one above, see the book [OrR70].

Linear Mappings on Countable Spaces

The case where X is countable (or, as a special case, finite) is frequently encountered in DP. The following proposition provides some useful criteria for verifying the contraction property of mappings that are either linear or are obtained via a parametric minimization of other contraction mappings.

Proposition B.3: Let $X = \{1, 2, \ldots\}$.

(a) Let $F : B(X) \mapsto B(X)$ be a linear mapping of the form

$$(FJ)(i) = b_i + \sum_{j \in X} a_{ij} J(j), \qquad i \in X,$$

where b_i and a_{ij} are some scalars. Then F is a contraction with modulus ρ with respect to the weighted sup-norm (B.3) if and only if

$$\frac{\sum_{j \in X} |a_{ij}|\, v(j)}{v(i)} \leq \rho, \qquad i \in X. \tag{B.4}$$

(b) Let $F : B(X) \mapsto B(X)$ be a mapping of the form

$$(FJ)(i) = \inf_{\mu \in M} (F_\mu J)(i), \qquad i \in X,$$

where M is parameter set, and for each $\mu \in M$, F_μ is a contraction mapping from $B(X)$ to $B(X)$ with modulus ρ. Then F is a contraction mapping with modulus ρ.

Proof: (a) Assume that Eq. (B.4) holds. For any $J, J' \in B(X)$, we have

$$\begin{aligned}
\|FJ - FJ'\| &= \sup_{i \in X} \frac{\left|\sum_{j \in X} a_{ij}\big(J(j) - J'(j)\big)\right|}{v(i)} \\
&\leq \sup_{i \in X} \frac{\sum_{j \in X} \big|a_{ij}\big|\, v(j) \Big(\big|J(j) - J'(j)\big|/v(j)\Big)}{v(i)} \\
&\leq \sup_{i \in X} \frac{\sum_{j \in X} \big|a_{ij}\big|\, v(j)}{v(i)} \, \big\|J - J'\big\|
\end{aligned}$$

$$\leq \rho \, \|J - J'\|,$$

where the last inequality follows from the hypothesis.

Conversely, arguing by contradiction, let's assume that Eq. (B.4) is violated for some $i \in X$. Define $J(j) = v(j)\,\mathrm{sgn}(a_{ij})$ and $J'(j) = 0$ for all $j \in X$. Then we have $\|J - J'\| = \|J\| = 1$, and

$$\frac{\big|(FJ)(i) - (FJ')(i)\big|}{v(i)} = \frac{\sum_{j\in X} |a_{ij}|\, v(j)}{v(i)} > \rho = \rho\, \|J - J'\|,$$

showing that F is not a contraction of modulus ρ.

(b) Since F_μ is a contraction of modulus ρ, we have for any $J, J' \in B(X)$,

$$\frac{(F_\mu J)(i)}{v(i)} \leq \frac{(F_\mu J')(i)}{v(i)} + \rho\, \|J - J'\|, \qquad i \in X,$$

so by taking the infimum over $\mu \in M$,

$$\frac{(FJ)(i)}{v(i)} \leq \frac{(FJ')(i)}{v(i)} + \rho\, \|J - J'\|, \qquad i \in X.$$

Reversing the roles of J and J', we obtain

$$\frac{\big|(FJ)(i) - (FJ')(i)\big|}{v(i)} \leq \rho\, \|J - J'\|, \qquad i \in X,$$

and by taking the supremum over i, the contraction property of F is proved. **Q.E.D.**

The preceding proposition assumes that $FJ \in B(X)$ for all $J \in B(X)$. The following proposition provides conditions, particularly relevant to the DP context, which imply this assumption.

Proposition B.4: Let $X = \{1, 2, \ldots\}$, let M be a parameter set, and for each $\mu \in M$, let F_μ be a linear mapping of the form

$$(F_\mu J)(i) = b_i(\mu) + \sum_{j\in X} a_{ij}(\mu)\, J(j), \qquad i \in X.$$

(a) We have $F_\mu J \in B(X)$ for all $J \in B(X)$ provided $b(\mu) \in B(X)$ and $V(\mu) \in B(X)$, where

$$b(\mu) = \big\{b_1(\mu), b_2(\mu), \ldots\big\}, \qquad V(\mu) = \big\{V_1(\mu), V_2(\mu), \ldots\big\},$$

with

$$V_i(\mu) = \sum_{j\in X} \big|a_{ij}(\mu)\big|\, v(j), \qquad i \in X.$$

(b) Consider the mapping F

$$(FJ)(i) = \inf_{\mu \in M} (F_\mu J)(i), \qquad i \in X.$$

We have $FJ \in B(X)$ for all $J \in B(X)$, provided $b \in B(X)$ and $V \in B(X)$, where

$$b = \{b_1, b_2, \ldots\}, \qquad V = \{V_1, V_2, \ldots\},$$

with $b_i = \sup_{\mu \in M} b_i(\mu)$ and $V_i = \sup_{\mu \in M} V_i(\mu)$.

Proof: (a) For all $\mu \in M$, $J \in B(X)$ and $i \in X$, we have

$$\begin{aligned}(F_\mu J)(i) &\le \big|b_i(\mu)\big| + \sum_{j \in X} \big|a_{ij}(\mu)\big| \, \big|J(j)/v(j)\big| \, v(j) \\ &\le \big|b_i(\mu)\big| + \|J\| \sum_{j \in X} \big|a_{ij}(\mu)\big| \, v(j) \\ &= \big|b_i(\mu)\big| + \|J\| \, V_i(\mu),\end{aligned}$$

and similarly $(F_\mu J)(i) \ge -\big|b_i(\mu)\big| - \|J\| \, V_i(\mu)$. Thus

$$\big|(F_\mu J)(i)\big| \le \big|b_i(\mu)\big| + \|J\| \, V_i(\mu), \qquad i \in X.$$

By dividing this inequality with $v(i)$ and by taking the supremum over $i \in X$, we obtain

$$\|F_\mu J\| \le \|b_\mu\| + \|J\| \, \|V_\mu\| < \infty.$$

(b) By doing the same as in (a), but after first taking the infimum of $(F_\mu J)(i)$ over μ, we obtain

$$\|FJ\| \le \|b\| + \|J\| \, \|V\| < \infty.$$

Q.E.D.

APPENDIX C:

Measure Theoretic Issues

A general theory of stochastic dynamic programming must deal with the formidable mathematical questions that arise from the presence of uncountable probability spaces. The purpose of this appendix is to motivate the theory and to provide some mathematical background to the extent needed for the development of Chapter 5. The research monograph by Bertsekas and Shreve [BeS78] (freely available from the internet), contains a detailed development of mathematical background and terminology on Borel spaces and related subjects. We will explore here the main questions by means of a simple two-stage example described in Section C.1. In Section C.2, we develop a framework, based on universally measurable policies, for the rigorous mathematical development of the standard DP results for this example and for more general finite horizon models.

C.1 A TWO-STAGE EXAMPLE

Suppose that the initial state x_0 is a point on the real line $\Re$. Knowing x_0, we must choose a control $u_0 \in \Re$. Then the new state x_1 is generated according to a transition probability measure $p(dx_1 \mid x_0, u_0)$ on the Borel σ-algebra of $\Re$ (the one generated by the open sets of $\Re$). Then, knowing x_1, we must choose a control $u_1 \in \Re$ and incur a cost $g(x_1, u_1)$, where g is a real-valued function that is bounded either above or below. Thus a cost is incurred only at the second stage.

A policy $\pi = \{\mu_0, \mu_1\}$ is a pair of functions from state to control, i.e., if π is employed and x_0 is the initial state, then $u_0 = \mu_0(x_0)$, and if x_1 is the subsequent state, then $u_1 = \mu_1(x_1)$. The expected value of the cost corresponding to π when x_0 is the initial state is given by

$$J_\pi(x_0) = \int g\big(x_1, \mu_1(x_1)\big)\, p\big(dx_1 \mid x_0, \mu_0(x_0)\big). \tag{C.1}$$

We wish to find π to minimize $J_\pi(x_0)$.

To formulate the problem properly, we must insure that the integral in Eq. (C.1) is defined. Various sufficient conditions can be used for this; for example it is sufficient that g, μ_0, and μ_1 be Borel measurable, and that $p(B \mid x_0, u_0)$ is a Borel measurable function of (x_0, u_0) for every Borel set B (see [BeS78]). However, our aim in this example is to discuss the necessary measure theoretic framework not only for the cost $J_\pi(x_0)$ to be defined, but also for the major DP-related results to hold. We thus leave unspecified for the moment the assumptions on the problem data and the measurability restrictions on the policy π.

The optimal cost is

$$J^*(x_0) = \inf_{\pi} J_\pi(x_0),$$

where the infimum is over all policies $\pi = \{\mu_0, \mu_1\}$ such that μ_0 and μ_1 are measurable functions from $\Re$ to $\Re$ with respect to σ-algebras to be specified later. Given $\epsilon > 0$, a policy π is *ϵ-optimal* if

$$J_\pi(x_0) \leq J^*(x_0) + \epsilon, \qquad \forall\, x_0 \in \Re.$$

A policy π is *optimal* if

$$J_\pi(x_0) = J^*(x_0), \qquad \forall\, x_0 \in \Re.$$

The DP Algorithm

The DP algorithm for the preceding two-stage problem takes the form

$$J_1(x_1) = \inf_{u_1 \in \Re} g(x_1, u_1), \qquad \forall\, x_1 \in \Re, \tag{C.2}$$

$$J_0(x_0) = \inf_{u_0 \in \Re} \int J_1(x_1)\, p(dx_1 \mid x_0, u_0), \qquad \forall\, x_0 \in \Re, \tag{C.3}$$

and assuming that

$$J_0(x_0) > -\infty, \quad \forall\, x_0 \in \Re, \qquad J_1(x_1) > -\infty, \quad \forall\, x_1 \in \Re,$$

the results we expect to be able to prove are:

R.1: There holds
$$J^*(x_0) = J_0(x_0), \qquad \forall\, x_0 \in \Re.$$

R.2: Given any $\epsilon > 0$, there is an ϵ-optimal policy.

R.3: If $\mu_1^*(x_1)$ and $\mu_0^*(x_0)$ attain the infimum in the DP algorithm (C.2), (C.3) for all $x_1 \in \Re$ and $x_0 \in \Re$, respectively, then $\pi^* = \{\mu_0^*, \mu_1^*\}$ is optimal.

We will see that to establish these results, we will need to address two main issues:

(1) The cost function J_π of a policy π, and the functions J_0 and J_1 produced by DP should be well-defined, with a mathematical framework, which ensures that the integrals in Eqs. (C.1)-(C.3) make sense.

(2) Since $J_0(x_0)$ is easily seen to be a lower bound to $J_\pi(x_0)$ for all x_0 and $\pi = \{\mu_0, \mu_1\}$, the equality of J_0 and J^* will be ensured if the class of policies has an ϵ-selection property, which guarantees that the minima in Eqs. (C.2) and (C.3) can be nearly attained by $\mu_1(x_1)$ and $\mu_0(x_0)$ for all x_1 and x_0, respectively.

To get a better sense of these issues, consider the following informal derivation of R.1:

$$
\begin{aligned}
J^*(x_0) &= \inf_\pi J_\pi(x_0) \\
&= \inf_{\mu_0} \inf_{\mu_1} \int g\big(x_1, \mu_1(x_1)\big)\, p\big(dx_1 \mid x_0, \mu_0(x_0)\big) && \text{(C.4}a\text{)} \\
&= \inf_{\mu_0} \int \left\{ \inf_{\mu_1} g\big(x_1, \mu_1(x_1)\big) \right\} p\big(dx_1 \mid x_0, \mu_0(x_0)\big) && \text{(C.4}b\text{)} \\
&= \inf_{\mu_0} \int \left\{ \inf_{u_1} g(x_1, u_1) \right\} p\big(dx_1 \mid x_0, \mu_0(x_0)\big) \\
&= \inf_{\mu_0} \int J_1(x_1)\, p\big(dx_1 \mid x_0, \mu_0(x_0)\big) && \text{(C.4}c\text{)} \\
&= \inf_{u_0} \int J_1(x_1)\, p(dx_1 \mid x_0, u_0) && \text{(C.4}d\text{)} \\
&= J_0(x_0).
\end{aligned}
$$

In order to make this derivation meaningful and mathematically rigorous, the following points need to be justified:

(a) g and μ_1 must be such that $g\big(x_1, \mu_1(x_1)\big)$ can be integrated in a well-defined manner in Eq. (C.4a).

(b) The interchange of infimization and integration in Eq. (C.4b) must be legitimate.

(c) g must be such that the function

$$J_1(x_1) = \inf_{u_1} g(x_1, u_1)$$

can be integrated in a well-defined manner in Eq. (C.4c).

We first discuss these points in the easier context where the state space is essentially countable.

Countable Space Problems

We observe that if for each (x_0, u_0), the measure $p(dx_1 \mid x_0, u_0)$ has *countable support*, i.e., is concentrated on a countable number of points, then for a fixed policy π and initial state x_0, the integral defining the cost $J_\pi(x_0)$ of Eq. (C.1) is defined in terms of (possibly infinite) summation. Similarly, the DP algorithm (C.2), (C.3) is defined in terms of summation, and the same is true for the integrals in Eqs. (C.4a)-(C.4d). Thus, there is no need to impose measurability restrictions of any kind for the integrals to make sense, and for the summations/integrations to be well-defined, it is sufficient that g is bounded either above or below.

It can also be shown that the interchange of infimization and summation in Eq. (C.4b) is justified in view of the assumption

$$\inf_{u_1} g(x_1, u_1) > -\infty, \qquad \forall\, x_1 \in \Re.$$

To see this, for any $\epsilon > 0$, select $\bar{\mu}_1 : \Re \mapsto \Re$ such that

$$g\big(x_1, \bar{\mu}_1(x_1)\big) \leq \inf_{u_1} g(x_1, u_1) + \epsilon, \qquad \forall\, x_1 \in \Re. \tag{C.5}$$

Then

$$\begin{aligned}\inf_{\mu_1} \int & g\big(x_1, \mu_1(x_1)\big)\, p\big(dx_1 \mid x_0, \mu_0(x_0)\big) \\ & \leq \int g\big(x_1, \bar{\mu}_1(x_1)\big)\, p\big(dx_1 \mid x_0, \mu_0(x_0)\big) \\ & \leq \int \inf_{u_1} g(x_1, u_1)\, p\big(dx_1 \mid x_0, \mu_0(x_0)\big) + \epsilon.\end{aligned}$$

Since $\epsilon > 0$ is arbitrary, it follows that

$$\inf_{\mu_1} \int g\big(x_1, \mu_1(x_1)\big)\, p\big(dx_1 \mid x_0, \mu_0(x_0)\big) \leq \int \inf_{u_1} g(x_1, u_1)\, p\big(dx_1 \mid x_0, \mu_0(x_0)\big).$$

The reverse inequality also holds, since for all μ_1, we can write

$$\int \inf_{u_1} g(x_1, u_1)\, p\big(dx_1 \mid x_0, \mu_0(x_0)\big) \leq \int g\big(x_1, \mu_1(x_1)\big)\, p\big(dx_1 \mid x_0, \mu_0(x_0)\big),$$

and then we can take the infimum over μ_1. It follows that the interchange of infimization and summation in Eq. (C.4b) is justified, with the ϵ-optimal selection property of Eq. (C.5) being the key step in the proof.

We have thus shown that when the measure $p(dx_1 \mid x_0, u_0)$ has countable support, g is bounded either above or below, and $J_0(x_0) > -\infty$ for all x_0 and $J_1(x_1) > -\infty$ for all x_1, the derivation of Eq. (C.4) is valid and proves that the DP algorithm produces the optimal cost function J^* (cf.

property R.1).† A similar argument proves the existence of an ϵ-optimal policy (cf. R.2); it uses the ϵ-optimal selection (C.5) for the second stage and a similar ϵ-optimal selection for the first stage, i.e., the existence of a $\bar{\mu}_0 : \Re \mapsto \Re$ such that

$$\int J_1(x_1)\, p\big(dx_1 \mid x_0, \bar{\mu}_0(x_0)\big) \le \inf_{u_0} \int J_1(x_1)\, p(dx_1 \mid x_0, u_0) + \epsilon. \qquad \text{(C.6)}$$

Also R.3 follows easily using the fact that there are no measurability restrictions on μ_0 and μ_1.

Approaches for Uncountable Space Problems

To address the case where $p(dx_1 \mid x_0, u_0)$ does not have countable support, two approaches have been used. The first is to *expand the notion of integration*, and the second is to place *appropriate measurability restrictions on g, p, and $\{\mu_0, \mu_1\}$*. Expanding the notion of integration is possible by interpreting the integrals appearing in the preceding equations as outer integrals. Since the outer integral can be defined for any function, measurable or not, there is no need to impose any measurability assumptions, and the arguments given above go through just as in the countable disturbance case. We do not discuss this approach further except to mention that the book [BeS78] shows that the basic results for finite and infinite horizon problems of perfect state information carry through within an outer integration framework. However, there are inherent limitations in this approach centering around the pathologies of outer integration, as discussed in [BeS78].

The second approach is to impose a suitable measurability structure that allows the key proof steps of the validity of the DP algorithm. These are:

(a) Properly interpreting the integrals in the definition (C.2)-(C.3) of the DP algorithm and the derivation (C.4).

(b) The ϵ-optimal selection property (C.5), which in turn justifies the interchange of infimization and integration in Eq. (C.4b).

To enable (a), the required properties of the problem structure must include the preservation of measurability under partial minimization. In particular, it is necessary that when g is measurable in some sense, the partial minimum function

$$J_1(x_1) = \inf_{u_1} g(x_1, u_1)$$

† The condition that g is bounded either above or below may be replaced by any condition that guarantees that the infinite sum/integral of J_1 in Eq. (C.3) is well-defined. Note also that if g is bounded below, then the assumption that $J_0(x_0) > -\infty$ for all x_0 and $J_1(x_1) > -\infty$ for all x_1 is automatically satisfied.

is also measurable in the same sense, so that the integration in Eq. (C.3) is well-defined. It turns out that this is a major difficulty with Borel measurability, which may appear to be a natural framework for formulating the problem: *J_1 need not be Borel measurable even when g is Borel measurable.* For this reason it is necessary to pass to a larger class of measurable functions, which is closed under the key operation of partial minimization (and also under some other common operations, such as addition and functional composition).†

One such class is *lower semianalytic functions* and the related class of *universally measurable functions*, which will be the focus of the next section. They are the basis for a problem formulation that enables a DP theory as powerful as the one for problems where measurability is of no concern (e.g., those where the state and control spaces are countable).

C.2 RESOLUTION OF THE MEASURABILITY ISSUES

The example of the preceding section indicates that if measurability restrictions are necessary for the problem data and policies, then measurable selection and preservation of measurability under partial minimization, become crucial parts of the analysis. We will discuss measurability frameworks that are favorable in this regard, and to this end, we will use the theory of Borel spaces.

Borel Spaces and Analytic Sets

Given a topological space Y, we denote by $\mathcal{B}_Y$ the σ-algebra generated by the open subsets of Y, and refer to the members of $\mathcal{B}_Y$ as the *Borel subsets* of Y. A topological space Y is a *Borel space* if it is homeomorphic to a Borel subset of a complete separable metric space. The concept of Borel space is quite broad, containing any "reasonable" subset of n-dimensional Euclidean space. Any Borel subset of a Borel space is again a Borel space, as is any homeomorphic image of a Borel space and any finite or countable

† It is also possible to use a smaller class of functions that is closed under the same operations. This has led to the so-called *semicontinuous models*, where the state and control spaces are Borel spaces, and g and p have certain semicontinuity and other properties. These models are also analyzed in detail in the book [BeS78] (Section 8.3). However, they are not as useful and widely applicable as the universally measurable models we will focus on, because they involve assumptions that may be restrictive and/or hard to verify. By contrast, the universally measurable models are simple and very general. They allow a problem formulation that brings to bear the power of DP analysis under minimal assumptions. This analysis can in turn be used to prove more specific results based on special characteristics of the model.

Cartesian product of Borel spaces. Let Y and Z be Borel spaces, and consider a function $h : Y \mapsto Z$. We say that h is *Borel measurable* if $h^{-1}(B) \in \mathcal{B}_Y$ for every $B \in \mathcal{B}_Z$.

Borel spaces have a deficiency in the context of optimization: even in the unit square, there exist Borel sets whose projections onto an axis are not Borel subsets of that axis. In fact, this is the source of the difficulty we mentioned earlier regarding Borel measurability in the DP context: if $g(x_1, u_1)$ is Borel measurable, the partial minimum function

$$J_1(x_1) = \inf_{u_1} g(x_1, u_1)$$

need not be, because its level sets are defined in terms of projections of the level sets of g as

$$\big\{x_1 \mid J_1(x_1) < c\big\} = P\Big(\big\{(x_1, u_1) \mid g(x_1, u_1) < c\big\}\Big),$$

where c is a scalar and $P(\cdot)$ denotes projection on the space of x_1. As an example, take g to be the indicator of a Borel subset of the unit square whose projection on the x_1-axis is not Borel. Then J_1 is the indicator function of this projection, so it is not Borel measurable. This leads us to the notion of an analytic set.

A subset A of a Borel space Y is said to be *analytic* if there exists a Borel space Z and a Borel subset B of $Y \times Z$ such that $A = \text{proj}_Y(B)$, where proj_Y is the projection mapping from $Y \times Z$ to Y. It is clear that every Borel subset of a Borel space is analytic.

Analytic sets have many interesting properties, which are discussed in detail in [BeS78]. Some of these properties are particularly relevant to DP analysis. For example, let Y and Z be Borel spaces. Then:

(i) If $A \subset Y$ is analytic and $h : Y \mapsto Z$ is Borel measurable, then $h(A)$ is analytic. In particular, if Y is a product of Borel spaces Y_1 and Y_2, and $A \subset Y_1 \times Y_2$ is analytic, then $\text{proj}_{Y_1}(A)$ is analytic. Thus, the class of analytic sets is closed with respect to projection, a critical property for DP, which the class of Borel sets is lacking, as mentioned earlier.

(ii) If $A \subset Z$ is analytic and $h : Y \mapsto Z$ is Borel measurable, then $h^{-1}(A)$ is analytic.

(iii) If $A_1, A_2, \ldots$ are analytic subsets of Y, then $\cup_{k=1}^{\infty} A_k$ and $\cap_{k=1}^{\infty} A_k$ are analytic.

However, the complement of an analytic set need not be analytic, so the collection of analytic subsets of Y need not be a σ-algebra.

Lower Semianalytic Functions

Let Y be a Borel space and let $h : Y \mapsto [-\infty, \infty]$ be a function. We say that h is *lower semianalytic* if the level set

$$\{y \in Y \mid h(y) < c\}$$

is analytic for every $c \in \Re$. The following proposition states that lower analyticity is preserved under partial minimization, a key result for our purposes. The proof follows from the preservation of analyticity of a subset of a product space under projection onto one of the component spaces, as in (i) above (see [BeS78], Prop. 7.47).

Proposition C.1: Let Y and Z be Borel spaces, and let $h : Y \times Z \mapsto [-\infty, \infty]$ be lower semianalytic. Then $h^* : Y \mapsto [-\infty, \infty]$ defined by

$$h^*(y) = \inf_{z \in Z} h(y, z)$$

is lower semianalytic.

By comparing the DP equation $J_1(x_1) = \inf_{u_1} g(x_1, u_1)$ [cf. Eq. (C.2)] and Prop. C.1, we see how lower semianalytic functions can arise in DP. In particular, J_1 is lower semianalytic if g is. Let us also give two additional properties of lower semianalytic functions that play an important role in DP (for a proof, see [BeS78], Lemma 7.40).

Proposition C.2: Let Y be a Borel space, and let $h : Y \mapsto [-\infty, \infty]$ and $l : Y \mapsto [-\infty, \infty]$ be lower semianalytic. Suppose that for every $y \in Y$, the sum $h(y) + l(y)$ is defined, i.e., is not of the form $\infty - \infty$. Then $h + l$ is lower semianalytic.

Proposition C.3: Let Y and Z be Borel spaces, let $h : Y \mapsto Z$ be Borel measurable, and let $l : Z \mapsto [-\infty, \infty]$ be lower semianalytic. Then the composition $l \circ h$ is lower semianalytic.

Universal Measurability

To address questions relating to the definition of the integrals appearing in the DP algorithm, we must discuss the measurability properties of lower semianalytic functions. In addition to the Borel σ-algebra $\mathcal{B}_Y$ mentioned earlier, there is the *universal σ-algebra* $\mathcal{U}_Y$, which is the intersection of all completions of $\mathcal{B}_Y$ with respect to all probability measures. Thus, $E \in \mathcal{U}_Y$ if and only if, given any probability measure p on $(Y, \mathcal{B}_Y)$, there is a Borel set B and a p-null set N such that $E = B \cup N$. Clearly, we have $\mathcal{B}_Y \subset \mathcal{U}_Y$. It is also true that every analytic set is universally measurable (for a proof, see [BeS78], Corollary 7.42.1), and hence the σ-algebra generated by the analytic sets, called the *analytic σ-algebra*, and denoted $\mathcal{A}_Y$, is contained in $\mathcal{U}_Y$:

$$\mathcal{B}_Y \subset \mathcal{A}_Y \subset \mathcal{U}_Y.$$

Let X, Y, and Z be Borel spaces, and consider a function $h : Y \mapsto Z$. We say that h is *universally measurable* if $h^{-1}(B) \in \mathcal{U}_Y$ for every $B \in \mathcal{B}_Z$. It can be shown that if $U \subset Z$ is universally measurable and h is universally measurable, then $h^{-1}(U)$ is also universally measurable. As a result, if $g : X \mapsto Y$, $h : Y \mapsto Z$ are universally measurable functions, then the composition $(g \circ h) : X \mapsto Z$ is universally measurable.

We say that $h : Y \mapsto Z$ is *analytically measurable* if $h^{-1}(B) \in \mathcal{A}_Y$ for every $B \in \mathcal{B}_Z$. It can be seen that *every lower semianalytic function is analytically measurable*, and in view of the inclusion $\mathcal{A}_Y \subset \mathcal{U}_Y$, it is *also universally measurable*.

Integration of Lower Semianalytic Functions

If p is a probability measure on $(Y, \mathcal{B}_Y)$, then p has a unique extension to a probability measure $\bar{p}$ on $(Y, \mathcal{U}_Y)$. We write simply p instead of $\bar{p}$ and $\int h dp$ in place of $\int h d\bar{p}$. In particular, if h is lower semianalytic, then $\int h\, dp$ is interpreted in this manner.

Let Y and Z be Borel spaces. A *stochastic kernel* $q(dz \mid y)$ on Z given Y is a collection of probability measures on $(Z, \mathcal{B}_Z)$ parameterized by the elements of Y. If for each Borel set $B \in \mathcal{B}_Z$, the function $q(B \mid y)$ is Borel measurable (universally measurable) in y, the stochastic kernel $q(dz \mid y)$ is said to be *Borel measurable* (*universally measurable*, respectively). The following proposition provides another basic property for the DP context (for a proof, see [BeS78], Props. 7.46 and 7.48).†

---

† We use here a definition of integral of an extended real-valued function that is always defined as an extended real number (see also Appendix A). In particular. for a probability measure p, the integral of an extended real-valued function f, with positive and negative parts f^+ and f^-, is defined as

$$\int f dp = \int f^+ dp - \int f^- dp,$$

where we adopts the rule $\infty - \infty = \infty$ for the case where $\int f^+ dp = \infty$ and $\int f^- dp = \infty$. With this expanded definition, the integral of an extended real-valued function is always defined as an extended real number (consistently also with Appendix A).

Proposition C.4: Let Y and Z be Borel spaces, and let $q(dz \mid y)$ be a stochastic kernel on Z given Y. Let also $h : Y \times Z \mapsto [-\infty, \infty]$ be a function.

(a) If q is Borel measurable and h is lower semianalytic, then the function $l : Y \mapsto [-\infty, \infty]$ given by

$$l(y) = \int_Z h(y, z) q(dz \mid y)$$

is lower semianalytic.

(b) If q is universally measurable and h is universally measurable, then the function $l : Y \mapsto [-\infty, \infty]$ given by

$$l(y) = \int_Z h(y, z) q(dz \mid y)$$

is universally measurable.

Returning to the DP algorithm (C.2)-(C.3) of Section C.1, note that if the cost function g is lower semianalytic and bounded either above or below, then the partial minimum function J_1 given by the DP Eq. (C.2) is lower semianalytic (cf. Prop. C.1), and bounded either above or below, respectively. Furthermore, if the transition kernel $p(dx_1 \mid x_0, u_0)$ is Borel measurable, then the integral

$$\int J_1(x_1) \, p\big(dx_1 \mid x_0, u_0\big) \tag{C.7}$$

is a lower semianalytic function of (x_0, u_0) (cf. Prop. C.4), and in view of Prop. C.1, the same is true of the function J_0 given by the DP Eq. (C.3), which is the partial minimum over u_0 of the expression (C.7). Thus, with lower semianalytic g and Borel measurable p, the integrals appearing in the DP algorithm make sense.

Note that in the example of Section C.1, there is no cost incurred in the first stage of the system operation. When such a cost, call it $g_0(x_0, u_0)$, is introduced, the expression minimized in the DP Eq. (C.3) becomes

$$g_0(x_0, u_0) + \int J_1(x_1) \, p\big(dx_1 \mid x_0, u_0\big),$$

which is still a lower semianalytic function of (x_0, u_0), provided g_0 is lower semianalytic and the sum above is not of the form $\infty - \infty$ for any (x_0, u_0) (Prop. C.2). Also, for alternative models defined in terms of a system function rather than a stochastic kernel (e.g., the total cost model of Chapter 1), Prop. C.3 provides some of the necessary machinery to show that the functions generated by the DP algorithm are lower semianalytic.

Universally Measurable Selection

The preceding discussion has shown that if g is lower semianalytic, and p is Borel measurable, the DP algorithm (C.2)-(C.3) is well-defined and produces lower semianalytic functions J_1 and J_0. However, this does not by itself imply that J_0 is equal to the optimal cost function J^*. For this it is necessary that the chosen class of policies has the ϵ-optimal selection property (C.5). It turns out that universally measurable policies have this property.

The following is the key selection theorem given in a general form, which also addresses the question of existence of optimal policies that can be obtained from the DP algorithm (for a proof, see [BeS78], Prop. 7.50). The theorem shows that if any functions $\bar{\mu}_1 : \Re \to \Re$ and $\bar{\mu}_0 : \Re \to \Re$ can be found such that $\bar{\mu}_1(x_1)$ and $\bar{\mu}_0(x_0)$ attain the respective minima in Eqs. (C.2) and (C.3), for every x_1 and x_0, then $\bar{\mu}_1$ and $\bar{\mu}_0$ can be chosen to be universally measurable, the DP algorithm yields the optimal cost function and $\pi = (\bar{\mu}_0, \bar{\mu}_1)$ is optimal, provided that g is lower semianalytic and the integral in Eq. (C.3) is a lower semianalytic function of (x_0, u_0).

Proposition C.5: (Measurable Selection Theorem) Let Y and Z be Borel spaces and let $h : Y \times Z \mapsto [-\infty, \infty]$ be lower semianalytic. Define $h^* : Y \mapsto [-\infty, \infty]$ by

$$h^*(y) = \inf_{z \in Z} h(y, z),$$

and let

$$I = \{y \in Y \mid \text{there exists a } z_y \in Z \text{ for which } h(y, z_y) = h^*(y)\},$$

i.e., I is the set of points y for which the infimum above is attained. For any $\epsilon > 0$, there exists a universally measurable function $\phi : Y \mapsto Z$ such that

$$h\big(y, \phi(y)\big) = h^*(y), \qquad \forall\, y \in I,$$

$$h\big(y, \phi(y)\big) \le \begin{cases} h^*(y) + \epsilon, & \forall\, y \notin I \text{ with } h^*(y) > -\infty, \\ -1/\epsilon, & \forall\, y \notin I \text{ with } h^*(y) = -\infty. \end{cases}$$

Universal Measurability Framework: A Summary

In conclusion, the preceding discussion shows that in the two-stage example of Section C.1, the measurability issues are resolved in the following sense: the DP algorithm (C.2)-(C.3) is well-defined, produces lower semianalytic functions J_1 and J_0, and yields the optimal cost function (as in R.1), and furthermore there exist ϵ-optimal and possibly exactly optimal policies (as in R.2 and R.3), provided that:

(a) *The stage cost function g is lower semianalytic*; this is needed to show that the function J_1 of the DP Eq. (C.2) is lower semianalytic and hence also universally measurable (cf. Prop. C.1). The more "natural" Borel measurability assumption on g implies lower analyticity of g, but will not keep the functions J_1 and J_0 produced by the DP algorithm within the domain of Borel measurability. This is because the partial minimum operation on Borel measurable functions takes us outside that domain (cf. Prop. C.1).

(b) *The stochastic kernel p is Borel measurable.* This is needed in order for the integral in the DP Eq. (C.3) to be defined as a lower semianalytic function of (x_0, u_0) (cf. Prop. C.4). In turn, this is used to show that the function J_0 of the DP Eq. (C.3) is lower semianalytic (cf. Prop. C.1).

(c) *The control functions μ_0 and μ_1 are allowed to be universally measurable, and we have $J_0(x_0) > -\infty$ for all x_0 and $J_1(x_1) > -\infty$ for all x_1.* This is needed in order for the calculation of Eq. (C.4) to go through (using the measurable selection property of Prop. C.5), and show that the DP algorithm produces the optimal cost function (cf. R.1). It is also needed (using again Prop. C.5) in order to show the associated existence of solutions results (cf. R.2 and R.3).

Extension to General Finite-Horizon DP

Let us now extend our analysis to an N-stage model with state x_k and control u_k that take values in Borel spaces X and U, respectively. We assume stochastic/transition kernels $p_k(dx_{k+1} \mid x_k, u_k)$, which are Borel measurable, and stage cost functions $g_k : X \times U \mapsto (-\infty, \infty]$, which are lower semianalytic and bounded either above or below.† Furthermore, we allow policies $\pi = \{\mu_0, \dots, \mu_{N-1}\}$ that are randomized: each component μ_k is a universally measurable stochastic kernel $\mu_k(du_k \mid x_k)$ from X to U. If for every x_k and k, $\mu_k(du_k \mid x_k)$ assigns probability 1 to a single control u_k, π is said to be *nonrandomized*.

Each policy π and initial state x_0 define a unique probability measure with respect to which $g_k(x_k, u_k)$ can be integrated to produce the expected value of g_k. The sum of these expected values for $k = 0, \dots, N-1$, is the cost $J_\pi(x_0)$. It is convenient to write this cost in terms of the following

† Note that since g_k may take the value ∞, constraints of the form $u_k \in U_k(x_k)$ may be implicitly introduced by letting $g_k(x_k, u_k) = \infty$ when $u_k \notin U_k(x_k)$.

DP-like backwards recursion (see [BeS78], Section 8.1):

$$J_{\pi,N-1}(x_{N-1}) = \int g_{N-1}(x_{N-1}, u_{N-1})\mu_{N-1}(du_{N-1} \mid x_{N-1}),$$

$$J_{\pi,k}(x_k) = \int \left(g_k(x_k, u_k) + \int J_{\pi,k+1}(x_{k+1})\, p_k(dx_{k+1} \mid x_k, u_k) \right) \mu_k(du_k \mid x_k), \qquad k = 0, \ldots, N-2.$$

The function obtained at the last step is the cost of π starting at x_0:

$$J_\pi(x_0) = J_{\pi,0}(x_0).$$

We can interpret $J_{\pi,k}(x_k)$ as the expected cost-to-go starting from x_k at time k, and using π. Note that by Prop. C.4, the functions $J_{\pi,k}$ are all universally measurable.

The DP algorithm is given by

$$J_{N-1}(x_{N-1}) = \inf_{u_{N-1}\in U} g_{N-1}(x_{N-1}, u_{N-1}), \qquad \forall\, x_{N-1},$$

$$J_k(x_k) = \inf_{u_k\in U} \left[g_k(x_k, u_k) + \int J_{k+1}(x_{k+1})\, p_k\big(dx_{k+1} \mid x_k, u_k\big) \right], \quad \forall\, x_k,\ k.$$

By essentially replicating the analysis of the two-stage example, we can show that the integrals in the above DP algorithm are well-defined, and that the functions $J_{N-1}, \ldots, J_0$ are lower semianalytic.

It can be seen from the preceding expressions that we have for all policies π

$$J_k(x_k) \le J_{\pi,k}(x_k), \qquad \forall\, x_k,\ k = 0, \ldots, N-1.$$

To show equality within $\epsilon \ge 0$ in the above relation, we may use the measurable selection theorem (Prop. C.5), assuming that

$$J_k(x_k) > -\infty, \quad \forall\, x_k,\ k,$$

so that ϵ-optimal universally measurable selection is possible in the DP algorithm. In particular, define $\overline{\pi} = \{\overline{\mu}_0, \ldots, \overline{\mu}_{N-1}\}$ such that $\overline{\mu}_k : X \mapsto U$ is universally measurable, and for all x_k and k,

$$g_k\big(x_k, \overline{\mu}_k(x_k)\big) + \int J_{k+1}(x_{k+1})\, p_k\big(dx_{k+1} \mid x_k, \overline{\mu}_k(x_k)\big) \le J_k(x_k) + \frac{\epsilon}{N}. \tag{C.8}$$

Then, we can show by induction that

$$J_k(x_k) \le J_{\overline{\pi},k}(x_k) \le J_k(x_k) + \frac{(N-k)\epsilon}{N}, \qquad \forall\, x_k,\ k = 0, \ldots, N-1,$$

and in particular, for $k = 0$,

$$J_0(x_0) \leq J_{\overline{\pi}}(x_0) \leq J_0(x_0) + \epsilon, \qquad \forall\, x_0.$$

and hence also

$$J^*(x_0) = \inf_{\pi} J_{\pi}(x_0) = J_0(x_0).$$

Thus, the DP algorithm produces the optimal cost function, and via the approximate minimization of Eq. (C.8), an ϵ-optimal policy. Similarly, if the infimum is attained for all x_k and k in the DP algorithm, then there exists an optimal policy. Note that both the ϵ-optimal and the exact optimal policies can be taken be nonrandomized.

The assumptions of Borel measurability of the stochastic kernels, lower semianalyticity of the costs per stage, and universally measurable policies, are the basis for the framework adopted by Bertsekas and Shreve [BeS78], which provides a comprehensive analysis of finite and infinite horizon total cost problems. There is also additional analysis in [BeS78] on problems of imperfect state information, as well as various refinements of the measurability framework just described. Among others, these refinements involve analytically measurable policies, and limit measurable policies (measurable with respect to the, so-called, limit σ-algebra, the smallest σ-algebra that has the properties necessary for a DP theory that is comparably powerful to the one for the universal σ-algebra).

APPENDIX D:

Solutions of Exercises

CHAPTER 1

1.1 (Multistep Contraction Mappings)

By the contraction property of $T_{\mu_0}, \ldots, T_{\mu_{m-1}}$, we have for all $J, J' \in B(X)$,

$$\begin{aligned}\|\overline{T}_\nu J - \overline{T}_\nu J'\| &= \|T_{\mu_0} \cdots T_{\mu_{m-1}} J - T_{\mu_0} \cdots T_{\mu_{m-1}} J'\| \\ &\leq \alpha \|T_{\mu_1} \cdots T_{\mu_{m-1}} J - T_{\mu_1} \cdots T_{\mu_{m-1}} J'\| \\ &\leq \alpha^2 \|T_{\mu_2} \cdots T_{\mu_{m-1}} J - T_{\mu_2} \cdots T_{\mu_{m-1}} J'\| \\ &\;\;\vdots \\ &\leq \alpha^m \|J - J'\|,\end{aligned}$$

thus showing Eq. (1.23).

We have from Eq. (1.23)

$$(T_{\mu_0} \cdots T_{\mu_{m-1}} J)(x) \leq (T_{\mu_0} \cdots T_{\mu_{m-1}} J')(x) + \alpha^m \|J - J'\|\, v(x), \qquad \forall\, x \in X,$$

and by taking infimum of both sides over $(T_{\mu_0} \cdots T_{\mu_{m-1}}) \in \mathcal{M}_m$ and dividing by $v(x)$, we obtain

$$\frac{(\overline{T}J)(x) - (\overline{T}J')(x)}{v(x)} \leq \alpha^m \|J - J'\|, \qquad \forall\, x \in X.$$

Similarly

$$\frac{(\overline{T}J')(x) - (\overline{T}J)(x)}{v(x)} \leq \alpha^m \|J - J'\|, \qquad \forall\, x \in X,$$

and by combining the last two relations and taking supremum over $x \in X$, Eq. (1.24) follows.

1.2 (State-Dependent Weighted Multistep Mappings [YuB12])

By the contraction property of T_μ, we have for all $J, J' \in B(X)$ and $x \in X$,

$$\frac{\big|(T_\mu^{(w)}J)(x) - (T_\mu^{(w)}J')(x)\big|}{v(x)} = \frac{\big|\sum_{\ell=1}^\infty w_\ell(x)(T_\mu^\ell J)(x) - \sum_{\ell=1}^\infty w_\ell(x)(T_\mu^\ell J')(x)\big|}{v(x)}$$
$$\leq \sum_{\ell=1}^\infty w_\ell(x)\|T_\mu^\ell J - T_\mu^\ell J'\|$$
$$\leq \left(\sum_{\ell=1}^\infty w_\ell(x)\alpha^\ell\right)\|J - J'\|,$$

showing the contraction property of $T_\mu^{(w)}$.

Let J_μ be the fixed point of T_μ. We have for all $x \in X$, by using the relation $(T_\mu^\ell J_\mu)(x) = J_\mu(x)$,

$$(T_\mu^{(w)}J_\mu)(x) = \sum_{\ell=1}^\infty w_\ell(x)\big(T_\mu^\ell J_\mu\big)(x) = \left(\sum_{\ell=1}^\infty w_\ell(x)\right) J_\mu(x) = J_\mu(x),$$

so J_μ is the fixed point of $T_\mu^{(w)}$ [which is unique since $T_\mu^{(w)}$ is a contraction].

CHAPTER 2

2.1 (Periodic Policies)

(a) Let us define

$$J_0 = \lim_{k\to\infty} \overline{T}_\nu^k \bar{J}, \quad J_1 = \lim_{k\to\infty} \overline{T}_\nu^k (T_{\mu_0}\bar{J}), \quad \ldots \quad J_{m-2} = \lim_{k\to\infty} \overline{T}_\nu^k (T_{\mu_0}\cdots T_{\mu_{m-2}}\bar{J}).$$

Since $\overline{T}_\nu$ is a contraction mapping, $J_0, \ldots, J_{m-1}$ are all equal to the unique fixed point of $\overline{T}_\nu$. Since $J_0, \ldots, J_{m-1}$ are all equal, they are also equal to J_π (by the definition of J_π). Thus J_π is the unique fixed point of $\overline{T}_\nu$.

(b) Follow the hint.

2.2 (Totally Asynchronous Convergence Theorem for Time-Varying Maps)

A straightforward replication of the proof of Prop. 2.6.1.

2.3 (Nonmonotonic-Contractive Models – Fixed Points of Concave Sup-Norm Contractions)

The analysis of Sections 2.6.1 and 2.6.3 does not require monotonicity of the mapping T_μ given by

$$(T_\mu J)(x) = F\big(x, \mu(x)\big) - J'\mu(x).$$

2.4 (Discounted Problems with Unbounded Cost per Stage)

We have

$$\frac{\big|(T_\mu J)(x)\big|}{v(x)} \le \frac{G_x}{v(x)} + \alpha \sum_{y \in X} \frac{p_{xy}\big(\mu(x)\big)\, v(y)}{v(x)} \frac{|J(y)|}{v(y)}, \qquad \forall\ x \in X,\ \mu \in \mathcal{M},$$

from which, using assumptions (1) and (2),

$$\frac{\big|(T_\mu J)(x)\big|}{v(x)} \le \|G\| + \alpha \|V\|\, \|J\|, \qquad \forall\ x \in X,\ \mu \in \mathcal{M}.$$

A similar argument shows that

$$\frac{\big|(TJ)(x)\big|}{v(x)} \le \|G\| + \alpha \|V\|\, \|J\|, \qquad \forall\ x \in X.$$

It follows that $T_\mu J \in B(X)$ and $TJ \in B(X)$ if $J \in B(X)$.

For any $J, J' \in B(X)$ and $\mu \in \mathcal{M}$, we have

$$\begin{aligned}
\|T_\mu J - T_\mu J'\| &= \sup_{x \in X} \frac{\Big|\alpha \sum_{y \in X} p_{xy}\big(\mu(x)\big)\big(J(y) - J'(y)\big)\Big|}{v(x)} \\
&\le \sup_{x \in X} \frac{\Big|\alpha \sum_{y \in X} p_{xy}\big(\mu(x)\big) v(y) \big(|J(y) - J'(y)|/v(y)\big)\Big|}{v(x)} \\
&\le \sup_{x \in X} \alpha \frac{\Big|\sum_{y \in X} p_{xy}\big(\mu(x)\big) v(y)\Big|}{v(x)} \|J - J'\| \\
&\le \alpha \|J - J'\|,
\end{aligned}$$

where the last inequality follows from assumption (3). Hence T_μ is a contraction of modulus α.

To show that T is a contraction, we note that

$$\frac{(T_\mu J)(x)}{v(x)} \le \frac{(T_\mu J')(x)}{v(x)} + \alpha \|J - J'\|, \qquad x \in X,\ \mu \in \mathcal{M},$$

so by taking infimum over $\mu \in \mathcal{M}$, we obtain

$$\frac{(TJ)(x)}{v(x)} \le \frac{(TJ')(x)}{v(x)} + \alpha \|J - J'\|, \qquad x \in X.$$

Similarly,

$$\frac{(TJ')(x)}{v(x)} \le \frac{(TJ)(x)}{v(x)} + \alpha \|J - J'\|, \qquad x \in X,$$

and by combining the last two relations the contraction property of T follows.

2.5 (Solution by Mathematical Programming)

If $J \le TJ$, by monotonicity we have $J \le \lim_{k\to\infty} T^k J = J^*$. Any feasible solution z of the optimization problem satisfies $z_i \le H(i,u,z)$ for all $i = 1,\ldots,n$ and $u \in U(i)$, so that $z \le Tz$. It follows that $z \le J^*$, which implies that J^* is an optimal solution of the optimization problem.

2.6 (Convergence of Nonexpansive Monotone Fixed Point Iterations)

For any $c > 0$, let $V_k = T^k(J^* + c\,v)$ for $k \ge 1$, and note that $J^* = T^k J^* \le V_k$. From condition (2), we have

$$H(x,u,J^* + c\,v) \le H(x,u,J^*) + c\,v(x), \qquad x \in X,\ u \in U(x),$$

and by taking infimum over $u \in U(x)$, we obtain $T(J^* + c\,v) \le J^* + c\,v$, i.e., $V_1 \le V_0$. From this and the monotonicity of T it follows that $\big\{V_k(x)\big\}$ is monotonically nonincreasing, and converges to some scalar $\overline{V}(x) \ge J^*(x)$ for each $x \in X$. Moreover, the corresponding function $\overline{V}$ is in $B(X)$, since $V_0 \ge \overline{V} \ge J^*$, and also satisfies $\|V_k - \overline{V}\| \to 0$ (since X is finite). From condition (2), we have $\|TV_k - T\overline{V}\| \le \|V_k - \overline{V}\|$, so $\|TV_k - T\overline{V}\| \to 0$ which together with the fact $TV_k = V_{k+1} \to \overline{V}$, implies that $\overline{V} = T\overline{V}$. Thus $\overline{V} = J^*$ by the uniqueness of the fixed point of T, and it follows that $\{V_k\}$ converges monotonically to J^* from above.

Similarly, define $W_k = T^k(J^* - c\,v)$, and by an argument symmetric to the above, $\{W_k\}$ converges monotonically to J^* from below. Now let $c = \|J - J^*\|$ in the definition of V_k and W_k. Then $J^* - c\,v \le J_0 = J \le J^* + c\,v$, so by the monotonicity of T, $W_k \le T^k J \le V_k$ as well as $W_k \le J^* \le V_k$ for all k. Therefore

$$\frac{\big|(T^k J)(x) - J^*(x)\big|}{v(x)} \le \frac{\big|W_k(x) - V_k(x)\big|}{v(x)} \le \|W_k - V_k\|, \qquad \forall\, x \in X.$$

Since $\|W_k - V_k\| \le \|W_k - J^*\| + \|V_k - J^*\| \to 0$, the conclusion follows.

CHAPTER 3

3.1 (Blackmailer's Dilemma)

(a) Clearly T_μ is a sup-norm contraction with modulus $1 - \mu(1)^2$. Hence J_μ is the unique fixed point of T_μ and we have

$$J_\mu(1) = (T_\mu J_\mu)(1) = -\mu(1) + \big(1 - \mu(1)^2\big)J_\mu(1),$$

which yields $J_\mu(1) = -1/\mu(1)$. The mapping T is given by

$$(TJ)(1) = \inf_{0<u\le 1} \big\{ -u + (1-u^2)J(1)\big\},$$

and $J \in \Re$ is a fixed point of T if and only if

$$0 = \inf_{0<u\leq 1} \big\{ -\big(u + u^2 J(1)\big)\big\}.$$

However, it can be seen that this equation has no solution. Here parts (b) and (d) of Assumption 3.2.1 are violated.

(b) Here T_μ is again a sup-norm contraction with modulus $1-\mu(1)^2$. For J_μ, the unique fixed point of T_μ, we have

$$J_\mu(1) = (T_\mu J_\mu)(1) = -\big(1-\mu(1)\big)\mu(1) + \big(1-\mu(1)\big)J_\mu(1),$$

which yields $J_\mu(1) = -1 + \mu(1)$. Hence $J^* = -1$, but there is no optimal μ. The mapping T is given by

$$(TJ)(1) = \inf_{0<u\leq 1} \big\{ -u + u^2 + (1-u)J(1)\big\},$$

and $J \in \Re$ is a fixed point of T if and only if

$$0 = \inf_{0<u\leq 1} \big\{ -u + u^2 - uJ(1)\big\}.$$

It can be verified that the set of fixed points of T within $\Re$ is $\{J \mid J \leq -1\}$. Here part (d) of Assumption 3.2.1 is violated.

(c) For the policy $\overline{\mu}$ that chooses $\overline{\mu}(1) = 0$, we have

$$(T_{\overline{\mu}} J)(1) = c + J(1),$$

and $\overline{\mu}$ is $\Re$-irregular since $\lim_{k\to\infty} T_{\overline{\mu}}^k J$ either does not belong to $\Re$ or depends on J. Moreover, the mapping T is given by

$$(TJ)(1) = \min\left\{ c + J(1),\ \inf_{0<u\leq 1} \big\{ -u + u^2 + (1-u)J(1)\big\}\right\}.$$

When $c > 0$, we have $J_{\overline{\mu}}(1) = \lim_{k\to\infty} (T_{\overline{\mu}}^k \bar{J})(1) = \infty$. It can be verified that there is no optimal policy, and the set of fixed points of T within $\Re$ is $\{J \mid J \leq -1\}$. Here part (d) of Assumption 3.2.1 is violated.

When $c = 0$, we have $J_{\overline{\mu}}(1) = \lim_{k\to\infty} (T_{\overline{\mu}}^k \bar{J})(1) = 0$. Again it can be verified that there is no optimal policy, and the set of fixed points of T within $\Re$ is $\{J \mid J \leq -1\}$. Here part (c) of Assumption 3.2.1 is violated.

When $c < 0$, we have $J_{\overline{\mu}}(1) = \lim_{k\to\infty} (T_{\overline{\mu}}^k \bar{J})(1) = -\infty$, and the $\Re$-irregular policy $\overline{\mu}$ is optimal. The mapping T has no fixed point within $\Re$. Here parts (c) and (d) of Assumption 3.2.1 are violated.

3.2 (Equivalent Semicontractive Conditions)

Let the assumptions of Prop. 3.1.1 hold, and let μ^* be the S-regular policy that is optimal. Then condition (1) implies that $J^* = J_{\mu^*} \in S$ and $J^* = T_{\mu^*} J^* \geq TJ^*$, while condition (2) implies that there exists an S-regular policy μ such that $T_\mu J^* = TJ^*$.

Conversely, assume that $J^* \in S$, $TJ^* \leq J^*$, and there exists an S-regular policy μ such that $T_\mu J^* = TJ^*$. Then we have $T_\mu J^* = TJ^* \leq J^*$. Hence $T_\mu^k J^* \leq J^*$ for all k, and by taking the limit as $k \to \infty$, we obtain $J_\mu \leq J^*$. Hence the S-regular policy μ is optimal, and both conditions of Prop. 3.1.1 hold.

3.3

The mapping H here is

$$H(x,u,J) = \begin{cases} b & \text{if } x = 1,\ u = 0, \\ a + J(2) & \text{if } x = 1,\ u = 2, \\ a + J(1) & \text{if } x = 2,\ u = 1. \end{cases}$$

The Bellman equation is given by

$$J(1) = \min\big\{b, a + J(2)\big\}, \qquad J(2) = a + J(1).$$

There are two policies:

$$\mu: \text{ where } \mu(1) = 0, \text{ corresponding to the path } 2 \to 1 \to 0,$$

$$\overline{\mu}: \text{ where } \overline{\mu}(1) = 2, \text{ corresponding to the cycle } 1 \to 2 \to 1.$$

The case where $S = \Re^2$ has been discussed in Section 3.1.2. Here μ is S-regular, as can be seen from the form of T_μ,

$$(T_\mu J)(1) = b, \qquad (T_\mu J)(2) = a + J(1),$$

but $\overline{\mu}$ is S-irregular, as can be seen from the form of $T_{\overline{\mu}}$,

$$(T_{\overline{\mu}} J)(1) = a + J(2), \qquad (T_{\overline{\mu}} J)(2) = a + J(1).$$

Briefly there are four cases of interest:

(1) $\alpha > 0$: Here Prop. 3.1.1 applies.

(2) $\alpha = 0$ and $b \leq 0$: Here Prop. 3.1.1 applies.

(3) $\alpha = 0$ and $b > 0$: Here Prop. 3.1.1 does not apply because the S-regular policy μ is not optimal.

(4) $\alpha < 0$: Here Prop. 3.1.1 does not apply because the S-regular policy μ is not optimal.

Consider now the case where $S = [-\infty, \infty) \times [-\infty, \infty)$. Then μ is S-regular in all cases (1)-(4), but $\overline{\mu}$ is S-irregular only in cases (1)-(3), and it is S-regular in case (4) because $J_{\overline{\mu}}(1) = J_{\overline{\mu}}(2) = -\infty$ and

$$\lim_{k\to\infty} (T_{\overline{\mu}}^k J)(1) = \lim_{k\to\infty} (T_{\overline{\mu}}^k J)(1) = -\infty, \qquad \forall\ J \in S,$$

while $J_{\overline{\mu}}$ is the unique fixed point of T within S. In cases (1) and (2), Prop. 3.1.1 applies, because the S-regular policy μ is optimal. In case (3), Prop. 3.1.1 does not apply because the S-regular policy μ is not optimal. Finally, in case (4), contrary to the case $S = \Re^2$, Prop. 3.1.1 applies, because the policy $\overline{\mu}$ is optimal and also S-regular. Case (3) cannot be analyzed with the aid of Props. 3.1.1, 3.1.2, or 3.2.1.

3.4 (Changing $\bar{J}$)

(a) By the definition of S-regular policy, we have $T^k J \to J_\mu$ for all S-regular μ and $J \in S$. Thus, changing $\bar{J}$ to $J \in S$ leaves the cost function of all S-regular policies unchanged.

(b) Here

$$H(x,u,J) = \begin{cases} b & \text{if } x = 1,\ u = 0, \\ J(2) & \text{if } x = 1,\ u = 2, \\ J(1) & \text{if } x = 2,\ u = 1. \end{cases}$$

When $\bar{J} = 0$, the $\Re^2$-regular policy is optimal and $J^* = b\,e$, as shown in Section 3.1.2. When $\bar{J} = r\,e$, the cost function of the $\Re^2$-regular policy μ $[\mu(1) = 0]$ continues to be

$$J_\mu(1) = J_\mu(2) = b,$$

while the cost function of the $\Re^2$-irregular policy $\overline{\mu}$ $[\overline{\mu}(1) = 2]$ is

$$J_{\overline{\mu}}(1) = J_{\overline{\mu}}(2) = r.$$

For $r \le b$, the $\Re^2$-irregular policy is optimal, but $J^* = b\,e$ continues to be the optimal cost over just the $\Re^2$-regular policies (there is only one in this example).

3.5 (Alternative Semicontractive Conditions)

We will show that conditions (1) and (2) imply that $J^* = TJ^*$, and the result will follow from Prop. 3.1.2. Assume to obtain a contradiction, that $J^* \ne TJ^*$. Then $J^* \ge TJ^*$, as can be seen from the relations

$$J^* = J_{\mu^*} = T_{\mu^*} J_{\mu^*} \ge T J_{\mu^*} = TJ^*,$$

where μ^* is an optimal S-regular policy. Thus the relation $J^* \ne TJ^*$ implies that there exists $\overline{\mu}$ and $x \in X$ such that

$$J^*(x) \ge (T_{\overline{\mu}} J^*)(x), \qquad \forall\ x \in X,$$

with strict inequality for some x [note here that we can choose $\overline{\mu}(x) = \mu^*(x)$ for all x such that $J^*(x) = (TJ^*)(x)$, and we can choose $\overline{\mu}(x)$ to satisfy $J^*(x) > (T_{\overline{\mu}} J^*)(x)$ for all other x]. If $\overline{\mu}$ were S-regular, we would have

$$J^* \ge T_{\overline{\mu}} J^* \ge \lim_{k \to \infty} T_{\overline{\mu}}^k J^* = J_{\overline{\mu}},$$

with strict inequality for some $x \in X$, which is impossible. Hence $\overline{\mu}$ is S-irregular, which contradicts condition (2).

3.6 (Convergence of PI)

We have

$$J_{\mu^k} \geq TJ_{\mu^k} \geq J_{\mu^{k+1}}, \qquad k = 0, 1, \ldots. \tag{3.1}$$

Denote

$$J_\infty = \lim_{k\to\infty} TJ_{\mu^k} = \lim_{k\to\infty} J_{\mu^k}.$$

Since for all k, we have $J_{\mu^k} \geq \hat{J} \in S$, where $\hat{J}$ is the optimal cost function over S-regular policies [cf. Assumption 3.2.1(b)]. It follows that $J_\infty \geq \hat{J}$, and by Assumption 3.2.1(a), we obtain $J_\infty \in S$. By taking the limit in Eq. (3.1), we have

$$J_\infty = \lim_{k\to\infty} TJ_{\mu^k} \geq TJ_\infty, \tag{3.2}$$

where the inequality follows from the fact $J_{\mu^k} \downarrow J_\infty$. Using also the given assumption, we have for all $x \in X$ and $u \in U(x)$,

$$H(x, u, J_\infty) = \lim_{k\to\infty} H(x, u, J_{\mu^k}) \geq \lim_{k\to\infty} (TJ_{\mu^k})(x) = J_\infty(x).$$

By taking the infimum of the left-hand side over $u \in U(x)$, we obtain $TJ_\infty \geq J_\infty$, which combined with Eq. (3.2), yields $J_\infty = TJ_\infty$. Since J^* is the unique fixed point of T within S, we obtain $J_\infty = J^*$.

CHAPTER 4

4.1 (Example of Nonexistence of an Optimal Policy Under D)

Since a cost is incurred only upon stopping, and the stopping cost is greater than -1, we have $J_\mu(x) > -1$ for all x and μ. On the other hand, starting from any state x and stopping at $x + n$ yields a cost $-1 + \frac{1}{x+n}$, so by taking n sufficiently large, we can attain a cost arbitrarily close to -1. Thus $J^*(x) = -1$ for all x, but no policy can attain this optimal cost.

4.2 (Counterexample for Optimality Condition Under D)

We have $J^*(x) = -1$ and $J_\mu(x) = 0$ for all $x \in X$. Thus μ is nonoptimal, yet attains the minimum in Bellman's equation

$$J^*(x) = \min\left\{J^*(x+1),\ -1 + \frac{1}{x}\right\}$$

for all x.

4.3 (Counterexample for Optimality Condition Under I)

The verification of $T_\mu J_\mu = TJ_\mu$ is straightforward. To show that $J^*(x) = |x|$, we first note that $|x|$ is a fixed point of T, so by Prop. 4.3.2, $J^*(x) \leq |x|$. Also $(T\bar{J})(x) = |x|$ for all x, while under Assumption I, we have $J^* \geq T\bar{J}$, so $J^*(x) \geq |x|$. Hence $J^*(x) = |x|$.

4.4 (Solution by Mathematical Programming)

(a) Any feasible solution z of the given optimization problem satisfies $z \geq \bar{J}$ as well as $z_i \geq \inf_{u \in U(i)} H(i, u, z)$ for all $i = 1, \ldots, n$, so that $z \geq Tz$. It follows from Prop. 4.3.3 that $z \geq J^*$, which implies that J^* is an optimal solution of the given optimization problem. Also J^* is the unique optimal solution since if z is feasible and $z \neq J^*$, the inequality $z \geq J^*$ implies that $\sum_i z_i > \sum_i J^*(i)$, so z cannot be optimal.

(b) Any feasible solution z of the given optimization problem satisfies $z \leq \bar{J}$ as well as $z_i \leq H(i, u, z)$ for all $i = 1, \ldots, n$ and $u \in U(i)$, so that $z \leq Tz$. It follows from Prop. 4.3.6 that $z \leq J^*$, which implies that J^* is an optimal solution of the given optimization problem. Similar to part (a), J^* is the unique optimal solution.

4.5 (Semicontractive Discounted Problems with Unbounded Cost per Stage)

(a) See Exercise 2.4.

(b) Since all policies in $\overline{\mathcal{M}}$ are S-regular and there exists an optimal policy within $\overline{\mathcal{M}}$, it follows that Prop. 4.4.1 applies, so that J^* is the unique fixed point of T within S. Similarly, the assumption that for each $J \in S$ there exists $\mu \in \overline{\mathcal{M}}$ such that $T_\mu J = TJ$, and the structure of H and S imply that Prop. 4.4.2 applies.

4.6 (Blackmailer's Dilemma)

(a) From Exercise 3.1, the cost function of any policy μ is

$$J_\mu(1) = -\frac{1}{\mu(1)},$$

so the policy evaluation equation given in part (a) is correct. Moreover, we have $J_\mu(1) \leq -1$ since $\mu(1) \in (0, 1]$. The policy improvement equation is

$$\mu^{k+1}(1) \in \arg \min_{u \in (0,1]} \big\{ -u + (1 - u^2) J_{\mu^k}(1) \big\}. \tag{4.1}$$

By setting the gradient of the expression within braces to 0,

$$0 = -1 - 2uJ_{\mu^k}(1),$$

we see that its unconstrained minimum is

$$u_k = -\frac{1}{2J_{\mu^k}(1)},$$

which is less or equal to $-1/2$ since $J_\mu(1) \leq -1$ for all μ. Hence u_k is equal to the constrained minimum in Eq. (4.1), and we have

$$\mu^{k+1}(1) = -\frac{1}{2J_{\mu^k}(1)}.$$

(b) Follows from Props. 4.3.14 and 4.3.15.

4.7 (Counterexample for Policy Improvement Under D - Infinite State Space)

(a) The policy μ that stops at every state has cost function

$$J_\mu(x) = -1 + \frac{1}{x}, \qquad x \in X.$$

Policy improvement starting with μ yields $\overline{\mu}$ with

$$\overline{\mu}(x) \in \arg\min\left\{J_\mu(x),\ -1 + \frac{1}{x}\right\},$$

so $\overline{\mu}(x)$ can be either to continue or to stop at every x. Let $\overline{\mu}$ be to continue at every x. Then $J_{\overline{\mu}}(x) = 0 > J_\mu(x)$ for all x. Moreover, the next policy obtained from $\overline{\mu}$ by policy improvement is μ.

(b) Follows from Props. 4.3.14 and 4.3.15.

4.8 (Counterexample for Policy Improvement Under D - Finite State Space)

(a) Essentially the same as the one of Exercise 4.7.

(b) Straightforward.

4.9 (Infinite Time Reachability [Ber72])

Let $\hat{E}(X)$ be the subset of $E(X)$ that consists of functions that take only the two values 0 and ∞, and for all $J \in \hat{E}(X)$ denote

$$D(J) = \big\{x \in X \mid J(x) = 0\big\}.$$

Note that for all $J \in \hat{E}(X)$ we have $T_\mu J \in \hat{E}(X)$, $TJ \in \hat{E}(X)$, and that

$$D(T_\mu J) = \Big\{x \in X \mid x \in D(J),\ f\big(x, \mu(x), w\big) \in D(J),\ \forall\ w \in W\big(x, \mu(x)\big)\Big\},$$

$$D(TJ) = \cup_{\mu \in \mathcal{M}} D(T_\mu J).$$

(a) For all $J \in \hat{E}(X)$, we have $D(T_\mu J) \subset D(J)$ and $T_\mu J \geq J$, so condition (1) of Assumption I holds, and it is easily verified that the remaining two conditions of Assumption I also hold. We have $\bar{J} \in \hat{E}(X)$, so for any policy $\pi = \{\mu_0, \mu_1, \ldots\}$, we have $T_{\mu_0} \cdots T_{\mu_k} \bar{J} \in \hat{E}(X)$. It follows that J_π, given by

$$J_\pi = \lim_{k \to \infty} T_{\mu_0} \cdots T_{\mu_k} \bar{J},$$

also belongs to $\hat{E}(X)$, and the same is true for $J^* = \inf_{\pi \in \Pi} J_\pi$. Thus J^* has the given form with $D(J^*) = X^*$.

(b) Since $\{T^k \bar{J}\}$ is monotonically nondecreasing we have $D(T^{k+1}\bar{J}) \subset D(T^k \bar{J})$, or equivalently $X_{k+1} \subset X_k$ for all k. Generally for a sequence $\{J_k\} \subset \hat{E}(X)$, if $J_k \uparrow J$, we have $J \in \hat{E}(X)$ and $D(J) = \cap_{k=0}^\infty D(J_k)$. Thus convergence of VI (i.e., $T^k \bar{J} \uparrow J^*$) is equivalent to $D(J^*) = \cap_{k=0}^\infty D(J_k)$ or $X^* = \cap_{k=0}^\infty X_k$.

(c) The compactness condition of Prop. 4.3.14 guarantees that $T^k \bar{J} \uparrow J^*$, or equivalently by part (b), $X^* = \cap_{k=0}^\infty X_k$. This condition requires that the sets

$$U_k(x, \lambda) = \left\{ u \in U(x) \,\middle|\, H(x, u, T^k \bar{J}) \leq \lambda \right\}$$

are compact for every $x \in X$, $\lambda \in \Re$, and for all k greater than some integer $\overline{k}$, or equivalently, that the sets X_k are compact for all $k \geq \overline{k}$.

References

[ABB02] Abounadi, J., Bertsekas, B. P., and Borkar, V. S., 2002. "Stochastic Approximation for Non-Expansive Maps: Q-Learning Algorithms," SIAM J. on Control and Opt., Vol. 41, pp. 1-22.

[BBB08] Basu, A., Bhattacharyya, and Borkar, V., 2008. "A Learning Algorithm for Risk-Sensitive Cost," Math. of OR, Vol. 33, pp. 880-898.

[BBD10] Busoniu, L., Babuska, R., De Schutter, B., and Ernst, D., 2010. Reinforcement Learning and Dynamic Programming Using Function Approximators, CRC Press, N. Y.

[Bau78] Baudet, G. M., 1978. "Asynchronous Iterative Methods for Multiprocessors," Journal of the ACM, Vol. 25, pp. 226-244.

[BeI96] Bertsekas, D. P., and Ioffe, S., 1996. "Temporal Differences-Based Policy Iteration and Applications in Neuro-Dynamic Programming," Lab. for Info. and Decision Systems Report LIDS-P-2349, MIT.

[BeS78] Bertsekas, D. P., and Shreve, S. E., 1978. Stochastic Optimal Control: The Discrete Time Case, Academic Press, N. Y.; may be downloaded from http://web.mit.edu/dimitrib/www/home.html

[BeT89] Bertsekas, D. P., and Tsitsiklis, J. N., 1989. Parallel and Distributed Computation: Numerical Methods, Prentice-Hall, Engl. Cliffs, N. J.; may be downloaded from http://web.mit.edu/dimitrib/www/home.html

[BeT91] Bertsekas, D. P., and Tsitsiklis, J. N., 1991. "An Analysis of Stochastic Shortest Path Problems," Math. of OR, Vol. 16, pp. 580-595.

[BeT96] Bertsekas, D. P., and Tsitsiklis, J. N., 1996. Neuro-Dynamic Programming, Athena Scientific, Belmont, MA.

[BeT08] Bertsekas, D. P., and Tsitsiklis, J. N., 2008. Introduction to Probability, 2nd Ed., Athena Scientific, Belmont, MA.

[BeY07] Bertsekas, D. P., and Yu, H., 2007. "Solution of Large Systems of Equations Using Approximate Dynamic Programming Methods," Lab. for Info. and Decision Systems Report LIDS-P-2754, MIT.

[BeY09] Bertsekas, D. P., and Yu, H., 2009. "Projected Equation Methods for Approximate Solution of Large Linear Systems," J. of Computational and Applied Mathematics, Vol. 227, pp. 27-50.

[BeY10a] Bertsekas, D. P., and Yu, H., 2010. "Q-Learning and Enhanced Policy Iteration in Discounted Dynamic Programming," Lab. for Info. and Decision Systems Report LIDS-P-2831, MIT; Math. of OR, Vol. 37, 2012, pp. 66-94.

[BeY10b] Bertsekas, D. P., and Yu, H., 2010. "Asynchronous Distributed Policy Iteration in Dynamic Programming," Proc. of Allerton Conf. on Communication, Control and Computing, Allerton Park, Ill, pp. 1368-1374.

[Ber72] Bertsekas, D. P., 1972. "Infinite Time Reachability of State Space Regions by Using Feedback Control," IEEE Trans. Aut. Control, Vol. AC-17, pp. 604-613.

[Ber77] Bertsekas, D. P., 1977. "Monotone Mappings with Application in Dynamic Programming," SIAM J. on Control and Opt., Vol. 15, pp. 438-464.

[Ber82] Bertsekas, D. P., 1982. "Distributed Dynamic Programming," IEEE Trans. Aut. Control, Vol. AC-27, pp. 610-616.

[Ber83] Bertsekas, D. P., 1983. "Asynchronous Distributed Computation of Fixed Points," Math. Programming, Vol. 27, pp. 107-120.

[Ber87] Bertsekas, D. P., 1987. Dynamic Programming: Deterministic and Stochastic Models, Prentice-Hall, Englewood Cliffs, N. J.

[Ber05a] Bertsekas, D. P., 2005. Dynamic Programming and Optimal Control, Vol. I, 3rd Edition, Athena Scientific, Belmont, MA.

[Ber05b] Bertsekas, D. P., 2005. "Dynamic Programming and Suboptimal Control: A Survey from ADP to MPC," Fundamental Issues in Control, Special Issue for the CDC-ECC 05, European J. of Control, Vol. 11, Nos. 4-5.

[Ber09] Bertsekas, D. P., 2009. Convex Optimization Theory, Athena Scientific, Belmont, MA.

[Ber10] Bertsekas, D. P., 2010. "Williams-Baird Counterexample for Q-Factor Asynchronous Policy Iteration,"
http://web.mit.edu/dimitrib/www/Williams-Baird Counterexample.pdf

[Ber11a] Bertsekas, D. P., 2011. "Temporal Difference Methods for General Projected Equations," IEEE Trans. Aut. Control, Vol. 56, pp. 2128-2139.

[Ber11b] Bertsekas, D. P., 2011. "λ-Policy Iteration: A Review and a New Implementation," Lab. for Info. and Decision Systems Report LIDS-P-2874, MIT; appears in Reinforcement Learning and Approximate Dynamic Programming for Feedback Control, by F. Lewis and D. Liu (eds.), IEEE Press, 2012.

[Ber11c] Bertsekas, D. P., 2011. "Approximate Policy Iteration: A Survey and Some New Methods," J. of Control Theory and Applications, Vol. 9, pp. 310-335.

[Ber12a] Bertsekas, D. P., 2012. Dynamic Programming and Optimal Control, Vol. II, 4th Edition: Approximate Dynamic Programming, Athena Scientific, Belmont, MA.

[Ber12b] Bertsekas, D. P., 2012. "Weighted Sup-Norm Contractions in Dynamic Programming: A Review and Some New Applications," Lab. for Info. and Decision Systems Report LIDS-P-2884, MIT.

[Bla65] Blackwell, D., 1965. "Positive Dynamic Programming," Proc. Fifth Berkeley Symposium Math. Statistics and Probability, pp. 415-418.

[BoM99] Borkar, V. S., Meyn, S. P., 1999. "Risk Sensitive Optimal Control: Existence and Synthesis for Models with Unbounded Cost," SIAM J. Control and Opt., Vol. 27, pp. 192-209.

[BoM00] Borkar, V. S., Meyn, S. P., 1900. "The O.D.E. Method for Convergence of Stochastic Approximation and Reinforcement Learning," SIAM J. Control and Opt., Vol. 38, pp. 447-469.

[BoM02] Borkar, V. S., Meyn, S. P., 2002. "Risk-Sensitive Optimal Control for Markov Decision Processes with Monotone Cost," Math. of OR, Vol. 27, pp. 192-209.

[Bor98] Borkar, V. S., 1998. "Asynchronous Stochastic Approximation," SIAM J. Control Opt., Vol. 36, pp. 840-851.

[Bor08] Borkar, V. S., 2008. Stochastic Approximation: A Dynamical Systems Viewpoint, Cambridge Univ. Press, N. Y.

[CFH07] Chang, H. S., Fu, M. C., Hu, J., Marcus, S. I., 2007. Simulation-Based Algorithms for Markov Decision Processes, Springer, N. Y.

[CaM88] Carraway, R. L., and Morin, T. L., 1988. "Theory and Applications of Generalized Dynamic Programming: An Overview," Computers and Mathematics with Applications, Vol. 16, pp. 779-788.

[CaR12] Cavus, O., and Ruszczynski, A., 2012. "Risk-Averse Control of Undiscounted Transient Markov Models," Rutgers Univ. Report, available on Optimization On-Line at http://www.optimization-online.org/

[Cao07] Cao, X. R., 2007. Stochastic Learning and Optimization: A Sensitivity-Based Approach, Springer, N. Y.

[ChM69] Chazan D., and Miranker, W., 1969. "Chaotic Relaxation," Linear Algebra and Applications, Vol. 2, pp. 199-222.

[ChS87] Chung, K.-J., and Sobel, M. J., 1987. "Discounted MDPs: Distribution Functions and Exponential Utility Maximization," SIAM J. Control and Opt., Vol. 25, pp. 49-62.

[CoM99] Coraluppi, S. P., and Marcus, S. I., 1999. "Risk-Sensitive and Minimax Control of Discrete-Time, Finite-State Markov Decision Processes," Automatica, Vol. 35, pp. 301-309.

[DeM67] Denardo, E. V., and Mitten, L. G., 1967. "Elements of Sequential Decision Processes," J. Indust. Engrg., Vol. 18, pp. 106-112.

[DeR79] Denardo, E. V., and Rothblum, U. G., 1979. "Optimal Stopping, Exponential Utility, and Linear Programming," Math. Programming, Vol. 16, pp. 228-244.

[Den67] Denardo, E. V., 1967. "Contraction Mappings in the Theory Underlying Dynamic Programming," SIAM Review, Vol. 9, pp. 165-177.

[Der70] Derman, C., 1970. Finite State Markovian Decision Processes, Academic Press, N. Y.

[DuS65] Dubins, L., and Savage, L. M., 1965. How to Gamble If You Must, McGraw-Hill, N. Y.

[DyY79] Dynkin, E. B., and Yushkevich, A. A., 1979. Controlled Markov Processes, Springer-Verlag, Berlin and New York.

[FeM97] Fernandez-Gaucherand, E., and Marcus, S. I., 1997. "Risk-Sensitive Optimal Control of Hidden Markov Models: Structural Results," IEEE Trans. Aut. Control, Vol. AC-42, pp. 1418-1422.

[FiV96] Filar, J., and Vrieze, K., 1996. Competitive Markov Decision Processes, Springer, N. Y.

[FlM95] Fleming, W. H., and McEneaney, W. M., 1995. "Risk-Sensitive Control on an Infinite Time Horizon," SIAM J. Control and Opt., Vol. 33, pp. 1881-1915.

[Gos03] Gosavi, A., 2003. Simulation-Based Optimization: Parametric Optimization Techniques and Reinforcement Learning, Springer, N. Y.

[HCP99] Hernandez-Lerma, O., Carrasco, O., and Perez-Hernandez. 1999. "Markov Control Processes with the Expected Total Cost Criterion: Optimality, Stability, and Transient Models," Acta Appl. Math., Vol. 59, pp. 229-269.

[Hay08] Haykin, S., 2008. Neural Networks and Learning Machines, (3rd Edition), Prentice-Hall, Englewood-Cliffs, N. J.

[HeL99] Hernandez-Lerma, O., and Lasserre, J. B., 1999. 'Further Topics on Discrete-Time Markov Control Processes, Springer, N. Y.

[HeM96] Hernandez-Hernndez, D., and Marcus, S. I., 1996. "Risk Sensitive Control of Markov Processes in Countable State Space," Systems and Control Letters, Vol. 29, pp. 147-155.

[HiW05] Hinderer, K., and Waldmann, K.-H., 2005. "Algorithms for Countable State Markov Decision Models with an Absorbing Set," SIAM J. of Control and Opt., Vol. 43, pp. 2109-2131.

[HoM72] Howard, R. S., and Matheson, J. E., 1972. "Risk-Sensitive Markov Decision Processes," Management Science, Vol. 8, pp. 356-369.

[JBE94] James, M. R., Baras, J. S., Elliott, R. J., 1994. "Risk-Sensitive Control and Dynamic Games for Partially Observed Discrete-Time Nonlinear Systems," IEEE Trans. Aut. Control, Vol. AC-39, pp. 780-792.

[JaC06] James, H. W., and Collins, E. J., 2006. "An Analysis of Transient Markov Decision Processes," J. Appl. Prob., Vol. 43, pp. 603-621.

[Jac73] Jacobson, D. H., 1973. "Optimal Stochastic Linear Systems with Exponential Performance Criteria and their Relation to Deterministic Differential Games," IEEE Transactions on Automatic Control, Vol. AC-18, pp. 124-131.

[Kle68] Kleinman, D. L., 1968. "On an Iterative Technique for Riccati Equation Computations," IEEE Trans. Aut. Control, Vol. AC-13, pp. 114-115.

[Mey07] Meyn, S., 2007. Control Techniques for Complex Networks, Cambridge Univ. Press, N. Y.

[Mit64] Mitten, L. G., 1964. "Composition Principles for Synthesis of Optimal Multistage Processes," Operations Research, Vol. 12, pp. 610-619.

[Mor82] Morin, T. L., 1982. "Monotonicity and the Principle of Optimality," J. of Math. Analysis and Applications, Vol. 88, pp. 665-674.

[OrR70] Ortega, J. M., and Rheinboldt, W. C., 1970. Iterative Solution of Nonlinear Equations in Several Variables, Academic Press, N. Y.

[PaB99] Patek, S. D., and Bertsekas, D. P., 1999. "Stochastic Shortest Path Games," SIAM J. on Control and Opt., Vol. 36, pp. 804-824.

[Pal67] Pallu de la Barriere, R., 1967. Optimal Control Theory, Saunders, Phila; republished by Dover, N. Y., 1980.

[Pat01] Patek, S. D., 2001. "On Terminating Markov Decision Processes with a Risk Averse Objective Function," Automatica, Vol. 37, pp. 1379-1386.

[Pat07] Patek, S. D., 2007. "Partially Observed Stochastic Shortest Path Problems with Approximate Solution by Neuro-Dynamic Programming," IEEE Trans. on Systems, Man, and Cybernetics Part A, Vol. 37, pp. 710-720.

[Pli78] Pliska, S. R., 1978. "On the Transient Case for Markov Decision Chains with General State Spaces," in Dynamic Programming and its Applications, by M. L. Puterman (ed.), Academic Press, N. Y.

[Pow07] Powell, W. B., 2007. Approximate Dynamic Programming: Solving the Curses of Dimensionality, J. Wiley and Sons, Hoboken, N. J; 2nd ed., 2011.

[Put94] Puterman, M. L., 1994. Markovian Decision Problems, J. Wiley, N. Y.

[Roc70] Rockafellar, R. T., 1970. Convex Analysis, Princeton Univ. Press, Princeton, N. J.

[Ros67] Rosenfeld, J., 1967. "A Case Study on Programming for Parallel Processors," Research Report RC-1864, IBM Res. Center, Yorktown Heights, N. Y.

[Rot79] Rothblum, U. G., 1979. "Iterated Successive Approximation for Sequential Decision Processes," in Stochastic Control and Optimization, by J. W. B. van Overhagen and H. C. Tijms (eds), Vrije University, Amsterdam.

[Rot84] Rothblum, U. G., 1984. "Multiplicative Markov Decision Chains," Math. of OR, Vol. 9, pp. 6-24.

[Rus10] Ruszczynski, A., 2010. "Risk-Averse Dynamic Programming for Markov Decision Processes," Math. Programming, Ser. B, Vol. 125, pp. 235-261.

[ScL12] Scherrer, B., and Lesner, B., 2012. "On the Use of Non-Stationary Policies for Stationary Infinite-Horizon Markov Decision Processes," NIPS 2012 - Neural Information Processing Systems, South Lake Tahoe, Ne.

[Sch75] Schal, M., 1975. "Conditions for Optimality in Dynamic Programming and for the Limit of n-Stage Optimal Policies to be Optimal," Z. Wahrscheinlichkeitstheorie und Verw. Gebiete, Vol. 32, pp. 179-196.

[Sch11] Scherrer, B., 2011. "Performance Bounds for Lambda Policy Iteration and Application to the Game of Tetris," Report RR-6348, INRIA, France; to appear in J. of Machine Learning Research.

[Sch12] Scherrer, B., 2012. "On the Use of Non-Stationary Policies for Infinite-Horizon Discounted Markov Decision Processes," INRIA Lorraine Report, France.

[Sha53] Shapley, L. S., 1953. "Stochastic Games," Proc. Nat. Acad. Sci. U.S.A., Vol. 39.

[Str66] Strauch, R., 1966. "Negative Dynamic Programming," Ann. Math. Statist., Vol. 37, pp. 871-890.

[Str75] Striebel, 1975. Optimal Control of Discrete Time Stochastic Systems, Springer-Verlag, Berlin and New York.

[SuB98] Sutton, R. S., and Barto, A. G., 1998. Reinforcement Learning, MIT Press, Cambridge, MA.

[Sze98a] Szepesvari, C., 1998. Static and Dynamic Aspects of Optimal Sequential Decision Making, Ph.D. Thesis, Bolyai Institute of Mathematics, Hungary.

[Sze98b] Szepesvari, C., 1998. "Non-Markovian Policies in Sequential Decision Problems," Acta Cybernetica, Vol. 13, pp. 305-318.

[Sze10] Szepesvari, C., 2010. Algorithms for Reinforcement Learning, Morgan and Claypool Publishers, San Franscisco, CA.

[TBA86] Tsitsiklis, J. N., Bertsekas, D. P., and Athans, M., 1986. "Distributed Asynchronous Deterministic and Stochastic Gradient Optimization Algorithms," IEEE Trans. Aut. Control, Vol. AC-31, pp. 803-812.

[ThS10a] Thiery, C., and Scherrer, B., 2010. "Least-Squares λ-Policy Iteration:

Bias-Variance Trade-off in Control Problems," in ICML'10: Proc. of the 27th Annual International Conf. on Machine Learning.

[ThS10b] Thiery, C., and Scherrer, B., 2010. "Performance Bound for Approximate Optimistic Policy Iteration," Technical Report, INRIA, France.

[Tsi94] Tsitsiklis, J. N., 1994. "Asynchronous Stochastic Approximation and Q-Learning," Machine Learning, Vol. 16, pp. 185-202.

[VVL13] Vrabie, V., Vamvoudakis, K. G., and Lewis, F. L., 2013. Optimal Adaptive Control and Differential Games by Reinforcement Learning Principles, The Institution of Engineering and Technology, London.

[VeP87] Verdu, S., and Poor, H. V., 1987. "Abstract Dynamic Programming Models under Commutativity Conditions," SIAM J. on Control and Opt., Vol. 25, pp. 990-1006.

[Vei66] Veinott, A. F., 1966. "On Finding Optimal Policies in Discrete Dynamic Programming with no Discounting," Ann. Math. Stat., Vol. 37, pp. 1284-1294.

[Whi80] Whittle, P., 1980. "Stability and Characterization Conditions in Negative Programming," Journal of Applied Probability, Vol. 17, pp. 635-645.

[Whi90] Whittle, P., 1990. Risk-Sensitive Optimal Control, Wiley, Chichester.

[WiB93] Williams, R. J., and Baird, L. C., 1993. "Analysis of Some Incremental Variants of Policy Iteration: First Steps Toward Understanding Actor-Critic Learning Systems," Report NU-CCS-93-11, College of Computer Science, Northeastern University, Boston, MA.

[YuB10] Yu, H., and Bertsekas, D. P., 2010. "Error Bounds for Approximations from Projected Linear Equations," Math. of OR, Vol. 35, pp. 306-329.

[YuB11a] Yu, H., and Bertsekas, D. P., 2011. "Q-Learning and Policy Iteration Algorithms for Stochastic Shortest Path Problems," Lab. for Info. and Decision Systems Report LIDS-P-2871, MIT; to appear in Annals of OR; DOI: 10.1007/s10479-012-1128-z.

[YuB11b] Yu, H., and Bertsekas, D. P., 2011. "On Boundedness of Q-Learning Iterates for Stochastic Shortest Path Problems," Lab. for Info. and Decision Systems Report LIDS-P-2859, MIT; to appear in Math. of OR.

[YuB12] Yu, H., and Bertsekas, D. P., 2012. "Weighted Bellman Equations and their Applications in Dynamic Programming," Lab. for Info. and Decision Systems Report LIDS-P-2876, MIT.

[Yu11] Yu, H., 2011. "Stochastic Shortest Path Games and Q-Learning," Lab. for Info. and Decision Systems Report LIDS-P-2875, MIT.

[Yu12] Yu, H., 2012. "Least Squares Temporal Difference Methods: An Analysis Under General Conditions," SIAM J. Control and Opt., Vol. 50, pp. 3310-3343.

[Zac64] Zachrisson, L. E., 1964. "Markov Games," in Advances in Game Theory, by M. Dresher, L. S. Shapley, and A. W. Tucker, (eds.), Princeton Univ. Press, Princeton, N. J., pp. 211-253.

INDEX